M000081507

ISRAEL HOROVITZ

The Primary English Class
and Six New Plays

ISRAEL HOROVITZ

The Primary English Class
and Six New Plays

CONTEMPORARY PLAYWRIGHTS SERIES

SK
A Smith and Kraus Book

A Smith and Kraus Book
Published by Smith and Kraus, Inc.
PO Box 127, Lyme, NH 03768

Copyright ©1997 by Israel Horovitz
All rights reserved
Manufactured in the United States of America
Cover and Text Design by Julia Hill
Cover Photo by Gaëla Blandy

First Edition: October 1997
10 9 8 7 6 5 4 3 2 1

CAUTION: Professionals and amateurs are hereby warned that the plays represented in this book are subject to a royalty. They are fully protected under the copyright laws of the United States of America, and of all countries covered by the International Copyright Union (including the Dominion of Canada and the rest of the British Commonwealth), and of all countries covered by the Pan-American Copyright Convention and the Universal Copyright Convention, and of all countries with which the United States has reciprocal copyright relations. All rights, including professional, amateur, motion picture, recitation, lecturing, public reading, radio broadcasting, television, video or sound taping, all other forms of mechanical or electronic reproductions such as CD-ROM and CD-I, information storage and retrieval systems and photocopying, and the rights of translation into foreign languages, are strictly reserved. Particular emphasis is laid upon the question of public readings, permission for which must be secured from the Author's agent, The William Morris Agency, 1350 Avenue of the Americas, New York, NY 10001, Attn: Jason Fogelson Tel: 212/903-1109. Fax: 212/903-1426. E-Mail address: jaf@wma.com. For West Coast inquiries, contact Jim Crabbe, Wm Morris Agency, 151 El Camino Drive, Beverly Hills, CA90212. Tel: 310/859-4156. Fax: 310/859-4462. In London, contact Jane Annakin, Wm Morris Agency, 31/32 Soho Square, London W1V5DG. Tel: (0171) 434-2191. Fax: (0171) 437-0238. Mr Horovitz is repre-sented in France by Marie-Cècile Renauld, Voyez Mon Agent, 10, av George V, 75008-Paris. Tel: (1) 47 23 55 80. Fax: (1) 47 20 15 86. He is represented in Germany by Daniel Fieldler, Felix Bloch Erben, Hardenbergstraße 6, 10623 Berlin. Tel: (030) 313 9028/29. Fax: (030) 312 9334. In Italy, Israel Horovitz is represented by Paola d'Arborio, D'ABORIO, S.N.C., Via S. Godenzo 70, 00189 Rome, Italy. Tel: (06) 3350801. Fax: (06) 3310849.

The amateur production rights in *The Primary English Class* are controlled exclusively by the *Dramatists Play Service, Inc.,* 440 Park Avenue South, New York, N.Y. 10016. No amateur performance of the play may be given without obtaining in advance the written permission of the *Dramatists Play Service, Inc.,* and paying the requisite fee. For production rights of all other plays in this volume, please contact The William Morris Agency at the above address.

The Primary English Class ©1976 by Israel Horovitz.
Fighting Over Beverley ©1994 by Israel Horovitz.
Free Gift ©1996 by Israel Horovitz.
Un Drôle de Mari Français ©1996 by Israel Horovitz.
Lebensraum ©1996 by Israel Horovitz.
My Old Lady ©1996 by Israel Horovitz.
One Under ©1997 by Israel Horovitz.

The Library of Congress Cataloging-In-Publication Data
Card Catalogue Number 93-46378

CONTENTS

The Primary English Class

For Henry Pillsbury and LuAnn Walther.

INTRODUCTION

This is mostly about Claude Roy's orange bathrobe. When I first started spending time in France, some twenty-five years ago, I spoke not a word of *le français*, and I mean nothing, *rien, nada*. I had managed to squeak through four years of high school Latin, and, at that point, my formal education following high school had been one year of teachers college in Salem, Massachusetts, and a two-year theatre program at The Royal Academy of Dramatic Art in London. The only exotic/foreign tongues I had come even close to mastering were Cockney, South Kent English, and Brooklynese. French might as well have come from Mars as Gaul.

Somehow, in the early 1970s, I found myself and my plays in Paris, not only oft-produced, but popular. *The Indian Wants The Bronx* and *It's Called The Sugar Plum* had been done with success by the French stage-star Laurent Terzieff, and *Morning* (of the Horovitz-McNally-Melfi Broadway trilogy, *Morning, Noon and Night*) had been done by Gérard Depardieu. *Line* had opened and was a kind of sensation at Théâtre de Poche-Montparnasse, where it would continue for eleven years! The French and I had begun our love affair. Only trouble was, I couldn't talk to them and they couldn't talk to me.

So, off I went to Paris, to bask in the oddly reflected light of my own incomprehensible French plays…and to study the language of these people who seemed to like me…and to be close with Samuel Beckett, with whom, I had begun a friendship that would last a lifetime and beyond. All of the above.

My late wife Doris and I borrowed the apartment of Claude Roy and Loleh Bellon. Claude, a famous/marvelous journalist/poet/novelist, had translated *Line* into French, and Loleh (now one of France's most important/popular playwrights) was playing the female lead in *Line*. They were visiting the Far East for a month and had given us their lovely, booklined Rue Dauphine apartment to use.

In those days, I wrote my plays on a tiny Olivetti portable typewriter, mornings, six A.M. to Noon. Frequently, then, as now, I did a very early morning run before writing, using the jog-time to plan out my morning's work. I returned to the apartment, showered, and used Claude Roy's magnificent bright-orange terry cloth bathrobe to cover my 128-pound real-man body, as I sipped my headache-guaranteed-strength French *café en grain* and munched my morning *croissant avec confiture à l'abricot*. See? I was learning. My writing went extremely well and, at a time in my life when I believed I was about to die (from a disease that had Anxiety as its only symptom), I was feeling, well, pretty good.

I figured that all good things could be credited to Claude's bright-orange bathrobe. Obviously, Claude was a great and successful writer, and his bathrobe was bringing me up the same ladder. (It would be too easy to say I was simply "crazy," back then. Let's say I was an imaginative young fellow...and that things have developed, nicely, into the present.

Anyway, when Claude and Loleh returned from China and reclaimed their apartment, I confessed to Claude that I had worn his lucky bathrobe, and begged to know where I could buy one of my own. He revealed that the great *bourgeois* department store *Printemps* was the source. Claude gave me directions by Metro, and off I went, alone, for the great American-in-Paris adventure called *le Shopping*. Claude thought I might need to know a few French expressions, just in case I happened to have a *vendeuse* who didn't *parle* the old *Anglais*...and so, he taught me *peignoir orange* (orange bathrobe) and *Ça coûte combien?* (How much does it cost?)...I memorized these six words and off I went. On arrival at the great *Printemps,* I asked the information-booth lady "*Peignoir orange?*" and she answered "third floor, in the middle." So far, no problem. In the middle of the third floor, I asked a corpulent vendeuse the same thing: "*Peignoir orange?*" and she answered: "*Juste là...*" pointing to a huge rack of men's bathrobes. And there, by God, it was: Claude's bright-orange star-maker bathrobe! Only one, in the midst of a half dozen inferior colors, like, for example, blue or, worse, yellow. I tried the thing on and, yes, it fit! No price tag, but, hey, not a problem for a bilingual *bon-vivant...*"*Écoute bien?*" I asked.

Now, "*ça coûte combien*" and "*écoute bien*" don't really look or sound all that different, do they? But one means "How much does it cost?" and the other means "Listen carefully!"...And I had just said, quite forcefully...you got it. So, the chubby vendeuse leaned in closer. "*Oui?*" she answered, ears aperk. "*Écoute bien?*" I repeated, confidently. She leaned in all the closer. "*Écoute bien?*"

"*Quoi?*" ("What?")

"*Écoute bien?*"

"*Quoi?*"

Within minutes, I had a large group of *vendeuses* around me, all stupefied by this skinny, hairy-headed American, who insisted they "*Écoute bien*" (and then said nothing else). Ultimately, a Supervisor arrived and asked "What ees zee problem?," to which I replied "*Écoute bien?*" and, he leaned in, thinking I had some bad news for him, and I repeated "*Écoute bien?*" and he, finally, asked in English what zee hell I wanted...

When I got back to Claude's, bathrobe in hand, not knowing in the least what had really happened back at *Printemps*, I repeated the event to Claude, Loleh, and Doris. Needless to say, Doris and I were amazed when Claude and Loleh fell to the floor, laughing. Within the month, Claude had published the story of me and my bathrobe in the magazine *Le Nouvel Observateur*.

Nearly thirty years and as many languages later, I am still not a comfortable fellow, but I can get a good bowl of soup in Brussels. I have learned that *metsa* means "the woods" to a Finn, and "only so-so" to an Italian. And to buy a pair of slacks in Berlin, I ask for a *hose;* and for a skirt I must ask for a *rock*. Out of this knowledge, *The Primary English Class* was born.

This play is, for me, a tribute to the countless moments I have spent staring, smiling into incomprehensible babble, as someone explained something important to me, slowly, carefully, clearly, in a language I didn't understand at all. (Surely, Germans stand on street-corners, laughing about how funny they sound!)

Some of my plays are produced in thirty different languages around the globe. I have visited my plays in Japan, Slovenia, you name it. Next year, I'm off to China! When *The Primary English Class* is done abroad, it usually becomes *The Primary Hebrew Class, The Primary Finnish Class,* etc. (In Spain, last year, the play had a hugely successful run in Spanish, with the title "Catalànish"...) I am often called to the stage after a performance and introduced to the audience, where I stand smiling through a speech that could well be announcing that I am a hell of a writer, or that the theatre is on fire. I wouldn't know the difference, until smoke hit my nostrils. (And had the announcer said "You'll smell smoke, but don't worry," the audience would see me leaping out the window.)

Recently, in France, I made a speech entirely in French, and a not-very-*gentil* Frenchie told me after the event how upsetting it was to hear someone he'd admired stammer his way through such inferior French. His advice: "Stick to English, keep up the mystery."

In the end, language is *not* the clarifier, neither a friend to thought, nor a twin to meaning. Language is the first mask, the fence between neighbors' emotions, between their ideas, their honest needs. Wars are fought over a word. Marriages stop or start over a simple "I do" or "I don't." One need only imagine Khrushchev holding his shoe in the air, screaming (in Russian, of course) "These shoes are killing me!" and his American-hating interpreter taking the chance of his life by mistranslating Nikita's words as "We will bury you!"...On this small, comic miscommunication, a world could turn. *The Primary English Class* exists to express my wonder and my love of language.

Postscript: This introduction wouldn't be complete without my acknowledging the (literally) hundreds of actors I have seen perform this play (in dozens of languages I don't speak). Diane Keaton must be thanked. She was an astonishing Debbie Wastba in the NYC premiere of *The Primary English Class*. Brilliant, hilarious, deeply moving. So was Paula Plum at Gloucester Stage. So was Sylvie Rolland in Paris. And Susanah Alexander in Mexico City.

This play has given me enormous pleasure. It creates a kind of microcosmic world, and puts together people of different cultures and backgrounds. It cuts to the quick of cultural differences overwhelmed by human similarities. It builds loving families of actors who came together as total strangers to simply do another play. This one is special. I hope you love it, too. One last thought, an apology. The non-English languages printed herein represent a virtual symphony of error. Please, native speakers, forgive us. It's nearly impossible to get it right. For actors approaching the non-English roles in this play, simply fix the language you'll be speaking. Make it modern and correct. I trust you. *Vraiment.*

ORIGINAL PRODUCTION

The Primary English Class was first presented by Jack Schlissel, Joseph Kipness, and Steven Steinlauf at the Circle in the Square Theatre, in New York City, on February 16, 1976. It was directed by Edward Berkeley; the scenery was supervised by Fredda Slaven; lighting was by Andrea Wilson; and the costumes were coordinated by Patricia McGourty. The associate producer was Irving Welzer. The cast, in order of appearance, was as follows:

Smiednik . . . . Tom Kubiak
Patumiera . . . . Richard Libertini
LaPoubelle . . . . Jean-Pierre Stewart
Male Translator . . . . Robert Picardo
Mulleimer . . . . Sol Frieder
Mrs. Pong . . . . Lori Tan Chinn
Female Translator . . . . Christine Von Dohln
Yoko Kuzukago . . . . Atsumi Sakato
Debbie Wastba . . . . Diane Keaton

THE PEOPLE OF THE PLAY

(In the order in which they appear)
Smiednik: A Polish man
Patumiera: An Italian man
LaPoubelle: A French man
Mulleimer: A German man
Pong: A Chinese woman
Kuzukago: A Japanese woman
Wastba: An American woman

THE PLACE OF THE PLAY

Classroom

THE TIME OF THE PLAY

Night

AUTHOR'S NOTE

I should like to herein gratefully acknowledge the support of The O'Neill Theatre Center, Waterford, Conn., Brandeis University, Waltham, Mass., and The Cubiculo, New York City, where early drafts of *The Primary English Class* were allowed public performance.

Further, I should like to thank Lynne Meadow of The Manhattan

Theatre Club, New York, and Paul Libin and Theodore Mann of The Circle in the Square Theatre, New York, for allowing workshop productions of *The Primary English Class* in their theatres, immediately prior to the play's New York premiere.

Finally, I gratefully acknowledge the generous assistance of Martin Esslin, Edith Fournier, Mario Fratti, Eugène Ionesco, Henry Pillsbury, Claude Roy, M. L. Thiersch, Carl Weber, and the performers of each production of *The Primary English Class,* prior to and including its New York premiere production, who enriched, improved, and made accurate the various languages of the play, not least of all the English.

I. H., Gloucester, Massachusetts,
August 1997.

N.B. The version of *The Primary English Class* collected herein was revised, slightly, in 1997.

The Primary English Class

ACT I

Night. Square box classroom, white plaster walls, wainscoting white as well. Trim color orange. Room reminiscent of handball court: orange lines cut room in court pattern. Twelve singular orange student desks, backs of five to upstage wall, four to stage-left wall, three downstage, between audience and center stage. Small bright orange teacher's desk, stage-right wall. Straight-legged variety teacher's legs and lower trunk constantly exposed to class. Orange wastebasket foot of desk. Wires on stage-left wall protrude from small circular cut: clock missing, taken from this spot. Circular shadow visible. A janitor, SMIEDNIK, is upstage left, mopping the floor of the classroom. He is stout, uses regulation-size mop. In dark, we hear Bulgarian folk music. Then SMIEDNIK sings. Then lights up. SMIEDNIK sings "I Can't Give You Anything But Love...Baby..." in Polish. Uses the recognizable melody. As he sings, we hear the MALE TRANSLATOR'S voice, over the scene, retelling the Myth of the Trashcan Family...

MALE TRANSLATOR'S VOICE: Once upon a time in Mesopotamia, approximately three thousand and ninety-nine years ago, there lived an unremarkable Mesopotamian family called Trashcano, with seven short, but friendly, sons. At the time of the Great Mesopotamian Purge, a thousand years before the birth of Christ, Mr. and Mrs. Trashcano believed the world was coming to an end. In that spirit, they sent each of their seven sons to a different corner of the Earth, and the Trashcano sons *all* survived. And they all procreated, enthusiastically, producing robust Trashcano families of their own. In this great year [1997], tonight, in fact, the Trashcanos will reunite for the first time in approximately three thousand and ninety-nine years...with a singular purpose...to learn English...quickly.

SMIEDNIK: Nie moge, ci dac niczego oprócz *baby*
  To jest wszystko co mam, *baby*
  Suij troszeczke, knuj tioszeczke
  Napewno znajdziesz...
  Szczescia i, mysle tak,
  Wszystko czego kiedys chciałes
  Gee, bym cheiał cie widziec
  w bujlautach, *baby*

Tahidi którzych nie ma u Woolworta
Ale dokad jeszcze nie mozemy, *Baby!*
(He stops mopping and gestures as though a nightclub performer in the throes of a big finish.)
Nie moge ci dac nic oprócz mnie!
Nie moge ci dac nic oprócz, baby!
(In silence now, he straightens row of chairs. SMIEDNIK empties trash can and notices that the clock has been stolen from the wall. He mutters in Polish.) Psaw krew skradły by buty, gdybym nie uwigzat do nóg. *(He spits.) Pteww! (SMIEDNIK gathers his mop into his pail now and goes to door. He opens door and sees that lights are out in the hallway.)* Gdzie do cholery swiatło? *(Pokes head out.)* Ciemno! *(Looks at light in room.)* Gówno! *(Pokes head outside.)* Jest tam kto???
(No response. He gathers mop and pail again and moves into hallway. Ten count. There is no one on stage. PATUMIERA enters the room. He believes himself to have movie-star looks. His shirt is silk, open, with a silk ascot, loosely tied. His sunglasses are blue. He carries a black leather briefcase, barristers' variety, plus a second case of the attaché variety, black. He also carries a small black canvas duffel bag. Several slips of paper are wedged between his teeth and lips. He spins twice in the center of the room, looking for a clock. He tries to lift his arm to look at his own wristwatch, but, due to the weight of his load, he cannot raise his wrist above his waist. He tries twice more and fails twice more. He finally stoops his face to his waist and reads his watch. He mutters, as he closes door to room. He is gasping for breath: winded.)
PATUMIERA: Chiamatemi un' ambulanza.
TRANSLATOR'S VOICE: Call me an ambulance.
(PATUMIERA falls into the center chair, downstage wall. Thus, he is alone on stage and his back is to the audience. He sits a moment, before muttering again.)
PATUMIERA: Chiamatemi un dottore.
TRANSLATOR'S VOICE: Call me a doctor.
(He throws his duffel-bag straight upstage. It lands at the feet of the second student-chair on the upstage wall. He throws his black attaché case to the same chair and then he throws his briefcase to the same spot. He stands, papers still in mouth, and staggers to the chosen upstage wall chair, falls into it, exhausted. He removes his ascot and blue gabardine suitcoat and folds them into his black attaché case. He removes a tangerine from the black duffel bag, peels it, and tries to eat it, but the papers are still in his mouth. He removes them and eats the tangerine. The door opens and PATUMIERA

wheels around to see who's come into the room. He smiles, assuming he's about to meet his teacher. MONSIEUR LAPOUBELLE enters. He is handsome, nearly bald, and diminutive. He wears extremely tight-fitting clothes: gray trousers and a black sweater with a silk scarf at the neck. He carries several papers in his mouth, but at the same time clenches a cigarette between his lips. He carries a cartable-type French book-satchel on his back and a brown leather briefcase in his left hand. In his right hand, he carries a sport coat and an overcoat and a smashed umbrella. He is also gasping air: winded. He collapses a moment on teacher's desk, causing PATUMIERA to believe that LAPOUBELLE is in fact the teacher. PATUMIERA stands and smiles. LAPOUBELLE mutters as he closes door.)

LAPOUBELLE: Appelez une ambulance.

TRANSLATOR'S VOICE: Call me an ambulance.

LAPOUBELLE: Appelez un médecin.

TRANSLATOR'S VOICE: Call me a doctor.

    (LAPOUBELLE staggers to exactly the same downstage chair first chosen by PATUMIERA. He drops his load and falls into it.)

LAPOUBELLE: Merde alors! Zut alors! Flûte! Bordel!

TRANSLATOR: Crap! Bitch! Damn! Heck!

PATUMIERA: Lei parla inglese?

TRANSLATOR: You speak English?

LAPOUBELLE: Quoi?…Répétez, s'il vous plaît.

PATUMIERA: *(Smiling.)* Lei parla Eengleesh?

    (LAPOUBELLE stands, drags his load across the room and sits beside PATUMIERA.)

LAPOUBELLE: Je comprends un peu.

TRANSLATOR: Yes, I understand a little.

PATUMIERA: Lei è Francese, vero? Stiamo fresch! Credo propria di essere l'unico Italiano el mondo che non parli Francese…

    Voi siete Francese? Io non parlo. Credo che sono l'unico Italiano nel mondo chi non parla Francese…

TRANSLATOR: You're French, right? That's a bad break. I must be the only Italian in the world who doesn't speak a word of French…

PATUMIERA: È straordinario quante lingue non parlo.

TRANSLATOR: It's amazing how many languages I don't speak.

PATUMIERA: Italiano è…come se dice…*tutta.*

TRANSLATOR: Italian is, you might say, *it.*

LAPOUBELLE: Je m'excuse, mais, je suis fatigué…

TRANSLATOR: Excuse me, but I'm a little tired…

PATUMIERA: *(Grabs LaPoubelle's hand; shakes it.)* Piacere della Sua

PATUMIERA: *(Grabs LaPoubelle's hand; shakes it.)* Piacere della Sua conoscenza. Il suo nome?

TRANSLATOR: It's a pleasure to meet you. Your name?

LAPOUBELLE: Quoi?

PATUMIERA: Signor Quoi?

LAPOUBELLE: Mister LaPoubelle.

PATUMIERA: Non capisco. Scusi.

LAPOUBELLE: *(Adds with a bit of embarrassment.)* La Patubelle. Je m'appelle Jean-Michel LaPoubelle.

TRANSLATOR: My name is Jean Michel LaPoubelle.

PATUMIERA: *(Taking his hand again.)* Come si chiama, signore?

LAPOUBELLE: Monsieur Chiama, alors?

PATUMIERA: Scusi?

LAPOUBELLE: Vous êtes Meester Chiama, n'est-ce-pas?

PATUMIERA: Meester...? *(Laughs.)* Heyyy! No, no, no...*(Speaks very slowly indeed.)* Io suo nomo Meester Carlo Fredriko Rizzonini LaPatumiera...

TRANSLATOR: My name is Carlo Fredriko Rizzonini LaPatumiera...

LAPOUBELLE: Patooo...miera?

PATUMIERA: *(Adds with a bit of embarrassment.)* La Patumiera.

LAPOUBELLE: *(Smiles.)* Parlez-vous anglais?

PATUMIERA: *(Smiling as well.)* Scusi?

LAPOUBELLE: Excusez-moi. *(Pauses; smiles.)* J'ai complètement oublié...*(Speaks in English with an extraordinarily thick accent.)* Do...yooo...speeks...in theee...Anglais?

(PATUMIERA smiles, but does not reply.)

LAPOUBELLE: Anglais? *(No reply. Suddenly LAPOUBELLE slaps his own forehead.)* Non pas *Anglais*...c'est *Eengleesh*, eh? *(Smiles and uses his hands now as he speaks, pantomiming the pulling of each word from his own mouth.)* Do...yooo...speeks...in the Eengleesh?

PATUMIERA: *(Misunderstanding the hand signals for gestures of eating.)* Una morte di fame Io. Qui mangiano solo roba da animali. Roba che ti distrugge il cervello. Buona per porci, forse. Non di certo per la gente!

TRANSLATOR: I'll say I'm hungry. All they eat here is animal food. It destroys the brain. Fit for pigs not people.

PATUMIERA: Ho ordinato una pastasciutta, giu...Cosi spappolata da restar tutta attaccata alla parete.

TRANSLATOR: I ordered a pasta downstairs...for snack...It was so overcooked, it stuck to the wall.

PATUMIERA: Non credo che siano stati contenti del fatta che l'ho sbattuta contro la parete ma…

TRANSLATOR: Hey, I don't think they appreciated me throwing it against the wall, but…

LAPOUBELLE: *(After a long pause.)* Dooo…yooo…speeks in the Eeengleesh?

PATUMIERA: Eeengleesh?

LAPOUBELLE: C'est quoi? Ce n'est pas "Eeengleesh?" *(Slaps head; laughs.)* Ahhh-oui! *(Corrects himself.)* C'est *Ahhng*leesh…

PATUMIERA: *(Smiling.)* C'est? *(Confused.)* Enngleesh? *(Recognizes word; he laughs.)* Ah! Si! Si si! Si si si! Eeengleesh!
(Silence.)

LAPOUBELLE: I…habit…à…from…Paris…up unteel…*Merde!*

PATUMIERA: Merda?
(LAPOUBELLE opens briefcase; finds French/English dictionary, begins to look for words.)

LAPOUBELLE: Excusez-moi, cher Monsieur Patchuli…

PATUMIERA: Patumiera!

LAPOUBELLE: *(Looking up; slightly annoyed.)* Ah, oui, bien, sûr…Patoo…

PATUMIERA:…eee—air—rah…Patumiera…

LAPOUBELLE: Oui. Bon.

PATUMIERA: Le piacciono le pellicole americane?

TRANSLATOR: Do you like American movies?

LAPOUBELLE: Qu'est-ce que vous avez dit?

TRANSLATOR: What did you say?

PATUMIERA: *(Pauses.)*…non si preoccupi! *(He rushes to his desk, opens briefcase and grabs his Italian/English dictionary.)*

LAPOUBELLE: *(Searching in his dictionary.)* Une seconde…*(Reading.)* Hibou…hic…hideux…ben, merde, alors!…*(Finds his words.)* Ahhh-oui! Hier! *(Reads.)* Yez-ter-dai…*(Corrects himself.)* Yester…dayii…

PATUMIERA: *(Smiling, doesn't look up from his own dictionary.)* Aspeta momento…

LAPOUBELLE: *(Suddenly angry.)* Merde alors! Fi donc! Zut alors! Bordel!

PATUMIERA: Che è successo?

LAPOUBELLE: *(Explaining in French.)* Ce n'est pas *yester*-quoi…vous savez…

PATUMIERA: Uno momento!

LAPOUBELLE: C'est avant hier…

PATUMIERA: Uno momento.

LAPOUBELLE:…non pas hier!

PATUMIERA: *(Looks up and smiles again.)* Non si preoccupi, eh? *(Back into his dictionary again.)*

LAPOUBELLE: *(Screams.)* Regardez-moi! Je veux qu'on s'occupe de moi!

PATUMIERA: *(Angrily.)* Basta!

LAPOUBELLE: Basta?

PATUMIERA: Basta!

LAPOUBELLE: *(Not laughing now, but instead quizzical.)* Basta?

PATUMIERA: *(Simply; confused.)* Si, basta.

LAPOUBELLE: Je connais le mot *basta*. C'est italien, alors!

TRANSLATOR: I know the word *basta*. It's Italian, right?

PATUMIERA: *(Ashamed of himself now.)* Si, basta. *(Shrugs.)* Scusi, eh?

LAPOUBELLE: C'est certainement italien…*(Smiles.)* Vous êtes italien?

PATUMIERA: Italien?

LAPOUBELLE: Oui, oui. Vous. Italien?

PATUMIERA: *(Realizes he is finally understood. Very pleased.)* Si. Si si. Si si si. *(Laughing and smiling. He shakes LAPOUBELLE'S hand again.)* Mi chiamo Carlo Fredriko Rizzonini LaPatumiera…*(Smiles; leans back. Smiles again.)* Come si chiama, signor?
(There is a long pause.)

LAPOUBELLE: Incroyable. Je parle anglais mieux que je parle italien.

TRANSLATOR: Incredible. I speak English better than I speak Italian.

PATUMIERA: Scusi?

LAPOUBELLE: Scusi? Je fais trois mille kilometre pour me trouver en face d'un plat de ravioli.

TRANSLATOR: I have to travel three thousand miles to end up in a room with a plate of ravioli.

PATUMIERA: Scusi?

LAPOUBELLE: Je crois bien que je suis le seul Français au monde qui ne parle aucune autre langue. Que la sienne—c'est notre tare familiale. Les langues.

TRANSLATOR: I must be the only Frenchman in the world who speaks absolutely no other language than French. Language is my family curse.
(PATUMIERA is working at dictionary and phrasebook.)

LAPOUBELLE: Je suis désolé d'avoir crié. Vraiment. Ce n'est pas dans mes habitudes. Pas du tout. Je suis en fait un type tranquille.

TRANSLATOR'S VOICE: I'm sorry I yelled. I really am. It's not like me. Not at all. I'm really a quiet guy.

LAPOUBELLE: A vrai dire je suis plutôt bien reputé pour ma…tranquillité.

TRANSLATOR'S VOICE: The fact of the matter is, I'm rather well known...for being quiet.

LAPOUBELLE: Je dois être stressé.

TRANSLATOR'S VOICE: I must be anxious.

LAPOUBELLE: Evidement que je suis stressé. Qui ne le serait pas à ma place?

TRANSLATOR'S VOICE: Of course I'm anxious! Who wouldn't be?

LAPOUBELLE: Se taper six étages et dans le noir en plus! Mais qu'est-ce qu'elles ont, ces fichues lumières?

TRANSLATOR'S VOICE: Climbing a million stairs in pitch black. What the hell's the matter with the lights out there?

LAPOUBELLE: Je crois qu'on vient de m'empoisonner. En bas. J'ai commandé et mangé un petit bout de saucisson. Pour boucher un trou. Comme nourriture, ça avait l'air d'être destiné à notre ami le cochon plutôt que d'en provenir.

TRANSLATOR'S VOICE: I think I was poisoned just now. Downstairs. I ordered and ate a little drop of sausage...for a snack...It wasn't food *from* our friend, the pig, it was food *for* our friend the pig!

LAPOUBELLE: Mon estomac fait de ces bruits impardonables. Je suis absolument navré.

TRANSLATOR'S VOICE: My stomach is making unforgivable sounds. I am desperately sorry.

(PATUMIERA suddenly throws down his dictionary after scratching forever on a piece of paper. He extends his arms, as if to say, "Now, I understand." LAPOUBELLE takes Patumiera's gesture to mean "Now, I understand." LAPOUBELLE smiles.)

PATUMIERA: *(With an enormous smile on his face and notes in hand.)* Dooo...yooo...liiiike...Ahhmerican...mooo fies?

LAPOUBELLE: Je ne comprends pas?

PATUMIERA: *(Pulling each word from his mouth; speaks extraordinarily slowly.)* Dooo...yooo...liiiike...Ahmerican moo-fies?

LAPOUBELLE: *(Still thinks PATUMIERA is commenting on his illness.)* Oui, j'ai mal à l'estomac...C'est affreux...

TRANSLATOR: Yes, I've got an awful bellyache.

PATUMIERA: *(Tries again, still smiling. This time he offers LAPOUBELLE an 8x10 glossy resume photograph of himself, which PATUMIERA holds next to his own face, for comparison.)* Dooo...yooo...liiiike...Ahmerican mofies? *(Smiles more than ever.)* Ahhh dooo lotz.

(LAPOUBELLE takes PATUMIERA'S 8x10 glossy photograph from him,

(LAPOUBELLE takes PATUMIERA'S 8x10 glossy photograph from him, comparing the man and the face. PATUMIERA takes LAPOUBELLE'S pen.)

PATUMIERA: Ha lei una penna?

LAPOUBELLE: Le stylo…? Oui, s'il vous plaît?

(LAPOUBELLE looks at photo, smiles. PATUMIERA takes back photo and autographs same and hands it back to LAPOUBELLE who looks at same and laughs. PATUMIERA pockets LAPOUBELLE'S pen)

LAPOUBELLE:…mon cher Monsieur…Ah, mon stylo.

(Patumiera gives back pen to Lapoubelle, who is laughing out of control now.)

LAPOUBELLE: C'est drôle!

PATUMIERA: *(Grabbing photograph away from LAPOUBELLE)* Che è successo?

TRANSLATOR: What's going on?

LAPOUBELLE: *(Laughing still out of control.)* Mon Dieu! *(Doubled over.)* Ma tête! *(Leaning on his desk.)* Excusez-moi, cher monsieur…c'est drôle, *hein?*

PATUMIERA: *(Angrily.)* Basta! Questa è la mia faccia a tu stai ridendo, biscotti.

TRANSLATOR: That's my face you're laughing at, cupcake.

LAPOUBELLE: Ça va, bien. Tiens! *(Pauses.)* Que j'ai mal à la tête! Mais mon Dieu! *(Turns to PATUMIERA again.)* Il faut que nous speekons thee Eenglish now, hein? *(Thumbs through his dictionary.)* Ecoutez! Yooo haf…how many…years?

PATUMIERA: Non capisco. Scusi. *(His feelings are hurt.)*

LAPOUBELLE: *(Repeats himself, but slowly.)* Yoo haf…how many years?

PATUMIERA: Non capisco. Scusi. *(Paces; refuses to answer. His feelings are still hurt.)*

LAPOUBELLE: *(Angry now.)* "Non capisco. Non capisco." C'est tout ce que vous savez dire? "Non capisco."

PATUMIERA: Calma, calma, Signor Pooblini…

LAPOUBELLE: Poubelle…LaPoubelle. Je m'appelle LaPoubelle. C'est facile, LaPoubelle! Vous voulez voir! *(LaPoubelle walks to the wastebasket that is positioned at front left leg of teacher's desk. He lifts wastebasket and waves it in PATUMIERA'S face.)* Regardez mon nom! LaPoubelle. Oui-oui, je sais. *(Shrugs. Sets down wastebasket.)* C'est exactement le même mot: LaPoubelle. Ce n'est pas banal, hein?

PATUMIERA: *(Extremely confused now.)* Scusi…*(Shrugs.)* Non capisco… *(Holds up hands so as to not be yelled at by LAPOUBELLE.)* I suo nome Lapoubelle? *(Smiles and picks up wastebasket.)* Mi chiamo la

Patumiera…*(No reply; louder.)* Io sono Carlo Fredriko Rizzonini La
Patumiera…*(Waves wastebasket.)* La Patumiera!
(LAPOUBELLE begins to understand. Points to wastebasket.)
LAPOUBELLE: Patumier…quoi?
PATUMIERA: Patumiera. *(Begins to realize.)* LaPoubelle?
LAPOUBELLE: Oui, LaPoubelle!
PATUMIERA: LaPoubelle?
LAPOUBELLE: Patumiera?
*(They both laugh now, understanding that they share the same name. They
embrace, clapping each other's back. LAPOUBELLE sets wastebasket down
again on its proper spot as they continue to laugh and point to wastebasket
time and time again, stretching the moment out as long as they can before
they fall again into embarrassed silence. They return to their seats. Each
begins to thumb through his dictionary. New man enters, MULLEIMER.
He is dressed in grey slacks black blazer with club patch, white shirt, striped
tie, maroon sleeveless vest-sweater underneath jacket. He carries several briefcases and sacks. He wears incredibly thick eyeglasses. He holds papers in his
mouth. Two cameras are strapped across his chest. He wears a raincoat over
all, which he will soon try to remove without first removing cameras. He is
totally breathless. He leans upon teacher's desk in state of near-collapse,
attempting to regain normal breathing. Both LaPoubelle and Patumiera
assume that MULLEIMER is the teacher, because he is at the teacher's desk.
They stand behind their desks and smile at MULLEIMER who finally
notices them and speaks, smiling as well.)*
MULLEIMER: Ach du liebe Scheisse! *(Collapses into chair.)* Ach du liebe
heilige Scheisse! *(Throws his briefcase on floor.)* Ich krieg noch einen
Herzschlag! *(Heaves his chest.)* Ich glaube ich hab' einen Herz Anfall!
TRANSLATOR: Holy crap! Holy jumping crap! I'm having a heart attack! I
think I'm in coronary arrest!
MULLEIMER: Warum brennen denn die Lampen draussen nicht? Bin doch
Kein Kananchen, ha, ha!
TRANSLATOR: Why the hell are the lights out out there? I'm not a rabbit!
MULLEIMER: *(Looks at other men.)* Was ist denn für eine beschissene
Schule hier? Sechs Treppen hoch und Kein Fahrstuhl!
TRANSLATOR: What the hell kind of a school is this anyway? Six flights up
and no elevator!
MULLEIMER: Für was halten die uns?
TRANSLATOR: What do they take us for?
MULLEIMER: Kancgeruhs? *(Laughs at his own joke.)* Hah-hah hah! *(Pauses;*

notices other men staring. Checks his fly zipper.) Was glotzen Sie mich
denn so an?

TRANSLATOR: What are you staring at?

MULLEIMER: Haben Sie noch nie jemanden mit einer Brille gesehen?

TRANSLATOR: Haven't you ever seen a man with eyeglasses before?

LAPOUBELLE: Qui êtes-vous?

TRANSLATOR: Who are you?

PATUMIERA: Credo di essere nella stanza sbagliata. *(Stands; smiles to
LaPoubelle.)*

TRANSLATOR: I think I'm in the wrong room.

PATUMIERA: Credo di essere nella classe sbagliata. *(Gathers his many briefcases and papers.)* Fottiti, piscione! *(Walks to door. Looks at number on
door. Looks at paper in teeth.)* Il numero e' lo stesso.

TRANSLATOR: The number's the same.

MULLEIMER: Tut mir leid, aber ich spreche kein Englisch.

TRANSLATOR: Sorry, but I don't speak any English.

PATUMIERA: Che hai detto?

MULLEIMER: Das ist doch nicht Englisch.

TRANSLATOR: That's not English.

PATUMIERA: Credevo che questa fosse la classe per l'Inglese elementare.

TRANSLATOR: I thought that this was the Primary English Class.

MULLEIMER: Mir Klingt das mehr wie Spanisch.

TRANSLATOR: That sounds like Spanish to me.

PATUMIERA: Sono nella stanza sbagliata. Scusi.

TRANSLATOR: I'm in the wrong room. Excuse me.

*(It is here that MULLEIMER begins to entangle himself in his raincoat,
which he has tried to remove without first removing the cameras that are
strapped across his chest.)*

MULLEIMER: Ich glaub' ich hab' mich in Zimmer geirrt. Entschuldigung.

TRANSLATOR: I'm in the wrong room. Excuse me.

LAPOUBELLE: *(Stands.)* Ca m'étonne que ça m'arrive à moi, mais il me
semble que je me suis trompé de salle. Sacre bleu!

TRANSLATOR: I'm in the wrorg room. Excuse me.

*(They all crowd to the door. They all exit and the stage is absolutely empty
for a count of ten. LAPOUBELLE is first to return.)*

LAPOUBELLE: Moi, j'ai raison, eux, ils ont tort.

TRANSLATOR: I'm right, they're wrong.

PATUMIERA: *(Enters quickly; smiling.)* Io ho ragione, loro hanno torto.

TRANSLATOR: I'm right, they're wrong.

MULLEIMER: *(Enters scratching head.)* Ich hab'recht, Sie nicht.

TRANSLATOR: I'm right: you're wrong.

PATUMIERA: Alemno ci sta la luce. Un po basso ma la luce.

TRANSLATOR: At least the lights are on. Dim, but on.

MULLEIMER: Wenigstens brennen die Lampen wieder, Trübe, aber doch.

TRANSLATOR: At least the lights are on. Dim, but on.

LAPOUBELLE: Au moins il y a de la lumière. Pas beaucoup, mais enfin.

TRANSLATOR: At least the lights are on. Dim, but on.

LAPOUBELLE: Je m'excuse, mais je ne parle pas norvègien.

TRANSLATOR: Excuse me, I don't speak Norwegian.

PATUMIERA: Mi dispiace, ma non parlo olandese.

TRANSLATOR: Excuse me, I don't speak Dutch.

MULLEIMER: Tut mir leid, aber ich spreche weder Flamisch noch Portugiesisch…Spreche auch weder Franzoesisch, Englisch, Italienisch, Griechisch noch Hebraeisch.

TRANSLATOR: Excuse me, I don't speak either Flemish or Portuguese. I can't speak French, Italian, English, Greek, or Hebrew, either.

MULLEIMER: Meine einzige Zunge ist und bleibt Deutsch.

TRANSLATOR: Actually, German's just about it for me.

(They all sit. Smile. Silence.)

MULLEIMER: Mein Namme ist Mülleimer. *(He picks up and points to wastebasket as he says his name.)*

TRANSLATOR: My name is Mülleimer.

MULLEIMER: Fritz Mülleimer.

LAPOUBELLE: *(Looks at wastebasket and then waves casually to Mulleimer.)* Oui, oui, je m'appelle LaPoubelle.

PATUMIERA: *(Looks at wastebasket at same time and also waves casually to Mulleimer.)* Si, si. Io sono la Patumiera…*(Smiles across to LaPoubelle.)* Si, si si, si si si. La Poubelle!

LAPOUBELLE: *(Smiles across to Patumiera.)* Oui, oui oui, oui oui oui. La Patumiera, aussi!

MULLEIMER: *(Smiling into his confusion.)* Ja. Ja-ja. Ja-ja-ja. *(Pauses sets basket down.)* Wie, bitte?

LAPOUBELLE: Comment vous appelez-vous? Je m'appelle La Poubelle.
(LAPOUBELLE and MULLEIMER smile at one another. After a long pause, Patumiera speaks, English phrasebook in hands. Waving to indicate that the room is warm.)

PATUMIERA: *(In English.)* I…canno breth. I…canno breth…*(Smiles. He offers a raisin to MULLEIMER and LAPOUBELLE after reading word on offers a raisin to MULLEIMER and LAPOUBELLE after reading word on box.)* Want uno ray-zeen?

MULLEIMER: Nein danke, bin satt.

TRANSLATOR: No thanks, stuffed.

LAPOUBELLE: Non, Merci. J'en ai jusque là...

TRANSLATOR: No, thank you. Stuffed.

(PATUMIERA waves his arm again to indicate that it is warm in the room. He repeats his newly learned English idiom.)

PATUMIERA: I...canno...breth...*(He is gaily popping raisins into his mouth.)*

(LAPOUBELLE repeats his last word, in English.)

LAPOUBELLE: Breth?...*(LAPOUBELLE begins to look for word in his French/English dictionary.)* Breth?...Je chercherai...

TRANSLATOR: Breth? I'll look it up.

(A raisin lodges in PATUMIERA'S throat. He chokes. He will begin now to make incredible sounds, wheezes, and groans. He will whack his own back, crawl about the floor near his desk, flail his arms and his face will become bright red in color. No one will pay close attention.)

MULLEIMER: *(Interrupting LAPOUBELLE'S dictionary search.)* Es tut mir Leid, aber ich spreche kein Portugiesisch.

(LAPOUBELLE looks up absently at MULLEIMER, who is standing next to him, smiling broadly.)

LAPOUBELLE: Comment?

MULLEIMER: Es tut mir Leid, aber ich spreche kein Portugiesisch.

TRANSLATOR: I'm sorry, but I don't speak Portuguese.

LAPOUBELLE: *(Takes phrasebook.)* Vous permettez, s'il vous plaît? I...canno' breth, eh? Breth?

PATUMIERA: *(Reads as he chokes. Repeats in English.)* I...canno...breth...

LAPOUBELLE: Breth, eh? Ça va. D'accord. Je chercherai...

TRANSLATOR: "Breth," huh? Okay, then. I'll look it up...

MULLEIMER: Das ist doch die Anfängerklasse für Englisch hier, ja?

TRANSLATOR: This is the primary English class, right?

MULLEIMER: *(After no response.)* Kann hier denn keiner sprechen?

TRANSLATOR: Well, how come nobody knows how to talk in here?

(No response. LAPOUBELLE is busily looking up the word "Breth" in his dictionary. PATUMIERA is whacking himself on the back and dying. MULLEIMER, cleaning his glasses, sees nothing.)

MULLEIMER: Sie müssen wissen Ich habe fast zehn Jahre gespart, un hier herzukommen...in dieses Land.

TRANSLATOR: I'd like you to know that I saved my money nearly ten years to come here…to this country.

MULLEIMER: Und Unterwegs wäre ich beinahe umgebracht worden, im Flugzeug. Von einem Luft-Piraten.

TRANSLATOR: And I nearly got killed on the airplane coming here. By a highjacker.

MULLEIMER: Auf der Untergrundbahn wär ich auch beinahe umgebracht worden.

(Pauses.)

TRANSLATOR: I almost got killed on the subway, too.

(PATUMIERA continues to choke and babble in Italian, calling for help.)

MULLEIMER: Auch von einem Piraten.

(Pauses.)

TRANSLATOR: Also by a highjacker.

MULLEIMER: In Hotel-Fahrstuhl wär ich auch beinahe umgebracht worden.

(Pauses.)

TRANSLATOR: I almost got killed in my hotel elevator too.

MULLEIMER: Nicht von einem Luft-Piraten. Was zum Tuefel hätte auch ein Luft-Pirat in einem Hotel-Fahrstuhl zu suchen?

(Pauses.)

TRANSLATOR: Not by a highjacker. What the hell would a highjacker do with a hotel elevator?

MULLEIMER: Das war ein "Mugger" im Fahrstuhl.

(Pauses.)

TRANSLATOR: *(German accent on word "mugger.")* There was a "mugger" in the elevator.

MULLEIMER: Zu meinem Gluck war er unglaubich alt.

(Pauses; no reply.)

TRANSLATOR: Lucky for me, he was incredibly old.

MULLEIMER: Heiss hier drinnen.

(Pauses.)

TRANSLATOR: It's hot in here.

MULLEIMER: Ich krieg keine Luft.

TRANSLATOR: I can not breathe.

LAPOUBELLE: I canno…breathe?

PATUMIERA: Si. Si si. Si si si.

LAPOUBELLE: Comment?

PATUMIERA: Non posso respirare.

LAPOUBELLE: Je ne peux rien trouver de pareil dans mon dictionnaire.

TRANSLATOR'S VOICE: I can't find anything like that in my dictionary.

LAPOUBELLE: Tout ce que je trouve de semblable c'est le mot "respirer."

TRANSLATOR'S VOICE: All I can find that's close is the word "breathe."

LAPOUBELLE: Mais, si vous ne pouviez pas respirer depuis la première fois que vous avez dit "Je ne peux pas respirer"...

TRANSLATOR'S VOICE: But, if you couldn't breath since the first time you said "I cannot breathe"...

LAPOUBELLE:...vous seriez...*ben*...*mort.*

TRANSLATOR'S VOICE:...You'd be...well...dead.

(PATUMIERA begins choking violently.)

LAPOUBELLE: Ca suffit ce cinema! Qu'est-ce qu'il y a?

TRANSLATOR: You're making a fool of yourself! What is it?

MULLEIMER: Sie machen sich ja laecherlich. Was haben Sie denn eigentlich?

TRANSLATOR: You're making a fool of yourself! What is it?

PATUMIERA: One canno...breathe! Non si respira un cavolo qui!

(PATUMIERA coughs violently and the raisin is released. LaPoubelle and MULLEIMER whack him on the back several times until it looks as though they are killing him. Small old Chinese woman enters, watches, sits. She is absolutely silent.)

PATUMIERA: Cosi e' maglio!

(PATUMIERA stops coughing, but men have now lifted him on to teacher's desk and continue whacking his back.)

PATUMIERA: Basta! Basta!

(They stop. PATUMIERA is furious that they have overwhacked him. He first punches LAPOUBELLES arm, as he smiles and says "Grazie.")

PATUMIERA: Grazie! (He now punches MULLEIMER'S arm.) Grazie tanto! *(MULLEIMER rolls with the punch and is the first to notice the old Chinese woman, MRS. PONG.)*

MULLEIMER: Ach! Guckt mal! Guten Abend, gnädige Frau...(He bows slightly, clicking his heels.)

LAPOUBELLE: Bonsoir, madame...(He bows.)

PATUMIERA: Bouna sera, signora...(He kisses her hand.)

MRS. PONG: Nay how mah?

LAPOUBELLE: Vous êtes japonaise?

MRS. PONG: M goi na, ngoi m sät yit gä fon wah wä...

TRANSLATOR'S VOICE: Excuse me, but I don't even speak a word of English...

MRS. PONG: Gim mon hai ngoi gä ai yit ngit ow coi gä fai wä.

TRANSLATOR'S VOICE: This is my very first day in the city...

MRS. PONG: Ngoi dieng-ä loi may gok dom mon se yä.

TRANSLATOR'S VOICE: I just got to this country yesterday...

MRS. PONG: Säle-lë...

TRANSLATOR'S VOICE: Sorry.

> *(The three men have been standing, staring at MRS. PONG as she spoke. They are astonished. LAPOUBELLE is first to speak, as he goes to his desk and sits.)*

LAPOUBELLE: Merde.

PATUMIERA: Merda.

MULLEIMER: Scheisse.

> *(Silence. A beautiful young Japanese woman enters, YOKO KUZUKAGO. She smiles and bows at everyone. Then she places a red apple on teacher's desk and giggles. She is breathing deeply, trying to catch her breath. She carries several small canvas bags, filled with books and papers. She has papers between her teeth.)*

LAPOUBELLE: Bonjour, ma jolie...*(LAPOUBELLE bows and smiles.)*

MULLEIMER: Guten Abend, mein Schatz. *(MULLEIMER bows and clicks heels and smiles.)*

PATUMIERA: Ebbene, ciao, tesoro...*(PATUMIERA straightens his spine and sucks in his stomach and smiles.)*

> *(YOKO giggles copiously. LAPOUBELLE takes her hand and kisses it. PATUMIERA moves in as a movie star might and takes her hand. By mistake, he actually finds that he has taken LAPOUBELLE'S hand and is about to kiss same. PATUMIERA hurls LAPOUBELLE'S hand away and takes YOKO'S hand, which he now kisses deeply, using his tongue for emphasis. YOKO giggles copious giggles.)*

PATUMIERA: Ah, tesoro...Tesoro mio...

YOKO: Daibu okure mashitaka? Ichijikan hodo maeni kitemimashitaga makkura deshita. Sorede shitano chisana resutoran de karui shokuji o shite kimashita.

TRANSLATOR: Am I terribly late? I stopped here about an hour ago, but all the lights were out, so I stopped at the little restaurant downstairs and had a bite.

YOKO: I no choshi ga chotto hendesu.

TRANSLATOR: I feel a little sick to my stomach.

LAPOUBELLE: Excusez-moi?

YOKO: Sukunakutomo akari ga tsuiteimasune. Kurai kedo tonikaku.

TRANSLATOR: At least the lights are on. Dim, but on.

PATUMIERA: *(Ushering YOKO to seat beside his.)* Mia cara signorina, nelle poche ore da me vissute in America, ho gia' visto, letteralmente, milioni di donne. Ma lei e chiaramente la pui belle di tutte. Che Dio la benedica.

TRANSLATOR: My dear young lady, in the scant thirty-six hours in which I've lived here in America, I have already looked at literally millions of women. But you are clearly the most beautiful of them all. God bless you.

YOKO: *(She turns to PATUMIERA, giggling.)* Sumimasenga anatano osshatteiru kotoga wakarimasen.

TRANSLATOR: I'm sorry, but I don't understand you.

PATUMIERA: *(Confused.)* Scusi?

MULLEIMER: *(Grabs YOKO; tries to lure her away from PATUMIERA.)* Meine name ist Mülleimer.

YOKO: Hai. Hai hai. Hai hai hai. *(Pauses.)* Moshiwake arimasenga eigoga hanasemasen. *(Smiles and bows.)*

TRANSLATOR: Yes. Yes, yes. Yes, yes, yes. Sorry, but I don't speak a word of English.

MULLEIMER: *(Confused.)* Gefällt ihnen denn mein Name nicht? Das wündert mich aber sehr.

TRANSLATOR: You think my name is funny? Well, who doesn't?

LAPOUBELLE: *(Smiling broadly.)* Vous êtes Chinoise?
(PATUMIERA moves behind YOKO with air of great secrecy. He puts his fingers to his lips as he whispers to her.)

PATUMIERA: Ho un segreto, Io!

TRANSLATOR: I have a secret!

PATUMIERA: Sono un membro del partito comunista.

TRANSLATOR: I am a member of the Communist Party.

MULLEIMER: *(Points to wastebasket.)* Weiss schon, die Leute machen sich immer über meinen Namen lustig.

TRANSLATOR: People always laugh at the obvious, I know.

LAPOUBELLE: *(Sees MULLEIMER pointing at wastebasket.)* C'est drôle, n'est-ce pas? Je sais, je sais.

TRANSLATOR: It's funny, isn't it? I know. I know.

MULLEIMER: Darf ich mich vorstellen, meine Fraulein…*(Extends his hand, leaning to her.)* Meine name ist Mülleimer.

YOKO: Hajimemashite.

LAPOUBELLE: *(Leans in as well.)* Je m'appelle LaPoubelle…

YOKO: Hajimemashite.

PATUMIERA: La Patumiera…
(All are amazed to discover they all share common name.)

YOKO: Watashi no namaewa Kuzukago Yoko desu. *(She points to wastebasket.)*

TRANSLATOR: My name is Yoko Kuzukago.

YOKO: Kuzukago Yoko. Kuzukago Yoko.

(All are smiling into each other's eyes as old Chinese woman moans, pitches forward out of her chair in a faint. YOKO is first to scream.)

YOKO: *Ta-i-ben!*

PATUMIERA: *Madonna mia!*

MULLEIMER: *Mein Gott!*

LAPOUBELLE: *Mon. Dieu!* De l'eau! *(He exits the room.)*

TRANSLATOR: Water!

MULLEIMER: Wasser! *(He exits the room.)*

TRANSLATOR: Water!

PATUMIERA: Acqua! *(He exits the room.)*

TRANSLATOR: Water!

YOKO: Ocha!

TRANSLATOR: Tea!

(YOKO also exits the room and, for a moment, the old Chinese woman is alone, on the floor. Slowly, she pulls herself over to her chair and, holding it for support, stands. She shakes her head. She sits in the chair, composed again. An American woman, DEBBIE WASTBA, enters. She is laden with bookbags, shopping bags, handbags, and briefcases: all hers. She has papers in her teeth. She is out of breath. She wears a long trenchcoat, British, with a colorful scarf, French. Her shoes are Italian and her bookbags a blend of Japanese, German, and Chinese. Her clothing is probably a skirt and blouse, slightly subdued, perhaps with black tights worn under the skirt. Her clothing gives her an air of competence. She looks about the empty room, seeing the many bookbags, attaché cases, jackets, etc. Finally, she sees the old Chinese woman, MRS. PONG, and smiles broadly.)

WASTBA: Hi. I'm Ms. Wastba. *(Pronounced "Wab-stah-bah.")* Odd name, huh? Dates all the way back to Mesopotamia. Wastba. *(Spells it.)* W-A-S-T-B-A. *(Pauses.)* My great grandfather shortened it…after his…uh…trouble. *(Pauses.)* Some muggy night, huh? I can't breathe. *(Pauses. Fanning the air.)* I've never been able to take heat, which is ridiculous, when you consider my family background. Three thousand years of rotten luck. All we had to do was stay put and we would have been swimming in gas and oil, but, no, we moved on and here I am. After six flights of climbing, I'd hate to be standing next to me on a bus. *(Laughs a bit at her own joke.)* Ah, yes…(Sets down a bag or two.)

Wouldn't you know the elevator would be on the fritz? That's a slang word: fritz. *(Pauses.)* You don't speak English at all, huh? *(Pauses, laughs.)* I forgot. That's why you're here. *(She laughs again.)* No English at all? *(No response.)* That's okay, really. Listen, that's all the better. No rotten habits, you know what I mean? *(Pauses; smiles, unpacking her notebooks.)* This is going to be total immersion. *(Smiles.)* Total. *(Pauses; smiles again.)* That means no speaking your base language. Which would certainly be Oriental in your case, right? *(Pauses, looks around room and sees men's bags and clothes in room.)* You sure brought a lot of stuff, didn't you? *(Pauses.)* There should be more of us. Maybe they're all late. *(Looks for clock; sees wires.)* There must be a clock…Look at that! Clock's been stolen. *(Shakes her head to express "What's the use?" as she unpacks more books.)* They'll steal anything nowadays, really. An old gentleman I know…*quite* well…he had his doorknobs taken. *(Pauses.)* It's true. Hard to believe, isn't it? *(Pauses.)* Listen, he was relieved they didn't get into his apartment altogether. *(Smiles.)* Of course, neither did he…not for hours. *(Giggles a bit; explains.)* No knobs. *(Pauses.)* At the time, I thought it was kind of…well…kinky…*You* might say "inscrutable," right?

(She laughs. No response from PONG. LAPOUBELLE rushes into room carrying a take-out container of water. He rushes to MRS. PONG.)

LAPOUBELLE: Voici. De l'eau! Pour vous…Buvez un coup…Ca ira mieux…Buvez, buvez, etc.…

(PATUMIERA, the same. Offers container.)

PATUMIERA: Acqua per lei, signora. *(And he bends near MRS. PONG, forcing her to drink as he babbles encouraging phrases.)*

(MULLEIMER rushes into room, carrying take-out container of water, as well. He forces MRS. PONG to drink same.)

MULLEIMER: Wasser, gnädige Frau.

(YOKO rushes into room. A teabag tag waves from her take-out container.)

YOKO: Ochao dozo. *(YOKO kneels near MRS. PONG and forces the old Chinese woman to drink tea.)*

(Each of them now pours liquid into the old Chinese woman, who squeals a lot, but seems nonetheless grateful. Each ad-libs in his or her own language such phrases as "Drink up. You'll feel better, etc.")

MULLEIMER: Trinken sie doch, meine Gute. Dann gehts ihnen gleich besser. Ja, ja. Ist schön gut.

(WASTBA watches them a while before speaking.)

LAPOUBELLE: *(Pointing to YOKO'S contribution.)* Ca, c'est pas de l'eau, n'est-ce pas?

PATUMIERA: *(Also pointing to teabag.)* Dev' essere qualcosa Orientale.

MULLEIMER: *(Slamming MRS. PONG'S back.)* Fühlen Sie sich besser? Ja? *(WASTBA now stands poised, her hand outstretched to greet them all.)*

WASTBA: Isn't that sweet of you all? Gifts for the Old Oriental!
(They all spin around and face her.)

WASTBA: Hi! *(She moves forward with overstated confidence and friendliness, pumping their hands in greeting.)* I'm your teacher. Debbie Wastba.
(Each rushes forward to deal with her outstretched hand. PATUMIERA will again grab LAPOUBELLE'S hand before finding WASTBA'S. He will again use his tongue for emphasis, but this time will be shocked by WASTA'S reaction, which will be shock.)

MULLEIMER: Darf ich mich vorstellen, mein Name ist Fritz Mülleimer.

WASTBA: Fritz? *(Laughs.)* Oh, the elevator…Yes.

MULLEIMER: Aber natürlich. Sie dürfen mich ruhig Fritz nennen.

WASTBA: Fritz?

MULLEIMER: Ja, Ja. Fritz. Ganz gewöhnlicher Deutscher Name. Bin Deutscher, aber ursprünglich stammen wir aus Mesopotamien. Während meine Vorfavern dort geblieben, so wäre ich jetzt Irake, ha, ha. Zum Gluck waren sie Nomaden.

WASTBA: I haven't understood a single word of what you've said. Do you know that?

MULLEIMER: *(Nonplussed. Chatty.)* Aber naturlich. Bin Deutscher, von Kopf…bis Fuss.

WASTBA: Look at that: bowing. Aren't you the polite one, now? *(To LAPOUBELLE.)* You? What's your name, hmmm?

LAPOUBELLE: Enchanté, Madame.

WASTBA: First or last?

LAPOUBELLE: *(Bows; takes her hand and kisses it.)* Moi, je m'appelle Jean-Michel LaPoubelle.

WASTBA: *(Giggles.)* Sheer poetry, I can tell you that.

PATUMIERA: *(It is here he executes his kiss.)* Io sono Carlo Fredriko Rizzonini La Patumiera…

WASTBA: *(She recoils from him.)* Just watch it, you!!
(She wipes her hand on her skirt. YOKO walks to the wastebasket and picks it up.)

YOKO: Watashi no namaewa Kuzukago Yoko desu.

WASTBA: Isn't that just simply one of the sweetest names you've ever heard?

YOKO: *(Picks up wastebasket.)* Kuzukago Yoko. Kuzukago Yoko.

PONG: *(Pointing to wastebasket.)* Ah, se-lop-pong. Ngoi gwä low Pong thlee

PONG: *(Pointing to wastebasket.)* Ah, se-lop-pong. Ngoi gwä low Pong thlee duk-ä se-lop-pong, wä.

WASTBA: *(Sees wastebasket.)* What's the matter with the wastebasket? (Pronounced as her name *WAH-STAH-BAH-SKET.*

(YOKO giggles. Puts wastebasket down. Giggles again.)

WASTBA: Okay, folks, take your seats…

(Nobody moves. She talks louder.)

WASTBA: Take…your…seats…

PATUMIERA: Take…you…zeets…

(PATUMIERA grabs his dictionary and starts looking for words. Smiling; he imitates WASTBA, calling to All. No response will follow.)

WASTBA: No no no. Sit down. *(She laughs nervously.)* Doesn't anybody speak a little English?

(They all continue to mill about her.)

WASTBA: Sit down. *(She laughs.)* Watch me now. *(She drags her chair out from behind her desk and sets it in the middle of the classroom. She slowly, carefully, demonstrates an act of sitting, first lifting out her skirts, then sitting, then folding her skirts demurely, and then folding her hands into her lap.)*

(All stand around her in circle, watching and smiling.)

WASTBA: See what I did?

(Nobody responds, but YOKO, who giggles.)

WASTBA: I sat.

(All smile and nod. WASTBA yells at them.)

WASTBA: Sit down!

(Nobody sits.)

WASTBA: Stay calm, everybody. *(She stands and walks the few steps to her desk. She turns away from the class.)*

(All watch, but for PATUMIERA, who is feverishly searching through his dictionary. WASTBA turns to class again, smiling competently now.)

WASTBA: Class, this could be one of the worst nights of our lives. *(To LAPOUBELLE.)* I want you to think seriously—deeply— about the following two words: sit down.

PATUMIERA: *(Suddenly screams.)* Eye!

WASTBA: What's the matter? Your eye? Soot?

PATUMIERA: *(Struts happily to front of room, reading from his pad of paper.)* Eye…have…eet! *(Turns and picks up his chair over his head, displaying same to Wastba.)* Eeet ees aye ki-eer.

WASTBA: Ki-air? Oh, no. No. It's *chair!* Chair. Good. It is a chair.

PATUMIERA: Alora, chair? Eeet ees a chair.

WASTBA: Good. Sit…in…it!

>*(She stands and takes chair from PATUMIERA. She places chair on floor and bends Patumiera into it. She fails. He will not bend. All, but for MRS. PONG, will soon assist WASTBA.)*

WASTBA: Sit! Sit! *(She motions to All to repeat word.)* Sit! Sit!

MULLEIMER: Ach sitz! Komm sitz. *(He begins to help push PATUMIERA into chair.)*

ALL: *(Repeat word.)* Sit, Sitz, Seet! etc. *(They all understand; push PATUMIERA downward.)*

PATUMIERA: *(He is panicked, as all are yelling at him. He stares at each with terror in his eyes.)* Scusi. Non capisco.

YOKO: Seet! *(She pushes his head from the top.)*

WASTBA AND OTHERS: Sit! Sit! Sit!

>*(PATUMIERA bends unwittingly and sits in chair, still confused.)*

WASTBA: *(Thrilled.)* Yes! He's sitting!

LAPOUBELLE: Seeting!

WASTBA: Right.

MULLEIMER: Zittsing!

WASTBA: Yes. *(To PATUMIERA.)* You're sitting!

>*(She applauds PATUMIERA. All applaud as well. PATUMIERA is no less panicked, but is smiling.)*

MULLEIMER: Zittsing!

WASTBA: *(To MULLEIMER.)* Now you!

MULLEIMER: *(Sits with enormous grin of pride on face. He stretches legs way out in front of him, leans back, as though in a steam bath and "Zitzes.")* Zittsing!

WASTBA: Wonderful! *(To LAPOUBELLE.)* Now you!

LAPOUBELLE: Ah, oui. Mais, voila. Seeting. *(He sits.)*

PATUMIERA: Eet ees aye chair.

WASTBA: *(To YOKO.)* And you.

YOKO: Sitty. *(She sits.)*

WASTBA: *(Looks at MRS. PONG.)* You did that on your own. Aren't you something?

>*(PATUMIERA tries to save face and crosses to his seat, pointing a finger to and lecturing old MRS. PONG.)*

PATUMIERA: Eeet ees aye chair.

WASTBA: Now then. Hello. I'm Debbie Wastba.

>*(All are sitting, smiling now.)*

PATUMIERA: Scusi?

WASTBA: Huh?

MULLEIMER: Was?

YOKO: Nani?

MRS. PONG: Häaaaaa?

LAPOUBELLE: Comment?

WASTBA: *(From her desk.)* Listen, now, I'll just go really slow. *(Pauses; smiles.)* My name is Debbie Wastba.

(She writes her name on blackboard. Each takes notebook and copies down name.)

WASTBA: W-A-S-T-B-A. That's pronounced Wass-tah-bah: Wastba. *(She links each of the three syllables together on board, in the following way: WA ST BA.)* Think of *Wah* as in wah-tah. Splash. Splash. *Stah* as in stah-bil-ity. And *Bah* as in Bah-dum...as in *(Sings* Dragnet *theme.)* Bum-tah-bum-bum. Well, listen. It was literally double its length in its ancient, biblical form. *(Pauses.)* Actually, that tune was wrong. It would be much more like...*(Sings again, to tune of "My Funny Valentine.)* Bum bum-bum bum-bum-bum...bum bum-bum bum-bum-bum...bum bum-bum baaahhhmmmmmmm...*(Pauses: sees they are confused.)* Well, anyway, really, you can easily check your bibles if you want. *(Rummages through stack of papers on desk, holds up lesson plan.)* This is our lesson plan. That's *lesson...plan.* Lesson plan. We're going to be together for several hours and I thought it would be highly professional and competent for me to make a plan. And I did. And here it is: *(She reads: smiling confidently.)* One. A pleasant welcome and normal chatter. For two, I've planned your basic salutations, such as the goods—good morning, good afternoon, good night, good luck, and good grief. *(She laughs.)* That was a mildly amusing joke: "good grief." Later in the night—after we've learned a bit of English—you'll be able to, well, get the joke. *(Pauses.)* Let's move along. Three will be basic customs: ours here. *(Reading again.)* Four will be a short history of our English language.

(As the students take their notes, they, as we, begin to realize that WASTBA is only writing the numbers one through six on to the blackboard—no words. They raise their hands in question, but she waves them away barging ahead.)

WASTBA: Five will be the primary lesson of the primary English class, according to the book. And six will be the very essential verb "to be." At some point, we shall also inspect the very basic concept of silence. *(Smiles.)* Now then, as you can see, there are only six points to cover and

(Smiles.) Now then, as you can see, there are only six points to cover and hours and hours ahead in which to cover them.

(All stare blankly at her smiling face.)

WASTBA: *Now* then: Questions?

(YOKO sneezes.)

WASTBA: God bless you.

MULLEIMER: Gesundheit!

PATUMIERA: Salute!

LAPOUBELLE: À tes souhaits!

(YOKO sneezes again.)

MULLEIMER: Nochmals. Gesundheit!

PATUMIERA: Salute, di nuovo.

LAPOUBELLE: À tes souhaits!

WASTBA: God bless you again! *(Laughs.)* That's a good one to learn. That's a basic custom, folks! *(Slowly: articulately.)* God bless you. Everybody. God bless you…

(All stare at her.)

WASTBA: God!…*(Waves arms above her head.)*

ALL: *(Repeating while looking up.)* God…

WASTBA: God bless…*(Touching her breasts on word "Bless.")*

ALL: God bless…

YOKO: God breast…

WASTBA: God bless *you!*

ALL: God bless you! *(All point to WASTBA on word "you.")*

WASTBA: Thank you very much and I certainly hope he's paying attention, huh? *(Smiles to LAPOUBELLE. Points overhead to ceiling.)* Him.

(All raise their hands to ask a question.)

YOKO: Shitsumon!

MULLEIMER: Duerfte ich Sie bitte etwas fragen!

(WASTBA mumbles "Let's see…" and pretends to be about to call on each of them; tantalizing them.)

LAPOUBELLE: S'il vous plaît, mademoiselle…

(WASTBA calls on LAPOUBELLE.)

WASTBA: I…choose…*you!*

LAPOUBELLE: Ah, merci, mademoiselle! Qu'est-ce que vous avez dit? Je ne comprends pas…comprends…*(Smiles.)* Même…enfin…même moi. *(He smiles again.)* Compris?

WASTBA: Huh?

LAPOUBELLE: *(Looking about class.)* Y a-t-il quelqu'un qui parle français?

(All stare blankly at LAPOUBELLE.)

WASTBA: I'm sorry, sir, but I don't speak...what you're speaking...French would be my first guess. Actually, that's quite obvious, right? *(Pauses; smiles.)* Right? *(No response.)* Parlez-vous français?

LAPOUBELLE: *(Instantly animated; speaks rapidly.)* Ou-ay! Français et seulement français! O là là!...je suis tellement heureux de vous entendre aussi parler français!

WASTBA: You're not French?

LAPOUBELLE: Comment?

WASTBA: Are you Swiss?

LAPOUBELLE: J'ai peur de ne pas avoir compris...

WASTBA: Don't the Swiss speak something like French?

LAPOUBELLE: Je ne comprends pas tout. Parlez plus lentement, s'il vous plaît, chere mademoiselle...

WASTBA: Are you from Luxembourg?

LAPOUBELLE: Dîtes-le en français, s'il vous plaît.

WASTBA: It must be your accent...

LAPOUBELLE: *Comment?*

WASTBA: I'm a little anxious tonight...

LAPOUBELLE: Si vous le disiez en français, chère mademoiselle...

WASTBA: What?

LAPOUBELLE: Quoi?

WASTBA: Yes, thank you very much. *(To the class.)* Listen, which of you speaks a little English?

PATUMIERA: *(After a long pause a short silence.)* Scusi?

WASTBA: Is that Greek?

PATUMIERA: Io...Non capisco...

WASTBA: Spanish, I'll bet.

PATUMIERA: Per piacere? Io...

WASTBA: *(She will tap out rhythm with her foot to Spanish words.)* I used to know a little Spanish...let's see...Me voy a lavar un poco para quitarme la arena que tengo pegada.

PATUMIERA: Scusi?

WASTBA: Don't you get it? It's beach talk. It means, "I'm going to wash the sand from my body." If some greaseball-type bothers you at the beach, that's what you say. My friend Ramon Vasoro taught me that.
(They all stare at her, blankly.)

WASTBA: Well, now, that's probably enough chatter. Do you have all your slips? *(No response.)* Slips? *(No response.)* Your slips. From the office. *(No response. She walks to LAPOUBELLE and begins rummaging through his briefcase.)* Excuse me.

LAPOUBELLE: Qu'est-ce que vous faites là?

(She continues to rummage.)

LAPOUBELLE: Pardonez-moi, mademoiselle, mais qu'est-ce que vous voulez?

(She continues to rummage.)

LAPOUBELLE: Si vous m'expliquez ce que vous cherchez, j'essayerai de la trouver! *(No response.)* Mais, chère mademoiselle…Bordel! Quelle belle soirée!

WASTBA: *(She finds his slip.)* This! *(She waves it to class.)* Give me your slips. *(All smile and rummage about looking for their slips, which each finds and hands to WASTBA. As she collects each slip, she reads each name, mispronouncing each.)*

WASTBA: LaPoo…Is this a name?

LAPOUBELLE: LaPoubelle. Je m'appelle Jean Michel LaPoubelle. C'est cela? C'est mon nom que vous voudriez? C'est tout?

WASTBA: That's very unique. *(To MULLEIMER.)* Where's yours? *(Takes slip, tries to read it.)* Is this of Slavic persuasion? *(Squints. She moves to MRS. PONG and plucks the slip that has been stapled to PONG'S sleeve, not looking away from MULLEIMER'S slip.)* Look at all these vowels.
(Hands slip to PATUMIERA, who is staring into YOKO'S blouse, not paying attention to WASTBA. He takes the slip from her.)

WASTBA: Can you pronounce this?

PATUMIERA: Grazie…

WASTBA: I don't think *that's* right. *(Squints. Looks again.)* Maybe. How's your eye? *(Smiles at all.)* I have new hard contacts. I hated the soft ones. Had to wash them every night. I went back to hard…
(Blank stares all around.)

WASTBA: Contacts. *(Smiles.)* Okay. There's a perfectly fine place to begin.
(She will walk to MULLEIMER and pluck his eyeglasses from his astonished face.)

MULLEIMER: Ah! *(He is nearly blind without glasses and will soon feel his way, looking for WASTBA.)*

WASTBA: These are…*(She reaches out. Plucks glasses.)*…eyeglasses.

MULLEIMER: Meine Brille!!
(He accidentally gropes WASTBA, grabbing her breast in one absolutely clean move. All see and are amazed. PATUMIERA stands. He is vaguely outraged.)

WASTBA: *Oh God!*

PATUMIERA: EEEAYY!

WASTBA: *(Shocked and amazed.)* I'm going to try to overlook that…*(Takes a deep breath.)* God! Let's go on. *(To all.)* These are eyeglasses. It's a new word. Learn it. Eyeglasses. *(Tries them on.)* Oooooo. You must be blind as a bat. *(Smiles again.)* Eyeglasses. Eye-glasses. Eyeee-glasssezzzz… *(Waves arms.)* Everybody! Eyeee-glassezzz.

YOKO: Everiii—Eyeee-grasssezzz…

WASTBA: Good! Eyeee-glasssessssszzz…*(Waves her arms.)* Eyeeee-glassezzz

LAPOUBELLE: Eye-glassée.

PATUMIERA: Eye-glasso.

WASTBA: Eye-glasses.

MRS. PONG: Eye…eye…gassieh.

WASTBA: *(Taps her foot to lead her students' chant of the word "eyeglasses.")* Everybody…eyeglasses…eyeglasses…etc. *(Smiling, but clearly in panic.)* Wonderful. Really. I wouldn't kid you. You're all just really wonderful.
(She applauds her students, who are so pleased by her approval, they all scream the word "eyeglasses" at her again, each with his or her own indigenous accent.)

ALL: Eyee-glassy (zes) (o) (ée) etc.
(N.B. MRS. PONG has been totally silent, but is awake, staring at all that goes on, smiling deeply; nibbling food.)

WASTBA: Just really and sincerely terrific. Really. Terrific. Sincerely. *(Pauses.)* Oh God…*(Smiles.)* Now watch. *(She points to her eye.)* These are…contacts. *(No reply.)* Contacts. *(No reply. She touches eye.)* Contacts. *(Suddenly, she stiffens, blinking. A contact lens has popped out of her eye and fallen on to the floor.)* Oh…my…dear…God!
(They all stare dumbly as WASTBA crawls around floor.)

WASTBA: Help me! It's on the floor!

LAPOUBELLE: *Floor!*
(He writes the word down. They look from one to the other, dumbly. YOKO and PATUMIERA move to her.)

WASTBA: Help me! I'm not insured! *(Suddenly, she stops them from stepping on lens.)* Don't anybody move!
(They all look away from her. She falls back down on the floor.)

WASTBA: I got it! *(She wets the tip of her index finger, right hand, with which she stabs at lens. When it sticks to the tip of her finger, she screams.)* I really got it! Oh! Lucky break! *(She transfers lens to her mouth.)* Thank God, huh? *(She takes it out of her mouth, holds it to light, looks at it, places it back into her mouth. She squints at class. She stands, smiling.)* I said, "Thank *into her mouth. She squints at class. She stands, smiling.)* I said, "Thank God, huh?" *(She looks at it, holding the lens toward the light, squinting.)* *(MULLEIMER, blinded, has raised his hand, politely, but high in air. He holds his position.)*

WASTBA: I'll have to go wash it off. *(She walks to door.)* I'll be right back. *(WASTBA exits. There is silence in the room for a moment. MULLEIMER breaks the silence, smiling to all.)*

MULLEIMER: Fräulein Lehrerin, hab ein kleines Problemchen! Bin ein bisschen schwer hörig. Gewöhlich bin ich ja Lippenleser, und das hilft schon, aber sie hat mir dock die Brille weggeschnappt, und jetzt kann ich nicht mehr sehen was ich nicht hören kann.

TRANSLATOR: Teacher, I've got a problem here. I'm a little hard of hearing, so usually I lip-read, which helps, but you took my glasses, so now I can't see what I don't hear.

(There is a moment of silence in the room, as all stare at spot where once there was a transparent contact lens. PATUMIERA is the first to break the silence. He seems angry with LAPOUBELLE.)

PATUMIERA: *(To LAPOUBELLE.)* Che cacchio gli hai detto?

TRANSLATOR: What the hell did you say to her?

YOKO: *(Very confidently; takes center.)* Kore wa akirakani totaru imashon no senjutsu desuyo.

TRANSLATOR: This is clearly a "total immersion" tactic.

PATUMIERA: Scusi?

YOKO: Konna hanashi o kiitakatoga arimasu. Otokono hito ga banana o te ni motte kyohitso ni haitte kitandesutte. Ban-ban to sakebinagara.

TRANSLATOR: I once heard of a man running into a classroom with a banana yelling "Bang-bang!"…

YOKO: Konna funi. *(YOKO runs out of classroom.)*

TRANSLATOR: Watch, I'll show you.

PATUMIERA: *(To LAPOUBELLE.)* E a lei, che cavolo gli hai detto?

TRANSLATOR: Now, what do you say to her?

YOKO: *(Runs back into classroom.)* Ban-ban. Tokyo deno dekigoto deshita. Amerikajin no bijinesuman no tame no nihongo no kurasu.

TRANSLATOR: It was in Tokyo. In a Japanese class for American businessmen.

YOKO: Kekkyoku Amerikajintachi wa sono hito o tatakinomeshite, motte ita banana o toriagechattan desutte.

TRANSLATOR: The way the story goes, the Americans beat the man up and took his banana.

PATUMIERA: Eh tu non vuoi rermare, eh?

TRANSLATOR: You're not going to stop, are you?

YOKO: Nani?

PATUMIERA: "Nani?" Se quella é inglese, tu' accenta è miserable…Un Orechio di stagno…

TRANSLATOR: "Nani?" If that's English, then your accent is intolerable. Language-wise, you've got a tin ear.

(PATUMIERA moves to WASTBA'S desk. Yoko begins copying down phrases from her phrasebook.)

MULLEIMER: Entschuldigen Sie, Fraeulein Lehrerin, dürfte ich Sie bitte privat sprechen?

TRANSLATOR: Excuse me, teacher. May I have a private word with you?

LAPOUBELLE: Excusez-moi?

MULLEIMER: Fraeulein Lehrerin! Fraeulein Lehrerin!

TRANSLATOR: Teacher! Teacher!

PATUMIERA: *(To LAPOUBELLE.)* E ma, che cazzo fai a tutti quanti?

TRANSLATOR: Now, what did you do to him?

LAPOUBELLE: *(To MULLEIMER.)* Que voulez-vous?

MULLEIMER: Entweder bringen Sie mir die Lehrerin oder lassen Sie mich in Ruhe, OK?

TRANSLATOR: Either get the teacher or get off my back, OK?

LAPOUBELLE: Une bonne classe, hein? Je suis très, très content.

(LAPOUBELLE has a small white paper bag filled with candies. He smiles and eats.)

TRANSLATOR: Quite a class, huh? I'm very pleased by the way things are going.

MULLEIMER: Kann nicht behaüpten, dass ich die Amerikaner verstehe. Warm und Freundlich sind sie ja, aber sie nehmen man die Brille weg, und warum, wenn ich Fragen darf, warum?

TRANSLATOR: I can't pretend to understand Americans. They're warm and friendly, but they take your eyeglasses and why, I ask you, why?

MULLEIMER: Und was mich so masslos aergert ist dass niemand von Euch Schweinehunden mir hilft!

TRANSLATOR: And why, I keep wondering, won't any of you sons of bitches help me get them back?

MULLEIMER: Falls ich Ihnen sage ein Baum stuerzt im Walde, und kein Mensch hier spricht ein Wort Deutsch, stuerzt dann der Baum, oder nicht?

TRANSLATOR: If I tell you a tree falls in the forest and nobody in here

TRANSLATOR: If I tell you a tree falls in the forest and nobody in here speaks any German, then does the tree ever realy fall?

(LAPOUBELLE offers candy to Mulleimer, placing piece on MULLEIMER'S desk. MULLEIMER stares down blindly. Angrily, MULLEIMER knocks the candy away.)

LAPOUBELLE: Est-ce que vous vous rendez compte combien vous êtes impoli?

TRANSLATOR: Do you have any idea how rude you're being?

(LAPOUBELLE picks up candy and sits; sulks. PATUMIERA crosses to YOKO again; sits.)

YOKO: *(Taking over class as though teacher.)* Ne. Minna kittekudasai. Hitotsu narai mashitayo. Eigo desuyo.

TRANSLATOR: Listen, everybody. I think I've learned something. I have some English here.

YOKO: *(In English, after checking her phrasebook and notes. Her accent is extremely heavy.)* I am starbing to…dess. *(She giggles.)*

TRANSLATOR: I am starving to death.

PATUMIERA: Si. Si, si. Si, si, si.

YOKO: *(In English; heavy accent.)* I would like my check, my rolls and my orangeee…*(YOKO teaches words to all.)*

MRS. PONG: Checoo…

PATUMIERA: Lolls…

YOKO: Lolls? Na. *Rolls.*

LAPOUBELLE: Orange.

YOKO: Watashiwa kotogakko de tomikakino seisekiga tottemo yokat-tandesuyo. Hontowa watashiwa kotobao umaku tsukaikonasemasu. *(Pauses; smiles at all.)*

TRANSLATOR: I got really good grades in high school for creative writing and public speaking. I've got a way with words.

YOKO: Watashino ie wa mukashikara benjutsu ni taketeite, sono rekishi wa mesopotamia made sakanoborundesu. *(She giggles at a blank-faced PATUMIERA.)*

TRANSLATOR: We have a history of oratory dating all the way back to Mesopotamia.

PATUMIERA: *(Frustrated by her incomprehensible language.)* Non ho capito nemmena una parole che tu hai detta, mia stuzzicadente. Ma perche tu sei cosi magra? Non piàce a mangiare o sei stanca di mangiare il riso?

TRANSLATOR: I haven't understood word one of what you've just babbled, toothpick. How come you're so skinny, huh? Don't you like food or do you just pick at your rice?

LAPOUBELLE: *(To YOKO.)* Je n'ai plus que douze heures et demie pour apprendre l'anglais, sinon je suis un homme mort. *(LAPOUBELLE grins as though his confession is totally unimportant.)*

TRANSLATOR: I've got twelve and a half hours left in which to learn English or else I might as well be dead.

YOKO: Nani?

(PATUMIERA sees that LAPOUBELLE has moved in on YOKO. Sits on desk next to YOKO, squeezing LAPOUBELLE off desk completely. YOKO and PATUMIERA each take candy from LAPOUBELLE, which they dislike and discard.)

LAPOUBELLE: Demain matin de bonneheure, j'ai un rendez-vous extrêmement important.

TRANSLATOR: I have an enormously important business meeting in the morning.

LAPOUBELLE: Si j'échoue, toute ma société d'assurance sera en faillite. Je perdrais mon job, ma jeune femme, mes enfants seraient obligés de quitter leur école privée...

(YOKO and PATUMIERA turn away from LAPOUBELLE.)

TRANSLATOR: If I fail, my entire insurance company will bankrupt. Then I'll lose my job, my young wife and my children will have to drop out of private school...

(LAPOUBELLE stands at center, talking to no one in particular.)

LAPOUBELLE: Je n'aurais plus qu'à me tuer.

TRANSLATOR: I'll have to kill myself.

(LAPOUBELLE sees that YOKO is no longer paying attention—is bored—and now smiling at PATUMIERA. LAPOUBELLE moves to MRS. PONG, as she nods to him, seeing that he is trapped and alone at center.)

MRS. PONG: Wa, wa.

LAPOUBELLE: *(To Mrs. Pong.)* Vous, vous êtes mariée, veuve, ou divorcée?

TRANSLATOR: Are you married, widowed, or divorced?

PONG: M goi nay. Ngoi m hieng gon nay mun mwut wä. Nay gong monmon yä-ä ye. Ngoi ännäm gai wä.

LAPOUBELLE: Veuve! Je suis désolé. J'espère que ça n'a pas trainé.

TRANSLATOR: I'm sorry to hear that. I hope it wasn't a lingering death.

PONG: Thlee mwut-ä Yea thlee, toi mä siek-ä?

TRANSLATOR: Give me a clue: animal? vegetable? or mineral?

LAPOUBELLE: Oui, ça va mieux comme ça. Moi même, j'ai perdu ma première femme...

TRANSLATOR: That's a relief. I myself lost my first wife...

MRS. PONG: Toi?

TRANSLATOR: Vegetable?

(PONG has taken a piece of candy from LAPOUBELLE'S bag during the above exchange.)

LAPOUBELLE: Non, elle m'a quitté.

TRANSLATOR: No. She ran away.

LAPOUBELLE: Elle m'a laissé un petit mot me disant qu'elle s'ennuyait avec moi.

TRANSLATOR: She left a note saying I was boring.

PONG: Haa?

LAPOUBELLE: Emmerdant, quoi.

TRANSLATOR: I said "boring."

PONG: Ahhhh.

LAPOUBELLE: Ma nouvelle femme est plutôt jeune. Elle aussi me trouve emmerdant.

TRANSLATOR: I have a young wife now. She finds me boring as well.

LAPOUBELLE: Heureusement, j'ai assez confiance en moi-même pour que ça ne m'ébranle pas.

TRANSLATOR: Luckily, I'm secure enough about my personality not to have to worry about such matters.

(MRS. PONG throws her head back, snores loudly. Her head drops down to her chest. She is asleep, snoring loudly. She has, possibly, spat LAPOUBELLE'S candy to floor. PATUMIERA and YOKO stare across to him. LAPOUBELLE is shocked and amazed and opens his suitcoat, trying to hide the sleeping MRS. PONG from his classmates.)

LAPOUBELLE: *(To MULLEIMER.)* Très vieille et visiblement trés fatiguée. Je lui ai conseillé de faire un petit somme.

TRANSLATOR: She's very old and is obviously exhausted. I've convinced her to get some rest.

MULLEIMER: Bitte keine ploetzlichen Bewegungen! Kann nur Schatten sehen. Es ist einfach schrecklich.

TRANSLATOR: Try not to make any sudden moves. I can only see shadows, and it's terrifying.

MULLEIMER: Wenn ich ganz still sitze und die Augen schliesse, ist es doch viel weniger beaengstigend.

TRANSLATOR: It's a lot less scary for me if I just sit here and close my eyes.

(MULLEIMER does so, allowing his head to drop in sleeping position. PATUMIERA and YOKO stare at LAPOUBELLE, who stares at MULLEIMER and MRS. PONG, thinking he has put both of them to

MULLEIMER and MRS. PONG, *thinking he has put both of them to sleep. LAPOUBELLE sits; bows his head, silence.)*

PATUMIERA: Ma quantomi manca Italia!

TRANSLATOR: I am homesick.

YOKO: Uchi ga koishiiwa.

TRANSLATOR: I am homesick.

PATUMIERA: *(Moving toward WASTBA'S desk.)* Ma fortunamento per noi abbiamo una buona maestra...simpatico, di namica, gentile... *(PATUMIERA touches Wastba's jacket on coat tree.)*

TRANSLATOR: Lucky for us we've got ourselves a great little teacher... warm...considerate...gentle...

(Suddenly we hear a bloodcurdling scream—Wastba's—from offstage, beyond the door, somewhere deep in a dark corridor. There is a moment of silence before each stands and comments.)

MULLEIMER: Was war das? Unser kleiner kürbis vielleicht?

TRANSLATOR: What was that? Could that be our little pumpkin?

PATUMIERA: *(Also stands.)* La madonna sta in un imbroglio.

TRANSLATOR: Sounds like that madonna's in trouble!

LAPOUBELLE: Notre adorable artichaut! Mon dieu!

TRANSLATOR: Our darling little artichoke! My God!

YOKO: *(Standing.)* Sensei wa amerika de tatta hitorino watashino tomodachi nanoni.

TRANSLATOR: She's the only true friend I have in America!

(LAPOUBELLE moves quietly to the door. Suddenly, WASTBA bursts into the room, slamming the door in LAPOUBELLE'S face. He disappears from our view, squashed behind door, into wall. WASTBA closes door now and presses her back against same. She holds SMIETNIK'S mop in her hand.)

LAPOUBELLE: Mademoiselle...

(He reaches for her and she screams, immediately handing mop to LAPOUBELLE, who places same behind coat tree, flat on floor, out of audience's view of same.)

WASTBA: Yaaa-iiiiii!!! *Git!*

(LAPOUBELLE scoots back to his chair and sits. WASTBA continues to lean heavily against door, keeping it closed. WASTBA is incredibly frightened. She begins to speak. Her mouth moves, her lips form words, but there is no voice under them. Finally, the words are audible. All have been staring intently, wondering no doubt if this has all been part of an intensive study of primary English.)

WASTBA: There's...there's a...there's a very dirty man...*(Rubs her face; looks down first.)* There's a very dirty man out there...*(She giggles.)* In the ladies' room. *(She waits for response. There is none.)* There's a man in the ladies' room. *(Pauses.)* He...touched...*(Pauses; then speaks in determined way.)* He tried to hug me but, thank God, he was on his knees so he couldn't reach. *(Wipes brow.)* I wouldn't want to tell you what he *did* reach, however.

PATUMIERA: Che successo?

WASTBA: I said I wouldn't tell you! What are you, a tell-me-a-story freak or something??

PATUMIERA: Scusi?

WASTBA: Yuh. Sure.

MULLEIMER: Ich kann weder hören noch sehen. Könnte mir Bitte jemand helfen???

TRANSLATOR: I can't hear or see. Could somebody help me?

LAPOUBELLE: Mais calmez-vous. Vous êtes affreusement tendue.

MULLEIMER: Wer ist das?

WASTBA: *(Completely panicked.)* Oh...my...God...*(Screams.)* Tranquility! *(Spins in circles.)* Got...to...get calm! *(Yells at class.)* Calm down!

MULLEIMER: *(Stands in front of WASTBA.)* Wo ist meine Brille?

WASTBA: I know you're upset, but can you imagine how *I* feel? *(She washes herself—her hands and arms—with "Wash-'n-Dri" napkins from her sack.)* He...was...enormous. Eight or nine feet tall!

MULLEIMER: Wo ist meine Brille, Fräulein?

WASTBA: For God's sake, this is no time for foreign language problems! *(Pauses.)* He couldn't have been eight or nine feet tall. I must be hysterical. Sit down.

(She sits, and they all sit, but for MULLEIMER.)

WASTBA: I'm sitting. Why don't you whistle something? *(She whistles.)* I'm whistling. *(She pauses.)* I'm hysterical. Why don't you change the subject? Class. I'm changing the subject— *(She smiles.)* We must move on. Whatever is happening is happening in the ladies' room and corridor and not in our room.

(Smiles, locks door again, Mulleimer stands nearby.)

WASTBA: Our door is locked. Our room is safe. *(Pauses.)* Things make sense here.

MULLEIMER: *(In front of WASTBA, near door.)* Meine Brille? Wo ist sie?

WASTBA: *(Pounds fist onto desk, loudly.)* Stop following me around, damn it. I said things make sense in here and now I really mean it!

MULLEIMER: *(Moves quickly, blindly, back to his desk. Students assist him— lead him.)* Wie bitte?

WASTBA: We're going to just have to continue our class in a sane and orderly fashion. Otherwise, we perish. *(To MULLEIMER.)* You want to perish?

MULLEIMER: Wie bitte?

WASTBA: Sit down.

LAPOUBELLE: Zeet! Zeet!

(MULLEIMER finds his way back to his chair and sits.)

WASTBA: *(To LAPOUBELLE.)* You! You want to perish?

LAPOUBELLE: *(Stands; recites the word, tentatively.)* Per...per-...per-ashh...

WASTBA: "Ish," not "ash." There's a good word to learn. Perish. *(Writes "Perish" on blackboard.)*

PATUMIERA: Mia cara signorina...

WASTBA: *(Turns to him; angrily.)* Sit down and learn the word "perish."

(Pauses. PATUMIERA stops, turns, rushes to his seat, sits.)

WASTBA: I'm getting calm. If you were smart, you'd go for calm, too. See? If I were any calmer, I'd be boring.

LAPOUBELLE: Ma chère mademoiselle, il y a encore un petit problème...*encore*...

WASTBA: I said "Boring."

YOKO: *(Stands suddenly; takes over. Points to her head in gesture of "I understand now.")* Ah! Bowling. *(She mimes bowling.)*

MULLEIMER: Wo ist meine Brille?

(WASTBA, MULLEIMER, LAPOUBELLE, PATUMIERA, and YOKO simultaneously.)

WASTBA: I don't understand a word you're saying!

MULLEIMER: Ich verstehe kein Wort von dem was sie sagen.

LAPOUBELLE: Je ne comprends pas un mot de ce qu'ils disent.

PATUMIERA: Non capisco una parola di quel che dicono.

YOKO: Watashiwa ka rerano hanashiteru kotoga wakarimasen.

WASTBA: *(Writes the word "English" beside the word "Perish" on the blackboard. Yells; stopping their words.)* I'm afraid you're going to have to just get it through your heads that this is an *English* class and the language I'm afraid I must *insist* we all speak is...for the love of God...*English.* *(She points to the words.)* Attention must be paid to these words: They both end in "i-s-h." *(Pauses.)* Let's hear them. *(No response. Waves her arms.)* English. Perish. *(No response.)* English. Perish. English. Perish. I demand you follow! *(She points at PATUMIERA.)* You! *English. Perish.* *(PATUMIERA is again in panic. He smiles and shrugs and tries to repeat what she has said: tries to please her.)*

PATUMIERA: *(Mimicking.)* English. Perish.

WASTBA: Very good. *(Waves arms.)* Everybody now: *Hit it! (Screams.)* English! Perish.

LAPOUBELLE: English. Per-*eesh.*

WASTBA: *English! Perish!*

ALL: *(Each yells the words "English! Perish!" in an accent indigenous to his or her own particular country.)* Iiingliish! Glishie! Anglish! *(Etc.)*
(MULLEIMER leans forward trying to whisper in the direction of WASTBA'S voice, but instead whispers in the clear.)

MULLEIMER: *Fräulein!...*

WASTBA: *(To all.)* That was wonderful! See? You can get it if you really want…But you must try…Just like the song says .

MULLEIMER: *(Whispers again.) Fräulein!*

WASTBA: Huh?

MULLEIMER: *(Whispers again; embarrassed to be without his glasses. Tries to appear as though all in his life is normal.) Fräulein!*

WASTBA: *(Whispers across to him.) What do you want?*

MULLEIMER: *(Whispers.) Wo ist meine Brille, Fräulein?*

TRANSLATOR: *(Whispers.) Where are my glasses, lady?*

WASTBA: *(Whispers.) Huh?*

MULLEIMER: *Wo ist meine Brille, Fräulein?*

WASTBA: *(Whispers.)* You will either get a goddamn English word out of that mouth of yours or just drop all talk!…*(Pauses; she still whispers.)*

MULLEIMER: *(Whispers.) Versteben Sie denn nicbt dass icb nicht verstehe?*

TRANSLATOR: *(Whispers.) Don't you understand that I don't understand?*

WASTBA: *(Whispers.) Don't you understand that I don't understand?*
(MRS. PONG stands and begins to walk to the closed door. She is holding her stomach and seems to be experiencing pain. She bows to WASTBA, who seems astonished to see the old woman's move to door.)

WASTBA: *(To old MRS. PONG.)* What are you doing?
(MRS. PONG bows to LAPOUBELLE and PATUMIERA, who stand and return her bow.)

LAPOUBELLE: Bon soir, madame.

PATUMIERA: Bonn sera…

WASTBA: Where are you going?
(MRS. PONG bows.)

WASTBA: Where do you want to go to do what?
(MRS. PONG bows again.)

WASTBA: Don't open that door! *(WASTBA leaps between MRS. PONG and the door.)* Didn't you hear me?

(WASTBA shoves MRS. PONG back away from door and knocks her down. MRS. PONG squeals. All go to PONG and help her up.)

LAPOUBELLE: Elle lui fait mal!

TRANSLATOR: She hurt her!

PATUMIERA: Le ho fatto male!

TRANSLATOR: She hurt her!

YOKO: Sensei wa ranbo o shimashita!

TRANSLATOR: She hurt her!

WASTBA: I'm sorry. I didn't mean to shove that hard. Push always grows to shove, I swear to God!

LAPOUBELLE: Nom de Dieu, vous avez vu ca? Elle a frappé cette vieille vietnamienne.

WASTBA: I didn't mean to push this old Chinese lady around...or *certainly* down!

(Looks at all, who are each staring amazed at WASTBA.)

YOKO: *(Yells.)* Dou shitanodesuka?

PATUMIERA: *(Yells.)* Che è successo?

LAPOUBELLE: *(Yells.)* Qu'est-ce qui se passe?

MULLEIMER: *(Yells.)* Ich flehe Sie an meine Brille!

WASTBA: What the hell is happening in here anyway?

(MRS. PONG makes another run at the door, more confirmed this time. She succeeds in reaching the knob this time. WASTBA whacks at her hand on the knob.)

WASTBA: Hey! *(WASTBA pulls MRS. PONG away from the door.)* I told you once, damn it! Now get away from this door! *(WASTBA drags MRS. PONG back to her desk and seats her.)* Now, damn it! I've told you there's a dirty man out there. *(She holds MRS. PONG by the back of her jacket.)* At your age, what the hell are you looking for, anyway?

(MRS. PONG whimpers, pulling back. All are shocked, staring.)

WASTBA: You could get hurt out there! *(Holding MRS. PONG still by back of her jacket.)* Try to understand...

MRS. PONG: *(She breaks free and runs to her desk, screaming.)* Ahhh-yiiiii...

WASTBA: Why are you screaming?

MRS. PONG: Ahhhh-yiiii!

WASTBA: Stop it!

MRS. PONG: Ooooo. *(She sits; whimpers. She eats.)*

WASTBA: *(Leaning over MRS. PONG.)* Did I hurt you, old Chinese woman?

MRS. PONG: *(Moving backwards as a crab.)* Ahhh-yiiiiii-*ahhhh*...

YOKO: Kio ochitsukete! Kitto nani ka riyu ga arundesuwa.

WASTBA: *(To class.)* I don't even know her name. *(To YOKO.)* What's her name? *(No response.)* Aren't you family? *(No response. WASTBA grabs large red tag from around MRS. PONG'S neck.)* There's a tag on her neck…*(Reads.)* "Hi. My name is *Zink?*" *(Strains to read.)* I can't read this!…*(To MRS. PONG.)* What's your name? *(No reply.)* Don't you even know your own name? *(Reads tag again.)* "I don't speak English…" *(To MRS. PONG.)* Oh, no need to be modest.
(Pats MRS. PONG, who moans.)
WASTBA: "Mrs. Pong…" Is that your name: Mrs. Pong?
MULLEIMER: Meine Brille…
WASTBA: *(In panic; to MULLEIMER.)* Hey, I've seen a lot worse on laundries and restaurants…Wing, Ling, Ding…*(Shrugs.)* But, listen. Pong's no picnic, either, I guess…
(WASTBA absently pats PONG'S head, unintentionally scaring the old lady again.)
MRS. PONG: Yiiii—iiii…
WASTBA: *(To MRS. PONG; leaning in to her.)* Don't you understand *any*-thing? *(No response.)* What I did I did for your own good…
(N.B. Throughout above, WASTBA has been holding MRS. PONG erect in her chair.)
LAPOUBELLE: Je pense que vous devriez vraiment vous expliquer. Après tout, vous l'avez poussé par terre.
WASTBA: Everybody here is my witness, right?
PATUMIERA: Ho bisogno di un splegazione, adesso.
WASTBA: I know you're all upset. I'm upset too…
(MRS. PONG whimpers.)
WASTBA: Now *you're* upset too…*(WASTBA smiles at all.)* We're just going to have to drop our mutual differences for a while and learn some English. A common goal is always for the common good…
LAPOUBELLE: Chérie mademoiselle…Personne ne comprend encore! Compris? Personne!
WASTBA: I said "common goal for common good." Don't you ever pay attention? *(WASTBA releases her hold on MRS. PONG and begins to move to the blackboard.)* These distractions will have to stop.
(She picks up apple that YOKO brought to class for her. WASTBA smashes apple on desk. YOKO screams.)
WASTBA: One rotten apple spoils a bunch. *(WASTBA throws apple into wastebasket.)* One must resist temptation. Mrs. Pong has managed to distract us…She has, in short, managed to become our mutual rotten

apple, but…I needn't remind you that the object of this class is clearly English and hardly some old Pong.

(MRS. PONG sings "I can't give you anything but love, baby" very quietly; a hum. Reading from sheet at same time all babble questions about MRS. PONG and WASTBA'S wrestling match.)

WASTBA:…so if you'll kindly and politely pay a little attention here, I'm going to give you the history of English. *(Pauses; smiles.)* I picked this sheet up in the office…early this morning.

(WASTBA has now written the words "The Great Vowel Shift" on the blackboard. PONG tries to calm herself down by singing more loudly now. The words are sometimes clear. "Baby" is sung in English.)

MRS. PONG: *(To the tune of "I Can't Give You Anything But Love.")* Bah, bah, bah, bah, bah, bah, bah, bah, bahhh…Ba-bee
Bah, bah, bah, bah, bah, bah, bah, bah, bahhh…Ba-bee.

WASTBA: "The Great Vowel Shift." *(Reading.)* "Compared to Old English, in phonological terms, Middle English's e, e…I"…*(She writes the letters on blackboard as she lectures.)*

YOKO: IIII…

PATUMIERA: Eeee…

WASTBA: I, e, u…

LAPOUBELLE: Ooooo…

WASTBA: Please just quietly take notes, okay. "O and e…"

MRS. PONG: *(Ill and faint.)* Aaaaayyyyiiii…

WASTBA: Oh. *(Without looking up, continues reading.)* "…and a were raised in their articulation. Middle English's a, which comes from Old English's short a, in open syllables, was fronted as well." *(Looks up at class.)* While this may seem to mean little to you, it means even less to me, and I was *born* speaking English perfectly! *(Reads again.)* "The highest two Middle English front and back vowels, i…"

YOKO: iiii

WASTBA: "and u respectively, became sounds traditionally known as dipthongs…"

MRS. PONG: *(Collapses in unconsciousness, her head crashing down forward on her desk.)* Oooooo…

WASTBA: *(Continuing.)* "These changes in the quality of the long or tense vowels constitute what is known as…" *(Underlining each word as she says it.)* "…The Great Vowel Shift."

LAPOUBELLE: *(To Yoko.)* Mon Dieu. Mais la vieille vietnamienne! Elle est tombée dans les pommes.

PATUMIERA: Forse è la vechiai. Mi sembra che questa vechia ha due centi anni.

YOKO: Toshi no seikamo shiremasenne. Nihyakusai gurai ni mierudesho.

MULLEIMER: *(Head down; sulking.)* Wo ist meine brille?

(All gather around MRS. PONG, rubbing her hands and ad-libbing encouraging remarks.)

YOKO: Shimpai shinakutemo daijobu desuyo.

LAPOUBELLE: Je vends des assurances de vie, et j'en ai vu de pires, croyez-moi!

PATUMIERA: Non fa paura, signora. Questa è una rechia. Ha bisogna di una riposa per un settimana e motto di medicazione. Conosca un dottore?

YOKO: Oisha san o shitte imasuka?

PATUMIERA: Conosca un dottore?

(WASTBA now turns and faces them. For the first time in this sequence, she is aware that no one is paying any attention at all. She is furious. She throws the blackboard eraser and hits LAPOUBELLE'S back. They all look up at her a bit frightened. MRS. PONG as well. PATUMIERA picks up eraser from floor. Silence.)

WASTBA: Supposing I were to spring a little pop quiz right now, huh? Huh huh? Huh huh huh? Which one of you would even pass? *(She points to Patumiera.)* You? Could you pass?

PATUMIERA: *(He has eraser and whacks himself on head with same for emphasis. Chalk dust flies.)* Ho un dolore di testa.

LAPOUBELLE: Que j'ai mal à la tête.

MULLEIMER: Mir zerspringt der kopf.

YOKO: Atama ga itai wa.

MRS. PONG: Aaaii, Ngoi gä hai tiek wah.

WASTBA: Okay, I'm now preparing the quiz…*(Turns to board; grabs forehead.)*…You over there, you're giving me a headache.

(Looks at PATUMIERA. PATUMIERA smiles and then coughs.)

PATUMIERA: *(To WASTBA.)* Ho una brutta tosse. *(Holds his chest.)* Ho un dolore qui.

WASTBA: *(Turns and faces him, slowly.)* Can I believe my ears? It sounds like an unwanted tongue…

PATUMIERA: *(Holds his stomach, in pain.)* Ho un dolore di stomaco… *(Holds his thighs.)* Mi fanno male le gambe…*(Grabs his back, suddenly.)* Mi fa male le schiene!

WASTBA: And now lewd gestures, too!

PATUMIERA: Mi fa male il bracchio. Mi fa male l'orecchio. Ho i brividi. Ho febbre.

WASTBA: That does it, wop! I'm giving you a pop quiz!

PATUMIERA: Da ieri.

WASTBA: Take your pen and a piece of yellow lined paper and explain the Great Vowel Shift. Ten minutes, no open books.

PATUMIERA: *(Paying no attention.)* Da ieri.

WASTBA: *(Screams.) Are you taking this quiz or what?*

PATUMIERA: *(Humiliated to be yelled at in front of the others, he screams as well.)* Non capisco un cavalo di quel che dici!
(LAPOUBELLE is still standing near MRS. PONG. He misunderstands the tension in the room, completely.)

LAPOUBELLE: *(In French.)* On dirait qu'elle vit encore mais à peine. Et ce n'est pas grâce à vous…Quelle belle soirée!

PATUMIERA: *Non capisco un cavolo do quet che dici! (Screaming at LAPOUBELLE.) Che cavolo dicono?*

LAPOUBELLE: *(Screams back at PATUMIERA.) Qu'est-ce que vous dîtes, tireur de spaghetti? Hein? Sale macaroni? (To the world.) Ben, merde, alors! Quelle belle soirée!*
(All continue their complaints, as MULLEIMER chimes in as well.)

MULLEIMER: *Himmel! Herr Gott! Donnerwetternocheinmar! Ich will meine Brille???*

WASTBA: What the hell do *you* want?

MULLEIMER: *(Groping his way toward the sound of WASTBA'S voice, his hand finds one of her breasts.) Meine Brille!*
(WASTBA pulls back violently.)

WASTBA: Oh…my…God!

MULLEIMER: *(Reaches toward her again.) Meine Brille, Fräulein!*

WASTBA: Goddammit, just keep your filthy little Dutch hands to yourself! Don't you think I've had enough sex for one night!

LAPOUBELLE: Sexe?
(MULLEIMER reaches out toward her again and she slaps his face.)

WASTBA: I can't believe it! You're trying it again!
(Silence in room as all stare amazed.)

MULLEIMER: *(Shocked and amazed; still blind without his eyeglasses. He staggers back.)* Fraulein!

WASTBA: I'm sorry to have had to do that in front of everybody, but you did what you did in front of everybody.
(MULLEIMER is not to be stopped now. He moves to WASTBA once more,

(MULLEIMER is not to be stopped now. He moves to WASTBA once more, reaches for her one final time.)

MULLEIMER: *Wo ist meine Brille?*

(He reaches out, she slaps.)

WASTBA: Now that is the goddamned limit! *(She slaps MULLEIMER again.)*

MULLEIMER: Arghhh!

WASTBA: I've told you five or six times, Dutchie! This is the twentieth century, ya' know! I don't have to take that kind of crap from anybody anymore.

MULLEIMER: Was ist denn? Wo bin ich?

PATUMIERA: Che sta succedendo?

(N.B. Throughout the entire section, MRS. PONG has been watching, wide-eyed. MRS. PONG will soon make a break for the door again and will not, this time, be stopped. Her moves will be enormous in that she will leap from the floor, high into the air, several times, as she screams at WASTBA in rage. MULLEIMER has bowed his head now in shame and humiliation and LAPOUBELLE is leading him back to his chair.)

WASTBA: If you ever…*ever!*…take such a horrid liberty again, I swear I will seek revenge…*(Pulls back; straightens herself.)*

MULLEIMER: *(Whispered.) Fräulein?…*

WASTBA: *If* you're getting my message!

(No response. She waits for an answer as she seats MULLEIMER. MRS. PONG begins her major move now. She leaps up, screams, and threatens to karate chop WASTBA.)

MRS. PONG: Eeiieewwwaamaaiiaaa!!!

WASTBA: Hey!

MRS. PONG: Nay kay kung wah! Nay kay kung mä ngoi de jom lon-nä nay lieng-gä siew äng nay gä gieng wah!

TRANSLATOR'S VOICE: Stay back! Stay back or I'll break both of your arms and your neck too!

MRS. PONG: How-lä.

(Stands straight now. Leans back and nods to WASTBA, who stands by the door, staring, astonished.)

MRS. PONG: Ngoi chut coi gä mwun wah.

(MRS. PONG moves closer to WASTBA and points to MULLEIMER, PATUMIERA, YOKO and LAPOUBELLE, one at a time, angrily they try to calm MRS. PONG down.)

MRS. PONG: Coi thlom gä gom ngoi ngim thlom boy sui äng cui de gom ngoy ngim yit boy chä äng coi se ngoi de chut coi gä mwun hun thlee ngoy ngim yit boy chä äng coi se ngoi de chut coi gä mwun hun thlee swa wah, how mah?

TRANSLATOR'S VOICE: I'm going out that door right now. Those three made me drink three glasses of water and she made me drink a cup of tea and now I'm going out the door and to the bathroom, okay?

MRS. PONG: Na hiew ngoi gong mah, hääää?

TRANSLATOR'S VOICE: Do you understand me?

MRS. PONG: *(Waves the terrified WASTBA away from the door and moves to it; stops, turns around, faces into room and yells at WASTBA.)* Ngoy sä-lä ngoy m sät gong fon wa, lë, hi ngoy sät gong fon wah, ngoi de m loy coi yä! *Nay hiew ngoi gong mä?! Hä?!*

TRANSLATOR'S VOICE: I'm sorry I don't speak English, but, if I did speak English, I wouldn't be here! *Don't you understand that?! Okay?! (Making a final attempt to save MRS. PONG, WASTBA leans in and pleads with her, as all surround MRS. PONG.)*

WASTBA: Old Chinese woman, hear me. Don't go out there. I beg you…

MRS. PONG: *(She chases LAPOUBELLE, screaming.)* Ngoi coi low yiek mieng gon gwä nä cow thlay hon-nieh wä! A sui gow näy cow-a, niek mä? Hä, hä-hä, hä-hä-hä?? *(In English to LAPOUBELLE.)* Sit! *(LAPOUBELLE hides behind chair.)*

WASTBA: My knee is bent to you. That's a beg. Please, Pong. Pong. Pong. I'm pleading, Pong. Back up to your student desk. Just throw it in reverse and back up. Please, Pong.

MRS. PONG: Nay hong huey lä-a. Ngoy chut de chut lë.

WASTBA: *(Moves to MRS. PONG.)* I'll have to forceably detain you. I know it must rub your religion the wrong way, but what the hell choice are you offering me, huh? *(Wastba reaches for old MRS. PONG'S sleeve.)*

MRS. PONG: *(Raises her hand to chop. She screams.)* Nay kay kung! *(WASTBA leans silently against blackboard now, head bowed.)*

MRS. PONG: Ngoy loy fon thlay ga fon jung yä…*(MRS. PONG holds up four fingers.)*

TRANSLATOR'S VOICE: I'll be back in four minutes…
    (MRS. PONG waves her four fingers.)

MRS. PONG: Thlay. Gä-wä.

TRANSLATOR'S VOICE: Four. Only.
    (Repeating Chinese word and waving. She thinks MRS. PONG has said good-bye.)

MRS. PONG: Thlay, Pong, thlay Gä-wä…

ALL: *(Waving.)* Thlay, Gä-wä.

(MRS. PONG stops, looks at WASTBA, shrugs, bows, opens door and exits. As soon as MRS. PONG has negotiated her exit, WASTBA slams door closed tightly by hurling herself against same. There is silence in the room.)

WASTBA: Well, listen…*(Smiles.)*…maybe an old Oriental of her years just isn't cut out for a stiff class like ours…*(Walks to Mrs. Pong's desk, finds her slip and walks back to wastebasket, where she throws slip away, after tearing it to bits. She moves to desk. She sits. Folds her hands, smiles.)* Let's hope old Mrs. Pong finds another class…something more to her…well…fancy. *(Pause.)* Here we are again; just us. *(Pauses; smiles.)* Any questions?

PATUMIERA: Non ho capito nemmena una parola che tu hai detta!

TRANSLATOR: I haven't understood even one word of what you've said!

MULLEIMER: *(With overstated calm.)* Okay…*(Smiles a big smile.)*…Jetzt sitze ich und bin ruhiger…

TRANSLATOR: Okay…I'm sitting now and I'm calmer…

MULLEIMER:…also, wo ist meine Brille? *(He is now, as if to prove calmness, smiling rather idiotically.)*

TRANSLATOR: Now, where are my glasses?

WASTBA: *(Calling back.)* I'm not answering a single question until you're asking in English…*(Pauses.)* Sorry…

MULLEIMER: Wo ist meine Brille?

WASTBA: Nope.

MULLEIMER: *(Through clenched teeth.)* Wo ist meine Brille?

WASTBA: Uh uh…

MULLEIMER: Wo ist meine Brille?

(No response, as WASTBA crosses her arms on her chest and shakes her head. MULLEIMER stands now and screams.)

MULLEIMER: In Ordnung! Dann eben nicht! Dann bin ich eben blind!

(MULLEIMER throws a tremendous temper tantrum. He screams. He throws his books. He breaks pencils and throws them onto the floor. He punches his desk. He beats the floor. Finally he sulks. Silence, as all stare in disbelief.)

WASTBA: Why did you do that?

LAPOUBELLE: De toute ma vie, je n'ai jamais vu une scène comme ça, jamais. Ça alors!

TRANSLATOR'S VOICE: In my entire life, I've never ever seen a scene like that! Wow!

PATUMIERA: Credi che abbia imparato qualcosa?

TRANSLATOR: Do you think he learned anything?

YOKO: *(She smiles and whispers to PATUMIERA.)* Eigo wa omottayorimo taihendesune…

TRANSLATOR: English looks a lot tougher than I thought...

(A soft knocking sound at door. All look up. WASTBA squeals in terror. Silence, as all look from WASTBA to door. Knocking resumes, as slow fade to black. Curtain.)

End of Act I

(N.B. Intermission is optional. If played without intermission, cut soft knocking at door from above.)

ACT II

Lights up on scene as it was, WASTBA at blackboard. She writes* the word "Silence" on blackboard. All stare at her. She stares back at them. There is silence.

*If intermission is taken, word "silence" should be already written on board. Also the sense of some time has passed wanted.

WASTBA: Silence. Can you hear it? *(Pauses; finger to word on blackboard.)* Silence.

LAPOUBELLE: Zi-lence?

WASTBA: Silence. That's what's wanted here: silence. Okay?

LAPOUBELLE: Ah, oui. C'est le même mot en francais: *silence. (Above "silence" in French.)*

WASTBA: Si-lonce. Right. Now let's hear you say the word in English: silence…

LAPOUBELLE: Oui, je comprends. *(Now in English.)* Silence.

WASTBA: *(Smiles.)* Perfect.

LAPOUBELLE: *(Puts his fingers to his lips and repeats word.)* Silence.

PATUMIERA: Silenco!

LAPOUBELLE: *(Looks sternly at PATUMIERA.)* Shhh.

WASTBA: Silence.

PATUMIERA: Zi-*lence?*

LAPOUBELLE: Shhhh.

WASTBA: Silence.

YOKO: Silence? *(Giggles.)*

LAPOUBELLE: Shhhh.

YOKO AND PATUMIERA: Silence!

LAPOUBELLE: *(Angrily.)* Shhh!

WASTBA: *(Smiling to PATUMIERA and YOKO.)* That's much better…Silence.

YOKO AND PATUMIERA: *(Happily.)* Silence! Silence!

LAPOUBELLE: *(Angrily, to both. In French again. He stands.)* Shhhh! Ecoutez! Silence, hein?

WASTBA: *(To LAPOUBELLE: angrily.)* Will you stop interrupting us?

LAPOUBELLE: Mais, mademoiselle…

WASTBA: *(Placing her finger to her lips.)* Shhh.

LAPOUBELLE: *(Angrily.)* Bon. *(He sits. He is silent a moment.)*

YOKO AND PATUMIERA: *(In unison. Pointing to LAPOUBELLE, they*

YOKO AND PATUMIERA: *(In unison. Pointing to LAPOUBELLE, they begin laughing.)* Silence.
(YOKO giggles.)

WASTBA: *(Moves to her desk, sits on it and MULLEIMER'S glasses.)* Now then...Ohhh! *(Finds glasses.)* Look! I almost forgot! Not broken. Not broken. Didn't break them. *(She turns to MULLEIMER.)* Your glasses... *(She puts them on his face.)* Here you go.
(MULLEIMER is shocked and amazed and thrilled.)

MULLEIMER: Meine Brille! *(He stands and looks at WASTBA and at class, overjoyed.)* Ahhhh! Meine Brille! Ssank you.

WASTBA: *(Thrilled.)* Ahhh!

MULLEIMER: Ssank you...veriii mich...

WASTBA: *(Pointing to his mouth.)* English!

YOKO: Ahhh!

PATUMIERA: Ahhh!

MULLEIMER: Veri mich, yah!

WASTBA: *(Pointing to his lips.)* English, class! English! Immersion is working!
(She applauds MULLEIMER, who bows.)

WASTBA: Bless you, Mr. Mancini...

MULLEIMER: *(Laughing and bowing.)* Veri mich, *yahhh!*
(The rest of the class now applauds, wildly laughing. They are extremely happy to be succeeding. They are now applauding and cheering. WASTBA turns to them, delighted. She bows. WASTBA laughs anxiously; bows.)

WASTBA: Oh, my goodness. You're all expressing such approval!
(MULLEIMER stands and bows as well.)

WASTBA: Oh, look at you! Excited...bowing, too...*(WASTBA straightens up.)* Okay, now, let's settle. Settle, now, settle. *(WASTBA is laughing quite happily. She searches through her satchels of books. She smiles to the class.)* I want you all to understand that while I have nothing...personally... against your tongues, I must teach this primary English class absolutely by...the...book. *(Smiles.)* I'm sure you understand. *(Pauses.)* Where's the book? *(Searches feverishly: finds book.)* I got it! *(Looks up, smiling. Produces small book covered in orange fabric, which she waves at class.)* I had to put ten dollars down on this. *(Smiles.)* A deposit. *(Pauses.)* In this country, it's assumed you're going to lose...something. Nor do I. Not at ten dollars a shot. *(Smiles.)*

LAPOUBELLE: *(Recognizes a word and smiles as well.)* Sumzing!

WASTBA: Hmmm.

LAPOUBELLE: Je comprends un peu. *Sum-zing,* par exemple: c'est quelque-chose, n'est-ce pas?

WASTBA: *Will you please and kindly pay some attention! Sit down!*

LAPOUBELLE: *(Humiliated.)* Enfin, merde! C'est quelquechose! Ce n'est pas compliqué!

(They all sit.)

ALL: Seetz…Sit dunn…Teetz…etc.

WASTBA: This is the book. Say it. Book. Book. Book.

ALL: Book. Book. Book.

WASTBA: *(Reads to them; clearly.)* "The object of the primary English class will be to teach the negative form." *(To the class.)* The negative should be right up your alleys. *(Reading again.)* "You will reach the negative through the positive…" *(To the class.)* Pay attention. *(Reads again.)* "You will reach the negative through the positive…" Okay…*(Reading.)* "Touch the floor and announce to class 'I can touch the floor.' " *(Pauses.)* Once again, I learn to lower myself in the name of higher learning. *(She drops to the floor.)* Okay. Here I am. Listen. *(She touches the floor and announces to class.)* I can touch the floor.*(Reads again from book.)* "Have they all said 'I can touch the floor'?" *(Looks up.)* Has *who* all said "I can touch the floor!?" This is just tawdry…If they think I'm going to make a life of this, they're barking up the wrong tree…

(LAPOUBELLE suddenly drops out of his chair onto the floor, on all fours, as might a hound.)

LAPOUBELLE: Flo-er! Flo-er! *(He moves toward WASTBA grinning and yelping.)* Flo-er! Flo-er!

WASTBA: What is it?

LAPOUBELLE: Flo-er! Flo-er!

(He moves closer to her, even more houndlike. She pulls away, frightened.)

WASTBA: What the hell are you doing? Get away from me! Sit! Scat! Heel! *(Screams.)* Sit!!!

MULLEIMER: *(Sits on the floor, touching it with two hands.)* Zeet? Zeet, fluur!

YOKO: *(Same.)* Flory.

PATUMIERA: *(Same.)* Scusi?

WASTBA: The floor! You're touching the floor! *(Demonstrates.)*

PATUMIERA: *(Shocked and amazed and thrilled; on his knees.)* Fleeer!

WASTBA: *(Flailing her arms about for them to follow.)* I can touch the floor! I can touch the floor. I can touch the floor!

ALL.: I can touch the floor! *(In unison, in their varying accents.)*

WASTBA: *(Reading.)* "If they can touch the floor and have said so, show them how to touch the desk." *(Looking up.)* Okay, you sneaky devils, I can touch the desk.

LAPOUBELLE: Comment?

WASTBA: *(She runs to her desk; slaps same.)* I can touch the *desk!*

LAPOUBELLE: *(Walks to her desk.)* "I can tooooch le dest!"

WASTBA: *(Flailing her arms.)* Everybody! *(Screaming and whacking the desk.)* I can touch the desk!

ALL: *(Screaming and whacking the desk as well.)* I…Tooooch…Desttie. *(Etc.)*

WASTBA: *(Reads from book.)* "Simple parts of the body." What's simple, these days? *(She dances and slaps her feet.)* Feet! I can touch my feet.

ALL: *(Imitate her as best they can.)* Tooochhhh…Feetz…*(Etc.)*

WASTBA: This is working! Oh my dear God! *(Laughs.)* I can touch my knees!

ALL: I can touch my knees…*(Etc.)*

WASTBA: I can touch my nose!

ALL: I can touch my nose! *(Etc.)*

(WASTBA stops them. They wait, fingers on noses.)

WASTBA: Just hang on a minute…this is truly exciting. *(She looks at book again, reading.)* "You will lead them to try to touch the ceiling. When they cannot, they will, of their own volition, offer 'I cannot touch the ceiling.' And then you will have succeeded in teaching the primary English class." *(Looks up.)* Do you understand that? *(Reading.)* "Command them to touch the wall…" *(Looks up.)* Touch the wall! I command you…*(No response. She reads again.)*…"and then act on your own command, leading them." *(Looks up.)* Okay. Touch the wall! *(She leads them to wall, waving arms for them to follow action and words.)* I can touch the wall!

ALL: I can tooch wall…I toochy wall…Eye tooch vall…*(Etc.)*

(WASTBA will lead them around room, as a group, screaming at them to touch various points and objects. MULLEIMER will follow, but always several beats behind rest of class.)

WASTBA: Touch the floor again!

(They do.)

ALL: *(But LAPOUBELLE.)* I can touch floor again…

LAPOUBELLE: Ah, c'est facile. *(Swaggers.)* Zee flooor again. Voila!

WASTBA: Touch the corner!

ALL: *(Ganging together at corner.)* I can tooch corner!…*(Etc.)*

WASTBA: Touch your elbow!

ALL: I can tooch my elbow!

   (They do. PATUMIERA embraces WASTBA from behind, grasping her elbow.)

PATUMIERA: I can touch your elbow!

   (WASTBA giggles.)

WASTBA: Stand by, my darling students, because here it comes! *(She staggers, giggling, to center. She points to ceiling and screams to them.)* Touch the ceiling! *(She pretends to try, stretching up high above her head toward ceiling. She wags her head "NO.")* Touch the ceiling! Naw-Naw-Naw...ceiling.

   (They all strain toward ceiling in attempt to please her, but none can touch ceiling, which is, of course, high above them. They all strain and moan.)

   (Simultaneously.)

ALL: Arggghhh...Ohhhh...Zeiling...Arghhh...

WASTBA: Touch the ceiling! Ooooo...Touch the ceiling! Ooooo...Touch the ceiling! Ooooo...

   (MULLEIMER, silently, at front of room, has climbed to the top of WASTBA'S desk. He reaches up and touches the ceiling.)

MULLEIMER: I...can...touch...zeeling...

   (He stands, fingertips on ceiling, grinning broadly. Keeping his fingers on ceiling, he smiles down to WASTBA for approval. All others in class applaud MULLEIMER'S success.)

ALL: Yayy...Ooooo...

WASTBA: *(Outraged; screams at MULLEIMER.)* You miserable Swiss son of a bitch!

MULLEIMER: Zeiling?

WASTBA: *(Screams.)* Get down!

   (He does; totally bewildered. She yells, as she slaps her textbook.)

WASTBA: There's nothing in here about Germans!

YOKO: Doshite ikenaindesuka? Tenjo ni sawaretanoni.

WASTBA: *(Yells; cutting YOKO'S line.)* Shut it up!!!

   (There is silence in the room. PATUMIERA smiles at YOKO and then at WASTBA as if trying to explain the problem.)

PATUMIERA: Eeengleesh...Parla Eeengleesh.

WASTBA: Oh yuh sure. You got it, champ!

PATUMIERA: *(Smiling even more broadly now.)* Eeeengleesh, si?

WASTBA: Right. Now put a little cheese and tomato sauce on that!

PATUMIERA: *(Thinks he's succeeding.)* Si?

WASTBA: *(Tight-lipped control.)* Look, my dear *touristies*, we could really roll up our sleeves and get down to good hard work, or I could just send you back the word "English" and you could go on saying "Eeeengliiish," back the word "English" and you could go on saying "Eeeeengliiish," just like we were playing ping-pong.

(Pauses. A knock is heard at door. Suddenly Wastba stiffens.)

WASTBA: Oh, my God!

(All watch her.)

WASTBA: Pong!

(All look from one to the other. WASTBA goes to the door and, cautiously, she cracks open door. WASTBA slams the door and leans against it.)

WASTBA: Him! Him! Him! Him! My heart! My God! Him!

ALL: *(Mimic her.)* Him?

WASTBA: Out the door. In the hall. On his feet.

ALL: Feet!

WASTBA: Crap!

(They will each pick up her word "crap" in their own accents and pass the word from one to the other, as a small ball thrown, rapidly.)

MULLEIMER: *(Mimics her.)* Crahrp?

LAPOUBELLE: *(Mimics MULLEIMER.)* Crêpe?

PATUMIERA: *(Mimics LAPOUBELLE.)* Cheptz?

MULLEIMER: *(Mimics PATUMIERA.)* Grepz?

LAPOUBELLE: *(Mimics MULLEIMER.)* Grecque?

PATUMIERA: Grekzi?

WASTBA: Grekzi?

PATUMIERA: Grekzi?

YOKO: Grassi?

WASTBA: Grassy?

MULLEIMER: Was?

WASTBA: Huh?

LAPOUBELLE: Hein?

YOKO: Nani?

WASTBA: Huh?

MULLEIMER: Was?

WASTBA: Huh?

MULLEIMER: Was?

WASTBA: What?

MULLEIMER: Huh?

WASTBA: *(Stands; moves to her desk.)* Listen, class, we've got to improve.

ALL: Improve!

WASTBA: If that old lady wants illicit sex, that's her business! We're here to learn English and that is, God damn it, precisely what I intend to do: so learn English and that is, God damn it, precisely what I intend to do: so get ready to learn!

(All smile. Blank stares all around.)

WASTBA: What did you all come here for if you don't speak any English? This is an English-speaking country!

YOKO: Ingrish.

WASTBA: Will you just shut it up, dopey!

YOKO: *(Correcting her.)* Yoko.

WASTBA: Okay?

YOKO: *(Chirps happily.)* O-kay…*(Giggles.)*

WASTBA: *(Pauses.)* I'm going to explain very slowly and carefully exactly what's going on here, so listen.

PATUMIERA: Non capisco un cavolo di quel che dici.

WASTBA: *(Furiously.)* Sit down and put a belt on it, you! *Sit!*

ALL: Sit. Sitz. Seetz. *(Etc.)*

(There is a pause as all settle into their chairs. WASTBA sits now in the chair behind her desk and folds her hands demurely. She is trying desperately to be calm.)

WASTBA: Class?

(All have notebooks and pencils poised now thinking the lesson is finally coming.)

WASTBA: In the simplest possible terms, here it is: there seems to be a maniac in the hall. *(Smiles.)* Okay?

YOKO: O-kay. *(Giggles.)*

WASTBA: You think a maniac is funny?

(YOKO giggles. WASTBA adds tersely.)

WASTBA: If I were Oriental, I would be ashamed of you.

(YOKO takes her cue from WASTBA'S tone of voice and is silent now.)

WASTBA: Right. In this particular city, we have a perfect balance between maniacs and non-maniacs: one-to-one. *(Looks up quietly.)*

PATUMIERA: Aspetta un momento.

(He has been studying his phrasebook and writing notes onto his pad of paper. He smiles proudly at YOKO. He smiles quietly at WASTBA, who is blowing her nose. All eyes on PATUMIERA now.)

PATUMIERA:…un momento. Diro qualcosa…*(He holds his pad in front of him and studies it. He smiles again.)*…Momento…*(Rummages through his phrasebook; smiles constantly to YOKO.)*

TRANSLATOR: Wait just a minute. I'll say something.

PATUMIERA: Solo un secondo!

TRANSLATOR: Just a second.

PATUMIERA: *(Finds a phrase he likes.)* Ne ho una!

TRANSLATOR: I've got one!

(PATUMIERA slithers to WASTBA, using his most practiced movie-star walk. He has memorized something from his phrasebook. WASTBA is unhappy. She senses that PATUMIERA has some words of consolation, hence, she looks up at him.)

PATUMIERA: *(Reads slowly.)* Signorina, may...I...smork?

WASTBA: *Smork?*

PATUMIERA: Posso fumare, signorina? *(Again, in English. Tries new pronunciation of word this time.)* May...eye...schmork? *(He waves his cigarette pack.)* Sigaretta!

WASTBA: Oh, sure, swell, smork. All of you, go on! You want to have sets of malignant lungs go on! Light up! Enjoy! Have your sigaretti...

PATUMIERA: *(Correcting her.)* Sigaretta! *(Smiles to all.)*

WASTBA: Sigaretta!

(PATUMIERA smiles; shrugs; lights up a cigarette, drags on it deeply, blows smoke into room. He will soon offer cigarettes to all, who will in turn begin to smoke. As each is quite anxious, quite a lot of smoke will be produced. Soon, in fact, the room will be filled with smoke and WASTBA will be coughing. At the moment, WASTBA is writing the words "Basic Salutations" on blackboard.)

PATUMIERA: *(Offers cigarettes to YOKO.)* Sigaretta?

YOKO: *Iie* kekko desu. Watashinoga arimasukara. *(She lights a Japanese cigarette.)*

PATUMIERA: *(To MULLEIMER.)* Sigaretta?

MULLEIMER: Nein, danke. Ich habe meine eigenen. *(He lights a German cigarette.)*

PATUMIERA: Si, Eigenen...*(To LAPOUBELLE.)* Sigaretta?

LAPOUBELLE: Non merci, j'ai ma pipe. *(He lights a French pipe.)*

YOKO: Ie kekko desu. Watashinoga arimasunode. *(She waves her Japanese cigarette.)*

PATUMIERA: Giapponese, quella sigaretta? Vuole cambiare?

TRANSLATOR: Japanese, that cigarette? Let's exchange...

YOKO: Sorewa Itaria no tabako?

TRANSLATOR: Is that an Italian cigarette?

MULLEIMER: *(He offers LAPOUBELLE a drag of his cigarette.)* Wollen Sie mal meine probieren? Vielleicht zu stark fuer Sie...

LAPOUBELLE: J'essaierai le vôtre, et vous le mien. Quoique le tabac francais soit probablement trop fort pour vous…*(He takes Mulleimer's cigarette and puffs on it, exchanging his pipe for cigarette.)*

TRANSLATOR: I'll try yours, you try mine. French tobacco's probably too strong for you though…

YOKO: Omoshiroi kedo. Yowai desune.

TRANSLATOR: Interesting, but too weak for my taste…

PATUMIERA: Interessante, ma un po leggiere per me. *(Puffing away happily.)*

TRANSLATOR: Interesting, but too weak for my taste…

MULLEIMER: Ganz interessant, aber etwas schwach fuer meinen Geschmack. *(Puffing away happily.)*

TRANSLATOR: Interesting, but too weak for my taste…

LAPOUBELLE: Intéressant, mais pas assez fort à mon goût. *(Puffing away happily.)*

TRANSLATOR: Interesting, but too weak for my taste…

(The room is full of smoke. WASTBA is gasping and coughing. PATUMIERA walks to her, offers his packette of cigarettes.)

PATUMIERA: Sigaretta?

WASTBA: Oh, c'mon, will you?

(They all puff away, smiling.)

WASTBA: I would like your…*(Coughs.)*…attention…*(Coughs.)* There is a slight problem.

(Coughs again. Room is full of smoke.)

WASTBA: For Christ's sake! *(She slaps at the smoke in the air.)* Open something, will you?

(WASTBA staggers to door and opens it, trying to add fresh air into room. She opens door fully, hiding herself behind door a moment, MRS. PONG is just outside door, smiling, reentering room. She is puffing away on a Chinese cigarette. She takes step on to threshold. All class members see MRS. PONG. WASTBA does not, as she is behind door. Suddenly WASTBA, remembering that there is danger outside of door, slams door in MRS. PONG'S face, knocking her out of threshold and sight. All are astonished.)

LAPOUBELLE: Elle vient de claquer la porte au nez de cette vieille Malaisienne! *(He nervously puffs his pipe.)*

PATUMIERA: Credo che sia stata lei ad uccidere la vecchia giapponese *(To WASTBA.)* Mi scusi, ma credo che lei ha appena ucciso la signora giapponese.

WASTBA: I know. I know. You must think I'm crazy to have opened the door with that maniac out there, but the smoke in here is so goddamned thick! *(Smiles; coughs.)* Please stop smoking, okay?

YOKO: *(Puffing away on cigarette nervously.)* Sensei wa toshiyorino gofu in o kizutsuke mashitayo.

WASTBA: Please, stop your smoking, okay, Yokè?

(YOKO smiles and puffs. Smoke hits WASTBA'S face. WASTBA takes her cigarette and drops it on the floor. Angrily.)

WASTBA: For God's sakes! I asked you politely!

YOKO: Toshiyori no gofujin o kizutsukete tabako o fumitsukete. Watashi wa seki ni modorimasu.

PATUMIERA: *(Confused.)* Sigaretta? *(He offers cigarette to WASTBA.)*

WASTBA: Oh, shove it, will you?

MULLEIMER: *(Puffing away on cigarette, he blows smoke right into WASTBA'S face.)* Ich lasse sie herein.

(WASTBA grabs his cigarette.)

MULLEIMER: Hallo!

WASTBA: *(She stomps cigarette out on floor.)* That's just about enough, okay?

MULLEIMER: Was ist denn?

(WASTBA has begun to snap. She will scream at each of them, until she will suddenly say, in the sweetest of tones, good morning.)

WASTBA: Sit down, Pilsner!

MULLEIMER: Wie, bitte?

WASTBA: *Down! Sit!*

(He sits.)

PATUMIERA: Non capisco nemmeno una parola di quel che sta dicendo.

WASTBA: Shut your mouth!

LAPOUBELLE: Excusez-moi, s'il vous plaît, mais…

WASTBA: *(Screams.)* All of you: listen!

(Silence in room. N.B. Change in her tone will be complete. She moves two steps into the center of the room, clasps her hands together and smiles demurely.)

WASTBA: Good morning.

(No response. She nods to LAPOUBELLE.)

WASTBA: Good morning. *(She rolls her arms at him, motioning for him to follow her words to repeat them.)* Good morning.

LAPOUBELLE: *(Stands; in disbelief.)* Goood morr-ning.

WASTBA: Perfect.

(To MULLEIMER, who stands. LAPOUBELLE sits.)

WASTBA: Now you.

(He stares dumbly at her.)

WASTBA: Good morning.

MULLEIMER: Gud morgan…

WASTBA: Morning…

MULLEIMER: Morging…

WASTBA: Morning!

MULLEIMER: Morning!

WASTBA: You see? You got a will, you got a way.
(To YOKO, after MULLEIMER sits.)

WASTBA: Right?

YOKO: *(YOKO stands for her turn. She turns to PATUMIERA and whispers.)* Good morning, eh?
(PATUMIERA nods.)

WASTBA: Okay, let's start you right out on the other essential…according to my plan. *(Smiles to YOKO.)* Good night.

PATUMIERA AND YOKO: Ohh.

WASTBA: Good night!

YOKO: Good nightie.

WASTBA: Good nightie! Is that supposed to be cute? Good nightie! *(Smiles ironically.)* It's not "Good nightie" but "Good night." *(Motions to her to repeat words.)* Good night. *(No response. She speaks the words again, but with tremendous hostility.)* Good night!

YOKO: *(Repeats tone.)* Good night!

WASTBA: *(To PATUMIERA.)* What's funny?

PATUMIERA: Good night.

WASTBA: What's funny? I asked what's funny?…

PATUMIERA: *(Shyly now.)* Good night?

LAPOUBELLE: *(Leans in correcting PATUMIERA, smiling to WASTBA for approval.)* Goooood night. *(Smiles again. Nods smugly.)* Goooood night.

WASTBA: You've got yourself a horrid oooo-sound. *(She squeezes his lips)* Gud, gud, gud. Gud night.

LAPOUBELLE: *(Repeats exactly.)* Gud night.

MULLEIMER: *(Leans in to correct LAPOUBELLE at the same time PATUMIERA and YOKO try the same words.)* Guden, guden, guden. Guden night.
(YOKO, PATUMIERA, and MULLEIMER, simultaneously, four times.)

YOKO: Good nightie…

PATUMIERA: God naght…

MULLEIMER: Guden, guden, guden…
(They each continue as LAPOUBELLE goes into a rage.)

LAPOUBELLE: C'est une catastrophe, cette leçon…et c'est de votre faute, je crois…

WASTBA: *Silence!*

MULLEIMER: *(Angrily now, to WASTBA.)* Ich komme micht mit. Tut mir leid, aber ich verstehe nicht was Sie sagen...

WASTBA: *(Screams.) I can't stand it!*
(All stop talking and look at her.)

WASTBA: Stop your goddamn babble! Stop! Stop! Stop! *(She stands.)* I *demand* you stop! *(She sits in MRS. PONG'S chair.)* I'm upset. *(She begins rocking MRS. PONG'S desk back and forth, moaning.)* Oh dear God, I'm upset...My heart is filled with such loathing for all of you!
(Her body heaves as she sobs. PATUMIERA walks to her, cautiously.)

PATUMIERA: Come si sente? Sta bene?

WASTBA: *(On hearing his Italian tanguage, sobs all the more.)* It's hopeless, hopeless...

PATUMIERA: Che t' è successo? Diccelo per favore.
(PATUMIERA touches WASTBA'S arm and she pulls back, violently, and screams.)

WASTBA: Don't you touch me! Oh, you would touch me! *(She is on her feet now.)*

PATUMIERA: Per amor del cielo!

WASTBA: Don't you know? Can't you tell?? *(Pauses; no response.)* Look at me! *(Nods ironically.)* Don't pretend it doesn't show. *(No response.)* Okay. Okay...*(Stands erect.)* This is my first class, too...They just called me last night. *(Waits for reaction. Gets none. Smiles, nods.)* Shocked, huh? Well...now you know...We must not fail here. *(Pauses.)* You fail and I fail. I fail and you fail. You fail and I fail and we all fail. I fail and you don't get to speak English. You fail and I don't get to *teach* English. We all fail and...*(Pauses.)* You see now, don't you? Language could be our mutual Waterloo! *(Pauses.)* Have I made myself perfectly clear?

YOKO: *(Smiling.)* Ware-ware wa ittai anataga doshte...

WASTBA: *(Screams.) I'm gonna stuff an eggroll in that mouth of yours, butter-fly!* (Silence.) The next three words out of my mouth will be the most important words in the English language. *(She has been holding her lesson plan book and leafing through it. Her calmness at this moment is icy.)* I certainly hope you'll have the decency to pay attention.
(She stares at her class. All look from one to another, wondering what it was they did that drove WASTBA crazy. Suddenly we hear three enormously loud raps at the door. The sound is quite terrifying.)

SMIEDNIK: *(Offstage. His lines are intercut with the pounding.)* Daj mi moja miotYe, pani! Hey, SYodka, bez mej moitYy nie moje pracowac! Nie zartuje, panno, dawaj miotYe i dawaj ja szybkó. Wchodze!! Otwieraj cholerne dzwi!

(There is a sharp intake of breath from all and then silence. WASTBA looks at class, bows head, speaks softly.)

WASTBA: Poor, poor Pong. *(She walks to MRS. PONG'S desk and gathers the four takeout containers together in a stack. She returns to the front of the room and drops the four takeout containers into the wastebasket.)*

LAPOUBELLE: Nom de Dieu, qu'est-ce que c'est que ça?

TRANSLATOR: What the hell is that?

PATUMIERA: Che é successo?

TRANSLATOR: What's happening?

YOKO: Dare ka hairitagatte irunjanaidesuka?

TRANSLATOR: I think somebody's trying to get into the room.

MULLEIMER: Was zum Teufel war das? *(Pauses; moves up from his seat.)* Was zum *Teufel* war das? *(Moves to WASTBA.)*

TRANSLATOR: What the devil was that?

PATUMIERA: *(Moves to WASTBA.)* Che è successo, signorina?

LAPOUBELLE: *(Moves to WASTBA.)* Qu'est-ce que c'est, mademoiselle?

WASTBA: Please, take your seats now…*(Smiles, calmly.)* All of you: sit down. Come on, now…*(Calmly.)* Please sit down.

MULLEIMER: Wir mussen die Tür aufmachen, und nachsehen, Fräulein.

(MULLEIMER moves to the door. WASTBA hurls her body between MULLEIMER and the door.)

MULLEIMER: Heh! *(MULLEIMER hops away from her, moving backwards.)*

WASTBA: Sit!

MULLEIMER: Fräulein, bitte…

WASTBA: *I* am the captain of this ship…not you!

(Backs him away from door by screaming and moving forward. MULLEIMER continues to hop.)

MULLEIMER: Fräulein!

WASTBA: *I'm* the one who killed the morning preparing…not you! *(Moves forward again.)*

MULLEIMER: *(Hops backward again.)* Fräulein!

WASTBA: *I'm* responsible here…not you!

YOKO: *(To LAPOUBELLE.)* Ittai do shitandesuka?

LAPOUBELLE: *(To YOKO as he stands.)* Qu'est-ce qu'elle fait?

PATUMIERA: *(Stands.)* Che sta facendo?

LAPOUBELLE: *(To WASTBA.)* Quand ce navire coulera, je serai le premier rat à se sauver.

WASTBA: We've got to stick together! *(Screams; panicked.)* We've got to stick together. *(Yells at MULLEIMER.)* Sit down and stick together.

MULLEIMER: Ich rühr mich nicht bis ich weiss was da draussen passiert ist!

WASTBA: *(Screams.)* Take your seats!

PATUMIERA: *(He recognizes phrase and repeats same, screaming word aloud trying to be helpful.)* Teetz...

WASTBA: I beg your pardon?

PATUMIERA: *(Pounds his desk; motions to all seats in room.)* Goood teetz...

WASTBA: Mister, do you know that I am an educated woman? I may be Business Administration and not Language Arts, which is only to say that while words may not be my way...my field...I am nonetheless degree-certified and educated. Furthermore, this is not a goddamn Latin country! We are civilized people here! Now, goddammit, *sit down!* *(Suddenly there is the sound of pounding on the door again.)*

SMIEDNIK: *(Screams offstage; screams are intercut with the pounding at the door.)* Potreba mi mej miotYy, kochanie. Pani, musze, isc dp domu. Wchodze! Otwieraj cholerne dzwi! *(Silence in the room again. LAPOUBELLE speaks first, under his breath. He is quite obviously frightened.)*

LAPOUBELLE: *Mais, enfin, merde, alors!...Qu'est-ce que c'est que ça??? La Guerre, Madame?...*

WASTBA: *(Intensely.)* Don't you understand that there is more of us than there is of him?

MULLEIMER: *Was ist passiert, Fraeulein? Kriegsausbruch vielleicht?*

PATUMIERA: *Che è successo, signorina? Una battaglia?*

WASTBA: He's probably only just another poor demented lunatic needing money for Godknowswhat kind of drug...That's all...It makes me want to spit. *Ptwew! (She actually spits on floor.)*

PATUMIERA: Signorina...Vietato sputare, eh?

WASTBA: Money!

PATUMIERA: Money!

WASTBA: Money! That's it! Money!

YOKO: *(Repeats word as well.)*...money...*(Giggles.)*

WASTBA: *(Grabbing her pocketbook.)* I'll chip in a dollar if you all will... *(Looks up at them.)* We can buy him off!

LAPOUBELLE: Mais, ma chère mademoiselle, il faut que vous nous donniez juste une petite chance, alors!...Nous sommes...

WASTBA: A dollar! *(To Patumiera.)* A dollar, you!

PATUMIERA: *(With dollar, proudly.)* Dollarr.

(She grabs his dollar.)

PATUMIERA: Eyyy!

WASTBA: Thank you. *(To LAPOUBELLE.)* C'mon, moustache, it's your life or a rotten dollar! What's to think about? Gimme' a dollar.

(LAPOUBELLE takes out his wallet. She grabs it and takes a dollar.)

LAPOUBELLE: Madame!

WASTBA: I'm only taking a dollar. One. See? *(To YOKO.)* You paying attention? *Hello?*

YOKO: *(Has a dollar now.)* Hello…Dolly.

WASTBA: To know you is to love you…Gimme'…*(Takes the dollar, counts people and then money.)* Who's not in? *(To MULLEIMER.)* You! A dollar. *(He takes out dollar.)*

MULLEIMER: Dollar, ja…

WASTBA: Good boy.

MULLEIMER: *(Proudly.)* Okay.

(WASTBA walks carefully to the door. All are frozen to see what will happen. She puts her hand on the doorknob.)

WASTBA: Five lousy bucks. Let's hope he's got a sense of humor. Get the picture? *(She looks at MULLEIMER.)* Hey! *(Grabs camera from him.)* That'll help.

MULLEIMER: Aääh…Das ist meine Yashika, Fräulein…

WASTBA: *(To YOKO.)* Okay, Yoko. *(Pauses; amazed.)* Just wait a goddam minute…*(To YOKO.)* Did you know that "Yoko" is "okay" spelled backwards. *(Pauses.)* I'm wrong…*(Pauses.)*…Okay is "yako." You're Yoko. *("Yako" should be made to rhyme with "Jack-o." Pauses; again in panic.)* Something of value! I need something of value! *(Sees YOKO'S gold make-up case.)* Gimme' that!

(Grabs for it. YOKO resists.)

YOKO: Aiiii…

WASTBA: Gimme'! Make-up case!

YOKO: *(Resisting.)* Aayyy-iiii…

WASTBA: Make-up casey!

YOKO: *(Suddenly giggles.)* May cupcasey…*(Gives over make-up case to WASTBA.)*

WASTBA: Six hundred million more of you, huh? That's just swell. *(Moves to door.)* Well, let's hope, right?

(Cracks door open a bit. LAPOUBELLE grabs umbrella for protection. Stands by his desk with umbrella raised over his head.)

WASTBA: I'll try what I assume is his tongue…Couldn't hurt. *(Yells out door.)* Me voy a lavar un poco para quitarme la arena que tengo pegada! *(And with that she throws money, make-up case and camera out of door into the hallway. She instantly slams the door closed. All are shocked and amazed and scream at her.)*

ALL: *(In own language.)* Hey! What the hell did you do! That was my dollar! Have you lost your mind? *(Etc.)*

(Mulleimer moves to the door. His attitude is "I'll take care of this.")

MULLEIMER: *(To all.)* Sit. *(To WASTBA.)* Heute meine Brille und meine Yashika; morgen was? *Meine Schuhe? Meine Hosen?* Was, Fräulein, was?

WASTBA: Stay back, I'm telling you. *(Raises her fist.)* I'm not above throwing a punch!

MULLEIMER: Das ist doch lacherlich.

WASTBA: I told you that we have to stick together and you *Goddammit!* are going to have to stick! *(And with that, she punches his shoulder. Her fist is to MULLEIMER'S shoulder what a mosquito is to a grazing cow.)*

MULLEIMER: Was machen Sie da, meine Dame?

WASTBA: My hand! *(She is bent in pain.)* My poor hand. *(She moves to her desk.)* I really hurt my hand on you.

MULLEIMER: Was ist passiert?

YOKO: Doshitanodes'ka?

LAPOUBELLE: Mais. Qu'est-ce qui est arrivé?

PATUMIERA: Che è successo?

WASTBA: *(Crying.)* I really hurt my hand on you…

MULLEIMER: Warum haben sie mich geschlagen?

YOKO: Senseiwa naze Doitsujin o naguttan desuka?

LAPOUBELLE: Pourquoi elle lui a tapé dessus?

PATUMIERA: Perché gli ha dato quella botta?

WASTBA: I'm upset!

PATUMIERA: Sono sturbato, Io!

WASTBA: I'm so upset!

MULLEIMER: Bin ganz ausser mich. *(He paces, as a cat, the length of the room, holding eye-contact with WASTBA.)*

YOKO: Iyani nacchau wa.

WASTBA: Am I ever upset!

YOKO: Honto ni iyani nacchau wa.

WASTBA: *(Sobbing.)* Oh, God! I'm upset!

MULLEIMER: Mein Gott! Ich bin ausser mich!

WASTBA: This is truly upsetting. I want you to know that this is truly very upsetting.

MULLEIMER: *(He stands, throws notebooks on the floor, gathers his belongings.)* Fräulein, ich geh' nach Hause. *(MULLEIMER moves to door; stops. He turns and faces WASTBA.)*

TRANSLATOR: I'm going home now, Lady!

MULLEIMER: Aber bevor ich geh', will ich Ihnen noch was sagen...

TRANSLATOR'S VOICE: But before I go, I gotta' tell you something...

MULLEIMER: Frueher dachte ich, dass Tod durch Ersticken das Schlimmste sie.

TRANSLATOR'S VOICE: I used to think that death by suffocation would be the worst.

MULLEIMER: Hab' mich geirrt.

TRANSLATOR'S VOICE: I was wrong.

MULLEIMER: *(He puts on his cap and coat.)* Sie sind das Schlimmste.

TRANSLATOR'S VOICE: *You* are the worst.

MULLEIMER: Tod durch Ersticken ist ein Stueck Apfelstrudel verlichen zu einem abend mit Ihnen...

TRANSLATOR'S VOICE: Death by suffocation is a piece of apple strudel next to a night with you...

MULLEIMER: Ich verlasse diese klasse, bevor ich meinen Verstand und meine Schuhe verliere.

TRANSLATOR'S VOICE: I'm getting out of here while I still have my mind and my shoes.

MULLEIMER: Und wenn Ihr Freund der "mugger" sie haben will, kann er sie haben. *(He moves to her desk.)*

TRANSLATOR: If your friend the "mugger" wants them, he can have them.

MULLEIMER: Was Ihr kostbares Englisch anbelangt...*(He rubs his hand through words written on blackboard.)*

TRANSLATOR: As for your precious English...

MULLEIMER:...So platzieren Sie es auf einen kleinen, aber eleganten stuhl...

TRANSLATOR:...stick it on the center of a small but elegant chair...

MULLEIMER: *(He pulls her chair out and motions to seat, on his line.)*...und sit! *(Pauses. Goes to door.)* Fräulein...Auf Wiedersehn.
(He bows, clicks his heels. All freeze for a moment. MULLEIMER exits. He leaves door open. All stare a moment.)

WASTBA: *(Realizes, yells to PATUMIERA.)* Close that door! *(She stands straight.)*

Close that door! *(She rushes to door.)* Close that door! *(She slams it closed.)* Oh, God!

(All stare, amazed.)

LAPOUBELLE: Elle a fermé la porte au nez de l'Allemand!

PATUMIERA: Dov'e lo Svizzero?

YOKO: Sensei wa doitsujin o Shimedashimashita!

WASTBA: Okay, everybody, just settle!

PATUMIERA: Hai sbattuto fuori lo Svizzero!

WASTBA: *(To PATUMIERA.)* Settle, you!

YOKO: *(Screams, to WASTBA.)* Sensei wa doitsujin o shimedashimashita!

(Sound of knocking at the door.)

LAPOUBELLE: Ecoutez!

WASTBA: Back to your seat.

LAPOUBELLE: Il y a quelqu'un qui frappe à la porte, Madame!

WASTBA: Sit, will you?

(Knocking at the door again.)

PATUMIERA: Senti, forse e' lo Svizzero, no? *(Stands, looks to WASTBA.)* Non dovremmo aprire la porta?

YOKO: Doitsujin wa hairitagatteirun ja nai desuka.

WASTBA: Settle, everybody, just settle!

LAPOUBELLE: *(Moving forward in room.)* Vaut mieux aller voir.

(He carries his umbrella for protection. The sound of knocking at the door.)

LAPOUBELLE: Ecoutez!

WASTBA: Go back to your seat!

(The sound of pounding at the door.)

WASTBA: I said "Back to your seat!"

(The sound of pounding at the door.)

LAPOUBELLE: Je vais ouvrir la porte.

WASTBA: It's your funeral.

(She steps back from the door, smiling and nodding magnanimously. LAPOUBELLE holds his umbrella as a club against door.)

LAPOUBELLE: Qui est là?

(Suddenly we hear the sound of three enormous pounding sounds, joined by hard knocking. LAPOUBELLE jams his umbrella against door to hold it closed, YOKO hides behind a frightened PATUMIERA. The door rattles under the pounding.)

SMIEDNIK: *(Offstage; screaming. His screams are intercut with enormous knockings of the pail against the door.)* Pani, musze isc do domu! Nie zaetuje, panno, dawaj miotYe i dawaj ja szybkó. Wchodze! Otwieraj cholerne dzwi!

(LAPOUBELLE is frozen in his tracks; there is silence. LAPOUBELLE finally backs away and hides near his desk.)

WASTBA: Now, perhaps, you'll take me seriously. *(Pauses.)* You're all... well...new to this, while I'm...well...not new to this...Please, every-body...sit down.

LAPOUBELLE: Ils sont dans de beaux draps...le Suisse et la vieille Hawaienne, aussi. *(Bows head.)* C'est certain maintenant. Mon Dieu.

TRANSLATOR: The Swiss and the old Hawaiian lady are in big trouble. My God, that's for sure.

WASTBA: *(Condescending tone.)* Yes...I know...It's never what our parents told us it would be. *(Touches LAPOUBELLE'S shoulder.)* Please sit down now, okay?

LAPOUBELLE: No seet.

WASTBA: Sit!

LAPOUBELLE: Non!

WASTBA: Yes!

LAPOUBELLE: Non. No seet!

WASTBA: Damn you!

LAPOUBELLE: Ne me touchez pas! *(Shakes loose from her. Moves to his seat. Stops. Smiles at her ironically.)* Tu es dingue, chérie...mais adorable... *(Waves.)* Je t'embrasse...(Pause.) Mon Dieu. Ma tête. Mon cul...

WASTBA: You're going to have to stop wagging that tongue of yours...

LAPOUBELLE: *(Suddenly screams.)* Je n'ai plus confiance en vous, made-moiselle. *Je vous déteste!*

WASTBA: I'm going to have to treat you like a child. *(She walks to LAPOUBELLE.)* Every time you speak your tongue instead of English...(She slaps his hand.) I'll slap you.

LAPOUBELLE: Pourquoi avez-vous fait ça?

(WASTBA slaps LAPOUBELLE again.)

PATUMIERA: Perche' t'ha preso a schiaffi?

WASTBA: *(To PATUMIERA.)* There's that tongue of yours now!

PATUMIERA: Eh?

WASTBA: I'll have to slap you, too. *(She slaps PATUMIERA.)* Okay?

PATUMIERA: *(He reacts as a movie star might for these lines.)* Non picchio mai una donna. Anche se ti sorprende, essendo io Italiano...

WASTBA: You're not learning...

PATUMIERA: *(He moves now as a movie star might for these words.)* Eh, Signora!…Io…

YOKO: Chotto kiite kudasai!

WASTBA: You, too? *(Walks to YOKO.)* Sorry. *(Slaps YOKO'S hand.)*

YOKO: Cho-to!

PATUMIERA: E' pazza!

(WASTBA slaps PATUMIERA'S face.)

LAPOUBELLE: Je m'en vais.

(LAPOUBELLE stands. WASTBA slaps him.)

LAPOUBELLE: Elle est complètement cinglée!

(She slaps him again, violently now.)

LAPOUBELLE: Bordel!

(She slaps him again. He looks to PATUMIERA.)

LAPOUBELLE: J'en ai assez!

(LAPOUBELLE begins to pack his belongings as rapidly as he can. He stuffs papers and notebooks and clothing into his briefcases and bookbags. He is now hysterical. WASTBA, equally hysterical, will slap him whenever she hears French language being emitted from LAPOUBELLE'S lips.)

LAPOUBELLE: Faites ce que vous voudrez, moi, je m'en vais.

TRANSLATOR'S VOICE: I couldn't care less what you're after here…I'm getting out!

(WASTBA slaps LAPOUBELLE. N.B. He is now slapped both for his own words and for the Translator's words.)

LAPOUBELLE: J'en ai assez!

TRANSLATOR'S VOICE: I've had enough!

(WASTBA slaps LAPOUBELLE again. WASTBA slaps LAPOUBELLE twice.)

LAPOUBELLE: Madame, votre anglais, vous pouvez vous le ranger…lá oú le soleil ne brille jamais!.

(WASTBA slaps him.)

TRANSLATOR'S VOICE: Lady, you can take your English and shove it where the sun never shines!

(WASTBA slaps him again.)

LAPOUBELLE: Maintenant, il faut absolument que je m'en aille.

(WASTBA slaps him again.)

TRANSLATOR'S VOICE: Now I'm really leaving!

LAPOUBELLE: Voilà!

(Slap. LAPOUBELLE places his hand on the doorknob. WASTBA pulls back from him, frightened. Silence, as all stare at LAPOUBELLE'S back as he faces door. Suddenly, he freezes.)

LAPOUBELLE: Ca alors! Attendez, un petit moment...

TRANSLATOR'S VOICE: Uhhh, let's just wait a minute...

LAPOUBELLE: *(Turning back into position of facing WASTBA and class-mates. He has a sick grin on his face.)* Je m'en vais pas!

TRANSLATOR: I'm not gonna' leave...

LAPOUBELLE: Je vais perdre mon boulot, ma jeune femme, mes enfants seront obligés de quitter leur école privée...

TRANSLATOR: I'll lose my job, my young wife, and my children would have to drop out of private school...

LAPOUBELLE: En plus, ce con-là, il va me tuer.

TRANSLATOR: Also I'll be killed by the maniac in the corridor.

LAPOUBELLE: *(He walks to WASTBA and offers his hand for her to hit.)* S'il vout plaît, mademoiselle.

(She hits his hand sharply. He clenches hand into fist, considers punching her; does not. He smiles instead. LAPOUBELLE now returns to his chair and sits. He has rejoined the class. All sit quietly; attentive.)

WASTBA: Quiet, huh? *(Smiles.)* You've learned, huh? *(Smiles again and makes a sudden pronouncement.)* I have seen The Miracle Worker! *(She returns to her desk and sits. She smiles, composed and erect now.)* Calmness prevails and I am pleased. *(Smiles.)* Now then, in accordance with our lesson plan, I would like to discuss the verb "to be." *(Pauses.)* I hope this will fullfill and satisfy your foreign expectations. *(She stands and writes the words "To Be" on the blackboard next to the word "English." She has thus created the sentence "To Be English.")*

PATUMIERA: Che stai cercando di dire?

(WASTBA turns and stares a moment at PATUMIERA, returns to black-board. There is absolute silence in the room. Her handwriting on blackboard is mere scribbles; almost more like Japanese characters than English.)

WASTBA: *(Speaks words as she writes.)* I am. You are. He, she, it is. We are. You are. They are. *(Smiles.)* How many of you know this already? *(Absolute silence in the room.)* Nobody. *(Stands; writes phrases on black-board; turns to class after each and reads. She calls for the class to repeat her words, slapping each word with pointer for emphasis.)* I am. You are. He, she, it is. We are. You are. They are. *(Motions with arms for them to fol-low.)* Repeat after me, please. *(Smiles and points to blackboard.)* I am.

ALL: I am.

WASTBA: You are.

ALL: You are.

WASTBA: He, she, it is.

ALL: He, she, it is.
WASTBA: We are.
ALL: We are.
WASTBA: You are.
ALL: You are.
WASTBA: They are.
ALL: They are.
WASTBA: Good.
ALL: Good.
WASTBA: Stop!
ALL: Stop!
WASTBA: *(Screams.)* I said "Stop!"
> *(LAPOUBELLE, who is humiliated, screams and pounds his desk, out of control.)*
LAPOUBELLE: *I said stop!*
WASTBA: Do any of you have any questions?
> *(Suddenly LAPOUBELLE stands. Smashed umbrella held as sword, he charges to the front of the room.)*
LAPOUBELLE: *(Stands with his belongings in his arms. He nods to PATUMIERA.)* Bon soir, Monsieur Ravioli…*(Nods to YOKO.)* Bon Soir, ma petite Mademoiselle Sukiyaki…*(Bows to WASTBA.)*…et au revoir, Madame le Hot Dog…*(He unlocks door; turns again to WASTBA.)*…Au revoir, ma chère femme…
TRANSLATOR: Good-bye, my wife…
LAPOUBELLE:…et au revoir à mes petits enfants et à leurs écoles privées…
TRANSLATOR:…and good-bye my children and good-bye your private schools…
LAPOUBELLE: *(Prepares to leap out of door.)* Salut, ange de la mort!
TRANSLATOR: Hello, Angel of Death!
> *(LAPOUBELLE exits play. WASTBA goes to door, closes it, locks it.)*
WASTBA: I repeat: do any of you have any questions?
YOKO: *(Stunned silence first.)* Furansujin ga nigemashita! *(She screams the same words again.)* Furansujin ga nigemashita!
> *(PATUMIERA, realizing YOKO will be slapped for speaking something other than English, leans in and whispers to her, using hand gestures for emphasis.)*
PATUMIERA: Sta zitto o quella ti prene a botte!
WASTBA: *(Thinking PATUMIERA is about to hit YOKO.)* Hey!
PATUMIERA: Eh?

WASTBA: I'll do the slapping around here, okay?
  (No response. PATUMIERA just smiles.)
YOKO: *(Hides her hands behind her back.)* Furansujin ga nigemashita!
WASTBA: *(To PATUMIERA.)* Did you hear me?
YOKO: Furansujin!
WASTBA: Don't let me hear that tongue of yours again! *(Pauses; raises hand.)*
  You hear me?
YOKO: *(Head bowed in guilt and shame.)* Sumimaszn.
WASTBA: Better. *(Rubbing her hands together, walking backwards to her desk.)*
  I am.
PATUMIERA: *(Repeats.)* I am.
WASTBA: *(To YOKO.)* You are. *(No response.)* You are. *You are!*
  (YOKO looks up; quietly.)
YOKO: *(Pronounced perfectly.)* You...are.
WASTBA: *(To PATUMIERA.)* He, she, it is.
PATUMIERA: *(Repeats.)* He, she, it is.
WASTBA: *(To YOKO.)* We are. *(No response.)* We are. *(No response.)* I said
  "We are!" *(No response.)* We are!
  (YOKO turns around to WASTBA.)
YOKO: *(Quietly smiling.)* Watashi ga Amerika ni tatta hi ni wa nihyaku-
  hachijunin mono hito ga eki made miokurini kitekuremashita. *(She slaps
  her own hand, sharply.)*
TRANSLATOR: There were two hundred and eighty people gathered at the
  train station waving good-bye to me on the day I left for America.
YOKO: *(She moves to position in front of WASTBA.)* Sonouchino nihyaku
  nanaju-nananin wa itoko deshita. *(She slaps her own hand again.)*
TRANSLATOR: Two hundred and seventy-seven of them were cousins.
YOKO: *(Sits in chair next to WASTBA so that WASTBA cannot avoid her eyes.)*
  Sonouchino hitori wa watashino haha, mo hitori wa watashino chichi.
TRANSLATOR: One was my mother and one was my father.
YOKO: *(Packing.)* Nokori no hitori was boi furendo no Jun deshita.
TRANSLATOR: The other one was my boyfriend, Jun.
YOKO: America ni kurutameni watashiwa minnato wakaretano desu.
TRANSLATOR: I gave up everybody to come to America.
YOKO: Kono heya kara derukoto wa nijyu-nanadai tsuzuita watashino ie no
  meiyo o kegasukoto ni narimasu. *(Goes to chair, collects her belongings.)*
TRANSLATOR: Walking out that front door represents more humiliation to
  me than the last twenty-seven generations of my family could even think
  about.

(Gathers belongings; nods to PATUMIERA to join her. PATUMIERA shrugs a "No." YOKO does an Italian put-down gesture. She moves to door.)

YOKO: *(Opens door, after peeking out carefully.)* Mohito ban anatato issho ni irukurainara roka de kichigai to rumba o odotta hoga mada mashidesu. *(Turns and faces WASTBA again.)*

TRANSLATOR: Sugar, I would rather dance a rhumba with the lunatic in the hall than spend another night with you.

YOKO: Sayonara, Misu American Pie.

(YOKO bows. She exits play. SMIEDNIK bursts into room. The knees of his trousers are visibly soaked. On seeing SMIEDNIK, WASTBA will recognize him and reach a near catatonic state of fear. PATUMIERA is confused and frightened.)

SMIEDNIK: StyszaYas teu kawat o Polaku i o sliwce, also teu o Polaku i ogòrku? StyszaYa's o Polaku i stzajku smieciarzy?

TRANSLATOR: Heard the one about the Pollack and the prunes? Heard the one about the Pollack and the pickle? Heard the one about the Pollack and the garbage strike?

SMIEDNIK: Ty myslisz ze to *zarty???* Ty myslisz mnie imie Smienczne?

TRANSLATOR: You think we're all *jokes???* Why? Just because I've got a funny name? *(Smiednik kicks wastebasket, violently.)*

SMIEDNIK: Czegòs mi miotYe ukradYa? Jamuzce podYoge myc, albo sie moge sie pojytce…gdzie jesta?

TRANSLATOR: Why'd you steal my mop? I gotta' mop floors, lady, that's how I put the food on the table. *(Pauses.)* Where is it?

SMIEDNIK: Jednego godzina wdomu chiat byYem. Widzic sie! Na kolany I wrence, podYoge wy mytem.

TRANSLATOR: I could'a' b'in home an hour ago, but for her. Look at me! I've b'in sponging the floor on my hands and knees 'cause'a her.

SMIEDNIK: *(Sees mop at hatrack; goes to it. He grabs his mop.)* Dawaj! Wy mytem podYoge wustepie kobiat I wtn samotny plazzek tutaj leci na schodach upada na palcach.

TRANSLATOR: I'm mopping the floor in the ladies' room and this maniac here comes running in all stooped over with her finger bent.

SMIEDNIK: Ona widzi mnie I zaczyna plakac. Ja chodzie do niej I chec uspokoic a una mnie voezy nad glowe z moje moitYe.

TRANSLATOR: She sees me and starts sobbing. I go and try to calm her down and she hits me over the head with my mop.

SMIEDNIK: I zamykà mnie wustepie, okolo jedna godzina asstara chinczy-ka kobieta przychodzie I otwiera dzwi.

THE PRIMARY ENGLISH CLASS 75

TRANSLATOR: Then she locks me in the ladies' room for nearly an hour until an old Chinese woman comes and opens the lock…

SMIEDNIK: *(He moves to WASTBA.)* Szytyry chas ja ukopnie twoj dzwi. I szytyry chas ty nie otwieraj. Wiedzirs ty jest sztrentny.

TRANSLATOR: Four times I come up here and bang on your door and four times you don't open your door. Don't you know that's nasty?

SMIEDNIK: *(At door.)* Tys scienczie nie jest whop appresivne.

TRANSLATOR: Lucky for you I'm not a violent man.

> *(He exits, stamming door violently. A pause. WASTBA speaks, to PATUMIERA who starts to pack his things.)*

WASTBA: We are. C'mon, mister, please we are. We really are. We are…

PATUMIERA: *(Repeats softly; gestures "you're nuts" to WASTBA first. Perhaps hums a tune, softly. He eyes his belongings; prepares to leave.)* We are.

WASTBA: *(Quietly.)* You are.

PATUMIERA: You are.

WASTBA: They are.

PATUMIERA: They are.

WASTBA: Good morning.

PATUMIERA: Good morning.

WASTBA: How are you?

PATUMIERA: How are you?

WASTBA: I am wonderful.

> *(PATUMIERA'S flight bags and brief cases are packed. He goes for his jacket.)*

PATUMIERA: I…wonderful.

WASTBA: Good.

PATUMIERA: Good.

WASTBA: Too bad…

PATUMIERA: Too bad…

WASTBA: What happens to women…

> *(PATUMIERA puts on his suitcoat.)*

PATUMIERA: Wha happens to women…

WASTBA: Like us…

PATUMIERA: Like us…

WASTBA: You are beautiful…

PATUMIERA: You…beautiful…

WASTBA: Debbie…

PATUMIERA: Deb…

WASTBA: So smart…

PATUMIERA: Smart…

WASTBA: Not wasting...
PATUMIERA: No wasting...
WASTBA: Time...
PATUMIERA: Time...
> *(Wastba bows her head and sobs. Patumiera stands, walks to five feet from her and watches, silently. She looks up and smiles.)*

WASTBA: English...
PATUMIERA: English...
WASTBA: Is not difficult...
PATUMIERA: Is no difficult...
WASTBA: Anymore...
PATUMIERA: Anymore...
WASTBA: Why?
PATUMIERA: Why?
WASTBA: Because...
PATUMIERA: Because...
WASTBA: Of Debbie...
PATUMIERA: Of Debbie...
WASTBA: Because of Debbie...
PATUMIERA: Because of Debbie... *(He smiles at her.)*
WASTBA: Because of Debbie Wastba...
PATUMIERA: *(Quietly; to her.)* Because of Debbie Wastba...
WASTBA: My teacher...
PATUMIERA: My teacher...
WASTBA: Who is certainly...
PATUMIERA: *(Nearly embracing.)* Who eeis certain...
WASTBA: ...competent.
PATUMIERA: ...compotentè.
WASTBA: ...competent.
PATUMIERA: *(Softly; smiling.)* ...compotentè?
WASTBA: ...compe*tent*.
PATUMIERA: ...compe*tent*?
> *(Wastba smiles. Nods.)*

WASTBA: Thank you. *(Pauses.)* Good.
> *(Patumiera smiles.)*

WASTBA: It's hot, huh. *(She wipes her brow.)* I can't breath... *(Smiles.)*
PATUMIERA: *(Recognizing the idiom as an old friend.)* Si. Si si. Si si si. I canno breth.
WASTBA: Huh?

PATUMIERA: *(Pulls at his shirt, mops brow, fans air.)* I canno...breth. *(Smiles.)* I canno breth.

WASTBA: Was that a negative I heard?

PATUMIERA: *(Confused.)* I canno breth?

WASTBA: Mister, this could be the second chance to end all second chances...

PATUMIERA: Scusi?

WASTBA: *(Suddenly.)* Touch the floor!

PATUMIERA: *Managa! l'America! Managa Christophe Columbe (Makes "you're nuts" gesture.)*

WASTBA: Touch the floor! *(She drops to her knees and touches the floor.)* I can touch the floor!

PATUMIERA: *(Drops to his knees; touches floor.)* Alora! I cain tooch the floor...

WASTBA: I can touch the desk!

PATUMIERA: Alora! I cain...tooch...the dest...
(She stands.)

WASTBA: *(She reaches up to ceiling above her head.)* Can you touch the ceiling?

PATUMIERA: *(He looks at her desk and starts to climb onto it.)* Si...é facile.

WASTBA: *(Moves quietly between PATUMIERA and her desk.)* No no, now...*(Reaches up again.)* Touch the ceiling! Please mister, I'm begging you. This could be the most important moment of my life.

PATUMIERA: *(Reaches up to ceiling, but of course, cannot reach it. Confused, he apologizes, in Italian.)* Signorina...

WASTBA: *(Screams; pleading.)* English! Speak English! *(She reaches again for ceiling.)* Touch the ceiling!

PATUMIERA: *Managa!* I canno...

WASTBA: *Say it!*

PATUMIERA: *(Reaching for ceiling, exasperated.)* I canno...I canno tooch the ceiling...
(WASTBA squeals with delight.)

WASTBA: *(She takes Patumiera's face in her hands and pulls his face down to hers.)* God bless you.
(They kiss. Going into the kiss, PATUMIERA is confused, thinking he has failed. After the kiss, he is changed; more confident somehow.)

PATUMIERA: Tesora...*(He reaches for her to kiss her again.)* Tesorai, mia...
(She pulls away from him, realizing.)

WASTBA: Oh, oh...no, no, no!

PATUMIERA: Ey?

WASTBA: *(She grabs his hand and shakes it enthusiastically, carefully holding her body back from his.)* I want to thank you. I really do. I'm really proud. English gets a lot easier, really. Just give it time. *(Pauses.)* You've learned. *(PATUMIERA suddenly grabs his various bags and briefcases and moves to the door. She backs away. He grabs knob.)*

WASTBA: Where are you going? Don't! Don't go! No! *No!!! Don't leave me!*

PATUMIERA: *(Quietly.)* Non ho capito ne un' acca ne un cavolo ne un cazzo di puello che hai detto.

(PATUMIERA exits the play, slamming door. WASTBA moves to door and leans her back against same. Turns. Locks doors. She pauses a moment. She moves to desk and chair. Music in. She stands facing blackboard. She bows her head. She writes "The Primary English Class" on board and then returns to her desk. She tidies desktop, stacking notebooks, pencils, etc. She places apple center of desk, sits, folds hands on desk behind apple. She weeps. The door opens, MRS. PONG re-enters, smiles at WASTBA.)

MRS. PONG: *(In Chinese language.)* Hsi wàng méi yòu lòu diào shé mǎ.

TRANSLATOR: I hope I haven't missed anything.

MRS. PONG: *(Burps, touches stomach, embarrassed.)* Wo tsài loú hsià chí le dian dóng hsi. (wo) Dù tzi gú…

TRANSLATOR: I had a little bite to eat downstairs. My stomach is making unforgivable noises. Excuse me.

MRS. PONG: *(In Chinese language.)*…lu gu lu de hsiang. Tsen dùi bu chì…Tzì shao dun hái liàng che. An í diàn, bú gùo hái liàng che.

TRANSLATOR: At least the lights are on. Dim, but on.

MRS. PONG: *(Sits in front row, folds hands, smiles at WASTBA. She speaks in Chinese, excitedly.)* Wo mén Jì hsu niàn bá!

TRANSLATOR: *(Simply.)* Let's go.

(WASTBA smiles, hopefully, happily, into MRS. PONG'S hopeful, happy smile. The lights fade to black.)

End of Play.

Fighting Over Beverley

For Gillian.

INTRODUCTION

Fighting Over Beverley was begun as a love letter to my wife, but, ended up being, instead, a quite serious warning to my mother and my daughters.

I started out writing a kind of valentine, thanking my wife Gillian for giving up what she did, in the name of love, when she married me, left England, and moved to the United States: my home. Gillian is English. She is a world-class runner, having been both British National Marathon Record-Holder, and English National Marathon Champion. She has placed #1 in the Paris, Barbados, and Essone Marathons, #2 in the New York and Stockholm Marathons, #3 in the London and Boston Marathons, etc, etc. When she moved to America, she left her friends, her family, and her fair bit of fame some 3,000 miles behind her.

And, like most English(wo)men abroad, she never stopped looking back. The English are never totally happy off their rainy rock. No matter how frequent their visits home to England, their appetite for things-English is never really sated. With rare exception, English expats never stop being recognizably English.

Fighting Over Beverley was first conceived as a devilishly tricky, unforgivably romantic comedy, in which the same three actors were to play their characters at age twenty (Act One), at age forty (Act Two), and at age seventy (Act Three). As first written, in Act One, a young English woman (Beverley) jilts her British fiancé (Archie), and runs off to America, with a twenty-year-old Yank (Zelly). In Act Two, Beverley and Zelly and their young daughter (Cecily) visit London, where Beverley has a chance meeting with Archie. In Act Three, Archie makes a surprise visit to Gloucester, Massachusetts, to Beverley and Zelly's home, where he confronts Beverley, proclaiming "I'm taking you home with me! He's had you for forty-five years. I want the rest. Enough's enough!"

As soon as I had a completed first draft, it was obvious that only Act Three was working, satisfactorily. In fact, the romantic triangle seemed to me to be only truly comic when the characters were age seventy, while, at the same time, Act Three's situation presented boundless *dramatic* possibilities. The latter revelation summoned me to quite another muse...and quite another play.

I put *Fighting Over Beverley* away for more than a year, and only dragged it out, again, at the start of the New York Playwrights Lab's sessions, in September 1991, making it my Lab project for the season. And I began writing *Fighting Over Beverley*, again, this time, *starting out* with Archie's visit to Gloucester. I reconceived Beverley as "a profoundly unhappy woman" on the brink of taking the single biggest step of her life...a step into independence.

I set out to write a seriously romantic play about three vital, sexy, *dangerous* seventy-year-olds, determined to…I'll stop, now. You'll read the play.

The earliest draft of the new, improved *Fighting Over Beverley* had its first public reading at Christmastime, in London, at the director Simon Curtis's apartment…for an audience of three (me, my British play-agent Jane Annakin, and Curtis). Elizabeth McGovern read the role of Cecily, and beautifully, showing me how much work I'd still have to do before Cecily held her own against the other, older characters. The actors reading Beverley and Zelly were so veddy veddy English, I couldn't hear the music of their characters' forty-five years in Massachusetts, together. So much so, I couldn't really judge what I had written. Only the character of Archie seemed to be working well.

I rewrote much of the play, again, in time for the NY Playwrights Lab's "retreat" in Gloucester, during the week following Labor Day, 1992. The script seemed stronger, tougher, more clear, on a better track. A month later, the Lab had its annual festival of readings of our fifteen newly completed plays, at The Joseph Papp Public Theater (on the Anspacher Theater's stage). Carole Shelly was an excellent Beverley, and Mary Beth Hurt was a clear-edged Cecily. The men were miscast. Again, more than anything else, I learned that I still had much work to do.

In the spring, Julie Harris did a reading of a newly revised text at Harvard's ART. The play was, finally, ready for production. I set August 1993, as the date for World Premiere of *Fighting Over Beverley* at Gloucester Stage. Alas, throughout the Summer of 1993, I was embroiled in a huge crisis at the theatre. The less said about it, now, the better, except to say that, in the end, crises come and crises go, and life does go on. And yesterday's newspaper is best used for wrapping fish. Unfortunately, I wasn't able to work on *Fighting Over Beverley* during its World Premiere production at Gloucester Stage. Although the play got excellent reviews, I was a totally uninvolved, totally absent parent.

In fact, *Fighting Over Beverley* was again shelved until 1994, when Steve Karp called me, saying his girlfriend had seen *Fighting Over Beverley* performed at Gloucester Stage and that she had "loved it." He asked if he could read a script. He called back, a few days later, with an offer to produce the play at his theatre in Stamford. A friend gave a script of *Beverley* to the actress Elizabeth Wilson, who called me, saying she "adored" the play, and would love to do it. And indeed she did. In reviewing *Fighting Over Beverley* for the *New York Times,* critic Alvin Klein, quoting one of Beverley's lines from the play, wrote of Elizabeth Wilson, "Her performance defines thrilling." I agreed.

The Fairbanks [Alaska] Drama Association produced *Fighting Over Beverley* during the following season with great success, but, I was unable to visit the production. (I did, however, manage to visit their production of my play *Barking Sharks* this past season, which was first-rate.)

A French production of *Fighting Over Beverley* (called *Quand Marie est Partie en français*) was produced this past season at Théâtre de la Madeleine, starring Simone Valère, Roger Pierre, and John Berry. My loving and talented French *frère*, Philippe Lefebvre, who adapted *North Shore Fish* (*l'Amour dans une usine de poissons*) for France, adapted and directed *Beverley*, as well. It was like a Broadway show, star-driven and powerful. It was fine, but, finally, it was the tiny Los Angeles production of *Fighting Over Beverley* that showed me my play at its largest…

The Fountain Theatre, whose production of my play *Park Your Car In Harvard Yard* had great success, also chose to present *Fighting Over Beverley*, this past season, starring Robert Symmonds, who had starred in *Harvard Yard*, and his real-life wife, Priscilla Pointer. Robert and Priscilla were brilliant beyond my wildest dreams. When Archie spoke to Beverley of his lifetime of loving her and no one else, there could be no doubt of his sincerity. The chemistry was perfect, and the play worked as never before.

After a season's SRO run at the Fountain, there were offers for me to adapt *Fighting Over Beverley* for the silver screen, which I am now working on with two seriously experienced film-producers, Robert Cort and David Madden, who both saw *Fighting Over Beverley* on stage, several times, and are as enthusiatic about the project as I am. I have, at this writing, had conversations with Julie Andrews, who could be a *great* screen Beverley. If the writing of my screenplay for *Fighting Over Beverley* comes slowly, it's mostly because I'm typing with my fingers crossed.

As for a major New York City production of *Beverley*, I've recently been warned that there "isn't a great deal of commercial interest in plays about older people" (*terrible* news for *King Lear!*), so, we'll have to wait and see. For my part, *Fighting Over Beverley* has already accomplished what I'd set out to do. In four substantial productions, it has held its audience. More importantly, it has *moved* its audience…and, after seeing the play, several times, in Stamford, Paris, and Los Angeles, I can report that *Fighting Over Beverley* pleases me. And it feels complete. And now, there are productions of *Beverley* planned for Germany and England. The child has its own legs and is walking in the world. It's time for me to move on.

Gloucester,
Summer 1997.

THE PEOPLE OF THE PLAY
ZELLY SHIMMA, Late 60s.
ARCHIE BENNETT, Late 60s.
BEVERLEY SHIMMA, Late 60s; married to Zelly.
CECILY SHIMMA, Early 40s; the daughter.

THE PLACE OF THE PLAY
The entire action of the play is contained in the Living Room of Beverley
and Zelly Shimma's home, overlooking the Inner Harbor, Gloucester,
Massachusetts.

THE TIME OF THE PLAY
Mid-winter, the present. From early morning of the first day, til late afternoon of the next.

THE SEQUENCE OF SCENES
Act One
   SCENE ONE: 7 A.M., Saturday.
   SCENE TWO: 7 P.M., Saturday.
   SCENE THREE: 6:30 A.M., Sunday.
Act Two
   SCENE ONE: Noon, Sunday.
   SCENE TWO: 2 P.M., Sunday.
   SCENE THREE: 5 P.M., Sunday.

Fighting Over Beverley

ACT ONE
SCENE ONE

In the darkness, WE HEAR: inspirational World War II song, "If You Love Me (I won't Care)," sung by Vera Lynn.

Living room, Beverley and Zelly Shimma's house, Gloucester, Massachusetts; noon. Prominent in upstage area of room, we see: Hammond electric (house) organ. Center of room, we see cushioned sofa and matching overstuffed chairs.

Front door to house is located upstage left; upstage right, we see swinging door to kitchen, and staircase to upstairs rooms. Upstage, we see two windows overlooking Gloucester Harbor. Outside, through windows, we see: snow falling. It is winter, deadly cold. In the distance, the wind howls, the odd hound bays, the copious buoys sway, causing their warning bells to chime; the lighthouse foghorn bleats its endless caution; a seagull screeches out in hunger. A seasonal thunderclap claps.

SPOTLIGHT on BEVERLEY SHIMMA standing in kitchen doorway, smiling, holding China teapot. BEVERLEY is beautiful; once a bombshell, now, simply, lovely. SHE speaks with an accent that combines Northeast England (Yorkshire) and Gloucester, Massachusetts. SHE stands smiling at ARCHIE BENNETT, Englishman. ARCHIE wears Norfolk-style jacket, belted, striped shirt, necktie. HE is white-haired, weathered; speaks with working-class English North Country accent.

BEVERLEY: If I didn't say this is a bit of a shock, seein' you at this current age of ours, Arthur, I'd be lying through my teeth. Not that you don't look well. You do: look well. You look very well, indeed. It's just that you look…well…*sixty-nine.*
(*LIGHTS WIDEN to include ARCHIE. HE sits on sofa, drink in hand. Outside the window, snow falls.*)
ARCHIE: I can understand your bein' rocked back on your heels a bit, Bev. I can. I half-expected to still see a skinny, full-breasted 18-year-old, meself. Seein' you old as you are, well…It is a bit of a shocker. Not that you aren't still attractive. You definitely are that: still attractive…It's just that you're not 18, any more, either, are you? Quite honestly, I expected

you to look like your mum, when I last saw her. But, thinkin' it through, Bev, I never actually knew your mum when she was any older than about *38* or *39!* I mean, she was a *kid* next to you and me as we are now, wasn't she?

BEVERLEY: She's just recently died, Mum.

ARCHIE: I'm sorry. The loss must be tremendous.

BEVERLEY: Mum was ninety, very nearly ninety-one.

ARCHIE: Bless her.

BEVERLEY: She wasn't actually current in my life, Mum. I mean, we didn't *make contact*, not on a day-to-day-week-to-week basis. I didn't *depend* on Mum. She was in a home for nearly 25 years...

ARCHIE: That long?

BEVERLEY: Might even have been longer.

ARCHIE: Must have been a tremendous blow, nevertheless. When me own m'am died, I was totally shattered...quite truly *devastated*. I didn't eat right for a year. Couldn't look at red meat or cooked chicken. *(Pauses.)* Influenza.

BEVERLEY: You got it?

ARCHIE: *She* got it. That what's killed her. *(Without warning.)* I never married, Bev. From the time you ran off with him...from the time you disappeared...right up til now. No wife, no other love of any solid...*significance*. No romance that was ever, ya' know, *estimable*. Just you in my head...in my *memories*...and nobody in my bed. *(Smiles.)* There's a rhyme in that: Beverley in Archie's head, and nobody in Archie's bed!...Now, that, to me, is poetic injustice! *(Laughs.)*

BEVERLEY: I...*(Pauses.)* Are you hungry at all? Have you eaten?

ARCHIE: I et a lovely fishy soup, in a caf' just across from the train station.

BEVERLEY: Maria's..."Seafood chowder"...

ARCHIE: That's it. "Seafood chowder." It was top class. Whacking great China bowl with just about every sort of seafood you can imagine, floating in the thing...scallops, clams, plaice, prawns...It came with a quite substantial side-portion of chips, as well, with lovely crispy bits. Very nice meal, that.

BEVERLEY: One of our favorites...When our daughter Cecily visits, she brings absolute buckets back with her to California, frozen in tubs. She adores Maria's chowder.

ARCHIE: Beats bangers and mash, doesn't it?

BEVERLEY: But, Arthur, it's only one o'clock. When did you eat lunch?

ARCHIE: I was early getting into Gloucester, this mornin'.

BEVERLEY: How early?

ARCHIE: Quite early. I et both me breakfast and me lunch in town...before comin' here to your house.

BEVERLEY: You should've come straight here.

ARCHIE: I had a look around Gloucester.

BEVERLEY: You shouldn't've wandered about in the cold, Arthur. That was silly. You should've come straight to us. *(Pauses.)* You came in by train?

ARCHIE: I did...but, not all the way from home.

BEVERLEY: *(Laughs.)* Well, I know that! You must have flown from home.

ARCHIE: I took a boat from home.

BEVERLEY: Did you?...A cruise ship?

ARCHIE: A freighter...a container ship...out of Liverpool.

BEVERLEY: *(Pours out fresh cups of tea.)* There's yours.

ARCHIE: Tar, very much, lovey. *(Sips; smacks his lips.)* Lovely! *(ARCHIE and BEVERLEY share a smile.)*

ARCHIE: I don't fly. Not since the war. It's too upsetting. I've had my fill of sky and clouds, thank you very much.

BEVERLEY: I can understand that, Arthur. I really can. Zelly doesn't like flying after his bad luck in the War.

ARCHIE: I shouldn't think he would.

BEVERLEY: Zelly has some terrible memories!

ARCHIE: As do I! I don't even try to sleep at night. My night dreams are too upsetting. I get whatever sleep I can in the daytime. Usually, no more than an hour or two.

BEVERLEY: And that's enough?...Rest.

ARCHIE: Rest? Rest is something other than sleep, isn't it?

(There is a pause.)

ARCHIE: You know, Bev, I'd known Zelly'd lost his leg, but, actually seeing it, actually meeting Zelly, I mean, and seeing, firsthand, that he's legless, I...well...

BEVERLEY: It's upsetting, I know, but, Zelly's adjusted to the artificial leg, totally. He takes two walks a day.

ARCHIE: Does he, then?

BEVERLEY: Two a day. One in the morning, one in the afternoon.

ARCHIE: Every morning, every afternoon?

BEVERLEY: Never misses.

ARCHIE: That's good to know, eh?

(ARCHIE smiles at BEVERLEY, flirtatiously. BEVERLEY giggles, girlishly.)

BEVERLEY: *Arthurrr!*

(Exits into kitchen with tea tray. ARCHIE calls after her.)

ARCHIE: We've got things to sort out, don't we, Bev? All this chat and back-chat we're doin' is bloody tiresome. Small talk, middle talk, grand talk: it's all just bloody useless *talk*, isn't it? We don't have time! It's not like we're *young people*!

(BEVERLEY re-enters.)

ARCHIE: Is your Zelly a good husband, then?

BEVERLEY: As husbands go, Zelly's a good one, yes.

ARCHIE: *(Without warning.)* You made a terrible mistake, Beverley. I'm sure you know that you did. I mean, it's obvious, isn't it? *(Pauses.)* I intend to take you back with me, Beverley. He's had you for 45 years. Enough's enough, isn't it? I may not have personally married, but, I know how these marriages work, Bev. Each one grows complaisant...mild...obliging. You get along, but, there's no fight left, there's no fire, no passion, no...excitement. We'll be starting fresh, you and me, Bev. It'll fire you up. You'll live longer. I promise you.

BEVERLEY: Arthur, you can't be serious!

ARCHIE: Oh, I am, Bev. I've loved only you. At first I thought it was just a kind of obsession...because of your jilting me as you did. But, after some years, I came to realize it was true love, Bev. Nobody's ever held a candle to you! You're the one.

(BEVERLEY is stunned.)

BEVERLEY: I'm just...flabbergasted!

ARCHIE: Are you, now? Well, then, you can easily imagine how bloody flabbergasted *I* was, can't you?...Waitin' at the station in Knutsford, alone, ring in a ring-box in me pocket, all paid for. Smile all over me face: ear to bloody ear! I'm watchin' couples re-couplin', kissin', huggin', passion in the air thick as mustard! I'm thinkin' ta' meself "Bev's *so in love with me!*"...Ten hours later, I trudge home, totally nackered, deeply depressed, bewildered, quite honestly devastated, and I hav'ta' tell m'am you never showed. She is stunned. Nearly falls backwards from the shock of it. I tell her I think you've bolted with your Yank. M'am says ta' me "Never!" She says "Bev's not that sort!" Two years later, almost to the day, that woman is in her grave.

BEVERLEY: You're not implying I was in any way *responsible* for your mum's death, are you? *(Stares at ARCHIE. Five count.)* You are.

ARCHIE: This is not a matter of implication, Miss Leach. These are hard cold facts of life!

BEVERLEY: I was eighteen, Arthur.

ARCHIE: As was I!

BEVERLEY: I'm so sorry, Arthur. I'm sorry that I did what I did. If I were able to live my life over, I would do things differently.

ARCHIE: How so?

BEVERLEY: I wouldn't've run off, so mysteriously. I would've talked with you, eye to eye, truthfully.

ARCHIE: Would you have changed the outcome?

BEVERLEY: Meaning would I still have married Zelly?

ARCHIE: Well…yes.

BEVERLEY: I don't know if I would have married Zelly, but, I do certainly know I wouldn't have married *you*, Arthur.

ARCHIE: *(After a pause; feelings hurt.)* I think I should be told why you've just said what you've just said.

BEVERLEY: Oh, Arthur…*please!* Entire *lifetimes* have passed between then and now. I will not be made to feel so profoundly *guilty*.

ARCHIE: No one can make a person feel guilt that isn't there, Bev. I hav'ta say this to you, because it's what I deeply feel to be true. *(New tone, suddenly sweet.)* Would you let me kiss you, Bev? I so much want to kiss you.

BEVERLEY: I'd prefer you didn't.

ARCHIE: For old time's sake.

BEVERLEY: I think not. *(SHE pauses, thoughtfully.)* The idea of a man wanting to kiss me…wanting me, romantically…is not an unattractive idea. And you're not an unattractive man, Arthur. But, I don't mean to hold out any false hope, especially to you, given our…history. I only want to be truthful with you. *(Without warning.)* Close your eyes, please. *(ARCHIE closes his eyes. BEVERLEY kisses him on lips, lightly.)*

ARCHIE: I love you, dearly, Bev…

(ARCHIE moves in for a major kiss. BEVERLEY backs away. HE pulls her to him, roughly. SHE pushes him away from her, angrily.)

BEVERLEY: Certainly not!

ARCHIE: Please, Bev…

BEVERLEY: *This is my husband's house! Kindly respect this!*

ARCHIE: *(Yells; a rejected lover.)* Why did you run off and marry him?

BEVERLEY: *Because I fell in love with him!*

ARCHIE: *Why?*

BEVERLEY: Zelly was exciting to me! He was forbidden by my parents. He was exotic, he was *American!*…Zelly was young and beautiful. He got into a plane and he flew against the enemy. Zelly fought to save me, my family, our little town…

ARCHIE: *So did I, all of the above!* What's so bloody great about what he did versus what I did?

BEVERLEY: There's a tremendous difference, Arthur. Zelly was shot down whilst protecting me...*us!* Zelly was decorated, made a hero. Even my father called Zelly "hero."

ARCHIE: Because he was shot down?

BEVERLEY: I beg your pardon?

ARCHIE: Him: Zelly. Gettin' shot down made the hero of him?

BEVERLEY: Of course it did.

ARCHIE: *Jesus!* That is *sickening!* That just makes me *sick.*

> (*ARCHIE moves to the window, turns his back to BEVERLEY. HE clenches his hands into fists; grinds his fists together.*)

BEVERLEY: I shouldn't have said "yes" to you, Arthur. It was wrong of me to have said "yes" to you. I do apologize. I wouldn't have hurt you, not knowingly, Art, not for the world. I adored you, Artie. I just didn't ever *love you.*

ARCHIE: Then, why ever did you say you'd marry me, then?

BEVERLEY: Because you asked me long before I met Zelly...Because you persisted...Because you wouldn't let me say otherwise...Because you wouldn't let me say "no." (*Walks to window, looks outside; then, turns to ARCHIE, again.*) I've just lied to you, Arthur. I was *thrilled* when you proposed marriage to me. But, you, personally, did not thrill me. Zelly, personally, did.

ARCHIE: And does he, Zelly, still thrill you, now?

BEVERLEY: Thrill me, now?...No.

ARCHIE: Then, leave him, Bev! He's had his time! He's had his chance! Let me have mine! I know I can thrill you. Maybe I couldn't when I was nineteen, but, I can thrill you, *now*...and he can't, now. You said so, yourself!...We can't let the most exciting times of our lives slip so far into the past. That's Death! We've got to have plans for the future! *Thrillin'* plans! We've got to find outrageous thrills! We got to have Life left! Beverley, please, trust me!...I understand that Zelly did all the right kind of talkin' ta' you, back then. But, back then's done and gone, and it's *me* who's bloody talkin' to you, *now*, my love! I'm talkin' and I'm sayin' I got me health, I've got a fair spot of wealth, and I've got all the time in the world to prove the tremendous lot of love I feel for you, Beverley Leach. You're the only woman I've ever bloody loved, Beverley. And, oh, God, I do still love you. What I lack in grace and charm, I make up for in the depth of my love for you, lass. What I lack in the way I look, I make up for in the way I look at *you!*...Let me prove myself to you, Bev. The worst that can happen is that you'll explode yourself out of this bloody *tedium!*

(Door slam. ZELLY calls from off.)

ZELLY: I'm hommmmme!

BEVERLEY: *(Pulls away from ARCHIE, stiffly.)* Zelly.

ARCHIE: At least, he's smart enough to announce himself...in case we were in the throes of *Copulatas Delecto sic.*

BEVERLEY: *(Astonished.)* Pardon?

ARCHIE: Don't say "yes" or "no," now, Beverley. Just promise me you'll think about all this.

BEVERLEY: *(Looks away, frowning. SHE then turns, looks at ARCHIE, smiles.)* I'll think about all this, Arthur. I do promise you.

(ZELLY SHIMMA, American, enters, carrying a white plastic shopping-bag. HE is ruggedly handsome, probably bald; has an artificial leg; walks with a pronounced limp. HE wears a storm coat, knit cap and scarf, over baggy cord trousers, baggy turtleneck shirt, baggy cardigan. His accent is North Shore Massachusetts "Pahk Yo'r Cah In Hah'vid Yahd.")

ZELLY: It's snowing, again, wick'id! The head of the harbor's frozen solid. Kids are skatin' on it...on the *ocean.* It'll kill you quick, this kinda' Win'tah, if you don't bundle up, but, it's beautiful to look at. At least, I, myself, think it's beautiful. *(Goes to BEVERLEY; removes cap.)* So are you. *(Kisses BEVERLEY.)* My wife hates Win'tah. If she ever leaves me, she'll leave me in Win'tah!...*(Kisses BEVERLEY, again; pats her bottom.)* The man loves his wife!...*(Smiles at ARCHIE, victoriously.)* I hope you like seafood chowder, Alf. I brought us back a gallon of the stuff! *(Hands shopping bag to BEVERLEY.)* Put this on the stove, mother, huh? It needs re-heatin'. *(To ARCHIE.)* Local chowder reheats perfect. *(ARCHIE looks at BEVERLEY; laughs. BEVERLEY laughs as well.)*

ZELLY: What's this? I miss something comical here?...Something funny about reheatin' chowder? *(Looks at BEVERLEY.)*...What?

BEVERLEY: Archie's actually had a bowl of chowder, already, today.

ARCHIE: Nooo! Please! It was my first chowder, ever, and I loved it! Really, Zelly, I'd love another go...Really!

BEVERLEY: Are you certain?

ARCHIE: Absolutely! It was lovely. I've never seen oversized prawns like that, before...certainly not in a soup. We're used to the tinned prawns at home. Aren't we, Bev?

BEVERLEY: Ah, yes. Terrible little salted prawns...tinned.

ARCHIE: "We're all just prawns in the game of life." My father used to make that joke, endlessly.

(BEVERLEY chuckles; ARCHIE repeats joke.)

ARCHIE: "We're all just prawns in the game of life, Arthur."

BEVERLEY: *(Chuckles, again; politely.)* It's rather sweet.

ARCHIE: No, you don't understand…My father said that very same thing…"We're all just prawns in the game of life, Arthur"…over and over, from the time I can remember right up til he *died!* Possibly once or twice, each day! Drove me round the bleedin' *bend!*

BEVERLEY: It's still rather a sweet little joke.

ZELLY: That's a *joke?*

ARCHIE: Prawns in the game of life…

BEVERLEY: Prawns are shrimp, dear.

ZELLY: We're all just shrimp in the game of life is a *joke?*

BEVERLEY: I'll re-heat the chowder. This won't take a minute.

(Exits into kitchen carrying chowder bag.)

ZELLY: (Sees reflection in mirror.) My goddam coat's still on! *(Slips out of his coat.)* How's *your* mind, Alf?

ARCHIE: I was never clever in school, but, I can remember things.

ZELLY: Hell of a thing, when a man's gotta' look in the mirror to find out if his coat's still on! *(Walks his coat and boots to hallway coatrack, calls to ARCHIE, from upstage.)* I never forget to put the goddam thing *on!* It's remembering the takin'-it-off part that's gettin' ha'hder. *(ZELLY laughs, then, crosses to liquor supply; stops, looks at wristwatch; squints at dial.)* Christ! My eyes are gone, too! *(ZELLY stretches his arm out; reads wristwatch at distance.)*

ZELLY: Quarter pah'st one. Normally, I'd say before supper is too early to drink, but, seein' as you're *company*…(Pours himself a straight whiskey.) What are you drinking, these days, Arch?

ARCHIE: I'm not allowed.

ZELLY: Me, neither. *(Drinks whiskey down in one gulp.)* What did you used'ta drink in the old days, Arch?

ARCHIE: Spirits? I never drank spirits. I was never allowed to drink spirits.

ZELLY: Never?

ARCHIE: Not ever.

ZELLY: Not even when you were young?

ARCHIE: Definitely not then. My father was caretaker in a village convent school.

ZELLY: So, your father didn't drink, either?

ARCHIE: Oh, I wouldn't go so far as to say *that!*...We lived in a Northern town called Knutsford. It's a little place. Everybody saw everything.

ZELLY: So, nobody in the town drank?

ARCHIE: That's not what I'm sayin' at all! Half the people were half sozzled half the time. The other half of the time, the other half of the people were *completely* sozzled!

ZELLY: *(Sudden, explosive anger.)* I can't follow nothin' comin' out'ta your mouth! You know this? Are you doin' this ta' mock me, or what?
(There is a substantial pause. A seagull screeches; a groaner groans. ARCHIE looks closely at framed photographs on TV set. Then, HE speaks again in a pleasant tone; no trace of anger.)

ARCHIE: She's lovely, isn't she?

ZELLY: Who? Bev?

ARCHIE: *(Suddenly tough.)* Aye, "Bev!"...Who in bloody hell do ya' think I'm goin' on about? Pope Pious the bloody *Third?* Are you givin' me stick?
(There is another substantial pause. Seagull screeches, again; groaner groans, again. Then, ZELLY speaks in a most pleasant tone; no trace of anger.)

ZELLY: I'm gonna' have myself another shot. Wanna' join me?

ARCHIE: *(Gentle, again.)* I'll have a belt of the brandy, if it's all the same. I see your Napoleonic Brandy bottle's out for public viewin' and, one might assume, *consumption*, yes? If it's all the same to ya', I'll have a belt of that.
(ZELLY walks to liquor cabinet with pronounced limp; pours two drinks; turns, faces ARCHIE.)

ZELLY: Here. *(Hands brandy to ARCHIE; catches ARCHIE staring at missing leg.)* You starin' at my leg?

ARCHIE: Nooo! *(Takes glass from ZELLY.)* Tar, Zelly, very much...*(Raises glass to ZELLY; recites schoolboy toast.)* Hair of the dog, tooth of the rat...Never eat flesh and you'll never grow fat. *(Downs drink.)*

ZELLY: *(Raises glass to ARCHIE.)* Cheers...Good health...May the best man win.

ARCHIE: It's the "*better*" man, not the "*best*" man. It's just two of us. Three of us, and it'd be the "*best*" man. *(Pauses.)* You're not implyin' there are more of us...other men?
(ZELLY downs his drink; never answers ARCHIE's question.)

ZELLY: The thing I've always hated about the English is that they're always correctin' your English. I've been speakin' English just like I'm speakin' now for my whole life and nobody ever didn't know what I was sayin'.

You follow me on this? *(Looks at photo of BEVERLEY in ARCHIE's hands.)* Bev was something, then, huh? How come we get so old, so fast, huh, Arch? We have all these big-deal plans...all these *wick'id* big-deal plans...but, then we finally get some time for ourselves, get a couple'a bucks in our pocket, and our wicked big-deal plans don't fit nothin'! They don't make sense for the people we are, now...for our age...It's wick'id awful depressin', huh?

ARCHIE: Oh, I dunno...Some people think their grand plans keep 'em goin', keep 'em *alive*. Some of our deepest thinkers say "without grand plans, you pack it in."

ZELLY: You got yourself some *grand plans*, Arch?

ARCHIE: Oh, yes, Zelly, I most assuredly do.

ZELLY: I was thinkin' you might.

(There is a small silence.)

ZELLY: You ready for another belt?

ARCHIE: Don't mind if I do.

(ZELLY moves toward ARCHIE. His limp is evident. ARCHIE stares.)

BEVERLEY: *(Calls from offstage)* Chow'dah's ready! *(Enters smiling.)* It's ready. We'll eat in the kitchen, if you don't mind. *(Exits into kitchen.)*

ZELLY: *(Stares at ARCHIE a moment, coldly. Then, HE smiles.)* Soup's on. *(Raises glass in toast to ARCHIE.)* Good health, Archie. May the best man win.

(Downs drink.)

(Lights fade to black.)

ACT ONE
SCENE TWO

Later, that evening. SPOTLIGHT [CROSS] FADES UP ON BEVERLEY at Hammond organ, playing and singing "Auf Wiederseh'n." SHE imitates Vera Lynn, quite well, indeed.

BEVERLEY: *(Sings.)*

"...We'll kiss again...Like this again.

Don't don't let the teardrops start!..."

(LIGHTS WIDEN to include ARCHIE and ZELLY. THEY are singing along, as well. ARCHIE is quite drunk; happy, openly sentimental. ZELLY is also quite drunk; unhappy, openly jealous of ARCHIE.)

BEVERLEY:

"...With love that's true, I'll wait for you.

Auf Wiederseh'n, sweetheart!"

ARCHIE: Vera Lynn was the greatest female singer what ever lived on the planet Earth.

ZELLY: She was pretty good, yuh.

(BEVERLEY changes tune; now sings "We'll Meet Again." ARCHIE and ZELLY chime in.)

ALL: *(Sings.)*

"We'll meet again…

Don't know where, Don't know when…

But, I know know we'll meet again

Some sunny day…"

(Speaks.)

It was an amazing time, wasn't it?

(BEVERLEY changes tune; now sings "Yours." MEN chime in.)

ALL:

"Yours, til the stars lose their glory.

Yours, til the birds fail to sing.

Yours, to the end of Life's story.

This pledge to you, dear, I bring…"

(BEVERLEY continues to play organ, lightly, under the scene.)

ARCHIE: *(Weeping, openly. HE wipes his eyes with his handkerchief.)* Oh, God bless us, it still brings tears to me eyes! I've said it once, and I'll say it, again: Vera Lynn was the greatest female singer what ever lived on the planet Earth!

ZELLY: Who da'ya think the greatest male singer was, Arch?

ARCHIE: In my opinion?…I never liked male singers.

ZELLY: Sinatra?

ARCHIE: I certainly never liked *Sinatra*.

ZELLY: Crosby?

ARCHIE: I couldn't *bear* Crosby!

BEVERLEY: Arthur never liked any Yanks at all, did you, Arthur?

ARCHIE: Not so much, no. I found Crosby a bit repulsive after his hair went thin.

BEVERLEY: My Dad hated Yanks, 'til he met Zelly. When the Americans first got into the War, my Dad always use'ta tell me and my sisters "Stay away from the Yanks!"…*(Imitates her father's voice.)* "Yanks are over-sexed, overpaid, and over here!"

(ZELLY and BEVERLEY share a laugh. ARCHIE stares, stone silent.)

ARCHIE: We used'ta say "Brit rhymes with grit. Yank rhymes with wank!" *(ARCHIE laughs at his own small joke, loudly.)*

ZELLY: Bev's dad and I got wick'id close, like family. I don't mean like in-laws kinda' thing. I mean like *family*.

ARCHIE: *(Smiles to BEVERLEY.)* I remember your dad well.

ZELLY: Bev's dad was like my best friend. Honest ta' God! I wouldn't make a move without askin' Den Leach, first. When I quit my job cuttin' at Gorton's and started my own fish business, I waited an extra three months, just so he could get over here, first, and check it out...

BEVERLEY: He's been gone about twenty years, now...

ZELLY: I miss Bev's father more than I miss my own father...I would've liked to have called him "Dad," honest ta' Christ!

BEVERLEY: He suffered, wick'id, Dad did...

ARCHIE: I'm sorry to hear this.

ZELLY: You wonder what God's thinkin', sometimes, makin' a man like Den Leach suffer like that...The man had Heaven's Touch. I swear to Christ! When they found me, I was barely breathin'...They thought I was a dead man! November of '44, November 12th...Two dozen of Adolph's flyboys, Heinkel III's, out'ta nowhere. Just six of us, mostly Mustangs. We were fighting in the clouds over the town of Beverley, Bev's Mum's town...

BEVERLEY: I was named for Beverley.

ZELLY:...A bunch'a Spitfires come up to help...Brits. I got hit from behind...first barrage. I fell out of the sky...My plane went down on Spaulding Moor, half a mile from the runway...Exploded...nothin' left of it. I parachuted clear, but, I was way too low for a soft touch. Both my hip joints shattered from the force of my hitting the ground. All the main nerves in this leg got cut. Bone was sticking out through the skin, every which way. *(Pauses.)*

I shouldn't complain, huh? I was one of the lucky ones! My best friend, Tommy Murphy, got hit direct, blown to bits. They only found pieces of 'im. They never found his head. Eighteen years old, bright, nice, smiley kid...They got me back to the base hospital, and they worked on me, 'round the clock...They told me I was gonna live, but, they had'da take my leg. That's what they told me...straight words, direct, no beatin' around the bush, no hedgin' any bets...Five doctors in a goddam circle around me...all educated, trained men...all of 'em dead wrong! They could've grafted bone and saved it! They just did what they did 'cause it was quick!...'cause it was easy for *them*!...*(Pauses; sadly.)*

...Two of 'em were Americans, two of 'em were Brits, and a little Czech runt son of a bitch!...Educated, trained doctors, all of 'em!...Imagine: takin' a kid's leg when you don't have to?!...*Shit!*
(ZELLY, suddenly, sobs. BEVERLEY reaches behind her head, without turning around, grasps ZELLY's hands.)

ZELLY: Once the leg was gone, alls I wanted ta do was roll over and die! I knew I wasn't goin' home, whole...You know what I mean? I knew I wasn't gonna' ever work no fishing boat on my own. I couldn't see any reason for staying alive! Den Leach taught me different, right off the bat. Soon as he sat down, he looked me in the eye and he goes "Zelly-lad, I never met a Yank didn't have more piss and fight than God himself! Get off your bottom, lad, and get a move on!"...And he gets 'em ta' strap a heavy old metal leg on me and then he shoves me out of my goddam bed! Can you imagine this? *He shoves me out of my goddam bed!* It was like God himself sent Den Leach to Zelly Shimma ta' do this! Between Bev and Den, I was up and walking, every day of my life, from then on. They saved my miserable goddam life, that's what!
(There is a small silence.)

ARCHIE: I was stationed just over the road, at Pocklington...

ZELLY: I knew this, yuh. Bev told me this.

ARCHIE: I was in the same skirmish. 12 November...

ZELLY: *(After a pause.)* I knew this, too, Arch, yuh.

ARCHIE: Auxilary Squadron #608...joint membership...us, you Yanks, Czechs, Poles...

ZELLY: I knew this, too.

ARCHIE: We were sergeants, gettin' thirty quid a month. You lot were lieutenants, gettin' (what?) five times that...

ZELLY: $255 a month, plus allowances...Big money, back then.

ARCHIE: My point, exactly...
(ARCHIE pauses; remembers.)

ARCHIE:...A squadron of Jerries made it through...one bomber, two dozen Heinkels. I went up with nine others...Spitfires. We chased 'em off.

ZELLY: I guess you Brits'd hav'ta' get the credit for chasin' 'em off, yuh.

ARCHIE: Terrifying thought...Jerries comin' in and out of England, at will, like it was no trouble for 'em at all! I meself think the Irish were in cahoots with Adolph...thick with him, teamed up..

ZELLY: I never heard that particular theory, myself.

ARCHIE: It's me own. I got no use for the Irish. I'd rather go to war *against* 'em, than with 'em! I'll tell the God's honest: I never met an Irishman

who wouldn't drink your vinegar and bugger your spaniel! *(Without warning.)* Late in the War, they dropped the length of the trainin' period for RAF flyers like me, from fourteen weeks, down to six, but, with you Yanks, they threw the bloody requirements out the *window*, didn't they? Nothin' cheered me more than watchin' your Yank "7-Day Wonders" tryin' ta' start their engines! Throttle in one hand, bleedin' engine specs in the other! Handbooks on their laps opened to Lesson #1! And they're goin' up ta' meet Adolph in the clouds! Quite a giggle! More humourous than your Bob Hope, I can tell ya' fuckin' *that*, mate!
(BEVERLEY stops playing. There is an astonished pause. ARCHIE smiles, awkwardly.)

ARCHIE: I hope you can pardon my Français, Bev. I shouldn't be thinkin' or talkin' about wartime. It's too upsetting. I get on about it, don't I, now? I get myself too worked up. I offer my apology.

BEVERLEY: I accept. And to Zelly?

ARCHIE: I said nothing to offend Zelly, did I?
(ARCHIE turns, faces ZELLY.)

ARCHIE: You not Irish, are you?

ZELLY: Me? Irish? Nope.

ARCHIE: Wouldn't surprise me none, if you turned out ta' be, after I said what I said about the Irish. I'm always sayin' the painfully incorrect thing. I've got a bleedin' *knack!* Me dad use'ta tell me I put me foot in me mouth so often, I had heel-marks on the back'a me throat!
(There is a moment's pause.)

ARCHIE: So, what are you, then?

BEVERLEY: Zelly's half Jewish.

ARCHIE: I think I knew that from your letters. *(Smiles at ZELLY.)* Well, now...half Jewish. Bein' half Jewish beats bein' *all* Jewish, doesn't it? *(Pauses.)* What's the other half?

ZELLY: "Portegee," mostly, with some Italian snuck in.

ARCHIE: *(Happy to hear the Portuguese connection.)* There you go, then! *(Explains.)* I had a lovely holiday in Portugal, a few years back. The Portuguese do very nice fish dishes. I love a nice piece of fish. *(Smiles a conspirator's smile.)* The Italian that snuck in's better left undiscussed.
(ARCHIE laughs. There is an embarrassed pause.)

ARCHIE: Stop me, if I'm sayin' painfully incorrect things. I'm sure you can understand my desperate case of nerves, mate...not seein' Bev in all these years...*(Pauses.)* It's a tricky situation we've got goin' among us, isn't it? I don't want you to think I don't appreciate your letting me stay under your roof, Zelly, mate. I do…I appreciate your hospitality…given who you are, in relation to Bev; and given who I am, in relation to Bev.

ZELLY: You're welcome in my house, Archie, 'cause you're one'a Bev's oldest friends. Also, I gotta' admit that Den Leach spoke well of ya', too, so, that in itself is more'n enough ta' let you through my door. But, I'm gonna' tell you som'pin, *bub!*…You so much as touch a finger to my wife and I'll rip you ta' pieces and feed you to the fuckin' seagulls! You get me on this?

(There is another small silence. Then, ARCHIE laughs, nervously. Then, BEVERLEY resumes playing and singing "Auf Wiederseh'n," quietly.)

BEVERLEY: *(Sings.)*

"…We'll kiss again, Like this again.

Don't don't let the teardrops start.

With love that's true…"

(BEVERLEY stops playing Hammond organ; turns, faces the MEN; speaks.)

BEVERLEY: I can't say it isn't flattering…you two…what's goin' on here…'cause, the odd thing is, it is: flattering. But, at the same time, I think you're both disgusting…absolutely and utterly disgusting.

(BEVERLEY resumes playing, this time without singing. After a few moments, SHE bangs her fists down on to the keyboard.

ARCHIE and ZELLY turn and face BEVERLEY, who looks first at ZELLY, then at ARCHIE…then, SHE bows her head.)

(The Lights fade to black.)

ACT ONE
SCENE THREE

7:30 A.M., next day. In the darkness, we hear the morning sounds of Gloucester Harbor: the straining engine of a dragger; a buoy bell clangs; a lighthouse foghorn groans its warning; copious screeching seagulls fly past the Shimma house in search of precious food.

LIGHTS FADE UP on ARCHIE facing CECILY SHIMMA. CECILY is in her 40s, looks younger. SHE is adorable; beautiful in the California style…thin and fit. In CECILY's beauty, we see BEVERLEY's past. She probably wears all black: designer jeans, and layers of 100% cotton.

CECILY's accent is a mix of L.A. and Gloucester. There is a British influence on her speech, as well. NOTE: CECILY's suitcases are in evidence in hallway, near front door.

ARCHIE speaks to CECILY, middle of a thought.

ARCHIE: [My name is] Archie Bennett...*(Corrects himself.) Arthur* Bennett.

CECILY: *(Almost laughing.) You're* Arthur Bennett?

ARCHIE: The man himself!

CECILY: My Goddd!

    (CECILY gives in to laughter. ARCHIE stares at HER, humiliated.)

ARCHIE: I must say, over the years, very few people have been as dead amused by that particular fact of my life as *you* seem ta' be.

CECILY: *(Giggles.)*

ARCHIE: What's so funny, may I ask?

CECILY: It's just that I've been hearing about you for years...

ARCHIE: Have you?

CECILY: I have...

ARCHIE: From whom, may I ask?

CECILY: *(Imitates his accent.)* From me mum...But, every time she talked about you, it was always in this darkly romantic-slash-sexual context...Oh, God, the same thing happened when I went to a Sinatra concert, when I was in college. I don't mean I got the giggles: I mean the *surprise*...the same kind of shock and surprise. All the time I was little, my parents went on and on about Sinatra. They played all his records, took me to a couple of his movies...But, when I went to his concert, years later, I was twenty, and it never once occured to me that in life Sinatra'd be this old old guy, still acting young and, ya' know, *cutesy*...He comes out on stage, and all these old ladies around me start screaming *"Frankeeeeee!,"* and he tosses his jacket over his shoulder, like this...*impish*...Then, this 200-piece orchestra starts playing "Try A Little Tenderness," and Sinarta starts doin' this boyish "I love you" with his baby blue eyes, and every old lady around me is instantly reduced to *tears*, and I don't *get* it! I mean, straight and simple, *I don't get it!* I mean, have you ever heard *Otis Redding* sing "Try A Little Tenderness?" Now, *that* is something to fucking *cry* about!...You know what I'm sayin' here? *(After a small silence, ARCHIE stares directly at CECILY. HE sings a travesty of "Smoke Gets In Your Eyes," with an overstated Yiddish accent.)*

ARCHIE: *(Sings.)*

    Dey asked me how I knew...Ginzburg was a Jew!

    I promptly replied..."He's been circumcised"...

    Dis is how I knew...

    (There is another small silence. ARCHIE breaks it; his voice suddenly stern.)

ARCHIE: I don't give a Tinker's damn *who* you are, sissy, Bev's kid or Bev, herself, I don't like havin' me piss taken! You wanna' try ta' take the piss out'ta me, you're gonna' be squashed! I'm the *master* of piss-takin'! *(BEVERLEY enters, smiling. SHE wears a "dress-up" dress: one that would normally be worn at night.)*

CECILY: Wow! Look at *you!*

BEVERLEY: *(Smiles.)* Thank you, dear…Have you introduced yourselves?

CECILY: Sort of.

ARCHIE: Not formally.

BEVERLEY: Cecily Shimma…Arthur Bennett. Arthur…Cecily. Cecily… Arthur. Cecily's my daughter.

ARCHIE: She *had* to be your daughter, 'cause you're berries from the same bleedin' bush, you are!

BEVERLEY: I've mentioned Arthur to you, haven't I, dear?…
(ARCHIE laughs.)

CECILY: Did you tell Daddy?

BEVERLEY: That you're home?…Yes.

CECILY: And?

BEVERLEY: Well…he's quite upset.

CECILY: And?

BEVERLEY: Well…he'll tell you, himself. He's just getting dressed. *(Looks at clock on wall.)* Goodness me! It's still terribly early, isn't it?

CECILY: The red-eye always gets into Boston, early. They say it lands at 6:30, but, it really lands at five-thirty. If they advertised five-thirty, nobody would ever take it, so, they lie. *(To ARCHIE.)* Sorry…I always babble when I'm sleep-deprived.

BEVERLEY: *(To ARCHIE.)* It's always something, isn't it? I mean, just when you think your troubles are *this*, then, suddenly, they're *that!*…Cecily's left her husband.

ARCHIE: Just?

CECILY: *(Looks at watch.)* Eight and a half hours, now. He drove me to the airport.

ARCHIE: What grounds?

CECILY: The airport?

ARCHIE: The divorce.

BEVERLEY: Are you getting *divorced?*

CECILY: On the grounds that enough is enough.

ARCHIE: I'll drink to that.

CECILY: On the grounds that men are selfish, heartless pigs. *(Imitates ARCHIE's accent.)* Do I not hear ya' drinkin' to *that*, mate?

BEVERLEY: Are you getting *divorced*, Cecily?

CECILY: I dunno.

BEVERLEY: What did you tell Arthur? Why did Arthur say what he said?

CECILY: He's *your* boyfriend, not mine. Ask him.

ARCHIE: I've known many a married man and wife to live separate from one another for years and years, but, never actually divorce. Better for the kiddies, they say. If you don't mind me givin' ya' a spot of advice, that'd be it, Sicily…live separate, but, never divorce.

CECILY: Did you call me *Sicily*? My name's not Sicily. It's *Cecily*.

ARCHIE: Oh, is it? Sorry, love. I thought your name was Italian. Your Dad said some Italian snuck into the family.

CECILY: You mean snuck in like through the *window* kind of thing? *(To BEVERLEY.)* What's he saying?

BEVERLEY: I don't know! *(To ARCHIE.)* What are you saying, exactly, Arthur?

ARCHIE: I thought you'd said you'd given your daughter an Italian name.

CECILY: *Sicily*? You thought my parents named me *Sicily*?

ARCHIE: I've known of many a Swiss-miss to be named Geneva.

(There is a small pause, as CECILY, confused, rolls her eyes Heavenward.)

CECILY: It must be the time change. *(To ARCHIE; explains.)* I'm still on L.A. time.

BEVERLEY: *(Brightly; to Cecily.)* Arthur's still on *English* time! It's already *afternoon* in Arthur's mind! He's six hours ahead of us!

CECILY: That explains it. By lunchtime, I'll know what he's talking about.

BEVERLEY: *(Brightly; to ARCHIE.)* Cecily's been living out in California. She's in the entertainment industry.

CECILY: I made this terrible career choice. I misheard my father. I thought he told me to go into *show* business. It turns out he'd told me to go into the *shoe* business. Of course, he also told me *The Lion, The Witch, And The Wardrobe* was *really* called "The Lying *Bitch* In The Wardrobe!" You boys do have your little prejudices, eh?

ARCHIE: *(Glares at CECILY, suspicious that HE's the butt of her small jokes.)* Is it just California men you find to be piglike, or is it *all* men you find to be piglike?

CECILY: Only a man would have to ask.

(After a small pause, BEVERLEY leaps in to save the moment.)

BEVERLEY: Cecily's a very successful talent agent. She represents film direc-

tors and screenwriters. Her husband's a screenwriter. He's working on a
screenplay with George Harrison, the former Beatle.

ARCHIE: The singing Beatles? From up home?

BEVERLEY: Not all of them. Just the one: George.

(ZELLY enters the room.)

CECILY: Hi!

ZELLY: Who's with Little Gerald?

CECILY: That's not my problem.

ZELLY: Fine.

(ZELLY exits into kitchen.)

ARCHIE: Is your husband not very tall, then?

CECILY: What?

(BEVERLEY smiles; explains.)

BEVERLEY: Little Gerald's her stepson.

CECILY: He's with his mother.

BEVERLEY: He's nine.

ARCHIE: He's *yours*? Not hers?

BEVERLEY: Pardon?

ARCHIE: You said "Little Gerald is mine"…

BEVERLEY: *Nine!* I said "Little Gerald is *nine!*"

ARCHIE: Me hearin's gettin' worse and worse.

(CECILY laughs. ARCHIE snaps at HER; annoyed.)

ARCHIE: You're not one of these nutter Feminists I've been reading about,
are you? Hairy legs and armpits…Feminists can't stay married more than
a matter of weeks! Both of the Queen's pathetic sons married Feminists,
didn't they? Is that what you are, then, a bleedin' Feminist?

*(Wordlessly, CECILY shows ARCHIE her armpit, just as ZELLY re-enters
from kitchen carrying mug of coffee. ZELLY sees CECILY's arm in the air.)*

ZELLY: What are you doing?

CECILY: *(Imitates ARCHIE's Northern accent.)* Nuthin' much, Dad. I'm just
showing Archie me hairy armpit.

ZELLY: *What?* *(There is a small embarrassed silence.)*

ZELLY: *(To CECILY.)* Take a walk with me.

CECILY: Outside?…

ZELLY: Yes, outside…

CECILY: It's snowing!

ZELLY: So what?

CECILY: My blood's thinner than yours!

BEVERLEY: They say this happens to East Coast people after they've lived in California a while: they become cold-blooded.

CECILY: *(Laughs.)* It's the essential nature of the film industry.

BEVERLEY: I beg your pardon, dear?

CECILY: Cold-bloodedness.

BEVERLEY: The *climate!*...I mean the climate...*(To ARCHIE; smiling; chirping, nervously.)* I meant the climate...When Easterners go West, they get cold. Their blood thins...

(Suddenly, ZELLY yells at BEVERLEY.)

ZELLY: Stop your goddam babble, will you?! You're makin' a fool of yourself!...You sound *stupid!*

(There is a hideous pause.)

CECILY: Nice. Really nice.

ARCHIE: Would you like me to take a walk, then, Zelly? I wouldn't mind, mate. I rarely see a snowstorm as violent as this one. I'd like very much to be out experiencing it, firsthand.

BEVERLEY: Noooo...

ZELLY: Yuh, that'd be great. We need to have a family powwow.

BEVERLEY: Meeting, he means.

ARCHIE: I know what "powwow" means...from the pictures.

BEVERLEY: *(To ZELLY.)* He means the movies.

ZELLY: *(Angrily.)* I know what he means!

BEVERLEY: I'll walk with you, Arthur. We could get the morning paper.

ARCHIE: Lovely.

BEVERLEY: *(To ZELLY.)* It'll give you two a few minutes alone.

ARCHIE: I'll leave you lot, then. *(To BEVERLEY.)* I'll have to borrow some boots.

BEVERLEY: Let me see your foot...*(Looks.)* Zelly's spare snowboots should fit you. They're in the pantry. We'll go out the back door. *(To ZELLY.)* Don't be angry with her without listening. Listen to her side, first.

ZELLY: Fine.

(BEVERLEY kisses CECILY.)

BEVERLEY: Don't be hostile toward your father, dear. He only wants the very best for you.

(And then SHE kisses ZELLY.)

BEVERLEY: Is a half hour enough?

ZELLY: Fine.

BEVERLEY: Come with me, Arthur.

(BEVERLEY and ARCHIE exit into the kitchen.)

CECILY: He's disgusting!

ZELLY: Don't change the subject!

CECILY: It's not your life, it's *my* life!

ZELLY: Oh, yuh? Whose house are you stayin' in?

CECILY: You want me to leave? Fine! Now? Tonight? When?

ZELLY: What about Little Gerald?

CECILY: What *about* Little Gerald? He's got a mother and a father! *(Suddenly.)* Doesn't it ever occur to you to put your arms around me and say "I can see you're unhappy and I love you!?"

ZELLY: Doesn't it ever occur to you to call yo'r motha' and yo'r fatha', first, and say "I love you and I need you…" and then maybe *ask* "Can I come to your house?" *before* you show up ?

CECILY: You think I should *ask permission* to see my own mother and father? You think this house is your house, not my house, too?

ZELLY: Yuh, lady, that's what I think!

CECILY: You are really fucked up!

ZELLY: Save the gutter language for your sophisticated show-business friends! *(Pauses.)* If I was forty, I'd never run home to my mother and father like I was twelve!

CECILY: That's what I started out telling myself…But then I thought, "uh uh…You get one mother and one father and they hav'ta count…They hav'ta figure into your life decisions…

ZELLY: Come off it! You're not lookin' for your mother and me ta' help you decide nothing! You're just looking for us to back you up, no matter what bullshit you pull!

CECILY: So, is that like *a bad thing*? I mean, aren't parents s'pose'ta be behind their children, no matter what?

ZELLY: Children, maybe! Forty-year-olds, hell, no! Marriage #1, fine! Marriage #2, *maybe!* Marriage #3, you're on your own, lady! Leave us out of it! You want help with a life decision, fine, here's help with a life decision: Go back to Gerald and Little Gerald and stay married.
(Pause. CECILY goes to brandy bottle, pours herself a drink.)

ZELLY: When did you start drinking brandy in the morning?

CECILY: I'm still on L.A. time.

ZELLY: Yuh, so, that makes it even *earlier*.

CECILY: Fine. This is my last drink of the night in L.A. Cheers! *(Drinks brandy; winces.)* That was just awful!…They say every man in France gets up in the morning, has a belt of brandy, and hits his wife. Now I know why.

ZELLY: Did Gerald hit you?

CECILY: No, Gerald didn't hit me. Believe it or not, there's more to hurt than sticks and stones.

ZELLY: Let me tell you something, loud and clear, lady: I never asked for kids. I never wanted 'em, and to tell the God's honest truth, I still don't. But, I got 'em, didn't I? I got you and you got me and we're stuck with each other. So, this is life and we put up with each other. We make the best of it…But, so help me God, I'm not gonna' just stand back, smilin', while you mess up some innocent little nine-year-old kid!

CECILY: Like *you* did?

ZELLY: What's that crack s'pose'ta mean?

CECILY: Remember me? I was the nine-year-old kid sleepin' in the pink room, and *I'm* messed up!…Dr. Weingarten thinks I can't stay married to Gerald or anybody, because of you, because of the marriage I grew up watching…I'm the only person Dr. Weingarten's ever met in his entire career who actually spent their childhood praying that their parents would get divorced.

ZELLY: Is that a true fact?

CECILY: That is a fucking true fact!…Your wife is miserable, you know this? Your wife has been unhappy for forty-five years. She has felt unwanted and unloved. She has felt homesick, disconnected from everything she loved. She's wearing dresses, again, in the daytime…and she is panting with excitement, now that that subhumanoid's here in the house, back in her life. You know why? I'll tell you why. It's 'cause, finally, she's feeling some connection to her youth! Finally, she's feeling some connection to *affection!* For the first time in forty-five years, she feels *loved!*
(ZELLY shoves CECILY backwards. SHE falls on to sofa.)

ZELLY: Shut your mouth!
(There is an astonished pause. ARCHIE appears in kitchen doorway wearing outlandishly bright-colored snow boots.)

ARCHIE: I don't mean to interrupt. I just want to tell you that we're off, now…Bev and me…into the fresh snow. *(Pauses; smiles, happily.)* I'm really very happy that I spent me time and money taking this trip. *Very* happy.
(ARCHIE smiles. CECILY and ZELLY stare at ARCHIE, and then, turn and face one another. The lights fade to black.)

End of Act One.

ACT TWO
SCENE ONE

Noon, the same day. In the darkness, we hear: Recording of Vera Lynn singing "When I Grow Too Old To Dream."

> *LIGHTS FADE UP in living room. CECILY and BEVERLEY sit in separate chairs, eating dinner from plates on their laps. The TV is playing soap opera, opposite them, sound off.*

> *MUSIC fades out.*

CECILY: He's nuts. You know this, yes?

BEVERLEY: Your father?

CECILY: Both of 'em! *(Eats.)* They weren't talking to each other at all at breakfast, so, I asked him (Archie) if he was enjoying America…

BEVERLEY: Oh, I think he is. What did he say?

CECILY: He said "Yank rhymes with Wank!"

BEVERLEY: *Did* he? Again?

CECILY: And then Daddy goes "Brit rhymes with shit!"

BEVERLEY: Dear me! They're not getting on at all well, are they?

CECILY: So, then, Archie goes… *(Will imitate ARCHIE's accent.)* "That's bloody grand talk comin' from a yob who's got one leg missing!"…

BEVERLEY: Goodness me! Arthur *said* that?! I am *shocked!*

CECILY: For a couple'a seconds, I thought they were going to have a fist-fight!

BEVERLEY: I dare *say!*

CECILY: They are both terminally *nuts!* Neither of 'em said another word after that! *(Eats.)* How could you even *know* somebody like that?

BEVERLEY: Arthur?

CECILY: Jesus, Mum, yes: Arthur!

BEVERLEY: It's sometimes difficult to determine which man you're so intensely hating, Cecily. You seem to hate them all.

CECILY: I'm just a little vulnerable at the moment, Mum. So, maybe you could hold your more intensely judgmental thoughts to yourself.

BEVERLEY: And you can't imagine *you're* being judgmental calling both my husband and my old friend "terminally nuts?"

CECILY: I'm not judging you. I'm judging them.

BEVERLEY: Are we saying that judgement is defined objectively versus sub-jectively?

CECILY: Don't get British on me, Mother. Stay mid-Atlantic, so we can keep talking. *(Paces, nervously.)* I'm either premenstrual or premigraine. I don't like my choices.

(CECILY checks to see if the portable telephone is working.)

BEVERLEY: Is it working?

CECILY: *It* is. I'm not. *(Checks the clock: time of day.)* Why does he sleep in the *daytime*?

BEVERLEY: Arthur?…Perhaps he's jet-lagged.

CECILY: He can't be jet-lagged. He came on a boat.

BEVERLEY: I suppose it's because he's unable to sleep in the nighttime. *(Explains.)* He has bad dreams.

CECILY: If Archie Bennett didn't have bad dreams, I wouldn't believe in God. *(Lights a cigarette. Puffs. Suddenly, jams cigarette out in ashtray.)* Jesus! *(Paces.)* I lived with a drummer like that for about six months. Did you ever meet Chick? He couldn't sleep in the nighttime, either. It was *Proustian*: as soon as there was a crack of daylight under the bedroom door, Chick would start snoring. I'd get up for work and leave him sleeping.

BEVERLEY: I remember the name Chick from your letters, dear, but, I'm quite certain I never actually *met* your Chick.

CECILY: He was nice to me and great looking, but, he used to lie awake in bed all night, worrying about everything…drumming his fingers on the night table…I didn't get a night's sleep for six fucking months!

BEVERLEY: Mind your language, dear.

CECILY: *(Pacing.)* Where's Daddy? He knows I'm only staying one day.

BEVERLEY: He's just having his walk. You could have gone with him. He would have greatly enjoyed your company.

CECILY: It's too cold…and I'm too jet-lagged to put up with his harangue. I'm exhausted.

BEVERLEY: Take a nap.

CECILY: I can't sleep in the daytime. *(Stands.)* I have to call my office. *(Goes to phone.)* It's Saturday. *(Returns to chair; sits; looks at TV.)* What's this? What are we watching? What is this "drech?"

BEVERLEY: I have no idea. You turned the television on, not I.

CECILY: I did?…I think you're right. You mind if I turn it off?

BEVERLEY: Not at all.

(CECILY switches off TV; goes to window; looks outside.)

BEVERLEY: You seem quite overwrought, darling.

CECILY: You're *under*wrought!…How is it you're so calm?

BEVERLEY: Why shouldn't I be calm?

CECILY: It should be obvious what your old friend wants here.

BEVERLEY: He wants me to leave your father and move back to England with him.

CECILY: Holy shit!

BEVERLEY: Language, darling, please!

CECILY: Does Daddy know this?

BEVERLEY: He *suspects* this. He doesn't know this.

CECILY: Daddy will kill this guy if he finds out. *(Considers this; laughs.)* Are you gonna'?

BEVERLEY: Tell Daddy?

CECILY: *Leave* Daddy.

(*There is a pause.*)

BEVERLEY: I haven't decided.

CECILY: *(Whispered shock.)* What?

BEVERLEY: *(Stands.)* I'm going to put the kettle on. I won't be a minute.

(*BEVERLEY exits into the kitchen. CECILY goes to portable telephone, dials a number; waits; speaks to an answering machine.*)

CECILY: Dr. Weingarten, this is Cecily Shimma, again. I'm sorry to leave so many messages, but, I'm having sort of a crisis. I'm still in Massachusetts, at my parents' house. I've left you the number here in my last couple of messages, but, in case your machine's broken, I'm at 508-281-4099. Please, call me as soon as possible…Thanks, Dr. Weingarten. I'm sorry to bother you, but, I guess you know I wouldn't if I didn't feel I had to…I hope your wrist is feeling better. Bye.

(*ARCHIE enters from upstairs. HE is wearing a circa1940 bathrobe. There is a white towel around his neck…and a small black, red and gold metallic label stuck to the center of ARCHIE's forehead.)*

ARCHIE: Oh, hullo.

CECILY: Hi. Sleep?

ARCHIE: A bit.

(*CECILY stares at the label on ARCHIE's forehead.*)

ARCHIE: Something on me head?

CECILY: There is, actually…Some kind of label's stuck to your forehead.

(*ARCHIE finds the label.*)

ARCHIE: *(Matter-of-factly.)* Oh, yuh, it's the label from me soap. Cussons' Imperial Leather. It's been me brand for more'n sixty years now. It was me Dad's brand, and his Dad's before *him*. I wouldn't dare wash meself without Imperial Leather! The scent suits me. *(Sniffs the label.)* Lovely! There's a a lifetime of memories in that scent. *(Smiles at CECILY.)* The label usually sticks pretty solid to the center of the bar, first three or four scrubbings. After that, it goes loose with the suds. I've found 'em in me mornin' scrambled'n'Spam, more than once. You never quite know *where* they're it's gonna' turn up! *(Without pause.)* Is your Dad around?

CECILY: Why?

ARCHIE: It's nothing special.

CECILY: He's out walking. Anything I can help you with?

ARCHIE: Actually, the lav I'm using upstairs is out of loo rolls.

CECILY: What's this?

ARCHIE: Do you have any loo rolls in the house?

CECILY: Lew Rawls, the singer?

ARCHIE: Pardon?

CECILY: You mean like his old records or tapes kinda' thing?

ARCHIE: I beg your pardon?

(BEVERLEY re-enters from the kitchen.)

BEVERLEY: Hello, Arthur. Did you sleep?

ARCHIE: A bit...

BEVERLEY: You're just in time for a cup of tea.

CECILY: He wants something.

BEVERLEY: And what would that be, Arthur?

ARCHIE: Do you have any spare loo rolls in the house? There's none in the upstairs lav.

BEVERLEY: In the vanity cupboard, under the sink.

(CECILY laughs.)

ARCHIE: I'm afraid I've looked there, already.

BEVERLEY: Then, try the ensuite lav in my bedroom. There should be a few spare loo rolls there.

ARCHIE: Thank you.

(ARCHIE exits upstairs. CECILY laughs, again. BEVERLEY smiles.)

BEVERLEY: Did you and Arthur have a misunderstanding?

CECILY: Arthur *is* a misunderstanding!...We had a mid-Atlantic language breakdown. I thought he was after Lou Rawls music, which is, in my book, absolute shit. He was after toilet paper. Well, at least, Archie and I are in the same ballpark.

BEVERLEY: You're so American, darling. It still amazes me. When you were little, it was amusing: having an American child. Somehow, I always thought I'd take you home, bring out the English in you. But, I never did, did I? Makes me sad, really...You look like me...like I did at your age...but, somehow, I can never find myself in anything you *say!*...I'm losing my Englishness, myself. I mean, listen to me: I don't sound English, and I don't sound American, either. I don't know what I am, anymore, really. It's a bit sad, isn't it? What I mean is, well, something's lost, isn't it?...*(WE HEAR: Teakettle's whistle whistles, offstage.)* I won't be a minute.

(BEVERLEY exits into the kitchen. CECILY dials another number, talks to another answering machine.)

CECILY: Gerald, it's me. I'm still at my parents. I know why I'm crazy, Gerald...Hullo?...*(New tone, suddenly. SHE is no longer talking to an answering machine.)* Gerald? Hiiii!...Are you still sleeping?...I'm sorry!...No, no, no, go back to sleep. Call me when you get up. I'm at my parents. I'll talk to you, later. Go back to sleep....What?...Is somebody there?...No, I just thought I heard somebody...Fine. No, no, it's fine...Bye, Gerald.

(CECILY switches portable phone off. SHE is terribly sad. BEVERLEY re-enters, carrying tea tray.)

BEVERLEY: Did someone call?

CECILY: No. I called someone. *(Tries not to say more, but, does.)* I called Gerald.

BEVERLEY: That's a good idea. *(Puts tea tray down.)* And how is Gerald?

CECILY: In bed with somebody.

BEVERLEY: Somebody?...Oh. I see. He told you this?

CECILY: I could hear.

BEVERLEY: Did you ask him?

CECILY: Mother, I could hear.

BEVERLEY: Sometimes, when you're overwrought, dear, the imagination plays tricks...

CECILY: Mum, *please!*

(CECILY fights back tears. SHE goes to window; looks out at the storm. Suddenly, tears overwhelm her. BEVERLEY watches her daughter weep. SHE keeps her distance. When SHE speaks, she speaks quietly.)

BEVERLEY: Are you alright, darling?

CECILY: I'm fine, Mum.

BEVERLEY: Is Gerald treating you badly?

CECILY: Yes. No. Yes.

BEVERLEY: Do you want to end your marriage?

CECILY: No. Yes. Those two things: No and Yes.

BEVERLEY: Is little Gerald difficult?

CECILY: That's not it.

BEVERLEY: *What's* it, dear?

CECILY: Why do we let them get away with it, Mum? *(Pauses; explains.)* Men. They can't bear any success we have, can they?

BEVERLEY: Things were different in my day, I suppose. Women didn't seem to want so much.

CECILY: You *didn't*, Mum? You always wanted to spend your life waiting for your husband to come home stinking of fish and female fish-packers? Waiting for him to come in from his homo nights out with The Boys, stinking of bar bimboes and beer?...

BEVERLEY: You have such a unpleasant way of putting things, dear!

CECILY: Yuh, well, maybe I do. Maybe I'm not telling you the honest-to-God truth, Mum. Maybe it's not just daddy. Maybe it's that I'm terrified of ending up like you.

BEVERLEY: That's charmingly put, as well, love.

CECILY: You know what I mean, Mum! Not you, personally! You, personally, are my *ideal!* You're beautiful, witty, composed, clear-headed...It's you, *married*, that terrifies me. I see what they're like, Mum...and I see what I'm like...what *we're* like. We're weak in their presence. We...*(Suddenly sobs; turns away from BEVERLEY.)* Shit!

BEVERLEY: Are you alright, dear?

CECILY: Never better. *(Goes to Kleenex box; dries eyes, blows nose.)* I know women who used to be vital, brilliant thinkers .. leaders...*world-beaters.* They had everything, except a husband and kids. So, they got married, got the husband, got the kids, got the big house, closed the door behind them and never saw daylight, again! I can't do this.

BEVERLEY: That's not necessarily been my life, thus far, Cecily.

CECILY: What has necessarily been your life, thus far, mum? Staying alone in this goddam house, day after day, waiting for him to come and go, when and if he wants?...What kind of life are you having?
(There is a pause.)

BEVERLEY: I had you...Your father let me go to school...

CECILY: Your husband *let you* go to school? You needed his *permission?*

BEVERLEY: It took money.

CECILY: Salem Teachers College took money? How much money? Five hundred a year? A thousand? Two thousand? Ten thousand?

BEVERLEY: That wasn't the issue, Cecily.

CECILY: What wasn't the issue?

BEVERLEY: Whether I worked and earned money, or whether I went to school and earned no money. Your father wanted me to go to school. He was proud of me.

CECILY: You believe that?

BEVERLEY: Yes, I do believe that.

CECILY: Did he ever actually "let you" *teach* school? Did he ever actually "let you" go out of this house for fifteen minutes without your having to make a full report? Did he ever actually "let you" take a breath of air without asking his *permission*?

BEVERLEY: We're different people, you and I. I tend to look on the brighter side of things. No marriage is easy, Cecily. Your father and I have had some lovely times together.

CECILY: He bullies you. He badgers you. He treats you like you're dumb and useless. He talks down to you. He expects you to listen to the same stupifyingly boring stories, over and over, again, ten thousand times!…He expects you to clean up after his endless mess. And he expects you to put up with the unspeakable…

BEVERLEY: I must ask you to stop, now…

CECILY: *And he expects you to put up with the unspeakable…*

BEVERLEY: *Cecily, stop talking! You are insulting me!…*

(*BEVERLEY sobs. CECILY goes to her, kneels at her feet, holds BEVERLEY's hand.*)

CECILY: Come away with me, Mum.

BEVERLEY: Pardon?

CECILY: I want you to come away with me.

BEVERLEY: On a holiday?

CECILY: On a *life!*…I want you to come back to California with me.

BEVERLEY: What are you saying, Cecily?

CECILY: I'm not going back to Gerald. I want you to come live with me, Mum. I make a lot of money. A *wick'id awful* lot of money. Plenty for both of us and then some! (*Pauses.*) California is warm. People are happy there…polite. They smile at you. They stop their cars at crosswalks! (*Pauses.*) It's like the walking dead here, mum. Everything's frozen, covered with ice. There's no work. People are dead broke, depressed. Gloucester's a dead place. You're married to a fisherman who doesn't fish. He limps around here, shouting orders at you, like you're some dumb lumper workin' his crew. He's *got* no crew. He's got no *hope*. He's just waiting to die. You're young enough to live, still, mum. In ten more years, who knows?…Leave with me, Mum. Do the exciting thing for yourself. Leave him. Come live with *me!*

BEVERLEY: Why do you hate your father so?

CECILY: Because I have been in psychoanalysis for fifteen years trying to sort through my nightmares…trying to find a way to stop believing that every man I meet isn't really, deep-down, a woman-hating murderer come to kill me.

BEVERLEY: Oh, darling Cecily! Surely, you can't blame your father!

CECILY: I can and I do! Come away with me, Mum. We're both still young enough. *You're* still young enough!…You can't seriously consider either one of them, mum! They're mean and they're old…In five years' time, they'll both be wearing pacemakers and colostomy bags! And you'll be wearing a nurse's uniform! Come with me, mum! *Live* with me!

ARCHIE: *(Offstage; from the staircase.)* An English nose can smell a good cup'pa tea through a stone wall!

(ARCHIE re-enters living room, smiling. HE has changed his clothes; now wears a dapper suit and tie: an Englishman on holiday. HE instantly senses CECILY's upset.)

ARCHIE: Am I interrupting somethin'?

(The telephone rings.)

CECILY: It's probably for me…*(CECILY answers the telephone.)* Hello?…Hiiii! *(To BEVERLEY.)* It's for me. I'll go in the kitchen.

(CECILY exits into kitchen with portable phone. BEVERLEY smiles at ARCHIE.)

BEVERLEY: Don't you look smart?

ARCHIE: Marks and Sparks. Thank you very much.

BEVERLEY: Cup'pa tea?

ARCHIE: Don't mind if I do.

BEVERLEY: You seem a bit more rested.

ARCHIE: I am, Bev, thank you. Very much so. *(Takes teacup from BEVER-LEY.)* Tar, very much, lovey.

(ARCHIE sips tea; smacks lips.)

ARCHIE: Lovely! *(Moves closer to BEVERLEY; looks in her eyes; smiles.)* I was dreamin' about ya' through my whole sleep. And it were very pleasant stuff I dreamed, as well!…

BEVERLEY: Oh, that *does* embarrass me.

ARCHIE: Does it, then? Good. *(Another sip.)* Your girl's upset, isn't she?

BEVERLEY: I'm afraid she is.

ARCHIE: She's a bit passé ta' be goin' on about men holding women back from success and all, wouldn't you say? Did she never hear of Mrs. Thatcher, then?

BEVERLEY: Were you eavesdropping?

ARCHIE: Not intentionally.

BEVERLEY: How much?

ARCHIE: Not much. It weren't all that interestin' ta' me.

BEVERLEY: Cecily's very successful out in California.

ARCHIE: What's the point of her bein' very successful if it brings her nothin' but misery?

BEVERLEY: I suppose...

ARCHIE: I *know*. Look at your singing Beatles her hubby's making moving-pictures with. Back home, they made bloody *heroes* of 'em. They're still a whacking great *industry!* Tour guides takin' tourists to their bleedin' *haunts!* And what's that about, really? The four of them are all misery, personified! Livin' in America...injecting drugs, studying bizarre religions with opportunist Pakistanis! Success? One of 'em got himself shot dead in New York City, didn't he? And they're still playin' his music on the radio, aren't they? I mean, that *is* Success, isn't it? But, the posh wanker's still bloody dead, isn't he, eh? So, what did Success do for the Beatles in the end, tell me? I'll tell you, Bev...in a word...*Nothin'!* *(Downs tea; smiles at BEVERLEY.)* I'm ready for another cup'pa tea, thank you...*(Hands cup to BEVERLEY.)*...So, why's the girl sniveling, really? She's had a row with her hubby, I expect. If she weren't livin' in such a posh manner, as she is, she'd have to face up to whatever's goin' wrong, wouldn't she? Instead, what's she doin' ta' solve her problems? I'll tell ya': she's on a jet, flyin' home to Mum. So, what's money doin' for the girl in the end, Bev? It's not solvin' her problems, is it? It's just feedin' the coffers of the bloody airlines! And that's as far as I see it. I'd personally rather be dead than be posh, and that's the truth! *(Takes cup of tea from BEVERLEY.)* Tar, very much, lovey. *(Sips tea; smacks his lips.)* Lovely!...

BEVERLEY: Are you still working, Arthur?

ARCHIE: Earning wages?

BEVERLEY: Yes...that, too.

ARCHIE: No. Not for more than twenty years, now.

BEVERLEY: I'd wondered.

ARCHIE: Twenty-five years, one job. That's bloody enough, wouldn't you say?...

BEVERLEY: I suppose...

ARCHIE:...My father always used'ta say "You can't be floatin' about. Life's too short. One job and one woman: That's all a man gets."

BEVERLEY: I suppose…

ARCHIE: I bloody *know!* I hated my job, by and large, but, a job's only a job, isn't it? I stuck with it for bloody forty years, didn't I? I've never been the sort to whine. I'm a sticker. You be amazed how many of the old lads are in their graves, or pokin' one toe in, already! Me best mate, Rod? Dead from drink. Alfie Bottoms, the one whose aunt met King George? Hit by the bus he was runnin' to catch! So sozzled, he thought he was behind the thing! He run into the front of it, full gallop! You remember Reg Farley and Rog Montgomery? Bo'sun Menges? Nobby Smythe? All pushin' up the daffodils. From what, you may wonder? From *hopelessness*. Things is tough, back home, Beverley. There's no work. There's this bloody Labour Council, but, there's no bloody labour! It's a bleedin' paradox, isn't it? So, they give up hope, one by one, and they die from the want of it!…Not me. I always had me hope, haven't I, then, lovey? Just before I left me job, I heard Mrs. Thatcher herself givin' a speech to the executives at the works. I wasn't in the audience, exactly…I was doin' my normal custodial duties…cleanin' up…but, I could hear her loud and clear. She talked about the stock market and investing in England. I listened hard. I thought about what was goin' on up North, and I said to meself "Artie, you gotta' learn ta' play the game by Mrs. Thatcher's rules, not by some Labour loser's rules!" And I bloody did! It were Mrs. T, herself, who made me wealthy! I withdrew all me pension money and I invested it in the stock market…but, always, based on Mrs. T's moves. Wherever Mrs. Thatcher went, I bet me quid on her. If she visited the Electrolux plant, I bought shares in Electrolux. If I saw a picture of her Hooverin' her bleedin' carpet, I bought Hoover. If she drank a cup of cocoa, I bought cocoa futures!…I stayed in the market for three years, with profits soaring every day. But, then, Bev, one Thursday night, without warning, I had the vision. Now, I must tell ya' that when I was a lad, me Dad use'ta say "Arthur-lad, you must never live a gambler's life. Gamblers don't gamble ta' win: They gamble ta' *lose!*…And, sooner (or later, gamblers get their wish and lose everything they have!" I remembered his words, every day whilst I was rakin' in the profits…It kept me in a sweat. But, this particular night, I actually had a *vision* of me Dad…a dream in which he appeared in front of me, vividly, sayin' what he'd always said ta' me about the gambler's life…but, this time, he ended his advice by screamin' "Sell, Arthur, sell!" It were terrifying! I screamed out loud…woke meself up!…Once I calmed down a bit, I said to meself: "Artie, you've made yourself a 2000% profit. It's bloody *enough!* Get out!

Do what Da says: Sell!" As soon as 9 A.M. Friday mornin' rolled around, I rolled out'ta me bed and phoned ta me broker, Mr. Charles Peabody. I sold every investment I had. Liquified me assets. I made meself a hundred and nineteen thousand quid, after taxes…clear profit.

BEVERLEY: Oh, that is *wonderful*, Artie!

ARCHIE: "Wonderful" is a colossal understatement, woman! You do know what happened, seventy-two hours later, don't you, love?

BEVERLEY: The market crashed?

ARCHIE: Crashed? It fell in a hole! The papers called it "Black Monday."

BEVERLEY: I remember this…

ARCHIE: For me, Beverley, "Black Monday" was the golden payoff. Property values all over Britain went spiralin' down, interest on savings shot up. There are certainly richer men than I, but, I am comfortable, Bev…Very, very, *very* comfortable. I bought meself a very substantial freehold property not far from Tatton Park…detached, four bedrooms, a double garage, a whacking great garden, with a small pond…

BEVERLEY: Oh, I love a fishpond.

ARCHIE: It's not a fishpond, woman…It's actually a *pond*.

BEVERLEY: How wonderful for you, Artie.

ARCHIE: It's so lovely, when me neighbors sold, they advertised that their cottage overlooked a beauty spot!

BEVERLEY: Did they?

ARCHIE: They did.

(ARCHIE stops talking; turns, faces BEVERLEY. HE smiles at HER, word-lessly for a moment.)

ARCHIE: I credit you, Beverley Leach, for every speck of me good fortune.

BEVERLEY: Me? Why ever for?

ARCHIE: Since the day I met you, Bev, I've always had the reason for livin'. And since the day I lost you, I've had the need to figure out what it was gonna' take…to get you back. I've dedicated my life to this…to you.

BEVERLEY: Are you serious?

ARCHIE: Deadly so! I always knew it was gonna' take some money…and probably a house…and probably my hoppin' up the class-ladder a rung or two.

BEVERLEY: All these years…thinking of me?

ARCHIE: Some many years back, I found a great and perfect love: a true love. And this true love sustained me…Sustained me hopes and me life. No matter how you've responded to me, or how you *will* respond to me, I love you, Bev. Nothin's gonna' change that.

(ARCHIE reaches out and touches BEVERLEY's cheek, ever so gently. BEV-ERLEY allows his touch.)

ARCHIE: When you used'ta sing Vera's songs to me, Bev...I was never happier. I believed you. I believed every word.

BEVERLEY: They were just songs, Artie.

ARCHIE: But, I believed them, Bev. They gave me such a thrill...such thrillin' hope.

BEVERLEY: We were young, Arthur. The bombs were falling.

ARCHIE: *(Sings.)*

"Yours, til the end of Life's story"...

(Speaks.) That's what I remembered all these years. It's kept me goin', Beverley...It's kept me young.

BEVERLEY: *(Weeps.)* Oh, dear...Look at us...

ARCHIE: You're weepin', Bev.

BEVERLEY: Yes. I know. *(Laughs.)* It's so sad...Us, grown old as we have. *(Weeps, again; laughs, again.)* Bein' young and beautiful, with bombs fallin'...*(Suddenly, sobs.)*

ARCHIE: What is it?

BEVERLEY: We should have died, then, Artie. All of us. They were the lucky ones, really, the ones that loved and died. The ones that loved and lingered, like us...grown old...We build nothing but our memories, Arthur. And then we die. And our memories die with us. It's like we never happened! It's so sad. It's such a tragic loss!...

ARCHIE: You don't mean what you're sayin', love!

BEVERLEY: I'm sure I don't. I'm sure you're right. There must have been some lovely moments, afterwards...with my family. But, what? I can't remember what?

ARCHIE: That's why I've come for you, Bev. That's why I come to take you back.

BEVERLEY: I can't...

ARCHIE: It's just what Vera was singin'...*Today* is the great day. Today is the day to *make love*. Today is the day we live! Tomorrow is the mystery...perhaps, the day we die!...Sing to us, Bev, will ya'?...*(BEVERLEY laughs.)*

ARCHIE: Sing to us. Give us a Vera.

BEVERLEY: Oh, Artie, please...I feel so silly...tears on me cheek...so sentimental...It's only that we've grown so old. It's only that Life has passed us by. That's all that moves us to tears, really...

ARCHIE: Stop that! Life's not bloody passed us by, Beverley Leach! Life's just been waitin' in the rain. Somebody's pushed the bleedin' *pause-button*!…But, now we're *talkin'* ta' one another, lovey, aren't we? And when lovers get ta' talkin', anything's possible, isn't it?…Please, give us a Vera, Bev, will ya'?

(Suddenly, ARCHIE drops down on to bended knee.)

ARCHIE: You've got a man on his knee, beggin' ya', Beverley!

(BEVERLEY laughs.)

ARCHIE: Do it! Don't let the chance pass! It's the best of Life for us, Bev. Do it, Bev.

(BEVERLEY sings, imitating Vera Lynn. ARCHIE puts his head on her lap; listening, lovingly)

BEVERLEY: (Sings.)

"We'll meet again…

Don't know where, Don't know when,

But, I know know we'll meet, again…"

(BEVERLEY stops singing; looks at ARCHIE, strokes his hair; speaks.)

BEVERLEY: I'm not Vera Lynn, Artie. I don't know quite who I am, any more, but, I do know I'm not her: not Vera.

ARCHIE: *I* know who you are: You're Beverley Leach, the woman I dearly love.

(ARCHIE kisses BEVERLEY. It is a long, loving kiss. CECILY re-enters from kitchen with portable phone; sees THEM kiss.)

CECILY: Oh, shit.

(CECILY exits into the kitchen. ARCHIE and BEVERLEY take a giant step back from one another.)

BEVERLEY: This is awful!

ARCHIE: No, it's not awful, Bev. It's *gorgeous!*

(ARCHIE moves to kiss BEVERLEY, again. SHE pulls back, quickly.)

BEVERLEY: Get away! Get back!

(CECILY calls out, loudly, from the kitchen.)

CECILY: *(Offstage.)* I'm done with my phone call! I'm coming back into the living room! You have been advised! *(CECILY re-enters; smiles.)* Hi, y'all! What's up?

(There is an embarrassed pause.)

BEVERLEY: I'm going to my room. I want to be left alone. *(To BOTH, sternly.)* I mean it!

(BEVERLEY exits upstairs. There is a pause. ARCHIE looks at CECILY; smiles. ZELLY enters from the kitchen. HE is no longer wearing his storm coat

or boots. HE seems to have been in the house a while. ARCHIE's smile fades.
ZELLY stands staring at ARCHIE, silently.)

ARCHIE: I thought you were out, walking, Zelly.

ZELLY: *(Unrelenting stare.)* I came back.

(CECILY laughs, nervously.)

CECILY: Hey, you guys probably wanna' talk about things on your own, huh?...undisturbed. I'll be in my room, packing.

(CECILY gathers together her portable phone, cigarettes, work folders, scripts; exits, upstairs. ZELLY continues staring at ARCHIE.)

ARCHIE: What are ya' starin' at, mate?

ZELLY: It's time, Archie.

ARCHIE: Time for what?

(No reply. ZELLY continues staring.)

ARCHIE: Time for what?

(No reply. ZELLY continues staring.)

ARCHIE: *(Angrily.)* I've asked you a question!

(No reply. ZELLY continues staring. ARCHIE meets ZELLY's stare for a moment, but, then, loses courage; looks down. ZELLY laughs.)

(Lights fade to black.)

ACT TWO
SCENE TWO

Same day, two hours later. In the darkness, we hear last moments recording of Vera Lynn singing "Yours."

LIGHTS FADE UP in living room on BEVERLEY, ZELLY, and ARCHIE, listening to conclusion of song.

BEVERLEY is absolutely silent, at the window, looking outside. ZELLY stands across the room, leaning against the bookcase. ARCHIE sits in overstuffed chair, weeping, as HE sings along with Vera.

ARCHIE AND VERA: *(Singing.)*

"...I never loved anyone the way I love you.

How could I? When I was born to be

Just yours...Just yours...

When I was born to be...Just yours!"

(We hear the scratch of needle against antique 78 rpm record, still turning on turntable. ZELLY walks to phonograph, lifts arm. Scratching stops.)

ARCHIE: That's what she sang to me.

ZELLY: Those were different times, Archie. Couples, ya' know, *got together*, pretty easy. It would'a be'n hard to expect Beverley ta' just stay, ya' know, *yours*.

ARCHIE: I didn't find it hard to expect. I expected it. We had an agreement, Bev and me, didn't we?

ZELLY: Nobody knew from one day to the next whether we'd be alive. They were bringing in the dead and wounded. It got to ya', somethin' wick'id. It changed the rules kinda' thing.

ARCHIE: You knew she was engaged ta' me, didn't ya'?

ZELLY: I...I guess I did. But, that sort'a thing didn't mean much...not with truckloads of war-wounded comin' in...boxcars on trains full'a the dead. You'd meet a girl, you'd like each other, you'd fall into each other's arms. It wasn't like boys on the make, just scorin'...It was much more desperate than that.

ARCHIE: I were in the same war, weren't I? It weren't so bloody desperate for me. We had a job ta' do, and we were doin' it bloody well. What kept us goin', we Brits, was the love of our country, and the love of our families...kiddies, if you had 'em...mums and dads...our women. Bev was mine, and you bloody stole her, didn't ya'? Makin' yourself exotic with your faraway stories...fishin' boats and this and that...half-Jewish/half-Portuguese with Italian snuck in...That sort of exoticism gets an innocent English girl's head swimmin'...She forgets herself, don't she? She falls right over, backwards, don't she?...Arms and legs spread akimbo...

ZELLY: Jesus, Archie, this is *nuts!* We're talkin' something that happened almost fifty years ago!

ARCHIE: True love never dies.

ZELLY: Okay, okay, okay! It's out in the open. I stole Bev from you. Okay? Fine. So, what's anybody s'pose'ta do about any of this?

ARCHIE: You've had her for forty-five years. I want the rest.

ZELLY: What's this?

ARCHIE: I'm takin' her back with me!

ZELLY: What?

ARCHIE: What can't you comprehend here, Zelly? I'm speakin' the King's bloody English, aren't I? I'm takin' Beverley Leach home to England, where she *belongs!*...

ZELLY: Read my lips. *(Points to lips; yells.)* Over my dead fuckin' body!

ARCHIE: That may well be. The choice is the lady's, isn't it?

(ZELLY and ARCHIE turn and look at BEVERLEY at the window. There is a moment's pause.)

ARCHIE: It's time, Bev. The moment of truth has come.

BEVERLEY: *(Calls offstage to CECILY.)* Cecily, come down the stairs and into the room. Join us. There's no point in hearing this on the sly.

(CECILY walks into view on the staircase.)

CECILY: Why does overhearing any conversation between your parents involving sex make you feel six years old and stupid? *(Goes to chair; sits.)* I'm sitting…I'm in the room…I'm one of the grown-ups…I'm really uncomfortable.

BEVERLEY: From the time Cecily was six until she was sixteen, I had a love affair with a local man.

ARCHIE: You what?

BEVERLEY: Be quiet, Arthur! It's my turn!…*(Pauses; composes herself.)* He was married, two children. A boy and a girl. James and Judy. He was an accountant…not very exciting, but, really very affectionate.

(BEVERLEY moves to a position behind CECILY's chair; touches CECILY's hair.)

BEVERLEY: Cecily knew about it. Children know everything that goes on in a house. *(Looks at ZELLY.)* Zelly knew about it, as well. Not every detail…but, you knew, didn't you, darling?…

ZELLY: What's the point of this, huh? This isn't anybody's business…

BEVERLEY: *(Angrily.)* The point is that I'm talking!…The point is that I'm speaking my thoughts!…I'm choosing my words! *Now, be quiet! (There is a pause.)* When Cecily was young, there was no end to Zelly's old girl-friends traipsing through this house. The one who cleaned for us…what's her name?…Shoes…

ZELLY: Bootsie.

BEVERLEY: Exactly. Bootsie. And the babysitter with the enormous bottom…ginger-haired, Irish…

ZELLY: Mary-Louise?

BEVERLEY: Mary-Louise.

CECILY: I remember Mary-Louise. I *loathed* Mary-Louise. She smelled bad.

BEVERLEY: Zelly used to kiss Mary-Louise hello and good-bye…on the mouth.

ZELLY: Mary-Louise was like a cousin.

BEVERLEY: You have Irish cousins?

ZELLY: I said *like* a cousin!

BEVERLEY: What about the Ciolino girl?

ZELLY: It wasn't the same thing! They all lived here! They were all local people! None of 'em traveled thousands of goddam miles to get to get here like this Archie Bennett person. I may not know much, but, I know men! No man comes halfway around the world for a bowl'a shrimpy chowder!…

BEVERLEY: Oh, I see. It's the mileage that determines the severity of the threat. It's a small point, but, England's not "halfway around the world" from here, darling. It's only three thousand miles…

ZELLY: Fine.

BEVERLEY: I think it's charming that you feel so threatened, dear. *(Pauses.)* Zelly had a string of extra women in his life. I just had the one extra man: Allen. Allen loved me. We met in Allen's office, Tuesdays and Fridays, from three til five, whilst Cecily had her piano lesson. Cecily learned Chopin's body of work, and I learned Allen's body.

ARCHIE: Bloody hell!

(CECILY laughs.)

ARCHIE: And where's he, now, then, this accountant?

BEVERLEY: Gone…dead. He wasn't young, not even then.

(BEVERLEY touches CECILY's cheek.)

BEVERLEY: Poor Cecily's seen it all, haven't you, dear?

ARCHIE: What'chu mean "Cecily's seen it all?" Was she bloody in the room wi' ya's?

BEVERLEY: *(Imitates ARCHIE's North country accent.)* No, she weren't, mate! Not wi' Allen, but, she were bloody in the room wi' me and Zelly, sluggin' it out.

ARCHIE: Zelly struck ya'?

BEVERLEY: Jesus! Belt up, will ya', man!? Ya' go on like an bloody *ignorant! (Pauses; her "Americanized" accent returns.)* Growing up with parents in a loveless marriage is a *disaster!*…I was too selfish to see it at the time for what it was, but, I see it, clearly, now. I've never talked with Cecily, mother to child…*woman to woman*…not once, not ever, before now…but, I am, now…I am talking. *(Pauses.)* I'm sorry, Cecily. I apologize for not making a good marriage. I know you're unhappy, and I know why. I take full responsibility for my part in it.

CECILY: It's not all your fault, Mother. Don't think it is.

BEVERLEY: I don't. I know it's not all my fault. But, a great deal of it is: my fault. And I'm sorry for all that. I love you, Cecily.

CECILY: I love you, too.

(CECILY weeps; then, laughs; then, turns to ZELLY, drying her eyes.)

CECILY: I've asked Mum to come out to California with me...to live with me.

ZELLY: Your mother lives here...with her husband: with *me!* *(To BEVER-LEY; angrily.)* These things are in the past, lady! These things are forgiven and forgotten.

BEVERLEY: Zelly's got another family.

ZELLY: Jesus, Bev!

(ZELLY goes to window, looks outside, his back now turned to BEVERLEY and OTHERS.)

BEVERLEY: He got a young Italian girl pregnant...about ten years into our marriage. I was nearly thirty. Cecily was five. The girl was twenty. She and her mother worked for Zelly, cutting fish on the line. The mother knew about it...about what was goin' on with her daughter and Zelly. In fact, she almost seemed to *approve!*...I knew the girl, myself, of course. She wasn't beautiful, but, she was what you'd call *good-looking* — dark-eyed, round-faced, large-breasted, strong. *(Pauses.)*

I didn't know what to do. I didn't want to go home...to England...My dad worshipped Zelly, and my mother would never take my part against him. Being so deeply unhappy in my marriage somehow made me feel *stupid*. *(Pauses.)*

She had his child. Everybody in Gloucester knew about it...my friends, Cecily's friends...And everybody knew we knew, as well. Nobody ever said a word about any of it to us, *directly*...But, couldn't you bloody hear the hushed whispers, the snide comments? How superior it made them all feel!...In this house, it was always the *unspeakable!* Zelly never let us talk about it, never let me bring it up. And I agreed with him, somehow. It was never spoken of, out loud, until now. *(Pauses.)*

She never married: the girl, I mean, not the child. He did: the child: he married, and moved away. He writes to Zelly from time to time, doesn't he, dear? He calls him "Dad." The girl's still in town. She's how old, now? Fifty-five? This all still hurts me, Zelly. *(Pauses.)*

When you're young, you trust in people...in marriage...Marriage seems...possible...natural. *(Wipes her eyes; smiles.)* There are so many secrets in a marriage, aren't there? So many lies. But, at the end of the day, all the empty excitement of love affairs and heart-pounding intrigue can't distract any of us from our essential unhappiness. I am a profoundly unhappy woman. I've been this for an unthinkable number of years, now. *(Pauses.)*

That's everybody's Big Secret, really, isn't it? Profound unhappiness…lack of purpose…lack of reason. I'm unhappy, Cecily's unhappy, Zelly's unhappy, and, Arthur, you're a *misery!* Take my word for it! *(Pauses.)*

There was only one thrilling time in my entire life, Arthur. I was seventeen years old and bombs were falling all around me. Up the road a mile or so from my house, there was this RAF base with about two thousand lads, mostly my age…you, Arthur, and nineteen hundred and ninety-nine others, all young, all beautiful to look at, all gorgeous to the touch, all scared to death to live or die. Up the road three miles or so, there was Zelly's American air base, with about a thousand more lads, same age, same life. All told, there couldn't've been more than a hundred unmarried girls my age in the entire area. Bombs falling from the sky almost every night of our lives, and a ratio of thirty lads to every one of us young girls. Now, this, for me, *defines* thrilling! *(Pauses.)*

Our parents were telling us to stay away from the flyboys, but, our hearts and our minds and our bodies were saying "Live for the moment, girl! Any one of Hitler's bombs could be the one with your name on it! Don't die unfulfilled! Don't die *unloved!* Don't die…*untouched!*" Don't talk to me about "a thrilling life," Arthur. I have known the ultimate thrill of my particular life, and only a fool would imagine such a thrill could be challenged, or, equalled…or, recaptured. *(Pauses.)*

For me, there have been very few discernable advantages to peacetime. My needs were always so different from Zelly's. He just needed a few chaps to remind him that he was once a hero. What I needed, quite honestly, was thirty men fighting over me. I needed to be young and beautiful, walking through tiny cobbled streets lined with hungry young men, all wanting me…all staring at my breasts and my bottom…touchin' me with their eyes…wanting me. I did need that. And, I'm afraid, I still bloody do. I had that. And anything less was and is…sadly lacking. *(Pauses.)*

Isn't it awful to hear this said out loud? *(Pauses.)*

It was, I admit, quite exciting when I knew that Zelly was actually cheating on me. It gave me a kind of freedom. I knew I could do whatever I wanted, with whomever I wanted…and I couldn't ever be blamed for me sins!…*(Pauses.)*

Isn't it awful to hear this said out loud? *(Pauses.)*

But, in the end, between us, between Zelly and me, it was dead. It felt like I was trapped in a cave, alone…only, I wasn't alone, was I? I was just bloody...*trapped*. *(Laughs; then.)* Don't you think that people like us finally die because they want to? I do.

ARCHIE: Think that?

BEVERLEY: Want to die.

CECILY: Don't say that, Mum...please.

ARCHIE: Sod that, woman! You're talkin' like a right nutter! What's ahead is The Big Sleep! No bloody more, no bloody less! You don't need rest, lady, as you've done nothin' to tire you out! Fancy you callin' me "a misery" and "an ignorant," when you're talkin' like a *pathetic spot!* Get off your bottom, Beverley! Life's precious! If you've missed the point, I'll give it ya'!

(ARCHIE grabs BEVERLEY; kisses HER. BEVERLEY breaks from the kiss; slaps ARCHIE's face, sharply. It is a stunning blow.)

BEVERLEY: Don't you dare! I'll decide who I kiss and when.

ARCHIE: *(Holding his cheek.)* That really hurt.

BEVERLEY: Come here!

(BEVERLEY pulls ARCHIE to her; kisses HIM. ZELLY watches, helplessly. BEVERLEY breaks the kiss; looks at ZELLY.)

BEVERLEY: Do you want a kiss, Zelly? *(ZELLY moans a "yes"; BEVERLEY giggles.)* Where am I getting this girlish *power?*...Come here, Zelly.

(ZELLY and BEVERLEY kiss. ARCHIE stares; helplessly.)

ARCHIE: I don't like this.

(HE makes a move toward ZELLY and BEVERLEY. CECILY suddenly steps in, interrupts ARCHIE.)

CECILY: *Don't!*

ARCHIE: Or what, Suzie?

(ARCHIE is enraged; pulls BEVERLEY away from ZELLY. A confession flies from his lips.)

ARCHIE: *I wish to God I had been the one who had you in my sights, 'stead'a the Jerry! I never would've botched it, believe you me!*

ZELLY: *(Stunned.) What?*

ARCHIE: You heard me! It's me life's one and only great regret. I was up there in the same bloody skirmish. If I'd'a had my sights on you, I wouldn't'a bloody missed. I would've made a corpse of you! The Jerry made a bloody *hero* of you, instead. It's the only reason she married you, mate. She told me that, herself. You can thank bloody Adolph for your marriage!

ZELLY: I should fuckin' kill you!

ARCHIE: You and what fuckin' brigade?!

(ZELLY stares at BEVERLEY.)
ZELLY: You told him this, Beverley?
   (BEVERLEY looks at ZELLY, then looks down.)
ZELLY: Is this why you married me?…Because of some cowboy-flyboy hero-
   ics?
BEVERLEY: *(After a pause.)* No.
ZELLY: Then, why did ya'?
BEVERLEY: I married you because I loved you…because I wanted to be
   your wife.
ZELLY: And now?
   (ARCHIE giggles.)
BEVERLEY: *(Holding back tears.)* Please, don't, Zelly.
ZELLY: I don't hear an answer to my question.
ARCHIE: Answer the man, Bev.
BEVERLEY: What's your question, Zelly?
ZELLY: Now: would you marry me, now?
BEVERLEY: Don't do this, Zelly.
ZELLY: *(Yells; roughly.) Answer me, goddammit!*
BEVERLEY: No. I wouldn't marry you, now, Zelly. No.
   (ARCHIE giggles.)
BEVERLEY: I won't ask the same question of you, Zelly, because I know the
   answer.
ZELLY: We don't get this time back, lady! It's *gone!* It's…
   (ZELLY turns away; suddenly, HE weeps.)
ARCHIE: I spent a bloody bomb on this trip, and it was worth it. Twice the
   cost would've been worth it! This is a dream come true!
   (ZELLY punches ARCHIE.)
ARCHIE: Jesus Christ! You struck me!
ZELLY: That's the way us Yanks do it, *mate!*
ARCHIE: I'll show you the way a Yorkshireman does it, *bub!*
   *(ARCHIE and ZELLY have a fistfight. As they are both rather old, it is a
   slow and careful fistfight. First, ARCHIE hits ZELLY, then, ZELLY hits
   ARCHIE. And so it goes. In the end, ZELLY runs ARCHIE to the door.)*
ARCHIE: Hey! Hey!
   *(ZELLY opens the front door; shoves ARCHIE outside; closes the door, locks
   it; faces BEVERLEY.)*
ZELLY: I would so marry you, now, Beverley. I would so! I swear ta' God I
   would!

BEVERLEY: No, you wouldn't, Zelly! Don't lie to me! I know you too well. Don't lie to me. Don't lie to *yourself!*

(The doorbell's chimes chime.)

ZELLY: Stay with me, Beverley. I know I haven't been much of a husband, but, I can be…I will be. Give me a chance, Bev, please…I'm begging you. *(Sees BEVERLEY laugh.)* What the hell is funny?

BEVERLEY: Your telling me that you "haven't been much of a husband for forty-five years," but, now, you want "a chance!" A *chance?* You don't think that's *funny?*

(Doorbell chimes chime, again. We see: ARCHIE running from window to window, shivering with the cold.)

BEVERLEY: I going to my room to pack my things. It's over, Zelly. Don't blame Cecily for my leavin', but, I must admit, it was she who finally got me off my bottom by telling me her biggest fear was that she might turn out to be just like me. That was my biggest fear, as well: that I'd turn out to be just like my mother. Not my mother, fully…Just my mother, *married. (Pauses.)*

    I wasn't strong enough for any of us, was I?…But, now, I will be. I'm leavin', Zelly. It's over. *(The doorbell chimes chime, again.)*

BEVERLEY: Let Arthur back in, please, dear. He's an old man. He'll die out there.

(ZELLY sobs. BEVERLEY goes to him, takes his hand, brings his hand to her lips; kisses his hand in an almost gentlemanly fashion.)

BEVERLEY: I'm not going with you, Cecily. That's your life, not mine!…I'm going to pack.

(BEVERLEY exits up staircase. There is a moment's pause. Then, the doorbell chimes chime, again. The lights fade out.)

ACT TWO
SCENE THREE

Late afternoon, same day. In darkness, we hear Chopin being played on the Hammond organ, lightly.

    LIGHTS UP in living room on ZELLY, CECILY, and ARCHIE. CECILY sits at the Hammond organ, playing a Chopin étude…and playing it well. ARCHIE wears his overcoat. HE paces from wall to wall. ZELLY stands at window, looking out. Suitcases, ARCHIE's and CECILY's, are in evidence near front door. We hear: Teakettle's whistle whistles, offstage.

CECILY: I'll get it.

(CECILY exits into kitchen.)

ARCHIE: If she'd have been my wife, I wouldn't've let her go, I can tell you that!

(ZELLY doesn't reply. ARCHIE looks at his watch; paces to front door; returns to living room.)

ARCHIE: Nothin' but broken homes out there! All over the world, "Family" means bloody nothin'. I read the papers! I see the bloody television! Divorce, divorce, divorce! People sayin' the til-death-do-us-part part with one foot out the bloody door! (To ZELLY; angrily.) Can't you control your own wife, for God's sake, man?! Can't you show the woman earthly reason?!…Bloody war hero, me arse! I know a man when I see one, and I see bloody none!

(ARCHIE paces to the front door, again, looks at his watch, again.)

ARCHIE: If I miss this bloody train ta' Boston, I'll miss me bloody boat back to England. And then what? I'll bloody tell ya' what? I'll be stranded! I'll be one of the bloody hundred thousand homeless beggars I stepped over since I've been in bloody America! If I'm gonna' be down and out, I'm gonna' be down and out in bloody England, where they know how ta' make a chip butty and a decent cup'pa tea!

(CECILY enters with tea tray.)

CECILY: Tea's up, lads!

ARCHIE: How come you're so cheery, dearie?

CECILY: (North Country accent.) I'm bloody happy for me Mum, mate!…That's what. Ready for a fresh cupp'a?

ARCHIE: Give us one, then…

CECILY: (Spooning sugar.) Was it two?

ARCHIE: Two.

CECILY: (Hands cup to ARCHIE.) Here ya' are, love.

ARCHIE: Tar, very much, lovey.

(ARCHIE sips his tea; winces.)

ARCHIE: Gawww! What's this?

CECILY: It's herbal. Better for you than caffeine when you're traveling.

ARCHIE: What is this stuff?

CECILY: Rose hips.

ARCHIE: Rose hips? Sounds like the name of a bloody exotic dancer!…

(Car horn sounds; offstage.)

ARCHIE: That's me. It's me taxi.

(ARCHIE goes out front door, leaving suitcase outside; yells to TAXI DRI-VER from o.c.)

ARCHIE: Won't be a minute!

(ARCHIE re-enters; goes to ZELLY, extends his hand for handshake.)

ARCHIE: All's fair in Love and War, mate. *(THEY shake hands.)* Thanks for lettin' me stay in your house, Zelly. We're the lucky ones, ya' know. We're the survivors. We've still got Life ta' live. *(Pauses.)*

   Maybe we'll see each other, again…I expect we will…don't know where, don't know when…*(Smiles.)* Vera. *(Pauses.)*

   God bless, Zelly. *(To CECILY.)* Oh, Cecily, love, a Dr. Weingarten called, whilst you were up talkin' with your Mum. I told him he was doin' a shitty job and that you'd committed suicide. Let's give *him* somethin' ta' worry about, eh, lovey? *(Goes to door; opens it, stands poised with suitcases.)* Take care of yourselves. If you don't, no one else will.

(ARCHIE exits the play. After a pause, CECILY goes to ZELLY with a cup of tea.)

CECILY: Here. This one's real tea. I made his cup up, special.

ZELLY: *(Smiles; takes cup.)* Thanks.

CECILY: You're welcome.

(ZELLY looks at it; sighs; looks at CECILY.)

ZELLY: You're gonna' hav'ta' help me through this, Cecie. I can't face this, alone.

CECILY: You want me to stay, awhile?

ZELLY: Could you?…Would you?

CECILY: Yes.

(ZELLY reaches out his hand to CECILY. SHE takes it: holds her father's hand.)

ZELLY: You think she'll come back?

CECILY: It's up to her, isn't it?

ZELLY: It can't end this way. Women can't just leave.

(LIGHTS CROSSFADE to SPOTLIGHT on BEVERLEY, downstage, facing ZELLY and CECILY, speaking words from a letter she has written to ZELLY.)

BEVERLEY: Dear Zelly. The oddness of being so far from you is indescribable. *(Pauses.)*

   I know it's unfair, my being the one to leave. The one who stays behind feels the loser, somehow. I know this is true, because I so often thought you'd leave *me*…*(Pauses.)*

I never imagined I'd be the one...the one to leave. It doesn't seem like me, does it?

(SPOTLIGHT FADES UP on ZELLY, downstage. HE holds Beverley's pink letter in his hand. BEVERLEY continues speaking the words of her letter, aloud.)

BEVERLEY: Don't worry about me. I'm in a safe place. I'd like to tell you where I am, but, I don't yet dare. I'm frightened you'll come after me, force me back. That wouldn't be good. I've spent much too much time in my married life planning what I would do after you died. Those were my secret fantasies, Zelly...the things I would do after you were gone. I never wanted you dead. I just wanted to leave, and I could never imagine any other way out the door. *(Pauses.)*

I have a chance to substitute-teach, Zelly. Two days a week. I know it doesn't sound Earth-shattering news, but, it's the most exciting thing that's happened to me in my life in the past thirty years! *(Pauses.)*

It must be terrible for you to read this. *(Pauses.)*

You are so present in my life, Zelly. Even though the thought of being near you fills me with dread, still and all, whatever I see, I think immediately that I should rush to tell you about it. *(Pauses.)*

After my dad died, when I went to see my mum, I remember how lost she seemed without her "darlin' husbin' Den"...She told me that the first thought she'd had after she knew for sure Dad was dead was "I can hardly wait to ring Den up and tell him who died!" *(Pauses.)*

I could hardly wait to write this letter to you, Zelly, because I could hardly wait to tell you the most amazing news: Beverley's left Zelly! *(Pauses.)*

I'll write to you, again, soon...Yours, as never before...Bev.

(LIGHTS FADE out on ZELLY. Beat. Then, LIGHTS FADE OUT on BEVERLEY. MUSIC IN: Vera Lynn "Yours.")

End of Play.

Free Gift

For Velma and Stephen, my friends.

INTRODUCTION

The courage of women is something that has touched and impressed me throughout my adult life. I have never really understood how Hollywood has been able to sustain the world's interest in so-called American Culture…or how men have gotten away with sustaining a world's interest in so-called Male Heroism. In fact, as we all know, we men are ridiculous blowers of hot air. And many women, thank God, smile and put up with it.

I have a close friend, Velma Branch, who has risen from the ashes of unthinkable tragedy to bring comfort to her children and her children's children. Velma is Barbadian, by birth, and has that magical Bajan way of smiling and laughing in the face of unimaginable disaster. Velma's husband, Ken, was killed by an out-of-control taxicab, whilst on a NYC sidewalk, groceries in hand. In fact, Ken died a few weeks after the accident, when a blood clot rose from his damaged leg to his heart. Velma was with him when he died…

The night after Ken's funeral, I put our children to bed. Oliver was tearful, saying "I don't know what I'll do when somebody I really love dies." And I explained Life to him, as best I could, saying that everyone is mortal and, as such, must be treated with compassion and respect…In the end, the expected daddy-lecture was thoughtfully given, mixed with profoundly deep compassion for the little boy who was getting the news so early in life. After a moment's thoughtful silence, Oliver spoke to me: "I hope you live for a long, long time, Daddy, so that when you die, I can die in the very same moment."

Never before had I heard such a beautiful and precise definition of love. And never before had I seen such a heroic statement of love than I continually witness in my friend Velma's life…in her relationship with her grandson/son, Stephen.

When Velma's daughter's life took a terrible turn and her fatherless child needed a home and normalcy, Velma took the boy in, and gave him a chance in life that he might have never had, otherwise. Stephen is flourishing under Velma's loving eye. And it is to him and his heroic "Mummy" that I dedicate my play *Free Gift*. I am in awe of my friend and so many, many other women in her circumstance.

And let me say it now, simply and clearly, of all the ills I have seen or experienced in my lifetime, and I have seen many too many, racism is the least acceptable. What I love the most about life is the differences between people, between different cultures. For me, New York City is a thrilling place, so diverse, so full of the unknown.

I am a playwright. I have little to offer as a solution to life's ills beyond my work...and my five wonderful children, who are totally and utterly "color-blind," and count among their intimate friends people of excitingly diverse backgrounds. I am proud to say that my children and I are only prejudiced against loudmouthed jerks. And, possibly, brussels sprouts.

So, here it is...a small, heartfelt free gift. From me to you, in celebration of a woman and her courage.

POSTSCRIPT. This story is not precisely true, not to be construed as literal details of my friends' lives. My play's story-details are imagined, invented. Life passes much more slowly than does time on stage. Stage-time and stage-stories must be compressed, compacted, telescoping years into minutes. So, then, this invented story isn't Velma's story...It is, more importantly, Velma's heroic spirit.

Gloucester, Mass.
July 1997.

THE PEOPLE OF THE PLAY

HEATHER, mid-20s; black, long-legged, undeniably beautiful. Heather wears a proper "business suit"...tailored skirt, matching jacket, silk blouse, sensible shoes. Heather was born in NYC...was "street," but, now, speaks with educated American accent.

ROSELLE, 50-ish; white, once cute, now, cute-ish. Roselle is instantly eccentric. She wears oversized men's shirt, blue jeans. Roselle was born in England, speaks somewhat like an American, but, with a clearly English accent.

THE PLACE OF THE PLAY

Music room, Greenwich Village (NYC) townhouse.

THE TIME OF THE PLAY

The present.

Free Gift

In darkness...Paul Simon's "Born At The Right Time."

LIGHTS UP ON...Music room, Greenwich Village townhouse; day. Sofa, coffee table, sideboard, grand piano...all antique. We discover... HEATHER, staring at framed photographs on sideboard of same little boy at various ages (up to age nine). We hear...

ROSELLE: *(Offstage.)* I couldn't decide between tea or coffee, and the kitchen's all the way downstairs, so, I made both.

(ROSELLE enters, carrying tea tray, upon which is stacked a coffeepot, a teapot, cups, saucers, plate of biscuits, sugar bowl, etc. Note: Roselle speaks with an accent that is more English than New York.)

ROSELLE: Which is it?

HEATHER: Tea, please.

ROSELLE: *(Sets down on coffee table.)* That's annoying.

HEATHER: Sorry.

ROSELLE: I *knew* you were a tea-person! I mean, you're *dressed* like a tea-person. I should have gone with my hunch.

HEATHER: It's just what I wear for work. I wear easygoin' stuff at home...on the weekends.

(ROSELLE stares at HEATHER. Beat. And then...)

HEATHER: I'm sort of allergic to coffee.

ROSELLE: Are you?

HEATHER: I get headaches.

(ROSELLE stares at HEATHER, again. This time, HEATHER notices. There is an embarrassed moment between the two women. And then...)

ROSELLE: Sugar.

HEATHER: Excuse me?

ROSELLE: Do you take sugar?

HEATHER: *(Laughs, nervously.)* Of *course*, that's what you meant! No...Thank you, no.

ROSELLE: That could've been one less thing to carry, as well! *(Pours out milk from milk-jug, then, the tea. A clock chimes.)* Is it quarter past two, already?...I won't have a lot of time. My son's school lets out at three. Once he's home, there's no possibility of conversation.

HEATHER: You pick him up at school?

ROSELLE: No. He walks home on his own. *(Beat.)* The school's just on the corner, here. *(Nods to photographs of little boy on sideboard.)* He's in fifth grade.

HEATHER: What's his name?

ROSELLE: His name's Maximillian. We call him Max.

HEATHER: Oh.

ROSELLE: Maximillian was my father's name.

HEATHER: Oh.

ROSELLE: He's adopted…*(Explains.)* My son, not my father. *(Laughs, and then, as if to explain her laugh…)* My mother taught high school English. In fact, she *is* English. *(Nods at photographs on table.)* I guess it's obvious…

HEATHER: That your mother taught high school English or that she *is* English?

ROSELLE: *(Laughs.)* You should have been my mother's daughter! *(Beat.)* It's obvious that he's adopted. Max…My son.

HEATHER: Yes…Unless, of course…

ROSELLE: Oh, no…Andrew was white. Totally white.

HEATHER: Well, yes, in that case…

ROSELLE: I have no other children. *We!*…I should say "we"…We had no other children, just Max.

HEATHER: Oh.

ROSELLE: Max is in fifth grade…on the corner.

HEATHER: Yes.

(ROSELLE stares at HEATHER for a small silent moment. And then…)

HEATHER: Did you say something else? Did you like ask a question I didn't hear?

ROSELLE: No.

HEATHER: I do that. I think too much. Sometimes, I look up and people are just staring at me, waiting for an answer to a question I never heard. *(The women smile at one another. And then…)*

ROSELLE: Freshen your tea?

HEATHER: I'm fine.

ROSELLE: So, what's my free gift? *(HEATHER looks up. ROSELLE explains…)* That's what the card I sent in said. I *think* that's what the card I sent in said.

HEATHER: It did. *(Takes book from her briefcase, sets it on coffee table.)* A desk-diary…

ROSELLE: Very nice.

HEATHER: Leather-bound. That's real leather. Cowhide.

ROSELLE: A cow died, so that I might have a desk-diary?...The card I sent in definitely didn't say that! *(Looking at diary.)* Very nice.

HEATHER: With my compliments.

ROSELLE: There's no...how do you say it?...obligation to buy?

HEATHER: Not at all, no.

(Laughs.)

ROSELLE: What's funny?

HEATHER: Nothing...It's just that you don't know what I'm selling, do you?

ROSELLE: That's true. I don't. I've just nervous about taking free gifts and having, you know, obligations. My husband used to refuse to take any kind of gift — even birthday gifts.

HEATHER: Was he a politician?

ROSELLE: My husband? No. He just didn't trust anybody. But, you seem so nice. *(Smiles.)* What are you selling?

HEATHER: Life insurance. .

ROSELLE: Oh. I see.

HEATHER: That always gets people really excited.

ROSELLE: When you tell them?

HEATHER: When I tell them. Exactly.

ROSELLE: You really think it does?

HEATHER: I'm being ironic.

ROSELLE: I thought you might be. How long have you been selling life insurance?

HEATHER: Oh, a long time. Nearly eight years.

(There is a pause. And then...)

ROSELLE: Did you have to go to school?

HEATHER: For this?

ROSELLE: For selling life insurance.

HEATHER: No. Not really. I did go to school, though...once I was doing this...once I was, you know, making money.

ROSELLE: Do you do well?

HEATHER: Moneywise? Yuh, I do.

ROSELLE: That's wonderful!...Do you live here in New York?

HEATHER: Uh uh. In New Jersey. Roselle.

ROSELLE: Yes?

HEATHER: That's where I live, now: Roselle, New Jersey.

ROSELLE: Oh, I *seeeee!*...Isn't that funny? My *name's* Roselle.

HEATHER: I know.

ROSELLE: You knew this?

HEATHER: It's on your doorbell...out front...when I rang your bell, just now. It's on your prospect card, too. *(HEATHER flashes index card for ROSELLE's benefit.)* Each potential customer — *prospective* customer — is written up on a card. A prospect card. This is yours. It's made up from the information on the card you sent in for your free gift...*(Looks at card.)* Roselle Clarke, widowed, one child...

ROSELLE: With an "e."

HEATHER: *(After a small pause to figure out what Roselle has just said.)* Your *name*...Clarke ....With an "e."

ROSELLE: My husband's grandfather changed their family name from Kleinwist to Clarke, because Kleinwist was constantly misspelled. He was evidently always saying "Klein...E-I-N...*wist*...W-I-S-T." For some inexplicable reason, he picked Clarke with an "e," so, now, his entire family is constantly correcting people, you know, saying "That's Clarke with an "e." *(Laughs.)* I don't know if that's exactly true. My husband told that story a million times, before he died. Who knows if he's been telling it *after* he died? *(Laughs)* You very rarely meet a Roselle.

HEATHER: I've known a few.

ROSELLE: Well, yes...I mean a *white* Roselle. I was born in a tiny village in England. There wasn't a Roselle within a hundred and fifty miles of us, but, at least four girls in my high school were named Heather. I mean, *your* name is Heather and *my* name is Roselle. Isn't that strange?

HEATHER: My grandmother's name was Heather.

ROSELLE: Was it? Please, don't feel that I was saying anything, you know, against black people. I would never! It's just a fact about names. My father was the village vicar and, according to my mother, for some inexplicable reason, he absolutely insisted that I be named Roselle.

HEATHER: Why do you think he did that?

ROSELLE: Why did he name me Roselle? I don't know. He died when I was three years old.

HEATHER: I'm sorry.

ROSELLE: Not as sorry as I was. My mother remarried...to an American minister, Methodist, when I was nine. I missed my father, terribly. My American father was never a replacement.

HEATHER: I can imagine.

ROSELLE: Is *your* father still living, or is he gone?

HEATHER: Gone. Beyond a question of a doubt. *(Beat.)* He was gone
before I was born.

ROSELLE: Dead, before you were born?

HEATHER: *Gone*, before I was born. Out the door.

ROSELLE: Oh, I see. I'm sorry.

HEATHER: Not as sorry as I was.

(There is a small pause.)

ROSELLE: Are you married?

HEATHER: No.

ROSELLE: Any marriage plans?

HEATHER: Big marriage plans!…To *never* do it!

ROSELLE: I can understand that. In my day, we married. It was the expected thing. If you got to be thirty and you still weren't married, people
thought of you as, you know…

HEATHER: A spinster.

ROSELLE: Exactly the word I was looking for: a spinster.*(Laughs.)* It's an
odd word: spinster, isn't it? Makes you think that old unmarried ladies
spin around or something!

(HEATHER looks up, smiles.)

ROSELLE:…You know, like a "roadster" goes on the road, or a "jokester"
tells jokes, or a "gangster" belongs to a gang…Ohhh! Maybe a spinster
spins wool? Knitting.

HEATHER: I suppose. *(Beat.)* How would you explain "hamster?"

ROSELLE: Hamster?…I can't explain hamster. *(Beat.)* Little pig.

HEATHER: Is he tall?

ROSELLE: Is who tall?

HEATHER: Your son.

ROSELLE: Max? Is Max tall? No, not tall. Good sized. Out of the boys in
his class, he's in the middle, I'd guess. Average height, but,
strong…healthy. Good sized.

HEATHER: Is he bright?

ROSELLE: Very. Bright and nice. He's a thoughtful boy. His teacher called
him "a new penny." She said "Having Max in my class is like having a
new penny." *(Beat.)* I'm not precisely sure what she meant, but, it has to
be good, wouldn't you think?

HEATHER: I'd say so. *(Beat.)* She didn't mean like *old* penny…?

ROSELLE: You mean tarnished penny?…Black penny?

HEATHER: Well, possibly.

ROSELLE: Good God, no! She said "new penny!"…

HEATHER: Well, then, it must have been a compliment.

ROSELLE: I took it as a compliment. Are you ready for another cup?

HEATHER: I am, thanks.

ROSELLE: *(As she pours out two fresh cups of tea.)* I won't be buying any insurance from you.

HEATHER: Why's that?

ROSELLE: I'd like to…I'd *love* to!…I can't qualify.

HEATHER: And why is that?

ROSELLE: Health.

HEATHER: I see.

ROSELLE: I could never pass.

HEATHER: The health exam?

ROSELLE: I could never pass.

HEATHER: You're not…healthy?

ROSELLE: Oh, I *feel* fine.

HEATHER: They've found something?

ROSELLE: They have, yes. *(Beat.)* I feel perfectly fine. I swim, every day.

HEATHER: In the ocean?

ROSELLE: What ocean?

HEATHER: Oh, well…The Atlantic.

ROSELLE: This is New York City! The Atlantic Ocean's not anywhere *near* New York City! The Atlantic Ocean's in New England…Maine, Massachusetts, Rhode Island.

HEATHER: It's in Brooklyn, too, actually.

ROSELLE: The Atlantic Ocean's in B*rooklyn?*

HEATHER: It is.

ROSELLE: When did that happen?

HEATHER: It's always been in Brooklyn.

ROSELLE: I suppose it *has*, when you think of a map. *(Beat.) I* wouldn't swim in it. I swim in the pool at the Printing House Health Club. I prefer the danger of chemicals to the danger of natural things. I'm terrified of fish! *(Beat.)* My mother once swam in the Ganges, every morning. She was in India for nearly a year, before I was born, when my father was doing missionary work. She took to swimming in the Ganges. English people feel they have to do things like that.

HEATHER: And did anything go wrong?

ROSELLE: With my mother? *(ROSELLE laughs. And then…)* Much. But, not from the Ganges.

HEATHER: And you?

ROSELLE: Me, what?

HEATHER: What went wrong?

ROSELLE: I don't know what you're asking?

HEATHER: What's the matter with your health? What did they find?

(ROSELLE looks up; stares at HEATHER. She doesn't answer Heather's question. Instead...)

ROSELLE: Are you hungry? Would you like a slice of chocolate cake? I have a lovely chocolate cake from Jon Vie.

HEATHER: No, thank you. I'm not hungry. I don't really like chocolate.

HEATHER: Good God! You don't? I *adore* chocolate! I've been eating a slice of Jon Vie's double-chocolate cake almost every day since I moved to the Village! Nearly sixteen years, now!

HEATHER: *(Smiles.)* Maybe that's what's made you ill.

ROSELLE: *(Smiles.)* I'd like that. I'd like to think that when I die, it'll be from eating Jon Vie's double-chocolate cake. *(Beat.)* Is your mother living?

HEATHER: No. Yours?

ROSELLE: Yes. She's in a kind of home, outside of London, near the Coast ....Folkestone. She's got the big "A." Did you ever read "The Man Who Mistook His Wife For A Hat?"

HEATHER: No.

ROSELLE: Doesn't matter. My mother mistook her fox fur hat for a skunk. She kept throwing books at this hat, and yelling "Go away, smelly old thing!"...About six years ago...I took Max with me. Just after my husband died, poor man. We were in the room with her...The director of the home was there, as well. Nobody knew what to do, except Max. He asked her what she was throwing her books at. She told him a skunk, and he just threw the hat out the window. She was fine after that. Matter closed.

HEATHER: Children have wisdom.

ROSELLE: Yes. She and Max love each other. They write lovely letters back and forth, once a week. He's one of the few people she recognizes. He loves his grandma. *(HEATHER looks off, sadly. ROSELLE watches HEATHER; continues.)* The closest she came to recognizing me was looking me straight in the eye and asking "Haven't we met?"

HEATHER: *(Looks up at ROSELLE.)* Excuse me.

ROSELLE: That was the closest my mother ever came to recognizing me. I mean in recent years, of course. When I was a child, she almost always knew who I was.*(Beat. ROSELLE smiles.)* I was bathing her. About two years ago. Max and I popped over to England for a visit. Virgin had one of their mid-winter specials. I'm cautious about depleting capital. As long as we live on the interest, we're fine. *(Smiles.)* Where was I?

HEATHER: England.

ROSELLE: Bathing my mother! Shampoo got into her eyes and she started crying like a little girl. I wiped her face with a flannel and she sort of looked up at me through the suds and asked "Haven't we met?" *(Beat.)* When she was first ill, she gave all of her money to my half-brother in Chicago. He was a lawyer, quite wealthy, himself. I didn't mind. I mean, I didn't want anything from her, but, I was curious as to why she would give everything she had to him, when he obviously didn't need money. She said she was afraid he wouldn't visit her if she didn't give him money. I suppose she was right.

HEATHER: *(Sadly.)* I suppose I was spared all that.

(Small pause as ROSELLE watches HEATHER deal with her sadness.)

ROSELLE: When did she die?…*(HEATHER looks up.) Your* mother.

HEATHER: Last Friday.

ROSELLE: Oh. I see. Just last Friday. *(Beat.)* Where was she living?

HEATHER: In Brooklyn, still. *(Beat.)* I asked her to live with me, but, she never wanted to. She liked being on her own.

ROSELLE: I can understand that. You are. *(Explains.)* On your own. *(And then…)* Am I just assuming something?

HEATHER: No, I am. On my own.

ROSELLE: Was she ill a long time? Did she suffer?

HEATHER: Stroke. Instantaneous.

ROSELLE: Lucky woman.

HEATHER: I suppose.

ROSELLE: My husband suffered terribly. The doctors promised him no pain, but, pain, I assure you, is not the only issue.

HEATHER: She was dead for three days before I found her.

ROSELLE: Oh. How ghastly!

HEATHER: I was in Chicago, for work. I called her the second and third days…and then, I took a plane back. I mean, I *knew* something had happened…that she was dead. I knew it.

ROSELLE: Yes, I'm sure you did.

(There is a small pause. Roselle and Heather share a sadness. And then…)

ROSELLE: Once somebody's dead, they're dead. I sat with my husband for a long, long while before I called the police. I can tell you, wherever spirits go, they're gone, immediately. I'm sure of it. The body is absolutely dead, empty, lifeless. When I was little, I watched a crushed squirrel, long after the offending car went God-knows-where. There was no hint of life, beyond an odd final moment of frenzy, frozen…It's not what you want to remember, is it?

HEATHER: I remember going to a funeral of a old friend's father…in Brooklyn, when I was maybe twenty. Stephanie. Stephanie was somebody I went to first grade with…The father had been married before, a long time before he'd married the mother. We knew there was another daughter somewhere, but, we didn't know that the father had been keeping up with her, with this other daughter…keeping in touch…being a kind of daddy, on some level. At the funeral, the casket was, you know, open. The father was dolled up in a blue suit and red tie and his skin was kind of this weird grey/green color. He was a really dark-skinned man, but you wouldn't've known this from lookin' at him. Well, the church was packed and the choir was into it, when, alls'a' sudden this woman about thirty years old starts yellin' "That's not my daddy! He's not my daddy!"…It was this other daughter. And we all start thinkin' "He really *doesn't* look like Stephanie's daddy!…Maybe they switched him with some other body by mistake? It was amazing, 'cause everybody had this very same thought at the very same time. People got the *giggles*, I swear to God! *(HEATHER laughs.)* That's the thing about being alive, isn't it?…You always want to laugh. No matter what, there's always, like, that energy. When you stop wanting to laugh, you're dead.

ROSELLE: You seem so…educated.

HEATHER: I go to school at night. I read a lot. *(Beat.)* I knew the English doctor, Oliver Sacks, wrote "The Man Who Mistook His Wife For A Hat." I just didn't read it. *(Smiles.)* He lives on City Island. You know that? I have a friend from work living up there. She told me that. She sees him a lot in the morning. They both walk in the same part of the woods. She told me she never says hello to him or nothing, because she knows who he is and she figures he must be busy, thinking.

ROSELLE: What sort of school?

HEATHER: It's part of Rutgers.

ROSELLE: What are you studying?

HEATHER: English.

ROSELLE: I thought so. At what…level?

HEATHER: I'm in a Ph.D. program.

ROSELLE: *Are* you?

HEATHER: I finished my B.A. with, you know, good grades, and I got accepted in the Ph.D. program in lit. It's going to be a long haul…sixty credits of coursework, plus exams, two languages, a book-length dissertation…

ROSELLE: I *am* impressed!

HEATHER: I've only finished ten hours of coursework, so far.

ROSELLE: It's slow because of my working full-time. Next September, my company's letting me do a semester, full-time, days, and work, part-time, nights.

ROSELLE: And they help with tuition-fees?

HEATHER: No. It's cheap enough. I'm doing it with loans.

ROSELLE: Will you teach?

HEATHER: I don't know. I s'pose. I might like to work with kids…not little kids…more like teenage kids…like my mother and me when we were, you know, fourteen.

ROSELLE: I *am* impressed.

HEATHER: Yuh, well…You've got to make an effort.

ROSELLE: That's true enough. *(Beat.)* What do you like to read?

HEATHER: Everything I can get my hands on. A book gives you a lot of answers, without anybody having to put up with your dumb questions.

ROSELLE: You're quite remarkable, Heather.

HEATHER: Not really. I'm passing through, one time, like everybody else. I'm just trying to make my pass-through the best I can for myself, just like everybody else…

ROSELLE: How old are you?

HEATHER: Twenty-six…last Friday.

ROSELLE: The day your mother…?

HEATHER: Exactly! See? Life's so crazy, it makes you almost wanna' smile. *(Beat.)*

ROSELLE: If you never marry, won't you miss out on…well…

HEATHER: Children? *(ROSELLE nods.)* I plan to have children.

ROSELLE: As a single parent.

HEATHER: I know a lot of women…

ROSELLE: So I read. I mean, look at *me*.

HEATHER: Exactly.

ROSELLE: Still and all, it's nice for a boy to have a father. When Andrew was ill, he really regretted not being there for his Maxie. He called him "Maxie." *(Laughs.)* Max is always after me to bring a man home. When he meets nice sort of grandfatherly men, he always asks them if they're married. It can be horrifying!…

HEATHER: Will you be really sick…ill?

ROSELLE: I'm not planning to wait it out. If it's as bad as they say it is, I'll, you know, do something about it.

HEATHER: Have you had a second opinion?

ROSELLE: Second opinion, third opinion, fourth opinion…I'm always ready for another opinion, but, it's never the news I'm looking for. So, now, I'm done looking.

(Beat. A clock chimes.)

ROSELLE: I meant what I said about your mother. No matter how painful it was…it is…for you, imagine how blessed she was to go that way. How old was she?

HEATHER: Forty-one.

ROSELLE: That young?

HEATHER: She was sixteen when she had me.

ROSELLE: That young. People must have mistaken you for sisters.

HEATHER: Not a chance. My mother always looked twenty years older than she was.

ROSELLE: Did she work?

HEATHER: Nothing but. She cleaned houses, when I was little. Later on, she cleaned a motel, out near the beach at Seagate. On the ocean. *(HEATHER smiles. And then…)* My mother worked, day and night. I remember her once sayin' ta' me that she could see it would be a relief to die. It made me feel scared when she said that.

ROSELLE: Was she ever a happy person?

HEATHER: I wouldn't say so. I wouldn't say she ever had a break in her whole life.

ROSELLE: Besides you.

(Beat. HEATHER looks up at ROSELLE, doesn't quite smile.)

HEATHER: Besides me. Yuh. *(Looks away, sadly; settles her stare on photographs of boy.)* He's cute.

ROSELLE: He's more than cute. He's beautiful. *(And then…)* Who would you say he looks more like?…Your mother or your father?

(HEATHER turns and looks at ROSELLE. THEY lock eyes, eyeball to eyeball. There is a long hold.)

HEATHER: Why did you ask me that? *(No reply. And then…)* My mother. When I first saw him in the schoolyard, I nearly fainted. He's got my mother's face on him, more than I do. If he had my father's looks, I wouldn't have recognized him. I've never seen my father. I have no idea what he looks like. My mother would never talk about him.

ROSELLE: Do you watch him a lot…in the schoolyard?

HEATHER: Yuh, I guess a lot. I'm in the city three or four times a week. I always try to get downtown to, you know…

ROSELLE: For a long time?

HEATHER: Do I watch a long time, or have I been *doing* this for a long time?

ROSELLE: Either. Both.

HEATHER: I started maybe five years ago, when he was little…in kindergarten. I stood on the corner, by Ray's Pizza, for a while…no plan or nothin'…just rememberin', you know…This bell went off, and all's a sudden there was this fire drill and all the kids started coming out of the school with their teachers, all at once. Kids comin' out of every door. The little kids came out of their own entrance, right on the corner, opposite where I was standin'. They were all holding hands. There weren't so many black kids, maybe ten in all, so, I could check each of 'em out, no problem,…And I saw him…Max.

ROSELLE: You knew right away it was him?

HEATHER: No doubt about it!

ROSELLE: Do you have your own name for him?

HEATHER: *(After a pause.)* No, uh uh. I guess I thought about names when I was pregnant and all…Martin…Malcomb…Mohammed…*(Laughs.)* The big M's.

ROSELLE: Max is an M.

HEATHER: Max is great!

ROSELLE: You like Max?

HEATHER: I love Max! Max fits him perfectly!…*(Beat.)* I remember the first time I saw him, thinking that he looked, I dunno, comical. He was little and his clothes were big. It was chilly and you put him in this big wooly coat. I asked one of the other kids what his name was and she said "Max," and I thought to myself "Max is perfect! He's a definite Max!"

ROSELLE: I've seen you watching the school, watching the house.

HEATHER: You have?

ROSELLE: Several times. I never told Andrew…my husband. He was too much of a pragmatist. I was afraid he would have…offered him back.

HEATHER: To me?

ROSELLE: Well…

HEATHER: I have no rights. I know this. I know that you've adopted him, legally and all, but, even without any of that, I have no rights. I gave him up.

ROSELLE: I saw you bring him to us.

HEATHER: You did?

ROSELLE: I didn't know what it was you'd left…At first, when the doorbell rang, I went down and saw this package and I thought it was, you know, a package…something for my husband from UPS, Federal Express, whatever…But, then, I thought "Nobody's asking for a signature"…I remember seeing you across the way by St. Vincent's, but, I didn't associate you with the package. I guess I was looking for a man, you know, a delivery man. Then, I remember getting worried. "A bomb?" I thought, "Could it be a bomb?" Then, Max cried and I knew it was a baby.

HEATHER: I remember that, hearing him wake up and start crying.

ROSELLE: For a split second, I wanted to yell at you. I mean, I knew you were connected to him…to the baby…but, I didn't think you were the *mother*. You were so young. I figured you were a sister…

HEATHER: Fifteen.

ROSELLE: Fifteen? That's all you were? Fifteen?

HEATHER: I had my fifteenth birthday, two days before he was born.

ROSELLE: How old was Max, exactly, when you left him here? The doctors figured a month.

HEATHER: Three weeks. I fed him a lot…from my breasts. He got big, fast.

ROSELLE: What was the date he was born? I'd love to know the exact date!

HEATHER: I'm October 29th, he's Halloween.

ROSELLE: Halloween. We've been celebrating October 23rd. *(Beat.)* Perhaps, I'll just leave it. Halloween's so *specific*. I mean, it'll dictate a sort of specific theme for every birthday party he'll ever have, don't you think?

HEATHER: It was pretty weird the night he was born, themewise, I can tell you that! And every person I saw was wearing some kinda' ghoulish Halloween mask!

ROSELLE: He was born at night?

HEATHER: Eleven o'clock on the button. The instant he was born, church bells started chimin'!

ROSELLE: I suppose he'll want to know these things. It's just human nature to want to know exact details.
(Beat.)

ROSELLE: It would be lovely, for his fortieth birthday, to give him the extra eight days as a gift. "Happy birthday, Max. You're not 40, yet. You have eight more days of being 39!"
(The WOMEN laugh. And then…)

ROSELLE: I took him inside, here. I didn't know what to do! I was afraid to tell my husband that somebody'd left a baby on the steps and I'd taken it in. I mean, I didn't know whether I'd done something *stupid*...picking him up, taking him inside. Andrew heard the crying and he poked his head down from the upstairs landing, and he saw me cuddling Max, and you know what he said? You know what my husband's very first words were?

HEATHER: What?

ROSELLE: "Oh, *shit!*"...I'll never forget that! Andrew said "Oh, shit," before he said anything else. It made me laugh. Here we were, home, together, in our miserable way...Andrew, alone, upstairs, in his study, reading, I don't know, *The Life of Dwight D. Eisenhower,* and me, alone, practicing the same Chopin étude for the nine-thousandth time...and then, the doorbell rings, and we are, suddenly, really and truly *together*...in a new life. I knew it and Andrew knew it. He said "Oh, shit," and I laughed, and we both laughed.

HEATHER: Me, too.

ROSELLE: You laughed?

HEATHER: I knew I was in a new life. As soon as you closed the door, I knew it. I knew I was in a new life, and he was, too. I owed it to everybody to get my act together. I went home to my mother...

ROSELLE: You hadn't been livin' at home, while you were pregnant?

HEATHER: For the last five months of it, from the time I told her what was goin' on. She freaked.

ROSELLE: Understandable.

HEATHER: Totally! I didn't really get mad at her, 'cause I knew it just brought her back to it, to when her own life fell apart. I knew what I had to do.

ROSELLE: With the baby?

HEATHER: With me, with her, with the baby, with all of it.

ROSELLE: The father?

HEATHER: Same age as me: fourteen when I got pregnant, fifteen when the baby was born. *(Beat.)* His name was Ray. *(Beat.)* His mother and father and brothers all worked, so, their apartment was empty til about 5:30, every day. It was the first time for both of us. We called it "Doin' the hoopie." *(Beat.)* I know exactly when I conceived Max. We were on his living room rug, listenin' to Run-DMC sing "My Addidas." *(Beat.)* He was nice about it...Ray. He would've run away with me, probably. I mean, he *said* he would've. I didn't trust him, so, I lied. I told him I was going to my aunt's in Boston. I never saw him, again.

ROSELLE: And now? Do you have any idea where he is, now?

HEATHER: I have an idea, yuh.

ROSELLE: And?

HEATHER: It's too stupid.

ROSELLE: I'm interested. I'm sure you can understand why. Wherever he is, he's Max's father.

HEATHER: You don't wanna' know. It's too stupid.

ROSELLE: Is he alive?

HEATHER: Nope.

ROSELLE: I see.

HEATHER: The only thing you can be sure of, when things are really bad, is that they can be really worse. There's no limit to how bad things can be!

ROSELLE: From the time he was three years old, he knew how he came to me. I told him as soon as he asked. For a long time, maybe even a year, he let it slide…never mentioned it. Then, at the most unexpected times, he would ask about you, very casually, as if it was unimportant. Once, when he was practicing piano, he played his piece particularly well, and he said to me "I'd love to play this for my other mummy."

HEATHER: He said that?

ROSELLE: That's what he's always called you: his "other mummy." Since he's been in school, you know, with other kids, once in a great while, he'll call you his "black mummy." *(Beat. A clock chimes, again.)* Why did you pick me, Heather?…*Us!* I should have said "us." Why did you pick us? Was it just random? Was it something you figured out and planned?

HEATHER: I planned the people next door…The Steins. They had a little girl and a big dog. I watched them from the sidewalk across the street a bunch'a times, but, they weren't home, that night. I pushed their bell, maybe twenty times. Nobody was home. I saw you in the window, next door, here, playing the piano. I thought "It's good growin' up in a house where they play the piano," so…

ROSELLE: Why the Steins? Why this neighborhood in the first place? Why this block? Did you just take him from the hospital to the first house across the street? Was it just chance…accidental…random?

HEATHER: It's a rich neighborhood…People live in houses…There's a school right on the block…And, I guess, there's the hospital…St. Vincent's. I can remember thinking that you could bring him there if he got sick. Maybe I was thinking, deep down, if you didn't want him, you could bring him across the street to the hospital and they'd take care of him. They wouldn't let him die.

ROSELLE: We did take him over there, when... *(And then...)* Are you saying that he wasn't *born* in St. Vincent's?

HEATHER: He was born in Central Park.

ROSELLE: In Central Park?!... *Outdoors?!*

HEATHER: Behind the boathouse.

ROSELLE: Were you alone?

HEATHER: I was with my girlfriend, Danine. She had had her baby a couple'a months earlier, so, I figured she would know what was happening, when the baby came...she was, you know, *experienced.* I asked her to hang with me...I gave her some stuff I had she wanted and she, obviously, stayed and helped. There wasn't that much to do. Fifteen's an excellent age for having babies.

ROSELLE: How old's Danine?

HEATHER: Then? Sixteen.

ROSELLE: And you all lived in the park, together?

HEATHER: Sometimes in the park, sometimes with Danine's cousin, Harold, in the Bronx. But, he didn't want the baby born in his place, so, when it was close to the time, we...

ROSELLE: He *let* you go to the park to have your baby?

HEATHER: I dunno...I guess he figured I was going to a friend. I dunno. I don't think he cared a whole lot.

ROSELLE: Was it terrifying, being in the park?

HEATHER: Uh uh. It was great. Sometimes, at night, I got scared. Weird people came around, but, once they saw our babies, they were great. Everybody loved playin' with them. It was pretty warm, still, and I could bathe him in the lake...and there were other kids my age livin' there.

ROSELLE: In the park?

HEATHER: Maybe twenty-five or thirty other kids my age.

ROSELLE: Living in Central Park?

HEATHER: That was just in our end of the park. We stayed pretty close to the boathouse. It's the safest part of the park. In the daytime, if it wasn't too crowded, the kid who worked the boats would let us take one out.

ROSELLE: You and Danine?

HEATHER: Me and Max. *(Smiles.)* Max and I. Danine knew this guy in Ohio she went to, about a week after Max was born. You don't wanna' know how she raised the money for their bus fare!...Max and I stayed put in the park for a couple'a more weeks.

ROSELLE: And you never thought about keeping him...about just...going on...you and the baby...together?

HEATHER: Not for a minute. The first cold night, I knew exactly what I had to do.

ROSELLE: And now?

HEATHER: And now what?

ROSELLE: Do you regret not keeping him?

HEATHER: Can you imagine what he'd be, or I'd be, if I kept him?

ROSELLE: But, now, you are what you are, and he is what he is.

HEATHER: He's your child.

ROSELLE: Yes, he is. He's my child.

(There is a small painful pause. And then...)

HEATHER: Does he play the piano well?

ROSELLE: Like an angel. We started him taking lessons, when he was five. He went from being the new kid to being number one in the group within the first year. He can play Chopin.

HEATHER: His father played the piano.

ROSELLE: Extraordinary!

HEATHER: Not Chopin, but, really, really well.

ROSELLE: Just extraordinary. The combination of the genetic and the conditioned...what you gave him, genetically, and what I...what *we* gave him by association...That's what Max is, and what Max will be.

(ROSELLE looks off, sadly, then, looks at Heather, again; smiles.)

ROSELLE: His father was musical...his biological father. Isn't it just extraordinary? *(Without warning...)* I feel sick. This is making me feel sick.

HEATHER: Your illness?

ROSELLE: You *knowing* I'm ill...knowing I can't keep him, be here for him, long enough...hovering over me like a goddam vulture!...

HEATHER: *I'm not!* Honest to God, I'm not!

ROSELLE: How long have you known I'm ill?

(No reply. HEATHER looks away, embarrassed.)

ROSELLE: Exactly.

HEATHER: Everybody's medical records are available to us from a central database. If anyone tries for insurance, anywhere, and gets turned down, well...*(Beat.)* I've known for maybe two years, maybe more.

ROSELLE: *(Sarcastically.)* You took your time getting here.

HEATHER: Yes, I well...

ROSELLE: You knew the quality of my illness, I suppose...

HEATHER: No, that's not...

ROSELLE: You knew I had a couple of good years before it…

HEATHER: *(Angrily.)* That's not it!

ROSELLE: What's it, then?

HEATHER: When my mother died, I couldn't not come here, I couldn't not make myself known.

ROSELLE: *(Angrily.)* Why not? You waited ten years…Why not fifteen? What not twenty? Why not wait and show up when he's getting out of college? Call in from…

HEATHER: *(Yells.) He's from me! He's a piece of me!*

ROSELLE: *You put him in a cardboard box from the A&P and you gave him away!*

HEATHER: *I didn't just give him to anybody! I gave him to you!*

ROSELLE: *And now, you want to take him back?*

HEATHER: *No!*

(*Beat.*)

ROSELLE: Then, why else are you here?

HEATHER: I don't know…To try to get you to share him.

ROSELLE: Well, know this: Whatever gets decided gets decided by *me*, not us: *ME!* My husband spent two years of his life in court, fighting for us to be able to keep Max! For nine years, I've held and nurtured Max, dressed him, fed him three meals a day, nursed him through measles, mumps, chicken pox and *where the fuck were you? You've done nothing!* (*HEATHER breaks down; sobs. ROSELLE watches her a while, then, goes to HEATHER, embraces her.*)

HEATHER: Shall I go?

ROSELLE: No. He'll be home, soon. *(Beat.)* I've always dreaded this day. I've probably dreamt it five hundred times. But, you were never as beautiful, never as clever, never as nice. (*ROSELLE goes to piano, picks out melody of Chopin piece, lightly. And then…*) My nightmare used to be that you would turn up and Max would run into your arms and beg you to take him back with you. I haven't had that particular nightmare for a long, long time. Not since I've been ill, not since I was diagnosed. Now, my nightmare's that you never show up at all. That I get sicker and sicker, and Max is on his own…totally without help.

HEATHER: Is that why you sent in the card?

ROSELLE: *(Nods "yes.")* That's why.

(*We hear the front door open and then slam close. We hear MAX, offstage, calling to Roselle.*)

MAX: *(Offstage.)* I'm home!

ROSELLE: Come upstairs, Max…I'm in the music room with your other mummy! Come upstairs, darling!

(ROSELLE turns. The WOMEN'S eyes meet. HEATHER bows her head. We gear…MAX's footsteps on the staircase, nearer and nearer. MUSIC IN…Reprise of Paul Simon's "Born At the Right Time," starting with lyric "Born at the instant the church bells chimed…" ROSELLE's head stays up, high, bravely, but a tear escapes from her eye, stains her cheek, betrays her courage. The door begins to open, as…the lights fade out.)

End of Play.

My Old Lady

For my Children.
On stage, so it needn't be in life.

We frail fathers
Doomed to failure,
Grow to apology.

Endless in your lives,
Endless in our love.

INTRODUCTION

My grandfathers both came to America, looking for something they called "A higher quality of life." I know little of my father's father, who died just before I was born...except for photographs of a formidably stern man and his eight, well-dressed, overachieving children. For me, as a child, my father's family was no fun.

By contrast, my mother's family was six laughing, childlike, aunts and uncles, unremarkable in their impact on a larger world, but remarkable in their love for each other, and for their parents. Nathan Solberg, my mother's father, will be the subject of a film that I am now working on with the Hungarian director, Istvan Szabo (with whom I have just completed a screenplay for Szabo's next film, *The Taste Of Sunshine*). As the story goes...somewhere in eastern Europe...when Grandpa Solberg was two years old, his mother died. Within a few weeks of the death, Grandpa Solberg's father married a seventeen-year-old girl...and put his eight children, little Nathan included, in a state-run orphanage. The oldest child, Lion, escaped from the orphanage and made his way to America, where he found work, saved money, and, two years later, returned to the orphanage to rescue his seven siblings. Lion took his brothers and sisters to America, by boat (steerage class). On arrival in America, the eight children all agreed to take a new name...and never to reveal who they had been or where they had come from. And this gave definition to my gradnfather's relationship to America. For him, all life was to begin in that very moment: arrival in the USA, the land of freedom and opportunity.

Yes, it is yet another compelling story of America, the beautiful. But, a scant few generations later, something has happened. The streets of American cities are littered with human life, the Homeless. If the American Dream hasn't exactly burst, it threatens to rupture, momentarily. And for my generation and my childrens' generation, there is small trickle of movement back to Europe for "*la qualité de la vie.*" Oui, c'est ça.

For American playwrights, a working-holiday in Europe is a shock. European theatre seats are mostly filled, theatres actually pay royalties, commission plays, newspapers and magazines seem to have an honest interest in plays and playwrights. In short, it's possible to *be* a playwright in Europe. In America, it's almost not possible. The Broadway theatre-scene is strictly for tourists. I know of only a very few playwrights who write with Broadway in mind, maybe three. The rest of us must be content with smaller theatres, smaller audiences, and livings essentially earned in Hollywood, not New

York…This harsh reality doesn't stop any of us from writing plays, not for a second. But it does make Europe quite attractive.

When I began writing *My Old Lady,* I wanted to break away from the sort of plays I'd been writing during the past ten years…working-class drama, set in my adored and adopted hometown, Gloucester, Massachusetts. After twelve full-length Gloucester-based plays, enough was becoming too much. I had never intended to be the Bard of Gloucester. During the past decade, I had been spending enormous amounts of time in Europe, particularly, in France, where my plays are popular, where I am able to combine writing, acting, and directing with controlled consumption of some of my favorite vegetables, such as *Crème Brulé* and *Châteauneuf du Pâpe.*

I had long been fascinated by an antique and odd French real-estate system called the "viager," wherein an apartment owned by a old person can be bought at a price well below market value. But, the buyer cannot actually take possession of the apartment until the seller (the old person) dies. And during the time between the purchase and the death of the seller, the buyer must pay an agreed-upon monthly charge. So, it's a crapshoot: Will the old person die, quickly, and make the apartment a good buy, or will the old person hang on for years, and turn the deal into a nightmare? In fact, shortly after I'd finished the first draft of *My Old Lady,* a story broke in the French press about the death of a lawyer, who had bought an apartment in the viager system from an old lady. The lawyer paid charges of the apartment for some sixty-five years, until *his* death. The old lady was named Jeanne Calmante. She was the oldest living person in the world, 122 years old. Ironically, she died during the writing of this essay.

My play is quite a different story. A dissolute New Yorker inherits an apartment in Paris from his recently deceased father. He borrows money to go to France and sell the apartment. In Paris, he finds an old lady living in the apartment: a viager. It is a story, essentially, of these two people…he, American, bankrupt, dissolute; she, European, too old, living in the past, yet with a grand *joie de vivre*…He sports an undeniable *joie de se plâindre* (joy of complaint). He wants to die, she *refuses* to die.

I'll stop here, before I spoil the play for you, except to note, it was a thrill to write this play, and an even greater thrill to see it in front of an audience. I won't go on, except to say the obvious: I really love this play.

The writing of *My Old Lady* was interrupted by the writing of *Lebensraum,* which was excellent good luck for *My Old Lady.* I returned to *My Old Lady* with the same sort of enthusiasm and vigor one feels at the *start* of writing a new play. It is no surprise to me that *My Old Lady* feels bouyant, strong.

The World Premiere production of *My Old Lady* was at Gloucester Stage, last summer, in tandem with *Lebensraum*. I had worried if Gloucester audiences would be at all interested in such work as these two Europe-based plays. In fact, *My Old Lady* was one of our most successful runs, ever, as was *Lebensraum*. David Wheeler directed a charming, talented cast for *My Old Lady*, including the profoundly appealing Miriam Varone as Mathilde (the old lady), beautiful Lisa Richards as Chloé (the daughter), and one of my most favorite actors, ever, Paul O'Brien, as the woeful Mathias (the American). O'Brien had acted in some six of my plays, before, but, his work in *My Old Lady* was off the charts: transcendent. I was so proud of my friend Paul, and so glad.

It's difficult to predict the future for *My Old Lady*. There is some pressure on me to alter the play's ending. Many people find it too harsh, too dark, too upsetting. I cannot say what I will do. For the moment, I want to live with this play. I want to see the German production in September, and assess my text from the hidden comfort of another language. I want to take great care casting the play for New York. I want this play to have a life, and I will do what I have to do to help it along…as I have with my five children, and my fifty-three other plays. In the final act of a full life, as in the final act of a full drama, there is a most amazing accumulation of people and things, and such unexpectedly enormous emotion.

I.H., Gloucester
August 1997.

ORIGINAL PRODUCTION

The original production of *My Old Lady* was presented at Gloucester Stage Co., Gloucester, Mass. on August 7, 1996. It was directed by David Wheeler, Scenery Design by Lisa Pegnato, Lighting Design by Ian McColl, Costume Design by Lisa Pegnato, Stage Manager Jeff Benish, Assistant Director Charlotte Vuarnesson and Light Board Operator Inge Berge, with the following cast:

Matilda . . . . Miriam Varone
Mathias . . . . Paul O'Brien
Chloé. . . . . Lisa Richards

THE PEOPLE OF THE PLAY

MATHIAS "JIM" GOLD, American, in his fifties, fading good looks.
MATHILDE GIFFARD, French, in her nineties, still beautiful.
CHLOÉ GIFFARD, French, in her fifties, fading good looks.

THE PLACE OF THE PLAY

The entire action of the play is contained in the living room of Mathilde's apartment, overlooking Jardin Luxembourg, Paris (France).

THE TIME OF THE PLAY

Mid-autumn, the present. One week, from Monday morning, til the following Sunday morning.

My Old Lady

ACT ONE
SCENE ONE

Monday morning. MUSIC IN...John Coltrane "Lush Life"...LIGHTS UP IN...Living room, Mathilde's apartment, Paris, overlooking Jardin Luxembourg. We are seeing the tip of the iceberg (so to speak) as the apartment beyond our view is enormous, perhaps 300M2, built in a grand style, but, is now sparsely furnished and seedy, obviously owned by somebody old, neither rich nor grand.

We discover MATHILDE sitting in an overstuffed chair, head back, eyes closed, deep in thought. Her back is turned to the door. Thus, SHE is hidden from MATHIAS, who has just entered apartment, looking around for a sign of life.

MATHIAS is thin, in his late fifties/early sixties, nervous. MATHILDE is thin, in her early to mid-nineties, relaxed.

MATHIAS: Hello?...Bonjour?...Anybody home? Il y a quelqu'un ici? Au maison? Hello?...*(Sees MATHILDE.)* Oh, hey! Hiii! I'm sorry. I kept knocking and the door was open and I...Oh, shit! Sorry!...*(Tries to say the same thing in French. HE speaks bad French, with a horrible American accent.)* Bonjour...Je suis desolé être ici, mais...la porte etait overt et je, uh, knockait, uh, frappait, uh, fait des knock-knock, beaucoup des fois, et...

MATHILDE: *(In beautifully correct English, with a charming French accent.)* I hope you take this in the best possible spirit, but, it would be much better for both of us if you spoke English.

MATHIAS: *(In English, with an educated American accent.)* English. Okay, well, *good!*...Hi. I, uh, I was knocking on the door and nobody answered and it sort of pushed open a little bit. I poked my head in, and I saw the lights were on, so, I sort of came in and, well...Hi.

MATHILDE: You're Mathias?

MATHIAS: I am Mathias, yes. I actually call myself "Jim"...How did you know my name?

MATHILDE: My lawyer told me you might be stopping by.

MATHIAS: He did? Your *lawyer?* I...

MATHILDE: Monsieur Gérard. Christophe Gérard.

MATHIAS: Oh, right…Oh, *right!* Christophe Gérard. The lawyer for the apartment. *(And then…)* I inherited this apartment…from my father. He died a few months ago and he, uh, owned it. *(Without pause; worried…)* This *is* the fourth floor, isn't it? I know the first floor is the Rez de Chaussée and the second floor is the first floor, and the second floor is the third floor…I mean, this has got to be the fourth floor because it's the top floor and the apartment I inherited is the top floor! *(A new worry…)* Have I got the wrong *number?* This is number forty-nine, right?

MATHILDE: You've got the right address, you've got the right apartment. I'm Madame Giffard…Mathilde Giffard.

MATHIAS: Oh…well…good.

(There is an embarrassed pause.)

MATHILDE: Didn't you speak with Monsieur Gérard?

MATHIAS: I did, but, not really. He…

MATHILDE:…Doesn't speak English.

MATHIAS: Exactly. Nobody in his office does, either.

MATHILDE: So, nobody's explained the…situation?

MATHIAS: No. Not really. *(Beat.)* What situation?

MATHILDE: This apartment is a "viager."

MATHIAS: Meaning what, exactly, in English?

MATHILDE: Oh, well, it means "for life," I suppose. The word "viager" doesn't translate, easily, because the system doesn't really exist outside of France.

MATHIAS: What system?

MATHILDE: When your father bought this apartment, he bought it well below the market price.

MATHIAS: I'm sure he did. My father was really good at that.

MATHILDE: Yes. I suppose he was. All "viager" apartments are sold cheaply. The buyer gets the apartment cheaply, for what we call a small "bouquet," but, he or she must agree to pay, well, fees — charges for the apartment — until the owner, well, dies.

MATHIAS: I don't follow you. My father bought this apartment twenty-five years ago and he…

MATHILDE: Twenty-*seven* years ago.

MATHIAS: Twenty-*seven* years ago…and he owned it, all that time, until *he* died…and then, he left it to me…in his will, which has just been probated.

MATHILDE: And you inherited quite a lot?

MATHIAS: *Me?* From my *father?*...Opposite. I inherited about two dozen books and this apartment. Period.

MATHILDE: In total?

MATHIAS: Period.

MATHILDE: And where did the rest go?

MATHIAS: To who?

MATHILDE: *(Correcting his English.)* To *whom*. *(And then...)* I taught English for many years. I've stopped teaching, now, but, I can't stop correcting people. I'm sorry.

MATHIAS: To whom. *(And then...)* He left his money to charity. He didn't feel comfortable leaving it to me, so, it went to charity, instead.

MATHILDE: Except for this apartment.

MATHIAS: Except for this apartment. And some books.

MATHILDE: Was he ill long?

MATHIAS: My father? Ill long? No, not long. Did you know him: my father? Of course, you must have! I mean, he bought the apartment from you, didn't he? Did he buy it from you or from the person who lived here before you?

MATHILDE: He bought it from me.

MATHIAS: And you never moved out?

MATHILDE: I never moved out.

MATHIAS: Well, that's really very interesting. Who's been collecting your rent?

MATHILDE: I don't pay rent. I pay charges.

MATHIAS: Your charges, then. Who's been collecting your charges?

MATHILDE: The "co-propriataire." Your father paid my charges and other expenses relating to this apartment from the time he bought it, up til now. That's what a "viager" *does. (Another small pause.)*

MATHIAS: I don't completely understand.

MATHILDE: Your father bought this apartment from me, cheaply, well below the market price. In return for the reduced price, he agreed to pay my charges...

MATHIAS: Until you *died?*

MATHILDE: But, not a minute, afterwards.

MATHIAS: Are you kidding me?

MATHILDE: No.

MATHIAS: So, now, *I'm* supposed to be paying your charges?

MATHILDE: If you in fact inherited the apartment, you are.

MATHIAS: Jesus!

MATHILDE: They're not huge charges. They're really quite fair, by today's standards, for an apartment of this size.

MATHIAS: And I'm *responsible?*

MATHILDE: Twenty-four hundred a month.

MATHIAS: Twenty-four hundred francs a month?

MATHILDE: Twenty-four hundred *dollars* a month. Your father always sent me dollars.

MATHIAS: And *I'm* supposed to be paying you that, now?

MATHILDE: No, I've been paid through the end of the year. But, after the new year begins, yes.

MATHIAS: Jesus! That's what I inherited? A twenty-four-hundred-dollar-a-month *debt?*

MATHILDE: Seems like it.

MATHIAS: So, what you're saying, really, is that I own this apartment, and I also own *you?*

MATHILDE: Not exactly…Well, I suppose, strictly speaking…yes. You own this apartment and you own me. Until I die. After I die, you just…

MATHIAS: Own the apartment.

MATHILDE: Exactly.

MATHIAS: How old are you?…*God!* I can't *believe* I just asked you that! I'm sorry. Forgive me. I'm being really really rude. I'm sure you can understand. This is kind of a *shock!* I mean, here I am, thinking I'll turn this place around…sell it, fast, get the money…I'm broke. My *father* was a wealthy man, not me. I'm broke. I own this apartment and a bunch of boxes of books and that's *it.*

MATHILDE: You had nothing, yourself, before your father died?

MATHIAS: Yuh, well, sure, I had stuff, a long time ago, when I was married.

MATHILDE: You're not married, any more?

MATHIAS: No. I'm divorced. Our divorce was American-standard. I took nothing, my ex-wives took the rest.

MATHILDE: Children?

MATHIAS: I'm sorry?…Oh…I see…No. No children.

(There is a small, thoughtful pause. And then…)

MATHILDE: I'm ninety-two.

MATHIAS: Jesus! This is *amazing*! You're *ninety-two*!? You were how old when my father bought your…? *Wait!* 27 from 92 is 65. You were 65! He ended up paying twenty-four hundred a month times twelve months is twenty-eight thousand eight hundred dollars a year times 27 years is…a *lot!*

(MATHIAS begins to laugh.)

MATHILDE: What's amusing you?

MATHIAS: He got screwed!

MATHILDE: *(MATHILDE smiles.)* He did. You could say that. Yes.

MATHIAS: *(Still laughing.)* Didn't he, like, try to kill you? I mean, after almost thirty years of shelling out that kind of money, didn't he, well, I dunno…yuh…try to kill you?

MATHILDE: Luckily, your father had other investments.

MATHIAS: *(Still laughing.)* I can just see the old son of a bitch, waiting for you to keel over! Ten years, twenty years…His shyster accountants advising him, cautiously, going…"We think you should unload that Paris apartment, Max." And him going "I dunno…She's over eighty, now. She can't hang on, forever!"…*I love it! (Suddenly, MATHIAS's laughter stops. His smile fades.)* Oh, my God! He did it, again! *(And then…)* He got me, again.

MATHILDE: Is something the matter?

MATHIAS: *(Not at all happy.)* No. I'm fine. *(Small silence. And then…)* I used the last penny I had on the plane ticket getting here. There's nothing left. There's *less* than nothing left! This was my last hope.

MATHILDE: This apartment?

MATHIAS: This apartment.

(MATHIAS goes to the window, looks outside.)

MATHILDE: Well, you do own it.

(MATHIAS looks at MATHILDE.)

MATHILDE: *(Explains.)* You just need to be patient.

(MATHIAS laughs, again…His laugh is a profoundly deep and unhappy laugh. MATHILDE watches him, carefully.)

MATHILDE: Where will you stay? Do you have friends in Paris?

MATHIAS: Nobody.

MATHILDE: Will you go back to New York?

MATHIAS: I dunno'. How? Why?

MATHILDE: You have an apartment in New York?

MATHIAS: Not any more, no.

MATHILDE: Weren't you planning to go back?

MATHIAS: After I had the money from selling this place…I guess. I dunno'. Maybe.

MATHILDE: You have a plane ticket home?

(MATHIAS doesn't answer.)

MATHILDE: How old are you?

(*MATHIAS doesn't answer.*)

MATHILDE: More than fifty?

MATHIAS: No. Well, yes. Fifty-*ish*. Fifty and three months.

MATHILDE: How did you get to be more than fifty and three months, and have so little to show for it?

MATHIAS: You shouldn't beat around the bush. I mean, don't be subtle. I mean, if you want to ask me something that's a little, you know, cruel, just, you know, *ask* it. Don't be subtle. Just ask it.
(*Beat.*)

MATHILDE: I'm ninety-two. Subtlety is not something that interests me, anymore.
(*Beat.*)

MATHIAS: I'm a loser. (*Beat.*) I've never actually said that out loud, before, but, it's true: I'm a loser. (*MATHILDE says nothing.*) Some people, basically, win; and some people, basically, lose. I lose. When I had some money, back when I was in my twenties, before my father dumped me, I invested in the market…the stock market…like my father, except, whatever *I* bought went down, immediately. My broker started advising me to buy short…you know…buy stocks with an *eye* to them going down. (*MATHIAS looks away. And then…*) Everything I bought short went up. After a while, my broker started investing his own money against me. He did very well. (*Beat.*)

My first wife left me nine months after we got married, twenty-five years ago. My second marriage lasted a bit longer, and I wish it didn't. My third wife ended up in an arcane Tibetan sect. (*Beat.*)

I've never had children. I didn't think it would be right to bring kids into this particular world…not with me as their father. Enough's enough. A joke's a joke. A loser's a loser.

MATHILDE: You're pathetic.

MATHIAS: Yes, I am. I am definitely pathetic.

MATHILDE: (*Goes to desk, finds a key, which SHE gives to MATHIAS.*) Take this.

MATHIAS: Why?

MATHILDE: It's the key to this door. The main door, the one on the street, opens with a code: R254. There, it's written on the key-holder. You can stay here for a while…until you know what you're doing. Do you have any luggage?

MATHIAS: Just the one bag.

MATHILDE: That's it? That's all you have?

MATHIAS: That's it.

MATHILDE: If you kill yourself, they win.

MATHIAS: Yuh. I know.

MATHILDE: So, be patient.

MATHIAS: I don't know why I'm telling you all this?

MATHILDE: It's because you're in a country that isn't your home. I've noticed that, myself, whenever I've traveled. Being in a strange country like France frees you. Nobody here in France remembers anything about you, because nobody *knows* you. You can reinvent yourself. Here, you can be whatever you want to be...Unless you're French. If you're French, you're screwed. *(Smiles at own use of "screwed.")* Go, take a walk for a while. Walk near the Seine. It's beautiful. But, don't jump in. You'd probably fail to kill yourself and just catch a dreadful cold, instead. Supper is at seven, sharp. Don't be late, or I'll start eating without you.
(MATHIAS smiles.)

MATHILDE: This is France. We French are known for our "joie de vivre"...a joy of life. You Americans seem to have more of a "joie de *se plaindre*" .. a joy of complaint. So, when you're out walking, act French. You'll feel happier. Just don't *speak* French, okay?

MATHIAS: Okay.

MATHILDE: Oh, I'll have to charge you rent for staying here. Not much, but, something. I'm an old lady. I always need extra money and I'm sure you have *some* money. I mean, your watch is gold.
(MATHIAS laughs, hands his watch to MATHILDE, who takes it, smiles.)

MATHIAS: You're a pirate, Madame Giffard.

MATHILDE: Oui. C'est vrai. This is true.
(Lights crossfade to...)

SCENE TWO

The next morning. MUSIC IN...Albinoni, pained, single cello. LIGHTS UP ON...CHLOÉ, wearing a winter coat, scarf, hat, and gloves. SHE stands near the door. CHLOÉ is Mathilde's daughter. She is beautiful, tall, and mysterious. CHLOÉ is just slightly younger than MATHIAS; just as nervous.

CHLOÉ: *(In French.)* Comment ça tu n'es pas seule? [What do you mean you're "not alone?"]

MATHILDE: *(In French.)* Je ne suis pas seule signifie que je ne suis pas seule. [I'm not alone means I'm not alone.]

CHLOÉ: *(Looking around room.)* Il n'y a personne d'autre dans cette pièce. [There's nobody else in the room.]

MATHILDE: Je n'ai pas dit que je n'étais pas seule dans cette pièce. J'ai dit que je n'étais pas seule. [I didn't say I wasn't alone in the room. I said I wasn't alone.]

CHLOÉ: Tu veux dire qu'il y a quelqu'un d'autre dans cet appartement? [You mean there's somebody elsewhere in the apartment?]

MATHILDE: Mais qu'est-ce qui te prend? [What is the *matter* with you?]

CHLOÉ: Où ça? C'est qui? [Where else? Who?]

(MATHIAS enters wearing a plaid bathrobe over his nonmatching plaid flannel pyjamas.)

MATHILDE: *(In English.)* Chloé, this is Mathias; Mathias, this is Chloé.

MATHIAS: Oh, hi…Bonjour. Do you speak English?

CHLOÉ: Who *are* you?

MATHIAS: Me? I'm Mathias Gold. From New York. I, uh, inherited this apartment. *(Smiles.)* I own the apartment and I own Madame Giffard… until she dies. After she dies, I only own the apartment.

(CHLOÉ stares, unamused.)

MATHIAS: That's sort of a joke. *(And then…)* Do you work for Madame Giffard?

MATHILDE: Chloé is my daughter. She's been on holiday in the Aveyron.

MATHIAS: Oh, well…*Hiii!* Your mother invited me to stay over, last night.

CHLOÉ: *Why?*

MATHIAS: Why? Well, I guess 'cause I was *planning* on staying here. I mean, I didn't know you and your mother were living here. I thought the apartment was empty and…

MATHILDE: He had no other place to stay.

MATHIAS: I had no other place to stay.

(Wordlessly, CHLOÉ turns and walks into the corridor leading to the back bedrooms. There is a small, embarrassed pause. And then…)

MATHIAS: She seems upset.

MATHILDE: Seems so.

MATHIAS: Did she leave?

MATHILDE: No, she's probably checking the bedrooms to see where you slept.

MATHIAS: Why would she…? I mean, where does she…? You don't think she thinks…? *(And then…)* Are you *kidding?*

(*CHLOÉ re-enters.*)

CHLOÉ: How long are you staying?

MATHIAS: In Paris?

CHLOÉ: *Here.* How long are you staying *here*?

MATHIAS: Oh, well, I don't know. *(Beat.)* I'm paying rent!

CHLOÉ: Why?

MATHIAS: Why what?

CHLOÉ: Why are you paying rent?

MATHIAS: Well, I…

MATHILDE: *(To CHLOÉ; in French.)* Et moi, je suis invisible? [Am I invisible?]

CHLOÉ: *(In French.)* Sors de cette pièce. [Leave the room.]

MATHILDE: Pardon? [Excuse me?]

CHLOÉ: Sors de cette pièce! Je veux lui parler, personnellement, sans tes interruptions! Sors de cette piéce! [Leave the room! I want to talk to him, privately, with you not interrupting. Leave the room.]

MATHILDE: Je crois plutôt que non. [I don't think so.]

CHLOÉ: *(Angrily, with great authority; in French.)* Sors de cette piéce! [*Leave the room!*]

(*Wordlessly, MATHILDE exits the room. CHLOÉ closes the door behind Mathilde, locks it; turns and sees MATHIAS drinking a whiskey "nip."*)

CHLOÉ: I know who you are and I know why you're here.

MATHIAS: Excellent! Let's start with those two things. Who am I and why am I here?

CHLOÉ: My mother is ninety-four years old.

MATHIAS: She told me ninety-*two*.

CHLOÉ: She always lies about her age. She wants people to think she's younger. She's ninety-four.

MATHIAS: She definitely had me fooled.

CHLOÉ: I want you out of here. By law, you have no access to this place, until she dies. Anyway, there's great question whether you can legally own this apartment in "heritage." If you continue to trespass, I'll have you arrested and I'll have the entire contract invalidated, immediately.

MATHIAS: How can I "trespass," if I'm paying rent?

CHLOÉ: It's exactly what I thought you'd say. Fine. I have a clear plan of legal action. I…

MATHIAS: To "trespass" connotes crossing some sort of forbidden line. The implication is *encroachment, infringement*…intrusion, invasion, *violation!* I am paying *rent!*…

CHLOÉ: Our lawyers will deal with this. Our lawyers and the police!...

MATHIAS: Wait a minute, wait a minute, wait a minute! Could we just start over, here? *(Big false smile and greeting.)* Hi. I'm Mathias Gold. My friends call me Jim. I'm visiting from New York. I'm renting a room here from your mother. I pay her money. We have a deal. I...

CHLOÉ: *(Not amused.)* I have no time for this! I think there's something I should say, simply and clearly: if you're not out of this apartment by two o'clock, this afternoon, our lawyers will petition the police to remove you.

MATHIAS: *Excuse me! Stop!...*Excuse me, but, I think there's something that *I* should say, simply and clearly...

(MATHIAS checks to see that Mathilde cannot overhear. And then...)

MATHIAS: Get the fuck out of my face, lady! This apartment is *my* apartment. My father paid kazillion dollars for it and he left it to me and I own it. I don't care if your mother's five hundred years old, I own it...not her, not you...not anybody but me! I own it and I'm going to sell it as soon as I can. Once I've got the money in my pocket, I will be gone, and not a minute sooner!

(CHLOÉ stares at MATHIAS, coldly, wordlessly. HE feels her hatred; tries a more reasonable voice.)

MATHIAS: Look, I've talked to a bunch of very savvy real estate people, and I know pretty much what this place is worth, so, I can understand what you're pissed off about...but, you can't change what is. What is, is. My father bought this place, legally. He paid through the teeth for almost thirty years. He left it to me, and, believe me, I need the money, and I intend to *get* the money! So, whatever ideas you've got in your head, *forget about it.* Save yourself a lot of grief.

(CHLOÉ walks to the door through which Mathilde exited the room. SHE unlocks and opens the door.

(We see...MATHILDE standing just inside. SHE has obviously heard everything that's been said, and SHE is not happy.)

CHLOÉ: *(To MATHILDE.)* Tu l'as entendu? Oui? Simple? Clear? He'll have you dead or out on the street. He owes you nothing. He cares nothing about you. He cares about nothing, but money. Tu l'ai entendu, ouais?

CHLOÉ: *(Walks to MATHIAS, squares off with him, eyeball to eyeball.)* I will destroy you.

(CHLOÉ turns, exits apartment through front door. MATHILDE and MATHIAS share a stare for a moment...and then...MATHILDE turns away, exits into the back rooms of the apartment. MATHIAS goes to the

*window, looks outside, down into the Jardin Luxembourg. HE bows his
head, sadly.)*
(The lights crossfade to…)

SCENE THREE

*Later, that night. MUSIC IN…John Coltrane, single sax, slow and pro-
foundly sad.*
    *LIGHTS UP ON…MATHIAS at table, napkin stuffed in his shirt,
finishing a meal. HE refills his wineglass. HE is slightly drunk. HE calls off
to MATHILDE.*

MATHIAS: I came here a few times when I was little. I remember some long,
    thin strips of tart, green-apple-flavored candy.
    (MATHILDE enters, wheeling small trolley with coffee and dessert.)
MATHIAS: *(Makes move to take trolley.)* I'll do that.
MATHILDE: *(Pulling trolley back, away from MATHIAS.)* No, please!…
    (MATHIAS stops in his tracks.)
MATHILDE: I enjoy doing this.
MATHIAS: Sorry.
MATHILDE: I'm fine. Really. The trolley gives me balance.
MATHIAS: I just wanted to help.
MATHILDE: If I allow people to help too much, they don't help at all.
MATHIAS: I see what you mean.
    (MATHILDE serves dessert.)
MATHIAS: I guess I never came to France, when I was older, because it
    would have pleased my father too much.
MATHILDE: Why would it have pleased him?
MATHIAS: My father liked France, a lot. He *loved* France. He was here,
    quite a bit, on account of his business, I guess. He had some family here,
    too, *before* the War. And he had his own place, a big apartment, some-
    where not far from here. So, he was in France a lot. My brothers never
    came here, either. My mother would have killed us if we did. France was
    like some kind of enemy for her.
MATHILDE: And why was that? Why was France like an enemy?
MATHIAS: Because *he* was here, so much. Because France was something he
    loved more than her, more than us, more than he loved his family.
MATHILDE: You have brothers?

MATHIAS: I *had* brothers. They're both gone. Dead.

MATHIAS: Why are there guns all over the walls in my room?

MATHILDE: They were my husband's. He was a hunter.

MATHIAS: Professionally?

MATHILDE: *(Laughs.)* Nooooo. He was a businessman. His passion was safari hunting in Africa. Tea?

MATHIAS: Thank you. *(Serves tea.)* Du sucre?

MATHIAS: No, thank you. Just milk.

MATHILDE: You're lucky you weren't staying here, a few months ago. We've just sold his animal heads. They were on the walls in the library. Lions, tigers, zebra…

MATHIAS: Carnage.

MATHILDE: *(Smiles.)* Exactly. Un carnage. *(Sits; smiles.)* You were telling me about your brothers.

MATHIAS: They were twins…Jacques and Alain.

MATHILDE: French names, all of you.

MATHIAS: French-Jewish. We were named for my father's French family. Jacques for our grandfather Jacob, and Alain for my father's favorite uncle. I don't know who I was named for.

MATHILDE: They were older than you?

MATHIAS: My brothers? Oh, yuh. A lot. Nearly ten years older than me. Alain died when he was still fairly young. Jacques *just* died, a few months before my father died. Heart attack.

MATHILDE: I see.

MATHIAS: My father's will was complicated, because, he'd left everything to Jacques, but, then, after Jacques died, he changed everything, and ended up leaving his money the way he did to…you know…charity.

MATHILDE: And not to you?

MATHIAS: And not to me.

MATHILDE: You were surprised?

MATHIAS: By that? Not really. My father and I weren't ever, you know, *pals!*…I mean, well, no, I wasn't surprised.

MATHILDE: Did your brothers have children?

MATHIAS: Jacques did. Jacques has a son who isn't quite right. *(Beat.)* In the head.

MATHILDE: Oh.

MATHIAS: Jacques and his wife were divorced, early on. Right after their son was diagnosed.

MATHILDE: It's sad.

MATHIAS: Not as sad as a bad marriage.

MATHILDE: I suppose.

MATHIAS: I *know!* I grew up in one. *(Beat.)* Not mine. My father's. But, then, I had my own.

MATHILDE: That's the classic way, I suppose. The sins of the father visited on the son.

MATHIAS: And vice versa.

MATHILDE: I suppose.

MATHIAS: I just said that. I don't actually know what it means. *(Beat.)* I do, actually. Children are like a terrible mirror. Children imitate their parents and parents see themselves, clearly…in the image of their children.

MATHILDE: I suppose.

MATHIAS: That's why so many parents smack their children…Because they recognize so many things in their children that they despise in themselves.

MATHILDE: I suppose.

MATHIAS: *(Laughs.)* Listen to me, pretending like I know something. *(Small pause. And then…)* Is your daughter married?

MATHILDE: My daughter? Married?…Non. Pas du tout. *(Beat. And then…)* Is *that* what you've been getting at?

MATHIAS: Noooo! *(Beat.)* I suppose I was. Your mind is awfully sharp for ninety-four.

MATHILDE: *(Quickly.)* Ninety-two.

MATHIAS: *(Just as quickly.)* Ninety-two.

MATHILDE: Why shouldn't it be?

MATHIAS: No reason.

MATHILDE: Irrespective of your disagreement with Chloé, in fact, ownership of this apartment is quite clear, legally. I own it, and I'll decide who stays here and who doesn't.

MATHIAS: Thank you.

MATHILDE: Not at all.

> *(MATHILDE looks away. Three count. SHE then turns; looks at MATHIAS, directly. Her mood has changed…)*

MATHILDE: I know you want me dead.

MATHIAS: I don't!…

MATHILDE: Of course, you do. I know what a "viager" is, what it causes. It's no matter to me. I have no intention of dying until I'm bloody well ready, so, no matter what you want or think, you'll have to be patient. You'll get your money when I'm ready, and not a moment before.

(The lights crossfade to…)

SCENE FOUR

Afternoon, next day. MUSIC IN…BACH, cello, slow, sad. LIGHTS UP ON…CHLOÉ and MATHIAS at table. CHLOÉ's coat is thrown over the back chair, next to her. THEY each have a cup of coffee in front of them. There is a coffee tray in front of Mathias that implies that he has served the coffee, not CHLOÉ. There is a manuscript on the table in front of Mathias…several pages of paper, a bottle of ink, a fountain pen. Also, a half-drunk bottle of Evian [water] and a half-filled (half-empty) glass.

CHLOÉ: It's really not that I hate you, personally, so much as I hate our circumstance.

MATHIAS: Exactly. You couldn't possibly hate me, personally. It's too soon. Give it another week or so.

CHLOÉ: I have no choice.

MATHIAS: This is true. How, exactly, do you see our circumstance?

CHLOÉ: Hopeless. Totally hopeless.

MATHIAS: Ahhhh, welllll! This is my kind of circumstance!

CHLOÉ: You cannot imagine what it's like for me knowing that I can never have the apartment I grew up in…that it's been sold out from under me…for money. That it's…

MATHIAS: It's only an apartment.

CHLOÉ: I remember my father saying that…exactly what you just said… when my dog died…"It's only a dog."

MATHIAS: Who was your father?

CHLOÉ: Only a father.

MATHIAS: Am I supposed to say "touché?"

CHLOÉ: My father was a businessman. He was older than my mother. He's been dead since I was twenty-two. I've done without him for a long time.

MATHIAS: Did you hunt with him? You seem to have a killing spirit.

CHLOÉ: *(Smiles.)* The guns.

MATHIAS: The guns. I'm sorry I missed the animal heads. Carnage on the wall can be quite comforting. You feel as if it's happened, already, rather than it's about to happen.

CHLOÉ: You're quite good-humoured.

MATHIAS: It's a racial thing. If you don't laugh, you cry. *(Beat.)* Was he Jewish?...Your father.

CHLOÉ: *(Smiles.)* No.

MATHIAS: Why'd you smile?

CHLOÉ: My father was not particularly friendly toward Jews.

MATHIAS: Oh. Was he like *against* Jews, in the War kind of thing?

CHLOÉ: I would have to say "yes."

MATHIAS: Oh. Well. How *about* that? I guess I'd heard that there were two or three Frenchmen who weren't in the Resistance. Hell of a coincidence that one of them would turn out to be your dad! Did he make a lot of money with the Germans?

CHLOÉ: Some.

MATHIAS: How about your mother?

CHLOÉ: *(Smiles, mysteriously.)* How *about* my mother?

MATHIAS: Was she against Jews?

CHLOÉ: I wouldn't think so.

MATHIAS: Was she against Mittérand?

CHLOÉ: Mittérand? She never liked Mittérand. He was her student, a hundred years ago, when she first started teaching school. I think she preferred De Gaulle. Actually, she didn't like De Gaulle, either. Politically, my mother always preferred Marcel Marceau.

MATHIAS: Is that a joke?

CHLOÉ: It is.

MATHIAS: I admire that. Your wit. I've always admired a rapid-fire, slashing wit.

CHLOÉ: I'm sure you have.

MATHIAS: Your mother's mind is, as they say, sharp.

CHLOÉ: Yes, it is. Her brain is the one muscle she never fails to exercise. My mother's imagination is somehow being liberated in her old age. Old people express their innermost thoughts, openly, directly, without constricting "politesse"...politeness. A lack of politeness seems to define the artistic nature. It's quite interesting, don't you think?

MATHIAS: Don't I *think*? Is that your question? Don't I *think*?

CHLOÉ: Don't you think it's interesting that a lack of politeness seems to define the artistic nature?

MATHIAS: No, I don't, actually.

CHLOÉ: Think it's interesting?

MATHIAS: Agree with you. Your lack of politeness doesn't give me the slightest *inkling* of an artistic nature. And my artistic nature doesn't so much connect to a lack of politeness as it does a lack of cash. Which brings us back to why I'm here, doesn't it?

CHLOÉ: I apologize. *(Glances at his manuscript.)* Am I interrupting your work?

MATHIAS: My work? *(Realizes.)* Oh, no…I was just trying to write something.

CHLOÉ: *(Glancing closer at top page.)* A story?

MATHIAS: *(Covers pages by stacking them.)* A kind of story.

CHLOÉ: Do you normally write? Is that what you do for work?

MATHIAS: Oh, no. I did write, quite a lot, actually, years ago, when I was younger. I wrote a couple of novels. Two.

CHLOÉ: Would I have read either of them?

MATHIAS: No. They were never published.

CHLOÉ: I see.

MATHIAS: I'm sure it's obvious. *(Beat.)* Do you work?

CHLOÉ: I teach.

MATHIAS: What?

CHLOÉ: What what?

MATHIAS: What do you teach?

CHLOÉ: English.

MATHIAS: Like your mother.

CHLOÉ: Like my mother.

MATHIAS: Where?

CHLOÉ: Where what?

MATHIAS: Where do you teach?

CHLOÉ: In my mother's school.

MATHIAS: I didn't know that. I mean, I didn't know your mother had a school.

CHLOÉ: She does. She did. In Neuilly. We sold it. She sold it.

MATHIAS: But, you still work there?…

CHLOÉ: I was part of the sale. As long as I live and the school continues to operate, I continue to teach. They are obliged to keep me there…to employ me.

MATHIAS: Your mother organized that?

CHLOÉ: My mother and her advisor.

MATHIAS: *(Makes quick note on manuscript page.)* That's great!…

CHLOÉ: Are we the story?

(MATHIAS looks up.)

CHLOÉ: Are you writing about us?

MATHIAS: *(Sings.)* "You're so vain…I'll bet you think this story's about you!…Don't you?…Don't you?…" *(Laughs.)* It interests me, that your mother sold this apartment with herself in it, as part of the deal, and she also sold the school with you in it, as part of that deal. It interests me.

CHLOÉ: She was in it, too…in the school contract. They were obliged to let her teach as long as she was able…as long as she wanted to, really. *(Beat.)* To teach. *(Beat.)* My mother taught English from the time she was twenty-two til last year…last January.

MATHIAS: *(Calculates in his head…)* Seventy-two years.

CHLOÉ: Seventy-two years.

MATHIAS: She's amazing! Why did she quit?

CHLOÉ: She had a fall, last winter. She broke her arm. It scared her, getting to school and back. It's in the *banlieue*…the suburbs.

MATHIAS: Why did she fall?

CHLOÉ: There was no underlying neurological reason. She slipped on some ice. I didn't mean to get your hopes up. Sorry.

MATHIAS: I'm not a vulture, by nature, Mademoiselle Giffard. In fact, I like your mother a lot. As you, yourself, said, so succintly, it's the circumstance.

CHLOÉ: Is that why you've talked with her doctors, three times, this week? *(Smiles.)* You call *them*, they call *me*. Does this surprise you? *(No reply. CHLOÉ continues.)* We have in France an old woman, the oldest in France, the oldest in the *world,* in fact. Jeanne Calmant. She's a hundred and twenty-[two] years old, at the moment, and still going strong. She sold her apartment in a "viager" contract with her lawyer, when she was seventy-five. Her lawyer paid her several thousand francs a month for nearly fifty years, until *he* died, several months ago. A "viager" can be a very bad gamble. French woman can live a long time. It's the red wine and the oysters.

MATHIAS: As I said before, Mademoiselle Giffard, it's only an apartment…May I call you "Chloé?"

CHLOÉ: No. Please, don't.

MATHIAS: *Really?*

CHLOÉ: Really.

MATHIAS: Okay, I won't. Is "Mademoiselle Giffard" okay?

CHLOÉ: "Mademoiselle Giffard" is fine, Mister Gold.

MATHIAS: *(Practices saying Chloé's name with a studied French accent.)* Mademoiselle Giffard…Mademoiselle Giffard…Mademoiselle Giffard…

Mademoiselle Giffard…*(Smiles.)* I like it. I like saying Mademoiselle Giffard better than Chloé.

CHLOÉ: I'm pleased to have pleased you, Mister Gold.

MATHIAS: And I'm pleased you're pleased I'm pleased. I have an offer for you, Mademoiselle Giffard.

CHLOÉ: I thought you might.

MATHIAS: Let me sell this apartment, now, and I'll divide the money between us, 75/25…meaning…

CHLOÉ: I imagine the 75 is you and the 25 is us.

MATHIAS: Well, I…Yes, that's what I propose. I'll keep 75% of the sale price, and you'll keep 25%…less legal fees, of course, which should come off the top.

CHLOÉ: We won't allow you to sell the apartment, Mister Gold.

MATHIAS: Most of the rooms in this apartment are boarded up, for Chris'sakes! I could sell off ten rooms and you wouldn't even notice they were gone!

CHLOÉ: It's not an acceptable offer, Mister Gold.

MATHIAS: *(Without hesitation.)* How's 70/30?

CHLOÉ: Not 50/50, not 40/60.

MATHIAS: You want 70% for *yourself!?* Jesus! I…

CHLOÉ: Not 30/70, not 20/80, not 10/90.

MATHIAS: What do you want?

CHLOÉ: I want to buy the apartment from you. I'm prepared to offer seven thousand francs a square meter.

MATHIAS: This apartment is worth five times that!

CHLOÉ: It's not a matter of it's monetary worth, it's market value. It's a matter of it's rightful owner. My mother's grandfather built this building. This apartment was designed and built for him. It's a matter of keeping this apartment in this family. It's a matter of…

MATHIAS: What family? *What family?* She's got one daughter: you. You've got to be close to my age, fifty, yes? What family are you talking about? Are you planning to have a bunch of kids? Is there a *famille cachée?* What family are you talking about?

CHLOÉ: I would pay you more if I could afford to. I have no money. Neither does my mother. We were renting out rooms for some time, but, it was too much for my mother, and it's not an acceptable way to live…not for a woman of my mother's intelligence and spirit.

MATHIAS: Fine. Okay. Fine. Let me try a whole other kind of idea. We can subdivide the apartment. We can make two apartments…a small one for you and your mother; and I sell the rest and leave.

CHLOÉ: Unacceptable.

MATHIAS: *(Angrily.) What the hell do you mean "unacceptable!"?*

CHLOÉ: Unacceptable can only mean one thing: unacceptable.

MATHIAS: Has anybody ever said "fuck you" to you, before?

CHLOÉ: Not in English.

MATHIAS: Fuck you, Mademoiselle Giffard.

CHLOÉ: It's easy to see why you've had no success in business.

MATHIAS: This is true.

CHLOÉ: For the moment, we are stuck with each other, Mister Gold…until I figure out what to do. I can't possibly find the kind of money you'll want. I mean, I *could*. I could borrow it from a bank, I suppose, using the apartment as security. But, then, the loan would be enormous and I couldn't possibly make the repayments, and the bank would take the apartment from me. So, here we are.

MATHIAS: Here we are. I'm sure we can find a way to settle this, rationally, if not amicably, *Mademoiselle Giffard*, if we both keep our wits about us, and our good humor, and our best manners. So, let's agree to stay calm, *Mademoiselle Giffard*. You stay calm, I'll stay calm. I promise.

CHLOÉ: I'm quite calm.

MATHIAS: As am I.

CHLOÉ: As long as my mother stays alive, you can do nothing. If she lives a while longer, she'll probably outlive you. You turn bright red when you yell, so, you probably won't live a particularly long life. We must remember, always, Jeanne Calmant, the woman who outlived her lawyer. She was one hundred and twenty-two when *he* died. We mustn't forget this.

MATHIAS: Fuck you, Mademoiselle Giffard.

CHLOÉ: Et nique ta Mère, pauvre crétin.

(MATHILDE, just risen from a midmorning nap, enters from back bedroom; sees CHLOÉ and MATHIAS at the table, together; smiles.)

MATHILDE: Ahhh! C'est gentil, ça! You're chatting and having a coffee, together. You're getting along. This pleases me.

(MATHIAS and CHLOÉ look up at each. THEY share a smile.)

(The lights crossfade to…)

SCENE FIVE

Thursday afternoon. Django Reinhardt music (possibly "In The Still Of The Night") plays lightly, under the scene.

    MATHILDE sits in her chair reading a fat novel. SHE wears thick eyeglasses. To further assist her reading/vision, she uses a large magnifying glass, from time to time. A notebook is opened on the table next to her. From time to time, SHE looks up from her reading to make a note or two in this notebook.

    A dinner tray is in evidence on the table next to her, set with soup, bread...There is a newspaper opened on the tray.

    MATHIAS sits at the dining table, writing. His stack of manuscript pages has grown. There is a bowl of soup on the table near his manuscript.

    After a few moments of this and nothing more, MATHILDE looks up from her reading...SHE speaks to MATHIAS.

MATHILDE: Sorry to bother you, again...

    (MATHIAS looks up from his writing.)

MATHILDE: What's another way of saying "wang?"

MATHIAS: What are you reading?

MATHILDE: An American novel by a former student of Philippe *[sic.]* Roth.

MATHIAS: Oh.

MATHILDE: "Wang" is an Oriental dynasty, isn't it?

MATHIAS: What's the context?

MATHILDE: *(Reads.)* "His blood-filled wang was in her mouth when the teakettle's whistle whistled."

MATHIAS: In that context, it's inexplicable.

MATHILDE: Inexplicable?

MATHILDE: Totally inexplicable.

MATHILDE: Does that mean it's smut?

MATHIAS: It does, yuh...It's smut.

MATHILDE: Thank you.

    (SHE goes back to her reading; HE to his writing. And then...)

MATHIAS: How would you translate...uh...*(Checks his notes.)*..."Nique ta mère, pauvre crétin"...?

MATHILDE: What's the context?

MATHIAS: It's something your daughter said to me.

MATHILDE: Did she?

MATHIAS: She did.

MATHILDE: It's untranslatable.

MATHIAS: I thought it might be.

(The music ends. The needle produces a loud, annoying scratching sound, as the turntable continues to turn. MATHIAS looks at the phonograph and then looks at MATHILDE. SHE seems unaware of the sound.)

MATHIAS: I'll get it. *(Pauses.)* Shall I?

MATHILDE: Please.

(MATHIAS stands, replaces the needle at the start of the record. The music recommences. HE goes back to the table; sits, begins writing, again. Only now, does MATHILDE acknowledge that the music had stopped...)

MATHILDE: *(Without looking up from her reading.)* Thank you.

MATHIAS: *(Looks up, surprised; smiles.)* You're welcome.

MATHILDE: *(Closing her book.)* I discovered the stories of Anaïs Nin when I was young. Discovering Philippe Roth and his friends at 92 is not as exciting.

MATHIAS: I s'pose that's true. Who gave you that particular book to read?

MATHILDE: My daughter.

MATHIAS: Really?

MATHILDE: We read as many American and British writers as we can, especially the more colloquial writers. We learn the most new language from the more colloquial writers.

MATHIAS: I've read a bunch of Roth novels. I've never read Anaïs Nin. Maybe I'll wait til I'm 92.

MATHILDE: It could be dangerous.

MATHIAS: Thanks for the warning.

(MATHILDE listens to the music for a moment.)

MATHILDE: Listen a moment! You hear this...?

(A particularly intricate phrase of improvised jazz passes.)

MATHILDE: Beautiful.

MATHIAS: Nice. I think that's called a "riff."

MATHILDE: Exactly. I watched Django Reinhardt play guitar at the Hot Club de Paris, often, during the 1930s...Perhaps fifty times. He had two damaged fingers. I had a romantic liaison with Django Reinhardt, briefly. It was more a flirtation than anything else. A diversion. I was married. It wasn't anything we'd planned. It was spontaneous. How do you say it? A *fling*. It was a fling.

MATHIAS: You had a fling with Django Reinhart?

MATHILDE: I did. I remember, in those days, jazz was considered to be hot.

Le Hot Club de Paris. And I remember, some years later on, jazz was considered to be cool. I can also remember, more recently, jazz was hot, again. If you live long enough, opposites collide...come together.

MATHIAS: Which is it, now? Hot or cool?

MATHILDE: I'm out of touch. I've lost track.

MATHIAS: Did you know Django Reinhardt's *wife*, as well?

MATHILDE: I did. Not well, but, I knew her.

MATHIAS: You taught Mittérand when he was a boy, and you had a fling with Django Reinhardt...?

MATHILDE: *(Interjects...)*...Briefly....

MATHIAS: Briefly.

MATHILDE: I did, both of those things, yes.

MATHIAS: Coltrane and Miles?

MATHILDE: I knew them both, quite well, yes. More recently, of course, than when I knew Django. I'd say the 1950s.

MATHIAS: Henry Miller?

MATHILDE: Well, yes, of course, I knew Henry Miller. Everyone in Paris knew Henry Miller.

MATHIAS: James Joyce? Ernest Hemmingway?

MATHILDE: I knew Joyce, quite well. I met Hemmingway. Not very interesting. Bulls, bells, balls...

MATHIAS: Could I ask you something?

MATHILDE: You could.

MATHIAS: Did you ever, like, date Sigmund Freud?

MATHILDE: Pardon?

MATHIAS: I was joking.

MATHILDE: I see.

(Beat.)

MATHILDE: If you live long enough, you meet the most wonderful people. If you live too long, you outlive them all. Nothing in life is only good or only bad. It's always a question of balance. *(Beat.)*

I knew Mittérand...not well, but, well enough. I was teaching English, part-time, in a Catholic school in Angoulème in the southwest. He was my student. He wasn't distinguished, but, I remember him. He was a clever boy. There was no question he would make a success of himself. He never walked away from his enemies. In some strange way, he knew how to seduce them into believing that they were friends...and then, he had his way with them. The kiss of the spiderman. He charmed his teachers, especially the ones who disliked him, initially. He was a natural

politician. He was extremely conservative, politically. I wasn't at all surprised that he was a collaborator in the Vichy government. I suppose,
near the end of the War, when he saw the Nazis couldn't possibly win,
he joined the Resistance. But, he never stopped being friendly with the
butcher Bousquet, did he? Or Kohl in Germany.

MATHIAS: Are you Jewish, Madame Giffard?

MATHILDE: No. I'm not. There were times in my life when I wished I were
Jewish. Somebody I loved a great deal was Jewish, and for him I wished
I could have been Jewish, too. Not that I admire the Jewish rules any
more than I admire the Catholic rules. I adore eating my "coquillages"
and "saucisson," shellfish and sausage, both of which are forbidden to
Jews. And I think that graven images, especially photographs, also forbidden to Jews, can be simply, absolutely, *thrilling*. I would have been a
sinning Jew, all of my life, much the way I have been a sinning Catholic.
But, I do know for certain that the Jews in France, no matter what they
ate or didn't eat, deserved a far greater apology than Mittérand offered
them in his "Mémoires," his apologia without apology. And now, I
would like to drink my soup, before it gets cold. It's filled with shellfish
and pork, and could send many Jews straight to hell. *(Samples soup, likes
it; smiles.)*

MATHIAS: Did you know my father well?

MATHILDE: I knew your father very well.

MATHIAS: How well?

MATHILDE: Your father and I were lovers from the time I was twenty-six
until last year, when he died. I loved your father more than I've loved any
other human being in my entire lifetime. If you want to know who you
were named for, I'll tell you, although, it's obvious. You were named for
me. I am Mathilde and you are Mathias. *(SHE allows a pause. And
then...)* Does this shock you?

MATHIAS: Madame Giffard, in the simplest possible terms, I would have to
say this shocks the living piss out of me!

MATHILDE: Bon. Good.

(SHE smiles. HE does not.)

(The lights fade out.)

ACT TWO
SCENE ONE

Late, same night. In the darkness, we hear John Coltrane playing tenor sax on "Lazy Bird" (Blue Train, Blue Note CDP7-46095-2).

LIGHTS FADE UP ON…MATHILDE and MATHIAS sitting at the dining table, side by side, studying photographs. There are three large hatboxes on the table, as well as a tea tray, and evidence of a casually eaten meal in front of MATHILDE. The hatboxes overflow with dozens of black-and-white photographs, many of which stand in tall, Giacometti-like stacks. MATHIAS is drinking from a half-empty bottle of wine. HE is drunk.

MATHIAS: He was handsome, in a sort of middle-European way.

MATHILDE: He was quite handsome, I suppose, but, it was his self-confidence that made him so attractive. He had a great inner strength. He had a great lifeforce.

MATHIAS: *(Staring at photograph.)* I think he may have had some Slovenian blood. Don't you think he has a kind of ex-Yugoslavian look about him? *(And then…)* Most of all, what I see when I stare at this photograph…what I find so really shattering…is that he…looks so…happy.

MATHILDE: I think he was, until your mother became ill. Then, it was difficult for all of us. Our relationship changed. *(Studies photograph.)* That's got to be fifty years ago. Almost. Look at *you*…You can't be more than three.

MATHIAS: *Me?* That's *me?*

MATHILDE: That's you. And that's Chloé in my arms. You were both such sweet children.

MATHIAS: That's *me?* I was *here?*…

MATHILDE: Five or six times.

MATHIAS: I was in this *apartment?* Five or six times?

MATHILDE: Once your mother became ill, he never brought you again.

MATHIAS: I don't remember…I have no memory of this…of my being here. I was *here?*…This is so *crazy!* I…*(Suddenly.)* Were my brothers here, too?

MATHILDE: A few times. Not more than twice, and both times, only for a moment. Wait! I think one of the twins…your brother Alain…took this photo. I think it was Alain…and Jacques stayed at the hotel with your mother.

MATHIAS: Are you *kidding* me?

MATHILDE: I think it was Alain.

MATHIAS: Alain *knew* about all this?…About you and my father? I mean, if I'm two, in this picture, he's twelve!

MATHILDE: Don't you think that children know everything that goes on in a family? Don't you think that…

MATHIAS: *I* didn't! I mean…I knew my father had a lot of business in Paris…I mean, I knew he kept coming here…I knew my mother hated his coming here. I knew…

(Beat. And then.)

MATHIAS: This's me? This's really me? You're *sure* of this?! This is so *crazy!*…Did you know my mother? I mean, were you introduced to one another? Mathilde, je te présente Hannah, Hannah…

MATHILDE: Non! *Jamais!*

MATHIAS: You didn't ever, like, meet her, accidentally?

MATHILDE: No. I saw photographs of her. I saw them together, once, at Chez Lipp. I was walking home and they were just there, eating a meal, talking, like any of the dozen other married couples. They never saw me.

MATHIAS: Did you tell my father that you'd seen them?

MATHILDE: No.

MATHIAS: Did it bother you, seeing them together, making it real…that he had a wife?

MATHILDE: No. It pleased me. She was so beautiful, so *refined*. I thought he must have thought a lot of me…to have chosen me…when he was married to her.

MATHIAS: You weren't jealous?

MATHILDE: Why would I have been jealous?

MATHIAS: He was married to somebody else!

MATHILDE: *I* was married to somebody else!

MATHIAS: Oh, God! I forgot about that! What about your husband?

MATHILDE: What about my husband?

MATHIAS: Did he know?

MATHILDE: About your father? He knew there was somebody, but, not specifically your father. He didn't know that.

MATHIAS: And Chloé?

MATHILDE: She knew quite a lot…especially, in recent years…after her father was gone.

MATHIAS: Right.

MATHILDE: It was different for Chloé and me. You and your father weren't close.

MATHIAS: *(Laughs.)* I've never put it like that. *(Explains.)* "Not close" is such a polite way of saying what we were…what we weren't. Close. Not close. *(Beat.)*

There were times I would have killed him, if I could have gotten my hands on his throat. I would have choked him to death with my bare hands. There were times I hated him that much.

MATHILDE: It's a pity. Your father was something marvelous and you've missed out. *(Beat.)* And he missed out.

MATHIAS: That was kind. Thank you.

MATHILDE: Not at all.

MATHIAS: Please, take this question in the right spirit, but, if I may be so bold as to ask…did my father leave you anything?

MATHILDE: Money?

MATHIAS: Money would be one of things I was thinking about, yes?

MATHILDE: There is a small fund.

MATHIAS: Forgive me, but, how small?

MATHILDE: Quite small. I do, after all, have a roof over my head for the rest of my life…as you well know.

MATHIAS: As I well know.

MATHILDE: Your father was extremely fair with me. The fund he set up is more than enough for my food and for incidentals.

MATHIAS: Excuse me, but, did he…? I'm sorry to be indiscreet…

MATHILDE: Not at all. If there's something I'm not comfortable answering, I simply won't answer.

MATHIAS: Did he…my father…did my father leave any money to your daughter, to Chloé?

MATHILDE: Certainly not!

MATHIAS: You seem…emphatic.

MATHILDE: That would have been up to Chloé's own father to do such a thing.

MATHIAS: She did, then, have her own father?

MATHILDE: What are you asking?

MATHIAS: I'm asking if Chloé had her own father.

MATHILDE: Of course, she did.

MATHIAS: I'm not sure why that's a relief, but it is. *(Exhales, smiles. HE is relieved.)* Now, that, to me, spells Rolaids.

MATHILDE: Excuse me?

MATHIAS: Excuse you? I don't think so. Was Chloé ever close with her father?

MATHILDE: Close?

MATHIAS: Loving. Affectionate. Palzy-walzy. My mother used to say that: palzy-walzy. Were Chloé and her dad palzy-walzy?

MATHILDE: No. Not really palzy-walzy.

MATHIAS: I'm probably way out of line asking this, Madame Giffard, but, did Chloé's father, uh, leave her, uh, some money?

MATHILDE: He had none to leave.

MATHIAS: Oh.

MATHILDE: My husband was penniless when he died.

MATHIAS: Oh. *(Beat.)* How did that happen?

MATHILDE: It happened. It happens. You should know.

MATHIAS: I should and I do. Was he involved with the Germans?

(MATHILDE looks up.)

MATHIAS: During the War.

MATHILDE: Why would you ask such a question?

MATHIAS: I…I'm sorry. I just wondered. Your daughter Chloé said something to me…not directly…I mean, she didn't say, directly, that her father was, you know…What she said was more offhand, oblique…

MATHILDE: He was.

MATHIAS: He was?

MATHILDE: I had this conversation with your father, so many times…Probably, five *thousand* times!…

MATHIAS: And?

MATHILDE: He was so completely American in his thinking. And so are you.

MATHIAS: What does that mean?

MATHILDE: I am Europe, too old, always looking backwards, as often as I can, because what's ahead of me is…obvious. *(Beat.)* You are America… cynical, dissolute, bankrupt…yet, at the same time, you cannot believe the essential cruelty of people. You are gullible, naïve… *(Without pause.)* Your father's family lost everybody. You know that?

MATHIAS: I know very little.

MATHILDE: They lived not far from here, on Rue Vavin. The Germans went into their building and killed everybody…even their dogs.

MATHIAS: I know very little.

MATHILDE: It's a lovely building. *Trés chic.* 40,000 francs par mètre carré. Mostly rich Americans and Japanese live there, now. *(Beat. And then…)* It's not so much that people solve life's problems, or even find new ways to live. It's more that people forget the cruelty they've seen, and they forget all traces of the pain they've inflicted on others. And life goes on.

With us, or without us. *(Hands a photograph to MATHIAS.)* This is your father and I on the Côte d'Azur, at Cap d'Antibes. Bathing costumes were quite modest, then.

MATHIAS: *(Looks at photograph; smiles.)* You were beautiful.

MATHILDE: Do you think so?

MATHIAS: It's obvious.

MATHILDE: If I was beautiful, it's because your father made me so.

MATHIAS: Madame Giffard, it's really not easy for me to…*(Stops himself, midsentence.)* Did you love your husband?

MATHILDE: In my way.

MATHIAS: As opposed to somebody else's way?

MATHILDE: To answer simply, I stayed married to him.

MATHIAS: That is among the most complicated simple answers I have ever heard!

MATHILDE: I met your father a few years after I was married…less than two, in fact. From the moment I met him, I knew he would be the love of my life. And he was.

MATHIAS: Where was my mother?

MATHILDE: Here. They'd just met.

MATHIAS: Wait a minute, wait a minute! Are you telling me that my mother and father weren't married when you started…you know…doing the hoopie?

MATHILDE: I assume that means…

MATHIAS: It does, indeed!

MATHILDE: I was married. Your father and mother were on their way to live in America. I knew I'd be seeing him. I knew he'd be back in France, often, because of family. I…

MATHIAS: Wait a minute, wait a minute! My father married my mother *after* you two were lovers?

MATHILDE: A few years after, yes. Their twins were born a few years after that.

MATHIAS: Amazing!

MATHILDE: We were terribly young. Your father was practically penniless. My husband was already quite successful. It seemed the best plan…

MATHIAS: Bloodless!

MATHILDE: Excuse me?

MATHIAS: Both of you…Totally bloodless! If you and my father had taken a moral stand, done the right thing, gotten together, right away, whether he had money or not, you would have left your husband, no children, and he…

MATHILDE: In my day, such things were simply not done. I was from a proper Catholic family. My husband…

MATHIAS: This is beaucoup bullshit, ma chère madame!

MATHILDE: My husband would never have divorced me, or allowed me to divorce him, under any circumstance. Never. Not ever.

MATHIAS: Was he faithful to you?

MATHILDE: Your father?

MATHIAS: I hadn't even *thought* of that! I meant your husband.

MATHILDE: No. Not at all.

MATHIAS: What about my father?

MATHILDE: If you don't mind, I'd rather not answer.

MATHIAS: *Really? (Beat.)* Why is it, at my age, I'm still able to be shocked? You're right: Human cruelty still takes me by surprise.

MATHILDE: Please, don't become self-righteous!

MATHIAS: In what possible way am I becoming self-righteous?

MATHILDE: Why do you possibly think you know what a moral stand would be?…*The "right thing to do?"* Why would you know the right thing to do and I *not* know and your father not know? What is so especially clever about you and your way of understanding people and life? *Tell me!* I am really very anxious to know!

MATHIAS: I know my pain! I know the pain you brought to my life, and probably nothing but. *I don't like it!* I just don't like it.
(HE pours another drink. SHE knocks bottle and glass from his hand. They crash to the floor.)

MATHILDE: *Stop drinking!*

MATHIAS: *Why?* Does it make you *uncomfortable?* Do you think it's immoral?…Do you think it's not the right thing?

MATHILDE: I think it's just escape!…

MATHIAS: You are on the fucking *nose*, lady! Why ever would I want to stay sharply focussed? To see what? Hear what? For whom? No one's depending on me, particularly…*Ahhh!* Did you hear that? *Particularly?* Nobody's depending on me, *period!* End of thought. Madame Giffard, I am invisible. I never happened. If I could live my miserable life over again, I certainly, clearly, *would not!* My father willed me here. He pushed me into this room with you. *He's pulling the strings!*…Sorry! It's not working! Sorry, Madame Giffard, but, I'm not seeing the wonder of you in the slightest. And you're not helping me in the slightest. You look at me and you see some sort of hope. You see some sort of justification for what you did to me and several generations of my family…in the name of love! *Give it up!* You're not getting off the hook! What you did did me in! Did me in and…*(Suddenly.) AND YOU DON'T EVEN KNOW HOW TO FUCKING SAY "I'M SORRY!"*

(MATHIAS throws the empty bottle against the wall; turns and stares, wild-eyed, at MATHILDE. SHE speaks, quietly.)

MATHILDE: I'm sorry.

(There is a small silence. MATHILDE weeps.)

MATHILDE: Do you think that's what he wanted? Do you think that's why he sent you here? So, that I would say that…for both of us?

(MATHIAS turns and looks at MATHILDE. THEY hold eye contact, silently. MATHIAS wants to say more, but, he cannot. Instead, HE turns, exits into the back rooms, leaving MATHILDE alone in the room. SHE bows her head, sadly.)

(The lights crossfade to…)

SCENE TWO

Friday night. MUSIC IN…a single violin. LIGHTS UP ON…MATHIAS, drunk, sitting in Mathilde's chair. HE recites a Yeats poem from memory…

MATHIAS: "An aged man is but a paltry thing,
    A tattered coat upon a stick, unless
    Soul clap its hands and sing, and louder sing…"
    (CHLOÉ enters from back-bedroom. MATHIAS looks up.)

MATHIAS: How the hell could soul "clap its hands and sing?"

CHLOÉ: *(Pours glass of brandy from nearly empty bottle.)* Excuse me?

MATHIAS: *(Quickly, from memory.)*
    "An aged man is but a paltry thing,
    A tattered coat upon a stick, unless
    Soul clap its hands and sing, and louder sing…"
    (Without pause.) How the hell could soul "clap its hands and sing?"

CHLOÉ: That's my book. *(Takes book from him.)*

MATHIAS: Fine. Your mother loaned me *your* book of Yeats poems to read. In the face of that, I ask you (as you own the goddam book): How could soul "clap its hands and sing?"

CHLOÉ: I don't know. I don't care.
    (HE drinks glass of whiskey. SHE exits for a moment, to check on MATHILDE. MATHIAS calls after her, drinking, laughing…)

MATHIAS: Nique ta mère. Is she sleeping?

CHLOÉ: What do *you* care?

MATHIAS: I care.

CHLOÉ: She's sleeping.

MATHIAS: *(Drinking another glass of whiskey.)* Lucky girl.

CHLOÉ: In what sense?

MATHIAS: Excuse me?

CHLOÉ: In what sense am I a lucky girl?

MATHIAS: I didn't mean you. I meant your mother. In *no* sense are you a lucky girl. Perhaps, in the unlucky sense.

CHLOÉ: It's a pity you didn't know my father.

MATHIAS: In what sense?

CHLOÉ: He would have had your head on the wall, next to the other beasts.

MATHIAS: Ahhh. In the *carnage* sense. *(Smiles; drinks.)* Isn't it lovely when things make sense.

CHLOÉ: How many times were you married?

MATHIAS: *(Looks up; bemused.)* What made you ask me that?

CHLOÉ: The mental image of you asking a woman to marry, and her saying "yes," is something I find *astonishing*.

MATHIAS: Do you? I suppose your being astonished comes from the mystery of it…of no one ever actually asking *you*…to marry him. *(Beat.)* That was unnecessarily cruel. I apologize.

CHLOÉ: Don't bother.

MATHIAS: I'll make a clean breast of it. I'll show you my breast, if you show me your breast. Sorry, sorry, sorry, sorry! Whenever I'm politically incorrect, I shudder with self-loathing. *(Playacts a huge shudder.)* Arrrgggggh! See that? I shuddered.

(Shudders again, comes at HER, romantically, drunkenly. SHE moves away from HIM, quicky, downstage.)

CHLOÉ: I was asked. And I answered.

MATHIAS: No?…

CHLOÉ: Yes.

(MATHIAS looks up.)

MATHIAS: No, your answer was "yes," or, yes, your answer was "no?"…

CHLOÉ: Yes, my answer was "no." Having my mother and father as marriage-models didn't inspire me to make the same mistake.

MATHIAS: I understand, but, I don't *agree*. I was married three times, and I *never* made a mistake. *They* all did.

CHLOÉ: I understand.

MATHIAS: *(Explains.)* The three women.

CHLOÉ: I understood. And I agree. Three women saying "yes" to your proposal of marriage…

MATHIAS:…HAD to be making a mistake.

CHLOÉ: Had to be making a mistake.

(Beat.)

CHLOÉ: Marriage was a misery for my father.

MATHIAS: You think he knew about *my* father?

CHLOÉ: How could he not?

MATHIAS: And you? You knew it was going on?

CHLOÉ: I was ten years old when I knew for sure what was going on. What do you think I should have done that I didn't do?

MATHIAS: Stopped it.

CHLOÉ: I was ten years old!…

MATHIAS: How about ten years later, when you were twenty? You'd know about it for ten years, by then, and you were, I'm sure, quite adult. What did you do about stopping it when you were twenty?

CHLOÉ: What's your point?

MATHIAS: Well, I suppose I'd like to know if you *couldn't* stop it, or if you didn't *try* to stop it?

CHLOÉ: What's your point?

MATHIAS: I suppose I'm wondering if you couldn't have, I dunno, insinuated yourself into the situation, somehow?…Perhaps, told your father what you knew?

CHLOÉ: I hardly think that would have been my place.

MATHIAS: What would have been your place, ma chère mademoiselle?

CHLOÉ: I suppose I felt that my place was to watch my father suffer…And to watch, to *feel*, my own suffering.

MATHIAS: Did you ever talk to your mother?

CHLOÉ: No. Did you ever talk to *your* mother?

MATHIAS: I never knew the way you knew. I never knew for sure…Not for sure. I…

CHLOÉ: C'est des conneries!

MATHIAS: What does *that* mean?

CHLOÉ: Bullshit. It means what you're saying is bullshit.

MATHIAS: *(Takes his notebook and a pencil.)* Could you just repeat that word, again, please? *(Spells it out…)* C-O-N…One "N" or two?…

CHLOÉ: *(Under her breath.)* Nique ta mère!

MATHIAS: Ah! This we can translate! Although, niquing the old mère, strictly speaking, was my *father's* hobby, and the old mère in question, was, of course, *your* old mère. *(Sings.)* The old grey mère, she ain't what she used ta' be...

CHLOÉ: Vous êtes complétement *détragué!*

MATHIAS: Back to you, and double it.

(MATHIAS refills his glass, emptying the bottle of its last drop of whiskey.)

MATHIAS: Now *that* is truly sad! All this we talk about has a kind of historical-hysterical sadness about it, but, this empty bottle is *in the moment.* I mean, dear darling Mademoiselle Giffard, this is an unalterable fact: this fucking bottle is dry! This is a dead soldier! *(HE drains his glass dry. And then...)* I saw my mother standing out on the balcony...I was about sixteen. She was looking down at Park Avenue and she was crying. There was no question about what she was thinking about doing. No question. She was leaned way, way over the front railing. I knew I had maybe ten seconds to do something. I smashed this crystal ashtray from Tiffany's that my father had won for some great business shit, and I cut my hand. *(Holds his hand for Chloé to see...)* See? *(Smiles.)* My mother came running. There was this blood spurting out on the coffee table and all over the rug. My mother snapped into serious mother-action. She had this kind of silk scarf that she was wearing and she wrapped it around my hand, really tightly. *(Beat.)* I bled for her. She bled for me. *(Smiles.)* All this talk of liquid makes me thirsty. What do we have in the house, dear darling Mademoiselle Giffard? An amusing Médoc? A meaty Margaux? A clair Sancerre? A nutty Côte du Rhone? A succulent Châteauneuf du Pâpe?

CHLOÉ: You drink too much.

MATHIAS: What? What did you say? What?

CHLOÉ: You drink too much. It's disgusting!

MATHIAS: Dégueulasse.

CHLOÉ: Excuse me?

MATHIAS: Disgusting. The word for disgusting is "dégueulasse." It's one of the few French words I've learned quite quickly. It's one of those words that people like me hear, used in close proximity, over and over, again. *(And then...)* What's the difference if I'm drunk or not drunk? What changes, really? When my first wife's mother was dying from drink, she was having DT's...seeing spiders and elephants. Her stomach was enormously distended from her devastated liver. I was terribly impressed by the treatment she got from her young doctor. He gave her enormous amounts of Absolute Vodka to drink. She died, anyway, but, she suffered a hell of a lot less. Absolute Truth. Absolute Death. *(And then...)* I need a drink.

CHLOÉ: There's a bottle of Pastis in that cupboard.

MATHIAS: *Pastis!* Thank you, dear darling Mademoiselle Giffard. Pastis and Nyquil are my two favorite cold remedies!

(MATHIAS finds Pastis bottle in cupboard, opens it, swigs directly from the bottle, shudders. Then, HE offers the bottle to CHLOÉ...)

MATHIAS: Wet your whistle?

CHLOÉ: Please, don't be vulgar.

MATHIAS: *(Another swig of Pastis.)* I came back to New York from college on a Saturday morning. I was due back on Friday night, but, I was acting in the Drama Department's production of *Where's Charley?* I had a dance and two songs. I had a knack for comedy. Go figure, right?...

(HE drinks another swig of Pastis. HE continues, quietly...)

MATHIAS: I used my own key to get in. I tossed my duffel bag on my bed and I called out for my mother, "I'm home, Ma!" She called back with this weird throaty voice, "In my room!" I went in. She had this gun. Not a hearty hunting rifle, like your dad's. Her's was a snub-nosed pistoly thing her husband gave her to keep near her bed at night, in case a stranger wandered in, and he was out. My father. Her husband. She put it in her mouth...the pistol...and she killed herself. No words, no complication, really...just this bahh-booom! She kind of flipped over, backwards, stiffly, like a gymnast. There was a tremendous mess. Dégueulasse. I sat on the floor and I held her. She died in my arms.

CHLOÉ: *(Clearly stunned.)* I...I'm sorry.

MATHIAS: I bled for her. She bled for me.

CHLOÉ: She was wrong to do that to you.

MATHIAS: You're right. It wasn't nice. Mademoiselle Giffard, I'm going to ask you to do me a little favor. This is not something I...It's upsetting...I know that I'm going to cry and it's terribly embarrassing for me. The English call it "blubbing." That's what's going to happen. I'm going to blub, any moment, now...Would you mind holding my hand? I know you won't think this is a romantic overture of any kind, because of who you are and who I am and how we feel about one another, but...

(Suddenly, sobbing.) I...am...so...upset.

(CHLOÉ goes to MATHIAS, embraces HIM. This tiny spot of human contact (and compassion) is too much for MATHIAS. HE begins to cry. Tears fall that have waited three decades to fall. HE folds into her arms...)

CHLOÉ: We must move beyond them, somehow. I can see this, now, when I see you. When I've been looking inward, it's been impossible. But, when I see you…suffer…Forgive me, but, it seems so unnecessary. My own years and years of living in the dark…of refusing laughter and love. *(CHLOÉ begins to kiss him. HE turns his head…)*

MATHIAS: If you kiss me, I'll drag you down. I do that to people. As soon as they kiss me, their lives change for the worse. There's nothing so bad that it can't grow worse. There's no limit to how bad things can be. *(CHLOÉ and MATHIAS kiss.)*

MATHIAS: Oh, my God, you're so beautiful.

CHLOÉ: I'm not. I'm nearly old.

MATHIAS: A perfect flower is nearly old. *(CHLOÉ reaches her lips to kiss MATHIAS, again.)*

MATHIAS: I warned you.

CHLOÉ: I know. *(THEY kiss, again, passionately.)* *(The lights crossfade to…)*

SCENE THREE

Afternoon, the next day. MUSIC IN…Coltrane, slow, sad. LIGHTS UP ON…MATHIAS, at table, drinking wine, writing in his manuscript.

MATHILDE sits in her chair, reading her newspaper. SHE looks over at MATHIAS, waits until HE stops writing and looks into space. And then, SHE speaks…

MATHILDE: Are you writing, or thinking?

MATHIAS: Are the two mutually exclusive?

MATHILDE: I don't want to disturb you.

MATHIAS: That, Madame Giffard, is a piece of *politesse* that boggles the old brain.

MATHILDE: Do you mind if I go back to what we were talking about? I was thinking about your mother.

MATHIAS: Please, go on, Madame Giffard.

MATHILDE: Thinking that she didn't know is naïve! Marriage is always a collaboration. Nothing passes unnoticed in a marriage. Believe me, on some level, your mother knew, and, trust me, she approved.

MATHIAS: She was stuck in a marriage with three kids! She didn't know where to turn! Women didn't walk out, in those days. Women didn't... *(Stops, midthought. Beat.)* Look, this is really stupid. I'm fifty and you're... whatever you say are. All of this is sort of ancient history, isn't it?...I mean, who cares?

MATHILDE: I care.

MATHIAS: I do, too. It's totally crazy. *Why* do I care? *(Without pause.)* Maximillian Gold was the meanest, cruellest, coldest son of a bitch I've ever known, and I have known some...

MATHILDE: *I simply won't hear this!*

MATHIAS: Wait a minute, wait a minute, wait a minute! You'll hear it, if I want to say it! I've just spent a couple of days with you telling me that my father was some kind of Cassanova and Saint John the Divine, combined, and I'm supposed to listen and nod, understandingly...but, when I try to point out that, as fathers go, my father, in his relationship with his wife and his children, was a little less like Cassanova and St. John, and a little more like Saddam Hussein, you *"simply won't hear it!"*?

MATHILDE: Your father was loving, kind, and generous to a fault!

MATHIAS: With *you*, lady! Not with me! Not with my brothers, and certainly not with his wife, who just happened to be our mother! I remember when I was a kid, watching my mother lean out over the balcony, and I knew...I *knew*...(Stops himself. Beat.)

This is stupid! Look, Mrs. Giffard...you're an old lady. You've got 92-to-94 years behind you. All real-estate considerations aside, you could have a good couple of years ahead of you, as well. Whatever my father was to you, he was...*to you.* I believe you. I don't doubt for a second that you're telling the truth. But, that particular truth is *your* truth, not mine...and, certainly, not hers...not my mother's. *(Beat.)* This is *crazy! (New tone of voice.)* May I tell you something? I don't have a friend in the world. Not one. I owe money, everywhere. I've put the touch on everyone. When people I used to know — former friends — if they see me coming, they don't even bother to ask for their money back! The fact is, they cross the street! They hide from me! Everything about me says "loser." It's like it's written on my face! It's like a kind of deadly virus they know I have and they think they're going to catch it, if they come too close to me.

MATHILDE: That's exactly what your father said about you!

MATHIAS: Excuse me?

MATHILDE: You have no confidence...no courage...no *vision*.

MATHIAS: Right! I have no confidence, no courage, no *vision!* Don't people like you and my father ever wonder *why?*

(MATHIAS pours and drinks a full glass of whiskey.)

MATHIAS: Do you think self-esteem is some kind of a *birthright?* Do you think self-esteem is some kind of, I dunno, *natural phenomenon,* like a physical fact? The baby's born; the doctor slaps his little ass and says "He's okay! He's got all his fingers and toes, he's got a little dick, he's got his self-esteem. He's okay." *(Drinks again.)* It doesn't work that way, lady. If you wanna' kill a kid, you don't shoot him! You just do *nothing!* You just withhold your love, and watch the child devote his loveless life to pleasing you. To *displeasing* you! At some point, the child says "I've got to stop trying!" *BUT, YOU CAN'T STOP TRYING!* You think everybody else in the world is loved, but not you. You've got this terrible secret that eats you alive! You think you're... *WHY AM I TELLING YOU THIS?... WHY DO I CARE?...* I cannot imagine that he and my mother spent a lot of time trying to organize my birth. I can only imagine my mother, desperately unhappy, sobbing in the night. And my father, home from travel, from your bed, throwing in a midnight mercy-fuck. Then, she's pregnant with me, with this endless reminder of...

(MATHIAS stops himself. Drinks, again.)

MATHILDE: You drink a lot.

MATHIAS: I do. I drink a lot. You're observant.

(Pours another glass of whiskey; drinks it.)

MATHILDE: I can't say your father was thrilled to get the news...that your mother was pregnant. He wasn't young. He was shocked, really...at first. But, then, he adjusted.

MATHIAS: Excuse me? You remember my mother being pregnant with me?

MATHILDE: I was pregnant at the same time.

MATHIAS: What are you saying?

MATHILDE: I was pregnant with Chloé at approximately the same time your mother was pregnant with you. That's probably why it stays with me...the memory...*(Beat.)* He was angry at first...with both of us. But, then, he was understanding with me. He had your brothers, of course...two sons...and he was quite proud of them, really. He knew I needed a child of my own. I mean, it wasn't balanced, was it?...Him, with two children; me, with none. *(Beat.)* I suppose it was inconvenient, having us both pregnant at the same time. I hadn't thought of it, that way...

MATHIAS: Inconvenient? That is the sickest...*(Beat.)* I ask it, again. Is there any chance that Chloé…? Is there any chance that he got two birds with one stone?

MATHILDE: I'm afraid I don't understand.

MATHIAS: Yes, I think you don't. Your daughter and I are attracted to one another.

MATHILDE: That pleases me.

MATHIAS: It does?

MATHILDE: Of course, it does. And I must tell you, when you were born, your father was quite pleased. I remember that. Your father was quite pleased.

MATHIAS: Thank you. It's a relief, after all these years, to find out that my father was "quite pleased" when I was born. *(Beat.)* What turned it around?

MATHILDE: Pardon?

MATHIAS: What turned it around? What made my father…hate me?

MATHILDE: Your father didn't hate you!

MATHIAS: I suppose that's true. I suppose he *didn't* hate me. That would have been passionate. He didn't *think* about me.

MATHILDE: In the end, I think that you sided too closely with your mother. He thought that you were more *her* child, than his.

MATHIAS: How about when I was twenty, and living away from her, on my own?

MATHILDE: Oh, I wouldn't know about that.

MATHIAS: How about when I was forty, lying near death, at Lenox Hill Hospital, about six blocks from his house?

MATHILDE: I didn't know.

MATHIAS: I'd had an…accident. I was taking a bath and my razor blade slipped and I cut both of my wrists, rather badly. The cleaning lady came back for her check and…

MATHILDE: *(Softly.) Bon Dieu!*

MATHIAS: In America, they don't let you die. You know this, don't you? It's so disrespectful. If they can possibly bring you back, they do, they bring you back. I left a note, explaining everything…a note, plus, two unpublished novels, and sixteen unpublished poems…my entire *oeuvre*. It was all pretty much the same message…what it feels like to be an orphan waiting to be born.

MATHILDE: And you tried to kill yourself?

MATHIAS: I did. I tried awfully hard, too. I am not terribly adept. But, then, you've noticed that, yourself, haven't you? Remember? "Don't jump in the Seine. You'll just get a headcold."

MATHILDE: It was a kind of joke…

MATHIAS: It was, indeed. A kind of joke.

MATHILDE: You mustn't, Mathias. You mustn't. You must get help.

MATHIAS: What help? I tried psychoanalysis. It made me feel even *worse* about myself. In point of fact, I've been ready to forgive my father since the beginning of time!...Well, since the beginning of *my* time, anyway...It just doesn't quite work that way, does it?...

MATHILDE: Mathias, you must live your own life! What went on between your father and I concerned no one. We were discreet. We were cautious. We were considerate.

MATHIAS: I don't mean to cloud your delusions, Madame Giffard, but, what went on between my father and you concerned me, rather significantly. You were hardly discreet, certainly not cautious, and, my God!, *considerate?*...In view of my mother's ten-to-fifteen suicide-failures before her ultimate suicide-success, I don't see where the word "considerate" fits in all this, exactly. I...*(MATHILDE turns away; stunned.)*

MATHILDE: *(Quietly.)* Your mother's what did you say? Are you saying that your mother attempted to take her own life?

MATHIAS: No, I'm saying that my mother *took* her own life. She died in my arms.

MATHILDE: I see.

MATHIAS: You didn't know? He didn't tell you?
(MATHILDE is suddenly weak. SHE grips the back of her chair to stop herself from falling.)

MATHIAS: Now, that's what I call considerate...not wanting to worry you with the details of my mother's...*(HE sees that MATHILDE is ill.)* Madame Giffard?...Madame Giffard?
(MATHILDE slumps against the back of the chair, and then, SHE falls to the floor.)

MATHIAS: Madame Giffard!
(The lights fade out.)

SCENE FOUR

Later, same day. MUSIC IN...Single cello, still sad. LIGHTS UP ON...MATHIAS, alone at table, writing in his manuscript. HE is drunk and still drinking. CHLOÉ enters from the back bedroom.

MATHIAS: *(Getting drunk.)* Ahhh, Mademoiselle Giffard, a face I remember.

CHLOÉ: *(Staring at MATHIAS.)* Yes.

MATHIAS: Why are you staring at me? Do I have spinach between my teeth? *(Drinks.)* I couldn't possibly have spinach between my teeth. I haven't eaten spinach in years! I must have…*(Reads label on bottle…)* …Châteauneuf du Pâpe between my teeth. *(Drinks.)* And how is your dear mother? I saw the doctor leave, but, I didn't dare to pop the question. *(Explains.)* Dead or alive? I assumed she was alive, as I didn't hear any hideous screams.

CHLOÉ: She's alive. She's doing well.

MATHIAS: I'm glad you didn't say she was doing "good." Doing good, as we both know full well, is not your particular mother's *raison d'être*.

CHLOÉ: The doctor says she's a living miracle.

MATHIAS: I suppose he means that it's a miracle she's living.

CHLOÉ: I suppose he does. *(Watches HIM drink.)* Are you planning to let her outlive you?

MATHIAS: *(Looks up; smiles. HE pats his manuscript.)* "My Old Lady."

CHLOÉ: Excuse me?

MATHIAS: That's my title…I found my title…"My Old Lady."

CHLOÉ: It's about your mother?

MATHIAS: At the very least. My mother, your mother…

CHLOÉ: Mathias, when she goes…when she *dies*…when my mother dies… this is apartment will be yours.

MATHIAS: Yes.

CHLOÉ: I'd like to go on, you know, living here.

MATHIAS: In the apartment?

CHLOÉ: *(Tentatively; bravely.)* Yes. I'd like to go on living here…with you.

MATHIAS: I'm afraid that won't be possible.

CHLOÉ: *(Hurt.)* Yes. I thought so. *(Beat. Then, simply…)* I'm prepared to accept your offer.

MATHIAS: Which offer would you be referring to?

CHLOÉ: 50%-50%.

MATHIAS: I'm afraid that won't be possible, either.

CHLOÉ: However you devise the split will be fine with me.

MATHIAS: That won't be necessary.

(CHLOÉ looks up. MATHIAS smiles. Pats the manuscript.)

MATHIAS: You're going to have to read the book to see how it all comes out…in the end.

(HE fills a large water glass with Châteauneuf du Pâpe; drinks.)

CHLOÉ: It's finished?

MATHIAS: It is. As books go, it's rather short and rather sketchy, but, it's still a hell of a read. I think you'll be totally engaged, from cover to cover.

CHLOÉ: I'd love to read it.

MATHIAS: No one else will, I'm sure.

CHLOÉ: My mother will.

MATHIAS: No one else, besides your mother.

CHLOÉ: Shall I read it now?

MATHIAS: Not now. Not with me in the room. It would be embarrassing for both of us. A major portion of the work is a kind of love letter, Mademoiselle Giffard. To you.

CHLOÉ: Is it?

MATHIAS: It is. It's a gift. I wish I could have given you something store-bought and pricier than just my scribbled thoughts and memories. I stayed awake, last night, after we made a clean breast of it with each other, after our souls clapped their hands and sang, I watched you sleep for quite a long while. Wait…*(Finds selection in manuscript; reads…)* "Mademoiselle Giffard is an astonishing beauty. She and her mother, and my mother, as well. My father and I are lucky men to have had such women in our…" *(Beat.)* Let me read a bit from the beginning of it…*(Reads…)* "When I first approached Madame Giffard's huge apartment house overlooking the Jardin Luxembourg, my heart quickened. I thought to myself, 'This has got to be the best neighborhood in Paris! I'll get a *fortune* for this place!'…*(From memory…)* At that point, I had one plan and one plan, only…To sell the apartment, to get the money in my hand, to send money to the shortlist of former friends I'd borrowed from who were truly in trouble because of me…and then, to kill myself…to rid the world of my odious presence, and to rid my life of this odious world. *(Beat.)*

I stood in the heart of the baroque faux-Henri-quartre lobby, pressed the call-button for an authentic Henri-quartre elevator…and waited twenty minutes for the goddam things to come for me. I ended up walking up the stairs, because the elevator wasn't big enough to hold me and my suitcase at the same time. You can never be in a French elevator with a woman, unless you plan to have an affair with her…and she with you, of course. More of this, later. *(Beat.)*

    I found the apartment and knocked on the door. No answer. I knocked again. Still no answer…The door to Madame Giffard's apartment was unlocked. When I entered, I somehow knew that I was taking the first steps toward the end of my life. I found…"*(Stops, looks up at CHLOÉ.)* It's all here. In the book. Please…Take it. *(Hands her the book, and then…)* I feel terribly weak.

CHLOÉ: Have you eaten anything?

MATHIAS: I wouldn't know, why? *(Beat.)* Could you help me to my bed?

CHLOÉ: Of course.

MATHIAS: It's not a romantic offer. I mean, it is, in a way, but, I'm not in the mood for making babies, if you know what I mean.

CHLOÉ: Yes, I do know what you mean.

    (SHE moves to HIM, three steps; stops short of HIM; speaks.)

CHLOÉ: Please, listen to me. When you came here, to this place, I would have been happy if you died. Now, I know you. I know you're not your father. And I know you're not *my* father. You're you, and I love you. I want you to live.

MATHIAS: That's so sweet!…It's such a pity we didn't meet each other, years ago, before we were born.

    (THEY share a long, affectionate look. MATHIAS exits, slowly, in dim light, as MATHILDE enters and…)

    (The lights crossfade to…)

SCENE FIVE

    The next morning. MUSIC IN…Coltrane, single tenor sax. LIGHTS UP IN…living room. The curtains are drawn closed. MATHILDE sits in her chair, head back, eyes closed, blanket over legs, as we discovered her at the beginning of the play. SHE is deep in thought.

    CHLOÉ enters from back rooms. SHE pulls the curtains open. Sunlight streams into the room.

    MATHILDE is startled, wakes.

CHLOÉ: We're you sleeping?

MATHILDE: No. How is he?

CHLOÉ: He's sleeping.

MATHILDE: Did you get him on to the bed?

CHLOÉ: I couldn't lift him. I got his shoes off…I cleaned his clothing as best I could…covered him.

MATHILDE: Did you talk with him at all? Did he say *any*thing?

CHLOÉ: No.

MATHILDE: He refused to speak?

CHLOÉ: It wasn't an issue. He wasn't really conscious.

MATHILDE: He said nothing?

CHLOÉ: Why do you keep asking me that? He said nothing.
    (After a pause.)

MATHILDE: Everything I believed is shaken.

CHLOÉ: In what sense?

MATHILDE: I'm too old. I've lived too long. Everyone I loved is gone. It's too sad. I have nobody to talk with. I have nobody but the dead to talk with.

CHLOÉ: *(A throaty whisper.)* How dare you say that, Mother?

MATHILDE: You know I mean "in addition to you," when I say this. You know I don't mean to exclude you. You know that you are all I have.

CHLOÉ: I know that I'm fifty years old and I have never had love in my life!

MATHILDE: You mean a husband?

CHLOÉ: Yes, I suppose I mean a husband. But, I also mean a mother. I also mean a father.

MATHILDE: You had a loving mother and a loving father…all through your childhood! If you don't know that, no amount of talk is going to convince you!

CHLOÉ: I know that when I sit and I stare at Mathias, I sometimes see his father's face on his face, and I want him dead!

MATHILDE: You can't mean that?

CHLOÉ: Why can't I mean that? Why can't I mean that?

MATHILDE: Because he's a person who is…so sad.

CHLOÉ: Like me?

MATHILDE: Like you.

CHLOÉ: And *defeated*, like me?

MATHILDE: I would never say that!

CHLOÉ: You would never say it, because you would never *see* it! You assumed that since I was your daughter, therefore, I was happy…I was fulfilled…You assumed that I was worldly, from living so close to *your* worldliness…that I was fulfilled and happy, because I was your daughter…

and how could a daughter of yours not be happy? This would be *unthinkable!*

MATHILDE: I gave you your life, not your lifetime. You created that. You lived that. You chose that.

CHLOÉ: How can you say that?

MATHILDE: How can you think otherwise? You're not a child, Chloé!

CHLOÉ: I'm *your* child!

MATHILDE: That was years and years ago.

CHLOÉ: What does that *mean*?

MATHILDE: It means that at age 15, you stopped being my child, and started being my *daughter*. What do you think it means?

CHLOÉ: I have been by your side for fifty years!

MATHILDE: *(Yelled.) I DIDN'T ASK YOU FOR THAT! (Spoken.)* I didn't ask you for that! *(Beat. MATHILDE continues...)* What should I have done? It's a given that everything I did was wrong. This is a given. I have caused every possible unhappiness in your life. It's all me. All my doing. So, then, tell me...We know what I should not have done...which is to say I should not have done every single thing that I did in my entire lifetime. I should not have followed my heart. I should not have stayed married to my husband. I should not have made a home for my daughter. All these things were wrong! All these things!...I am ninety-four years old and I have made nothing but mistakes. So, tell me, Chloé, my daughter...You are so knowing...so, tell me. What should I have done?...

CHLOÉ: Is he my brother? Mathias...Is Mathias's father my father? There is so much about him that is familiar, so much that is me. Is Mathias my brother? That's what he thinks. That's what he's written in his story. Please, mother, tell me.

MATHILDE: Yes.

CHLOÉ: That's why he hated me.

MATHILDE: Mathias?

CHLOÉ: My father...your husband.

MATHILDE: He didn't hate you! He loved you! You were his daughter!

CHLOÉ: He knew.

MATHILDE: Not at all.

CHLOÉ: He knew!

MATHILDE: Not at all!

CHLOÉ: *I know he knew!* How would you know what he knew and what he didn't know? *I know! I know what he knew!* You weren't thinking you were his daughter, like I did, looking for love in his eyes!...

MATHILDE: There was love!

CHLOÉ: There was no love! There was no love!...*(Realizes...)* No wonder Mathias and I depised each other, when we first met. Somewhere, deep inside, we both...*(Beat.)* Why didn't you tell him the truth about us?

MATHILDE: He asked. I lied to him.

CHLOÉ: Why?

MATHILDE: Why did I lie?

CHLOÉ: Yes, mother, why did you lie?...

MATHILDE: For you.

CHLOÉ: For me?

MATHILDE: So, he might love you.

CHLOÉ: Thank you, mother. That was sweet. A little crazy, but, sweet.

MATHILDE: I see nothing wrong with the two of you bringing comfort to each other. You're certainly not having children at your age.

CHLOÉ: *(Bitterly.)* Yes, mother, you're certainly right. We're certainly not having children. It certainly stops with us.

MATHILDE: It's a pity, but, what is, *is*, and what was, *was*. We can only change what's ahead, Chloé...and only that, if we're very determined, and very lucky. *(Beat. And then...)* Chloé, please, what would you have had me do? Stay faithful to a man who was unfaithful to me, who I did not love and who did not love me?...I wanted a child. I wanted *you!*

CHLOÉ: People like us, like Mathias and me, we keep telling ourselves none of this matters. Childhood is a human invention, not God's invention, not something *natural*. That's what we tell ourselves, but, our pain tells us something different. Our pain tells us that we have been cursed. We have no reason to live and no courage to die. So, we go on, in a place reserved for the least-liked, the least-known...*(Beat.)* Listen, Mother. This is from his book...

CHLOÉ: "I found the apartment and knocked on the door. No answer. I knocked again. Still no answer..."

(MATHIAS appears in spotlight, upstage, center, reciting a section of his writing. His voice will overlap CHLOÉ's voice...and then take over the narration, on its own, singularly.)

CHLOÉ AND MATHIAS: *(IN UNISON.)* "The door to Madame Giffard's apartment was unlocked."

(MATHIAS takes over narration.)

MATHIAS: *(Singularly.)* "...When I entered, I somehow knew that I was taking the first steps toward the end of my life..."

CHLOÉ: He writes of how he spent his first days in Paris...

MATHIAS: "I sat in cafés, writing and sampling the imported whiskeys. I was astonished by the intensity with which French people talk with one another. The French talk about life, endlessly. In fact, they never really seem to *live* life, properly. This is, no doubt, because they're always sitting in cafés *talking* about Life."

CHLOÉ: And about meeting you, *Maman*.

MATHIAS: "Madame Giffard is a sphinx of a woman…She is *that* wise…*that* mysterious…*that* beautiful…But, sometimes, when she talks about her past, she reveals a self-absorption that was profound, allowing her a heart, like a sphinx, made entirely of stone. When she is not self-absorbed, of course, she is generous, loving, and glorious. She is, as my father would say, a peach."

CHLOÉ: And this is how he felt on meeting me for the first time…

MATHIAS: "Mademoiselle Chloé is the nastiest person I've met in my entire life. I should add that here this is true in a life that has been *dedicated* to ferreting out and finding the very nastiest of people."

CHLOÉ: And later on, of he and I, in more recent times…

MATHIAS: "Even though I've come to love Mademoiselle Giffard, I find that I've come back to my original plan, though somewhat altered. I won't liquidate the apartment, I'll liquidate myself. If I clear out of the big picture, entirely, Mademoiselle Giffard gets to keep her precious apartment, *soi-même*, and I will be perfected in my passing. She will love me til the day she dies, which, given her mother's medical history, should come to pass about a hundred and fifty years from now! *(Beat.)*

For years, I'd wanted to commit suicide as a kind of metaphysical fuck you to my father. Now, thanks to *les belles femmes* Giffard, I've moved by all that. Now, I will be killing myself in the name of love. Love for Chloé and Mathilde Giffard, so I won't stain their affection for me…love for my few old friends, who cannot bear another moment of me…love for the memory of my mother…and my brothers…and my father…who must not be remembered for their connection to me, not for an instant…and love for myself, which I cannot seem to find in the slightest. *(Beat.)*

Were I to stick around, *ad nauseam*, I would lose Mademoiselle Giffard's love, as surely as I have lost the love of everybody else. The wine flows too freely in a place like this for a fellow like me. *(Beat.)*

And so, I will one day soon be saying "adieu," which is the French word for "I'm out of here"…The flash with which the sulphur, charcoal, lead, and potassium nitrate will combine, may be heard, sooner, or later.

That depends upon the fervor with which I pursue my half-sister, Chloé, and she, I. It's rather sweet to think of us playing "Doctor and Nurse" at our age, innocently, as children, without a chance, at our age, of procreating even one of the little beasts. *(Beat.)*

But, whether it's to be sooner, or later, it is to be. Be sure of that. It is my God-given right to say "adieu," to whom I want, where I want, when I want.

(WE HEAR...GUNSHOT, offstage, loud, terrifying, fatal. MATHIAS bows his head. CHLOE and MATHILDE look at each other, sadly. MUSIC IN...Coltrane. Loud, full, plaintive. CHLOÉ walks slowly across the room to the photograph of herself, as a child, with her father. SHE carries the photograph with her across the room...in front of MATHILDE. CHLOÉ sits in a small chair, opposite Mathilde, stiffly. CHLOÉ looks across at MATHILDE. The WOMEN hold eye-contact for a moment, before MATHILDE breaks it, leans her head, closes her eyes...as SHE was at the play's start. And then, CHLOÉ turns from her mother, bows her head; weeps.)

(The lights fade to black.)

End of Play.

Un Drôle de Mari Français

(A Funny French Husband)

For Gillian, seriously...

INTRODUCTION

As the new millennium approaches, theatre in New York City is in a fearful state. While I'm far too young to remember Broadway's great old salad days, I'm plenty old enough to recall a time when a good play was written, sent to a commercial producer, who liked it, found a director, who cast it, and the play was put on stage for a crapshoot unlimited run. If it was a success, people bought tickets and the play continued for as long as income exceeded expenses. Life was simple.

Let me give you some details from my particular life during the days of, say, *The Indian Wants The Bronx*...1968. My guaranteed royalty from the NYC production of *Indian* was $100 a week. Al Pacino's salary was $52.50 a week. Sounds awful, yes? In fact, it was pretty awful...but, vaguely possible to squeak by. I was in my late twenties with three small children. My rent was $187 a month; Al's rent was $0, as he was superintendent (janitor) of a fairly crummy Uptown West Side apartment building.

When *Indian* opened, we both knew our lives would change. We had a runaway hit. I quit my day-job writing and directing TV commercials and never "worked" again. And Al quit his job, as well. Al and I both got movies...I wrote one forgettable script for $25,000, and *The Strawberry Statement,* which got produced, for $100,000. I gave up my rent-controlled apartment and bought a house in Greenwich Village. Al got to kiss Patty Duke in something forgettable, but, quickly made his mark in *The Panic In Needle Park,* and soon got cast in *The Godfather.* Within eighteen months of *Indian* opening in NYC, I had a total of six plays open in NYC, all in commercial productions. One of the plays, *Morning,* was actually done on Broadway. My plays were being translated and performed in Europe and Asia. And Al Pacino was, already and forever, a movie star.

I was the son of a truck driver, Al had been a street-kid, virtually abandoned. And now, still in our twenties, we had a fair share of Fame and Flow, and no end in sight. We even had the war in Vietnam to focus our purpose and our rage. Sound like the American dream? It was. In Randy Newman-speak, it was good to be an American.

At this time, nearing 2001, it is practically impossible to even *identify* a "commercial theatre producer," let alone stick a play in the mail to one. They're not a dying breed, they're extinct. While Times Square is two stops on the seventh Avenue IRT from my house, it is two billion miles from my sensibility. Broadway is for tourists...refried musical trifles...popularized serious ideas, cynically sloganizing real agonies..."Hate that AIDS!" "Stomp that Racism!" It's all so silly and life's so short. I can't bear it. The idea of

Broadway being the vital political/poetic/social arena that it once was for the likes of Clifford Odets, Robert Sherwood, Eugene O'Neill, Tennessee Williams, Arthur Miller, or Sidney Kingsley is long gone, a kind of nostalgic cliché, really.

So, is this one of those bleak, death-knell essays heralding the end of the thing we love…no more Cool-Whip, no more Popsicles? Hardly. This is, like every play I've written, an attempt to record what life was like in our time on our little dot on the planet Earth. And like every serious work of art ever created, it wrestles with the essential question: Why are we alive?

Playwrights write plays, producers or not. The greatest showbiz cliché of all, "Hey, kids, this barn would make a great theatre!," is only truly silly because of the absence (and cost) of *barns*. Theatre is in human blood cells. Little kids act out stories. No one shows them how. They dress up, they perform. It's, well, natural. And for grown-ups wrestling with the old "Why are we alive?," why not see a show? It reminds of our tiny, simple years, and it brings in close contact with something lifelike, but slowed to a speed at which life is watchable, considerable. (Sidenote: very rarely do husbands say to their wives "Let's go see a play, tonight, and try to figure out why we're alive!," but, believe it, that's what's going on, every time. And how irresponsible it is to give 'em the old song and dance…everything's going to be peachy in the end, when, in fact, we're looking at old age and death, if we're lucky, and disease, suffering, and death, if we're like most humanoids.)

So, serious writers write, no matter what. And somehow, there's a possibility of theatre, even without producers and beautiful theatres. Several years ago, I founded a group called The New York Playwrights Lab. We are fifteen fairly well-known playwrights. We start a new play on approximately the same day in September. We meet, weekly, and read and criticize our new pages. We have retreats, in Spring and Fall, to read and criticize our completed drafts. We have public readings, in NYC, in early winter, to show and sell our plays. Not one single playwright in the room ever talks about Broadway. For us, it simply doesn't apply. In the twenty-two years that The New York Playwrights Lab has been in existence, every play written in the Lab has gone on to be produced, professionally. Every one. These are real, working playwrights, estimable…who have, by necessity, found an alternative way to get their voices heard.

What happens in NYC, just now, is, approximately, this: There are literally hundreds of tiny performance spaces where plays are done for extremely limited runs, with actors, playwrights, and directors being paid either nothing or next to nothing. And there is a small, vital audience for these plays. And the great *impresarios* have been replaced by groups of often quite young men and women who somehow raise needed money, put on plays, and insist that theatre continue, no matter what, until somebody figures something out for the better.

And group-shows happen, frequently. Sharing the burden of responsibility, a group of theatre artist/producers often show their own work...or the work of their friends. Or raise needed money by asking known writers to contribute to a group effort, mixing unknown names with known. At almost any time in NYC, one can find a dozen or so group-shows...omnibus evenings featuring the short plays by several playwrights writing on a single theme. I am forever hearing my friends say things like "I'm late with my gun-play for Naked Angels!" or "Rocco wants to produce an evening of 10-minute wedding-cake plays"...(In fact, I, too, owe Rocco a wedding-cake play.)

And it was for such a group-show that *Un Drôle de Mari Français (A Funny French Husband)* was first created. Damien Gray, an enormously talented young director I've just worked with on my play *Stage Directions* at Redford's Sundance Theatre Institute, was, last year, running a small Tribeca theatre called The Workhouse. To raise money, the theatre created a group show...ten-minute plays that each contained a mysterious box. I was asked to be a contributor.

I had just returned from France, where I'd won a prize, and made a speech, in halting French, in which I promised that within the next year I would attempt to write a French play...which is to say, write a play *in French*. I don't know why I promised that. I hadn't planned to. And, in fact, I'm nothing even close to capable. I suppose I was just so happy to win the prize...and I felt like I wanted to give something back to this French-speaking country that had embraced me, given such volume to my voice...So, as I so often do in my crowded life, I put the things together — joined promise to invitation — and set out to write a 10-minute play in French, that could be performed in NYC for a non-French-speaking audience, and contained a mysterious box. And I guess I wanted, also, to say something about lousy husbands...and jokes...Much as I love the French, they are often so totally weird in marriage, and, *désolé de dire ça*, they tell the worst jokes...the absolute worst. I tried to write a sort of *film noir* little play...about a woman who finds the strength to kill her joke-telling husband...Anyway, you'll read the play.

I've included *Un Drôle de Mari Français (A Funny French Husband)* in this collection, as much as a reason for writing this small essay...about theatre in NYC in our time, as for itself. Would *Un Drôle de Mari Français (A Funny French Husband)* have been written in 1968? Consider my short play *Rats,* written that year for a group-show called "Collision Course"...a group of young playwrights including Israel Horovitz, Terrence McNally, Sam Shepard, Lanford Wilson, Leonard Melfi...

Vive le changement!
Vive le changement!
Vive le changement!
Quel changement?

THE PEOPLE OF THE PLAY
MATHILDE, beautiful, affluent, bored; in her 30s
MATHIAS, handsome, affluent, bored; in his 30s
DELIVERY MAN, quirky, seedy, bored; any age

THE PLACE OF THE PLAY
Mathilde and Mathias's 16th Arrondissement studio apartment (Paris).

THE TIME OF THE PLAY
Now.

A NOTE FROM THE AUTHOR
In this text, the Delivery Man announces that he has traveled from White Street, Tribeca (NYC). This reference should be changed to the location of the theatre producing the play, i.e., the address of the theatre to which the audience has just arrived. The play is designed to be played, simultaneously, in two languages, French and English. Dialogue is to be spoken first, in French, and then, almost instantly, in English, translated by off-stage actors, over a loudspeaker system. Translators' voices should be discreet, essentially friendly. Translations should almost always overlap the primary language. The first speeches of the play, however, will not be translated, allowing non-French-speaking audiences some moments of serious worry.

Un Drôle Mari Français
(A Funny French Husband)

LIGHTS UP IN…MATHILDE and MATHIAS's 16th Arrondissement studio-apartment (Paris). MATHILDE and MATHIAS are in their 30s. MATHIAS wears expensive outfit, floppy jacket and pants, baggy shirt, bright tie. MATHILDE wears the female equivalent. HE is handsome, SHE is beautiful. WE are envious…for the moment.

MATHILDE is setting the table, preparing an elaborate dinner that she has cooked. Candles will blaze, crystal will gleam, the event will be quite festive.

MATHIAS stands at the doorway talking to a DELIVERY MAN, a small, mysterious, foreign fellow. HE wears a motocycle helmet, carries several brightly colored boxes.

DELIVERY MAN: J'ai une boîte pour un Mathias et une autre pour une Mathilde.

MATHIAS: Génial! C'est nous! Mathias et Mathilde…

DELIVERY MAN: *(Gives MATHIAS slip to sign.)* Signez ici, s'il vous plaît.

MATHIAS: *(Signing.)* Vous travaillez tard! Vous savez l'heure qu'il est?

DELIVERY MAN: *(Whilst completing various forms…)* Y'avait une circulation infernale. C'etait comme conduire dans un champ de spaghetti!
(NOTE: Translation begins. TRANSLATORS' voices should always be discreet, almost whispered. Care should be taken to pick up cues, quickly. There should never be "air" between ACTORS' speeches and TRANSLATORS' reactions.

If there is only one male TRANSLATOR, an effort should be made to create two distinctly different male voices; one for translation of the DELIVERY MAN's speeches, and another for translation of MATHIAS's speeches.)

TRANSLATOR: I was in traffic from Hell! It was like driving through spaghetti!

MATHIAS: Vous êtes à moto?

TRANSLATOR: You're on a motorbike?

DELIVERY MAN: J'y étais, oui jusqu'à ce que j'ai crevé!

TRANSLATOR: I was, til I broke down.

MATHIAS: Vous, personnellement, ou la moto?

TRANSLATOR: You, personally, or the bike?

DELIVERY MAN: *(Gives MATHIAS a nasty look.)* La moto.

MATHIAS: Où avez-vous crevé?

TRANSLATOR: Where'd you break down?

DELIVERY MAN: Rue Blanche, Tribeca.

TRANSLATOR: White Street, Tribeca.

MATTHIAS: Où c'est, Tribeca?

TRANSLATOR: Where is Tribeca?

DELIVERY MAN: J'ai pas envie d'en parler.

TRANSLATOR: I don't want to talk about it.

DELIVERY MAN: Vous connaissez les règles: Vous choisissez chacun votre boîte. Quelque soit le contenu de la boîte, il doit être utilisé avant minuit ce soir.

TRANSLATOR: You know the rules: You choose one box, each. Whatever is in the box must be used before midnight, tonight.

MATHIAS/MATHILDE: *(In unison.)* D'accord.

DELIVERY MAN: Faites vos choix, s'il vous plaît.

TRANSLATOR: Make your choices, please.

MATHILDE: *(To Mathias.)* Toi…vas-y.

MATHIAS: Je'n reprends une rose pale.

TRANSLATOR: I'll have another pale pink.

> *(MATHILDE hears her husband's choice of boxes. SHE is shocked; obviously upset. The DELIVERY MAN sees this.)*

DELIVERY MAN: Vous êtes sûr, monsieur?

MATTHIAS: Ouais. Absolument sûr. Aucun doute.

> *(MATHILDE motions to the DELIVERY MAN to move close to HER. HE does. SHE now nods to MATHIAS, who, by prior arrangement, covers his ears and turns away. HE cannot see or hear Mathilde's choice of box. MATHILDE now whispers her choice to the DELIVERY MAN.)*

MATHILDE: *(Confidentially.)* Je veux la rouge-sang, cette semaine.

TRANSLATOR: *(As confidentially.)* I want bloodred, this week.

DELIVERY MAN: *(A bit shocked.)* La rouge-sang? Vous êtes sûr?

MATHILDE: Ouais. Je suis sûr.

> *(DELIVERY MAN hands box to MATHILDE, after pulling off small bloodred dot (sticky label) and pasting it down on his delivery list. HE moves close to MATHIAS, who uncovers his ears, nods to MATHILDE, who signals MATHIAS by yelling "Coo-Coo!")*

DELIVERY MAN: Aucun de vous ne veut la boîte bleu roi?

TRANSLATOR: Neither of you wants the royal blue box?

MATHILDE: Non. Pas moi.

MATHIAS: Moi, non plus. *(Beat.)* Je reconnais votre visage. Vous êtes déjà venu ici, n'est-ce pas?

TRANSLATOR: I know your face. You've been here before, haven't you?

DELIVERY MAN: Au moins deux fois.

TRANSLATOR: At least twice.

DELIVERY MAN: Ouais. La semaine dernière, il y a deux semaines, et le mois d'avant, je pense. Vous avez pris une boîte le mois dernier, non?

TRANSLATOR: Last week, two weeks ago, and I think last month. Didn't you get a box last month?

MATHIAS: Oui.

DELIVERY MAN: Bien. *(Hands pink box to MATHIAS.)* Votre boîte, monsieur…

MATHIAS: Merci.

DELIVERY MAN: *(Hands bloodred box to MATHILDE.)* Et la votre, madame.

MATHILDE: Merci, monsieur…

(MATHILDE places her box on the table. DELIVERY MAN waits in the doorway, smiling. There is an awkward moment.)

MATHIAS: Ah, bien, c'est *génial!* Merci.

TRANSLATOR: Ah…well…*brilliant!.* Thanks.

(DELIVERY MAN doesn't move.)

MATHILDE: *(Calls to MATHIAS, discreetly, from the table.)* T'as pas un petit quelquechose pour lui…

MATHIAS: De quoi tu parles?

MATHILDE: Allez fais un geste.

TRANSLATOR: He wants a tip.

MATHIAS: *(To DELIVERY MAN.)* Ne portez jamais de chaussettes Écossaises avec un costume en plaid!…

TRANSLATOR: Never wear argyle socks with a glen plaid suit!…

DELIVERY MAN: Commencez pas, hein?!

TRANSLATOR: Don't start, okay?!

MATHIAS: Ne m'en voulez pas! Le petit geste c'était l'idée de ma femme.

TRANSLATOR: Don't blame me! The tip was my wife's idea.

MATTHIAS: Ma femme et moi…nous avons une compréhension parfaite.

TRANSLATOR: My wife and I have a perfect understanding.

MATHIAS: Je n'essaie pas de contrôler sa vie, et je n'essaie pas de contrôler ma propre vie.

TRANSLATOR: I don't try to run her life, and I don't try to run my own.

DELIVERY MAN: Nique ta mère, pauvre type! Je livre ces machins-là depuis quatre mois, sans arrêt! Je suis crevé! Je…

TRANSLATOR: Fuck you, wiseass! I've been delivering these things for four months, nonstop! I'm exhausted. I…

MATHIAS: *(Grabbing DELIVERY MAN's arm…)* Attendez une minute, attendez! Je vous ai déjà dit que ma femme travaillait comme ventriloque nue…?

TRANSLATOR: Wait a minute, wait a minute! Did I tell you my wife used to work as a nude ventriloquist ..?

MATHIAS:…Mais, qu'elle a dû démissionner. Tout le monde voyait ses lèvres bouger!…

TRANSLATOR:…She had to quit. Everybody saw her lips move!…

DELIVERY MAN: *(Turns to leave. HE is angry.)* Oubliez le pourboire. J'ai pas le temps pour ça!

TRANSLATOR: Forget the tip, *comedian!* I've got no time for this!

MATHIAS: *(Pulls HIM closer.)* Alors, elle a eu un travail comme serveuse dans un restaurant seins-nus. Elle croyait qu'elle avait des brûlures d'estomac, jusqu'à ce qu'elle voit que son sein gauche trempait dans la soupe de poisson!…

TRANSLATOR:…Then, she got a job as a waitress in a topless restaurant. She thought she was having terrible heartburn, til she saw that her breast was in the soup!…

(MATHILDE pulls at her left brastrap, unconsciously.)

MATHIAS: C'est étonnant le peu de gens qui commande du lait dans un restaurant seins-nus.

TRANSLATOR: You know, it's amazing how few people order milk in a topless restaurant!

DELIVERY MAN: *(To MATHILDE.)* Demerdez-vous, chéri!

TRANSLATOR: You're on your own, lady!…

(The DELIVERY MAN exits. MATHIAS opens the box, extracts a slip of paper; laughs; reads…)

MATHIAS: Cette blague est formidable! *Écoute!* Ma femme s'est mariée tellement de fois avant moi, que quand on s'est rencontré, elle avait plein de "marques-de-riz" sur le visage! *(HE taps MATHILDE's face, playfully.)*

TRANSLATOR: This one's hilarious! *Listen!* My wife was married so many times before me, when I met her, she had rice marks on her face!

MATHILDE: *(Pulling away, annoyed.)* Arrête! Arrête!

(MATHIAS reads another slip…laughs.)

MATHIAS: *Écoute!* J'ai su dés que j'ai rencontré ma femme qu'elle allait me rendre heureux. Elle avait déjà rendu six mecs heureux la semaine d'a-vant.

TRANSLATOR: Listen! I knew when I met my wife she was going to make me happy. She made six other guys happy the week before.

(Frustrated, MATHILDE begins to eat her meal. SHE will continue to eat — first her meal, then, his meal — until all of the food is consumed…by her.)

MATHILDE: S'il te plaît, assieds-toi et mange, Mathias. Si le chèvre refroid-it, encore, la soupe sera dégueulasse!

TRANSLATOR: Please, sit and eat, Mathias. If the goat cheese recongeals, the soup will be disgusting.

MATHIAS: *(Reads another joke; laughs.)* Ahhh, c'est vraiment drôle! Ma femme et moi…nous vivons un mariage heureux depuis trois ans. Trois sur dix c'est une bonne moyenne!

TRANSLATOR: This one's *really* funny! My wife and I have been happily married for three years. Three out of ten's not such a bad average!

MATHILDE: S'il te plaît, pas maintenant, Mathias. J'ai perdu trois heures et demi à faire les courses pour ce repas…

TRANSLATOR: Please, not now, Mathias. I wasted three and half hours shopping for this meal….

MATHILDE: Je suis aux fourneaux depuis midi! C'est notre anniversaire de mariage! Je…

TRANSLATOR: I've been at the stove since noon! It's our anniversary! I…

MATHIAS: *(Reads another joke; laughs.)* J'ai rencontré ma femme dans un bar pour célibataires. C'était vraiment gênant! Je croyais qu'elle était à la maison avec les gosses!

TRANSLATOR: I met my wife in a singles bar. It was really embarrassing! I thought she was home with the kids!

(MATHILDE crosses to MATHIAS's seat, inspects his soup, sits; drinks his soup.)

MATHILDE:Regarde le chèvre dans ta soupe! Regarde-le! Il est compléte-ment caillé!

TRANSLATOR: Look at the goat cheese in your soup! Look at it! It's total-ly clotted!

MATHIAS: Comment veux-tu que je sois drôle, si tu m'interromps tout le temps?

TRANSLATOR:How can I ever be funny, if you keep interrupting me?

MATHILDE: Je m'en fous que tu ne sois pas drôle! Tout le monde ne peut pas être drôle! Il faut qu'il y ait des gens rasoirs, autrement, qui achèterait les *billets?*

TRANSLATOR: I don't *care* if you're not funny! Everybody can't be funny! Some people have got to be boring, otherwise, who would buy *tickets?*

MATHIAS: *(Takes new group of slips from his box; reads…)* Ma belle-mère avait un corps étonnant. Ses mensurations étaient 58-34-44. Son autre sein était légèrement plus petit.

TRANSLATOR: My wife's mother had this amazing body…Her measurements were 58-34-44. Her other breast was slightly smaller.

MATHILDE: Est-ce que t'a essayé le gingembre flambé? C'est exquis!

TRANSLATOR: Did you try the seared ginger? It's exquisite!

(SHE offers HIM a stick of seared ginger. HE ignores it. SHE eats it. HE continues…)

MATHIAS: Sais-tu pourquoi le Roi Solomon avait mille femmes?

TRANSLATOR: You know why King Salomon had a thousand wives?

MATTHIAS: Pour que la nuit y'en ait au moins une qui n'ait pas la migraine!

TRANSLATOR: So, at night, at least one of them wouldn't have a headache!

MATHILDE: Mathias, s'il te plaît, je…

MATHIAS: Ma femme est si froide, si frigide, quand elle ouvre la bouche, une petite lumière s'allume!

TRANSLATOR: My wife is so frigid, when she opens her mouth, a little light goes on!…

MATHILDE: Mathias, s'il te plaît, je…

MATHIAS: *(A burst of hideous anger.)* NE M'INTERROMPS PAS!

TRANSLATOR: *DON'T INTERRUPT ME!*

(MATHILDE's head goes down; her feelings have been hurt.)

MATTHIAS: *(HE continues reading jokes, calmly.)* Ma femme souffre d'une maladie appellé "l'Agoraphobo-Renverso." Elle a peur de quitter la place du marché!

TRANSLATOR: My wife suffers from a disease called "Agoraphobia-Reverso." She has a fear of *leaving* the marketplace!

MATHILDE: Tu ne veux pas gouter ma truite?

TRANSLATOR: Aren't you going to try my trout?

MATHIAS: Ma femme ne peut cuisiner que le poisson. Elle me fait manger du poisson si souvent que j'ai commencé à respirer par le cou!

TRANSLATOR: My wife can only cook fish. She has me eating fish so often, I've started to breath through my neck!

(MATHILDE unwraps and opens her box.)

MATHIAS: Avant, je sortais ma femme tout les soirs, mais, elle arrêtait pas de revenir!

TRANSLATOR: I used to take my wife out every night, but, she kept coming back!

MATHIAS: *(Reads another joke; laughs.)* Ahh, c'est génial! J'étais dans une ville étrangère, et solitaire. Ce soir la, je suis allé au bordel. J'ai dit à ma petite pute: je veux tirer ce soir le plus mauvais coup de ma vie…

TRANSLATOR: This one's *brilliant!* I was out of town, and lonely, so I went to a whorehouse. I told my hooker I wanted the worst sex she could muster up…

MATHIAS:…Je lui ai demandé de regarder la télévision pendant qu'on faisait l'amour, et peut-être, aussi, de s'épiler les sourcils en même temps…

TRANSLATOR:…I asked her to watch television while we were making love, and maybe pluck her eyebrows at the same time…

MATHIAS: Elle m'a demandé pourquoi. J'ai expliqué que je n'étais pas en manque, que ma femme me manquait!

TRANSLATOR: She asked me why. I explained that I wasn't horny, I was *homesick.*

(MATHILDE takes a gun from her box, aims at MATHIAS, who is amazed…)

MATHIAS: Ne me tue pas! Ce ne sont que des blagues!

TRANSLATOR: Don't kill me! They're only jokes!

(MATHILDE shoots MATHIAS. SHE makes the sound of the gunshot…)

MATHILDE: *Blam!*

(MATHIAS flies backwards, crashing to the floor. SHE shoots him again.)

MATHILDE: *Blam!*

(MATHIAS is near death. HE crawls to the table, on his back, like a mad crab. Is he trying to hide from Mathilde, or trying to reach her? HE gasps his final few thoughts…)

MATHIAS: Écoute…Cette blague est pas mal. C'est trés mauvais signe de voir la mariée juste avant le mariage, et, parfois, pendant les dix années qui suivent!

TRANSLATOR: Listen. This one's pretty good. It's bad luck to see the bride just before the wedding, and, sometimes, for about ten years, afterwards.

(MATHILDE shoots him, again.)

MATHILDE: *Blam!*

MATHIAS: Dis à l'Oncle Miltie que je suis vraiment désolé de l'avoir plagié. Sincèrement.

TRANSLATOR: Tell Uncle Miltie I'm really sorry I stole from him. I really am…

MATHILDE: D'accord.

MATHIAS: Je t'ai aimé quand je t'ai aimé.

TRANSLATOR: I loved you when I loved you.

MATHILDE: Moi aussi, je t'ai aimé quand je t'ai aimé.

TRANSLATOR:And I loved you when I loved you.

MATHIAS: Je pense nous avons choisi les mauvaises boîtes.

TRANSLATOR: I think we chose the wrong boxes.

> (*MATHILDE reaches under the table, shoots him, again.*)

MATHILDE: *Blam!*

MATHIAS: (*His final words…*) Au revoir, Mathilde…ma femme…Au revoir et merci. *Ughhh.*

> (*Dies. His death-rattle rattles.*)

TRANSLATOR: *Ugggh.*

> (*WE HEAR: TRANSLATOR's death-rattle rattle. MATHILDE blows out the candle flames. SHE sips an amusing 1986 Merlot; considers it. SHE walks to the front of the table.SHE looks directly at the AUDIENCE; speaks. NOTE: Mood is now totally "Film-Noir"…*)

MATHILDE: Il s'est arrêté de m'appeler "la petite femme," quand j'ai commencé à l'appeler "la grande erreur!"…(*Shoots MATHIAS, again.*) Blam!

TRANSLATOR: He stopped calling me "the little woman," when I started calling him "the big mistake!"…

MATHILDE: Il me disait que j'étais obsédé par son pénis, mais, je lui ai assuré que ce n'etait pas la peine de s'inquiéter pour si peu. (*Shoots MATHIAS, again.*) Blam!

TRANSLATOR: He used to tell me I was obsessed with his penis, but, I assured him there was very little there to worry about!

MATHILDE: Un mari, c'est ce qui reste quand on en a extrait les nerfs. (*Shoots MATHIAS, again.*) Blam!

TRANSLATOR: A husband is what's left after the nerve has been extracted.

> (*MATHILDE responds to a male laugh from the audience; turns, looks, speaks directly to the man in the audience who laughed…*)

MATHILDE: Est-ce que vous trouvez ça drôle?

TRANSLATOR: You think that's *funny?*

> (*SHE aims her gun at the MAN IN THE AUDIENCE who laughed. SHE is clearly about to shoot, when…*)
> (*The lights fade out.*)

End of Play.

Lebensraum

To countless unborn Jewish and German artists.
Nie wieder.

INTRODUCTION

Two years ago, my German play-agent reprimanded me, quite sternly, saying that I'd repeatedly rejected invitations to visit productions of my plays in Germany. He pointed out that my plays were getting quite popular in Germany, but that I was doing nothing to help him. Simply said, people knew my plays but didn't know *me*. I was actually quite surprised. I hadn't realized that I'd turned down any invitations to visit Germany at all...well, maybe a few...And then, I added it up. In recent years, by my own calculations, I'd found reasons not to visit Germany some fifteen times. In fact, I'd *never* seen a play of mine in the German language. Never. Never isn't a lot.

I thought it through, starting from when I was a five-year-old, in my bed at night in Wakefield, Massachusetts, thinking that the Nazis would be soon coming through my window to kill me and my family. But, that was fifty-three years ago. A few things have changed, since then.

So, okay, I accepted my agent's proposition for a whirlwind visit to some then-current German productions of my play, and to some German theatres considering my plays, and to a couple of my German translators. My first stop would be Bonn, for an important production of *Park Your Car In Harvard Yard.* And then, Cologne, where I would see an old friend (pen-pal variety) at WDR (Westdeutschen Rundfunk), a radio network that's done my plays over the past twenty-five plus years. And then, Frankfurt, Hamburg, Berlin...

In Bonn, first station of my particular cross, I had a drink with my play's producer, who told me that there would be a small press conference, after that night's performance. Using a quickly bought dictionary, I prepared a small speech, in German, saying how happy I was to be in Bonn, etc, etc. As I watched the performance, which struck me as being excellent, I wondered what the reaction would be to the lead character's speech about being a Yankee-Jew. I didn't sit with held breath, I just *wondered*. In fact, the speech never got spoken. (At least, I didn't *think* it got spoken. I don't speak German. It's a language that's always seemed to me to be rather comical, so many *fahrt*-words...I've always imagined Germans standing around on street corners, laughing about how funny they sound.) Anyway, after the show, which got a strong and positive audience response, I stood with the actress, waiting for our press conference to begin. Making friendly conversation (I thought), I asked her, cautiously (I thought)..."Did the old man ever make his speech about being a Yankee-Jew?"...Her answer took my life around a corner I didn't even know was there..."Oh, no!" she said. "You can't have Jews on stage in Germany. It doesn't smell good."

Smell good? *Smell* good? Before I could start to talk this out with her, the press conference began. I was introduced in glowing terms. I repocketed my little speech and in English (the language of international business, which most everybody seems to speak in Germany), I said…"Being in your country — hearing your language being spoken — is an act of heroism for me. It brings me back to when I was five years old, in Wakefield, Massachusetts, lying in my bed at night, thinking the Nazis were about to come through my window to kill me and my family…" Needless to say, there have been more popular speeches made in Germany, before and after mine.

The next day, in Cologne, still extremely angry, I told the story to my WDR-friend, Angela, who was amazed, but smiled, knowingly, as if she had the answer that would calm me…"The actress probably doesn't speak English very well. It was a problem of language, that's all…The actress was trying to say was that a Jewish character on stage sends a German audience into thinking the play is about the Holocaust. And your play is not about the Holocaust. It would have confused them." This was not calming news.

In Berlin, a few days later, I stayed at the apartment of one of my German translators, Miriam Mueller. Miriam is the daughter of a highly regarded German playwright, Harald Mueller (*Totenfloss, Stille Nacht*). Arnaud, her live-in boyfriend (now live-in husband), is French. Miriam speaks English. I speak English and French. We could all talk about this thing that happened to me…

First off, Miriam told me that, growing up, she "didn't have any casual Jewish friends, whatsoever," meaning, no Jewish school chums, no Jewish neighborhood kids. Why? "There were none. They were dead." In fact, Miriam told me that she didn't have any Jewish friends at all until she was in her twenties and went to translation school in London. And Arnaud talked about the guilt that young German people feel concerning what their parents and grandparents did more than fifty years ago…and about the unthinkable pain young Germans have inherited…The German legacy…

We three stayed up most of the night, talking. I never slept. At six A.M., sleep-deprived, I left the apartment and took my morning run in the Charlottenberg *Shlosspark*, around the castle. I was obsessed by all this…by Miriam's never having a Jewish friend…by Jews being unknown, abstract, even to sophisticated people like the children of successful playwrights…and by what Anaud had said about the profound guilt Miriam and her young German friends feel, forced on them by parents and/or grandparents… (Miriam told me she'd been given a name thought to be Jewish, because "My parents wanted to replace a dead Jewish child")…

As I ran, I thought to myself, "If Jews are totally abstract and are causing young Germans so much guilt, it's only a matter of time before young

Germans say to themselves 'These abstract Jews are a major pain in the ass to me!'...and we're here we go, again!"...

And then, out of the sky and into my head came the first image of my play *Lebensraum*...Germany's Chancellor wakes from a nightmare and calls a press conference that he promises will contain "the news of the Century." In front of politicians, citizens, reporters, radio microphones, television cameras, he speaks the following words to Germany: "We face the start of a new millennium...a new beginning. As Chancellor of this great German republic, I extend an invitation to six million Jews from anywhere in the world to come to live their lives in Germany. I speak to you, now: You will be given citizenship and full privileges in this great nation. You will be German. It is my heartfelt desire to re-establish a Jewish community in Germany, and to reduce, as much as humanly possible, the immeasurable shame we Germans feel each day of our lives for what this country did to our German-Jewish neighbors, sixty years ago. What I am saying to you six million Jewish people is quite simple, really. Please, come home. Please."

As soon as I had the idea, I felt faint. I stopped running and grabbed hold of a bench, next to a small, rectangular trashcan upon which a Nazi *swastika* had been hand-drawn by Magic Marker. I was weak, sweating. Suddenly, a pack of unattended dogs rushed past me, barking ferociously. At first, I thought I would die of fright. And then, I actually laughed aloud...It was all so shabbily *theatrical*.

I ran back to Miriam's apartment and began to write my ideas into my notebook. When Miriam and Arnaud woke, I told them my plan for the new play...and that I might call it *Lebensraum*..."Living Space"...Hitler's initial promise to the German nation when he first set out to conquer the world. Miriam and Arnaud were instantly supportive.

I wrote the first draft of *Lebensraum,* obsessively. I had been in the midst of writing a new play, *My Old Lady.* I stopped work on that play...and on the screenplay I was writing for the recent movie based on my play *North Shore Fish.* In fact, I stopped almost everything in my life but for the writing of *Lebensraum.* I read fifteen to twenty new pages a week to the other playwrights of The New York Playwright Lab. I only half-listened to their criticism. In Sylvia Plath-speak, I was "seized by a savage God."

I gave the play an odd, theatrical form, calling for three actors to play some eighty characters. I felt that any play dramatizing Jews, Germans, the Holocaust, at this point in history, needed a fresh approach, both formally and substantially. Without realizing it at the time, I called for three actors who precisely fit the description of the main actors of the Hercub Company, with whom I have been working successfully during the past six years in

France. It is they who are doing the European Premiere of *Lebensraum*, at this moment, at Festival d'Avignon, in a translation they've created with my young friend Charlotte Vuarnesson. *Lebensraum* opened at Théâtre du Balcon, Avignon, a week ago, to a packed house. I'm told there is a standing ovation, each night.

The World Premiere of *Lebensraum*, was given, of course, at my own theatre, Gloucester Stage, in tandem with my other new play, *My Old Lady.* Both plays brought tearful audiences to their feet...: *My Old Lady* (*Meine Alte Dame*) will have its European premiere in Dormund, Germany, in September; and the Gloucester Stage production of *Lebensraum,* under Richard McElvain's inventive direction, will re-open in NYC at The Miranda Theatre in October. Several productions of *Lebensraum* are planned for Germany during the next few seasons.

For what it's worth, I am certain that at age fifty-seven, I somehow wrote my best work (thus far)...thirty years after *The Indian Wants The Bronx, It's Called The Sugar Plum, Line* and *Rats* opened, one after the other, in my incredible "First Season" as a produced playwright in New York City. But, in the end, it is quite difficult to comment intelligently on one's own work... i.e., what's important work, what's not important work. Such self-assessment feels wrong...asburd...like a snail explaining its shell...except to say that it does often seem to me that all of life exists as preparation for the next day. All past is prologue. Such is the nature and condition of Hope. And, in the end, one cannot possibly have the fullest life without dreaming it, first. But, if we allow ourselves the dream, yes, oh, yes, all things are possible.

I.H., Gloucester, Mass.
Summer, 1997.

ORIGINAL PRODUCTION

The original production of *Lebensraum* was presented at Gloucester Stage Company, July 10, 1996. It was directed by Richard McElvain, Scenery Design by Lisa Pegnato, Lighting Design by John Ambrosone, Costume Design by Jane Alois Stein, Music Design by Catherine Goldwyn and Richard McElvain, Stage Manager Jeff Benish, Assistant Stage Manager Jana Mestecky, Assistant Director Charlotte Vuarnesson, Light Board Operator Inge Berge, with the following cast:

Actor #1	Ari Fliakos
Actor #2	Scott Richards
Actor #3	Emme Shaw

Lebensraum was first produced on the New York stage, October 14, 1997, presented by The Miranda Theatre, Valentina Fratti, Artistic Director.

THE PEOPLE OF THE PLAY

ACTOR #1 (Younger, Male), Narrator; also plays Political Announcer, Steffen Von Menck, TV Talk Show Host, Götz Witzenbacher, Sammy Linsky, Zev Golem, Jacob Brontheim, High School Teacher, Pierre Chambray, Günter Friedlander, Sign-In Centre Clerk, Various Voices.

ACTOR #2 (Older, Male), Narrator; also plays Rudolph Stroiber, Gustav Geisling, Professor Viktor Spretz, Reverend Hans Schnabel, Michael Linsky, Rabbi Shlomo Brechtman, History Teacher, High School Teacher, Axel Rosensweig, Maximillian Zylberstein, Jacques Burstin, Ludwig Hess, Götz Burger, Sign-In Centre Clerk #2.

ACTOR #3 (Younger, Female), Narrator; also plays Eva Mueller, Bessie Mandelbaum, Gertrude Moskowitz, Millie Brontheim, Lizzie Linsky, Anna Giesling, High School Teacher, Berta Giesling, Reba Golem, Katrina Keitel, TV Interviewer, Rifka Borenstein, Fishpacker, Esla Krebs, Various Voices.

THE PLACE OF THE PLAY

Various locations around the world, including Gloucester, Massachusetts, U.S.A., and Bremerhaven, Germany.

THE TIME OF THE PLAY

The start of the 21st century.

AUTHOR'S NOTE

This play is designed to be performed by three actors on an essentially barren stage. Scenery should be limited to platforms, ramps, and racks draped with various costumes and props. I strongly suggest imaginative use of props and costumes to indicate character. Puppetry techniques, such as portrtaits with cut out spaces for heads and hands, add-on fat stomachs, handheld masks, and objects in miniature, can be liberally employed. Music should be used, throughout, to underscore action. Practical lighting — lamps turned on and off by the actors — can be freely used, in addition to conventional stage lighting. In short, great invention is asked of you, in keeping this sometimes grim story forever entertaining.

I. H., New York City
May 1996

In diesem gro(en Haus
— von den ratten,
die um den Abflu(wissen,
bis zu den Tauben,
die nichts wissen —
wohne ich und ahne vieles.

In this big house —
from the rats
who know about the sewers,
to the doves,
who know nothing —
I live and learn much.

From *Saturn,* a poem by Günter Grass.

Lebensraum

As AUDIENCE enters theatre, the stage is illuminated by work-lights. The scenery is primarily wooden platforms and wooden racks, upon which hang various costumes, masks, props, etc. At curtain-time, STAGE MANAGER calls out from the booth...

STAGE MANAGER: *(Offstage.)* Okay, actors...The stage is yours. We're ready!
(THREE ACTORS enter and casually check their costumes and props. Eventually, they get into their starting positions. ACTOR #2, lying on a ramp, center, is covered by a blanket by ACTOR #3, as if in bed. ACTOR #2 calls to STAGE MANAGER, offstage...)
ACTOR #2: We're ready, stage manager!
STAGE MANAGER: *(Offstage.)* Thank you. Stand by for music and lights. We're going.
*(LIGHTING SHIFTS, suddenly, from preshow work-lights to dramatic stage-lighting. MUSIC IN, pulsating, nightmarish. ACTOR #2, grey-haired, 60ish, is now sleeping, in the throes of a frightening dream. Suddenly, HE screams out from his sleep. The play has begun.
LIGHT UP ON...ACTOR #1, an affable, handsome young man, who speaks to AUDIENCE.)*
ACTOR #1: At three A.M., Rudolph Stroiber woke from a most terrible nightmare.
(ACTOR #2 screams, again, sits up, sharply. Then, moves to platform, dresses in his next costume.)
ACTOR #1: Although it was winter and his window was half open, his body was drenched with perspiration. He was trembling with excitement. He had formulated an astonishing plan.
(ACTOR #2 re-enters, as RUDOLPH STROIBER, carrying a framed "official" cut out portrait through which his head and hands appear. HE smiles a politician's smile...)
ACTOR #2: Guten Morgen...Guden Morgen...Guden Morgen...
ACTOR #1: Herr Stroiber called together his family, his closest friends, his most learned advisors, and the very highest leaders of the German government. Every newspaper, every radio and television network was in

attendance for what Herr Stroiber announced would be "the news of the century."

(ACTOR #3 holds briefcase on shoulder as TV Camera, yells out countdown "Finf, fier" SHE motions "3, 2, 1." ACTOR #1 continues...)

ACTOR #1: Ladies and gentlemen, I give you Rudolph Stroiber, the Chancellor of the German Republic...

(WE HEAR...APPLAUSE, CHEERING.)

RUDOLPH STROIBER: We face the start of a new millennium...a new beginning. As Chancellor of this great German republic, I extend an invitation to six million Jews from anywhere in the world to come to live their lives in Germany. I speak to you, now: You will be given citizenship and full privileges in this great nation. You will be German. It is my heartfelt desire to re-establish a Jewish community in Germany, and to reduce, as much as humanly possible, the immeasurable shame we Germans feel each day of our lives for what this country did to our German-Jewish neighbors, sixty years ago. What I am saying to you six million Jewish people is quite simple, really. Please, come home. Please.

(LIGHTS CROSSFADE TO...ACTOR #3, young, blonde, blue-eyed, adorable; instantly appealing. SHE speaks directly to AUDIENCE...)

ACTOR #3: Herr Stroiber's speech ended as quickly as it had begun. At first, there was a shocked silence. And then, Steffen Von Menck, a senator from a suburb of Cologne, clapped his hands together, ten claps. He, alone, applauded.

(LIGHT FADES UP ON...ACTOR #1, now playing VON MENCK. HE claps his hands together, ten claps.)

ACTOR #3: After ten solitary claps, Herr Von Menck stopped. There was a most deafening silence...(Silence. ACTOR #1 drops a pin.)...Before the screams began.

(Silence. And then, on tape, we hear...SHOUTS, CROWDS YELLING.)

ACTOR #1: In Bremerhaven, Gustav Giesling, a dockworker and father of six, shouted into the microphone of a roving reporter from Westdeutscher Rundfunk...

(LIGHTS UP, suddenly, on...ACTOR #2 as GUSTAV GEISLING. ACTOR #3 shoves a microphone at HIM)

ACTOR #2: *I'm* not shy. *I'll* tell you what's going on. I can't feed my children, that's what going on! Last year, in my sector, alone, 900 dockers lost their jobs! In one year! I was one of the lucky ones! I kept my job, but, there's no work! There are no ships coming into port to load or unload! There are no fish, no containers, no work! I earned 10,000 marks, last year, before taxes, and my house-payments and car-payments, combined, were *20,000* marks! Where do we put six million new people, Jews or not? I don't personally care if these six million are Jews or if they're monkeys…Where do we put them, and how do they feed themselves?!…Ask yourselves *that?*

ACTOR #1: In Dusseldorf, Frau Eva Mueller had a different sort of reaction, which she discussed on "Open Your Heart," a popular daytime television talkshow…
(LIGHTS UP ON…ACTOR #3 as EVA MUELLER, holds a framed TV-screen in front of her face, speaks…)

ACTOR #3: I have three unmarried daughters. The oldest is twenty, and the youngest is seventeen. Do you not think that Jews will be looking for young German girls to marry, as soon as they arrive? If you think they won't be, you are crazy! They will romance our young daughters, and do you know how sorry our daughters will feel for them, when they hear their sad stories? Their tears and their knickers will be on the ground in no time!…I tell you, young German girls will be a prize for these Jews!
(ACTOR #1 sits facing EVA.)

ACTOR #1: Frau Mueller, it is a fact that, historically, Jews marry their own. Throughout history, since the bible, Jews marry Jews. I understand your anxiety, but, deep in your heart, won't you feel better about yourself if the shame we feel as a nation is lessened, if not erased?

ACTOR #3: What shame? *What shame?* You are a homosexual and a fool!
(LIGHTS CROSSFADE TO…ACTOR #2.)

ACTOR #2: At the University in Bonn, Viktor Spretz, Distinguished Professor of Psychology, stood before 200 of his university colleagues and delivered a hastily written, deeply sincere paper on the events of the past two days. *(ACTOR #2 looks up at AUDIENCE as pipe-smoking, tweedy VIKTOR SPRETZ; taps microphone; speaks to people at rear of auditorium…)* Can you hear me back there? Can you hear me?…

STAGE MANAGER: *(Offstage.)* Yuh, yuh, we hear you!

SPRETZ: Thank you. What I want to say to you wants to be said, calmly, without my worrying about projecting my voice like an actor. I want to speak to you, quietly, from my heart. Normally, I have no interest in politics. But, suddenly, what our government is proposing interests me, deeply. *(Takes notes from his pocket.)* I hope you won't think I'm in any way insincere because I have notes. I'll try not to read everything I say. I'll try to speak somewhat spontaneously, when it's…How shall I say it? Appropriate. When it's appropriate. *(Clears his throat; reads…)* This

Republic has, for sixty years, been drowning in a sea of guilt. Especially our children...our young people...two generations away from the shameful crimes of their grandfathers against the Jewish people. In the last forty-eight hours, incredibly, a solution has come, not from our philosophers, not from our psychoanalysts, not from our artists, not from our writers, not from our clergymen, but from our *government!* We have been encouraged to welcome six million Jews to Germany...to welcome them to live here among us as Germans...as equals...and to this, I say, emphatically, "Yes!"...How beautifully direct is this idea, how totally uncomplicated, how astonishingly achievable...

ACTOR #3: Unnoticed, at first, in the center of the auditorium, Doctor Götz Witzenbacher, Vice-Chairman of the Psychology Department, celebrated scholar of Freud and Wittgenstein, stood on his chair and took the chance of his life...

(ACTOR #1 stands on a chair — if possible, in the center of the AUDITORIUM, amongst the actual theatre-audience — and gives the salute of the 3rd Reich...)

ACTOR #1: Heil, Hitler! Heil, Hitler! Heil, Hitler!

ACTOR #3: What followed was a kind of mayhem. Doctor Witzenbacher was, at first, screamed at...and then, he was applauded by a quartet of skinhead-students at the rear of the auditorium, but, then, he was pulled from the chair and punched by Helmut Vogel, a promising young professor from the University's History Department. Dr. Witzenbacher fell to the ground and he was stomped by several important young faculty members, including professors of literature, science, and the plastic arts. *(ACTOR #2 throws ACTOR #1 to the ground and kicks him, viciously. DRUMBEATS, as WITZENBACHER dances being punched.)*

ACTOR #2: *Pig! Pig!*

(On tape, WE HEAR...SHOUTS OF ANGER AND PROTEST. WITZENBACHER is on the ground, now, on his back, center. ACTOR #3 approaches him, ripe tomato in her hand. ACTOR #2 covers SPRETZ with a white plastic sheet. And then...)

ACTOR #3: Dr. Witzenbacher's skull was crushed. He died, almost immediately.

(ACTOR #3 crushes the tomato. Its inner juice and pulp falls on to the white plastic sheet, which ACTOR #2 folds and removes.)

ACTOR #2: The crowd was astonished. No one knew what to do. They backed away from Dr. Witzenbacher's still-trembling body, leaving him alone in death, face down, in the center of the crowded auditorium.

ACTOR #3: Just three months earlier, Dr. Witzenbacher had been short-listed for the Nobel Prize in Science. He was a frequent guest on important German television panel-shows, and was well-known throughout the world as a liberal-minded German intellectual.

(ACTOR #1 rises; speaks to AUDIENCE, directly, quietly...)

ACTOR #1: What demon had seized Götz Witzenbacher? Was it a kind of momentary madness? Whatever it was, it had cost him his life. The academic community was shocked and outraged...and profoundly sorrowful. At the funeral of Doctor Götz Witzenbacher, Reverend Hans Schnabel, a reknowned Lutheran minister, added fuel to a fire that was already burning out of control...

(ACTOR #2 steps forward, speaks as MINISTER at a funeral. CHURCH MUSIC IN...under the scene.)

REVEREND SCHNABEL: Many of us have known Dr. Götz Witzenbacher for several years. We have known him as a great thinker, as a great writer, as a great pillar of our university community. I have personally known Herr Witzenbacher as a devoted father to his children, an exemplary husband to his wife, and as a man of God. His violent death leaves us stunned and confused. What our government has proposed will light the fuse of violence throughout the German Republic. I implore Herr Chancellor Stroiber and the government of this great German Republic to witness Herr Doctor Witzenbacher's death and to withdraw their invitation, immediately. When I speak against this issue, I am not speaking against Jews. I have no negative feelings about Jews. But, the manner in which our government is trying to undo sixty years in sixty minutes is unthinkable. Now, we must bury our friend Götz Witzenbacher. His four hundred students are without a professor. His four children are without a father. And this great German Republic is without one of its greatest thinkers. Let us bow our heads and pray.

ACTOR #1: And now, the clergy-population of Germany was in a hideous flap. Most clergymen called for Herr Reverend Schnabel's immediate resignation from the altar. But, several ministers and church laypeople proclaimed Herr Reverend Schnabel "a modern-day German hero"...a courageous speaker of what many came to know as "the great and undeniable German truth"...

ACTOR #3: *(Carries a rubber fish, wiggles fish's mouth, "throws" her voice, as though fish is speaking...)* In America, in Gloucester, Massachusetts, a fishing port, north of Boston, at land's end, Michael Linsky, an unemployed dockworker, spoke to his teenaged son.

ACTOR #2: *(With working-class Boston accent, as MIKE LINSKY…)* I dunno, Sammy…This offer could be wick'id appealing. I mean, we can't do worse than we're doin' here! You see what I'm sayin' on this?

ACTOR #1: *(As SAMMY, cap backwards; bouncing basketball…)* Germany? Are you *crazy?* They speak *German* in Germany!

ACTOR #2: *(To AUDIENCE, as NARRATOR.)* And in Tel Aviv, Israel, Bessie Mandelbaum, a survivor of Auchswitz, heard the news and wept…

(ACTOR #3 wears dark shawl, as BESSIE MANDELBAUM…)

BESSIE MANDELBAUM: My mother, my father, my two brothers, Edgar and Isaac…my little sister, Becca…my cousins Asher, Yisak, Izzie, and Shem, my tante Rachael…

ACTOR #2: *(To AUDIENCE, as NARRATOR.)* South of Jerusalem, in Beersheba, Zev Golem, a high-ranking officer in the Israeli Army, heard the news over a meal of blini and smoked salmon and alerted his wife, and cautioned his wife, angrily…

ACTOR #1: *(As ZEV GOLEM.)* Any Jews who go to live in Germany are fools. They are as good as dead. The Germans will finish the job, the first opportunity they have. These Jews will be shot in the back, the first time they try to take a stroll. No one will bury them. Their bodies will rot in the streets. Dogs and rats will eat the flesh from their bones!…

ACTOR #3: *(To AUDIENCE, as NARRATOR.)* And in Jerusalem, Rabbi Shlomo Brechtman read the news and called together a meeting of the most intelligent men and women of his congregation.

(ACTOR #2 enters as REB BRECHTMAN, wearing mask with talmudic beard.)

BRECHTMAN: We must go. We must do this. We must bring our young people with us. We must reclaim this place for Jews.

ACTOR #1: *(As NARRATOR.)* Not all of Reb Brechtman's friends agreed with him.

ACTOR #3: *(As older woman, MRS. MOSKOWITZ.)* I would rather put a knife in my son's heart than send him to live among the Germans!

ACTOR #1: Gertrude Moskowitz, who lost her entire family to the ovens of Buchenwald, who was raped by Nazi soldiers at the age of twelve, was overcome by a savage rage she could not begin to control. Reb Brechtman tried to reason with her, but, to no avail…

ACTOR #2: *(As REB BRECHTMAN.)* Mrs. Moskowitz, please! We must discuss this, together, intelligently.

ACTOR #3: *(Screams, as MRS. MOSKOWITZ.)* I'll gladly discuss this, intelligently, but, not with Nazi-lovers the likes of you, Herr Fuehrer Brechtman!

(Mrs. MOSKOWITZ spits at BRECHTMAN. ALL THREE ACTORS make a sound with sharp intake of breath. Then…)

ACTOR #1: *(As NARRATOR.)* There was a terrible shocked silence after Gertie Moskowitz spat on Reb Brechtman. But, then Jacob Brontheim did something that made Mrs. Moskowitz's spittle seem like a gentle tear of regret. He walked to Reb Brechtman…*(Walks to BRECHTMAN, grabs HIM by the throat…)*…grabbed him by the throat…*(Chokes BRECHTMAN.)*…and began to kill the kindly old Rabbi with his bare hands…*(Yells, as BRONTHEIM…)* They tied my hands and legs and made me watch them rape my mother and my two sisters. There were ten of them. When they were done with their sex, they cut my mother's throat and they took my sisters away with them. I never saw my sisters, again. It took me three days to free my hands. For three days I watched my mother's dead body…

(BRONTHEIM removes BRECHTMAN's beard and mask, which HE now strangles, as though it were the old man, himself…)

ACTOR #3: Suddenly, Brontheim's wife, Millie, began screaming and swatting at Brontheim, begging him to stop! *(Screams, as BRONTHEIM's wife…)* Jacob, stop! Stop, Jacob, darling, stop!

ACTOR #1: But, Brontheim could not stop…and Rabbi Brechtman's heart exploded. He slumped to the floor…

(Beard and mask fall to the floor. The old rabbi is dead.)

ACTOR #2: He's dead.

ACTOR #3: He's dead.

(ACTOR#2 steps forward, talks to AUDIENCE, directly…)

ACTOR #2: And so, within fifty hours of Rudolph Stroiber's invitation to the Jews, two intelligent men lay dead…Götz Witzenbacher, who had dared to salute Hitler, and Rabbi Shlomo Brechtman, who had dared to think the return of six million Jews to Germany was a good idea.

(SPRETZ's hat and pipe are put in a bucket along with BRECHTMAN's mask and beard. FLASH-PAPER is hidden in the bucket and ignited.)

ACTOR #3: In Gloucester, Massachusetts, Lizzie Linsky, née Elizabeth O'Donnell, wife of Michael Allen Linsky, made her husband say it to her, again…*(As LIZZIE LINSKY.)*…slowly, this time…

ACTOR #2: *(With working-class Boston accent, as MIKE LINSKY; speaks slowly…)* I…want us…to move…to Germany. *(Beat.)* I'm serious, Lizzie!… This offer makes sense on every level. You gotta' imagine they're gonna' come through with jobs, right? I mean, they can't pull six million new people into their country and not have work for us, right? So, why not? Nothin's happenin' here.

LIZZIE LINSKY: *(Same Boston accent.)* How can you even *think* about moving to Germany?! What's your mother gonna' say if you tell her we're moving halfway around the world?

MIKE LINSKY: Germany's not halfway around the world. It's maybe four thousand miles from here, that's all.

LIZZIE LINSKY: Fine. Four thousand miles. That's all.

MIKE LINSKY: I was thinking maybe my mother would, I dunno', maybe move with us kind of thing.

LIZZIE LINSKY: Did you, like, talk to your mother on this, already?

MIKE LINSKY: Course not! I wouldn't do that, Lizzie, would I? I know you and I've got to talk together on this, first.

LIZZIE LINSKY: I mean, what do we know about Germany? We'd be, like, *immigrants.* We'd be like the Italians and "Portegees" who come over here. You hear them in the Stop'n'Shop tryin' ta' ask questions. Nobody can understand what they're sayin'! Nobody wants them here!...

MIKE LINSKY: It's only a *language*! We'll study it. Bennie Krantz's brother went to music school in Germany. Bennie says everybody there speaks English, too.

LIZZIE LINSKY: Bennie said that?

MIKE LINSKY: Ask him. His brother didn't speak any German for the first year he was there and had no problems, whatsoever.

LIZZIE LINSKY: Why would Germans speak English?

MIKE LINSKY: It's the language of international business.

LIZZIE LINSKY: They speak *English*?

MIKE LINSKY: I'm thinking so positively on this, Elizabeth. I feel so *stupid* hanging around the house, no real job. It makes me feel stupid. Thinkin' about moving *excites* me. It could really be different.

LIZZIE LINSKY: What if it isn't?

MIKE LINSKY: Isn't different?

LIZZIE LINSKY: Isn't different. What if we move all the way there, and there's no work? Or supposing we just don't like it? What then?

MIKE LINSKY: We move back.

LIZZIE LINSKY: Just like that?

MIKE LINSKY: Just like that.

LIZZIE LINSKY: How? We swim?

MIKE LINSKY: We take a plane, same as we got there.

LIZZIE LINSKY: How are we even gonna' buy the plane tickets in the first place?

MIKE LINSKY: We sell off the land my father left me.

LIZZIE LINSKY: You'd do that?

MIKE LINSKY: Sooner or later, I'm gonna' have to, anyhow. It's almost three years since I worked, full-time.

LIZZIE LINSKY: *(New tone; somewhat frightened.)* I can see what you're sayin'. I really can. It's just that it scares me. I'm not Jewish, so, I've got no particular gripe with Germans. It's just the pickin'-up-and-movin' part. Goin' someplace totally different. It really scares me, Mike.

MIKE LINSKY: It scares me, too, Lizzie. Don't think it doesn't, cause it does.

LIZZIE LINSKY: What about Sammy?

MIKE LINSKY: Sammy's a kid. He'll love it, ten minutes after he gets there. Kids learn languages a lot quicker than grownups. Everybody says that. Sammy'll be fine.

LIZZIE LINSKY: He's not gonna' want to go. He came running to me, first time you mentioned any of this to him!

MIKE LINSKY: He'll go. He's a kid. He's got no choice. If we go, he'll go.
(ACTOR #1 steps forward, as SAMMY. HE is not happy. HE yells...)

SAMMY: *I won't! I won't! I fucking won't!*

MIKE LINSKY: You open up a filthy mouth like that in the house, I'll deck you! I swear ta' Christ!

SAMMY: It makes no sense!

MIKE LINSKY: It makes *plenty* of sense! There's work, there's money, and we're going. We're your mother and father and you're fifteen, so, you're going. For all I know, we won't like it and we'll be coming back in six months. Or maybe we'll like it. All's I know for sure is that we're gonna' try.

SAMMY: What if you like it and I don't? Then what?

MIKE LINSKY: You're gonna' have yourself a serious problem.
(Beat. And then...)

ACTOR #3: In Bremenhaven, Gustav Giesling, was having a similar problem with his teenaged daughter, Anna.

ACTOR #2: *(As GIESLING; black moustache.)* I am your father. I love you and I know what's best for you. I have *forbidden* you to go to that meeting!

ACTOR #3: I don't accept your ruling.

GUSTAV GIESLING: Your don't *what?*

ANNA GIESLING: I don't accept your ruling. The meeting is public and important. Almost everybody from my school will be there — my teachers, my friends — and I'll be there, too. If you want to take away my allowance, do it. If you want to scream until you give us both headaches, do it. I'm going to the meeting.

(After a substantial pause, GUSTAV calls, upstage, to his wife...)

GUSTAV GIESLING: *Berta!* Get in here and talk sense to your daughter!

ACTOR #1: *(To AUDIENCE, directly...)* Anna Giesling was one of four hundred and sixty Bremenhaven students who gathered in the high school auditorium, that night, to hear their teachers explain Chancellor Rudolph Stroiber's invitation to the Jews.

ACTOR #3: Like Anna, many students had no idea why Chancellor Stroiber made such an offer to so *many* Jews. Anna had nothing against Jews. In her entire life, she had never met a Jew. And, as far as she knew, she had never read a story by a Jewish writer, or seen a play by a Jewish playwright, or heard a song by a Jewish composer.

ACTOR #1: Thus far, in her public-school education, when Anna's teachers had reached the years 1933 through 1948, they'd told their students...

ACTOR #2: *(As a HISTORY TEACHER.)*...For an in-depth analysis of this particular period of German history, you should talk to your grandparents.

ACTOR #1: By contrast, many older high school students and university students had heard and read so much about the Nazis and the Holocaust, they were, frankly, bored by the very thought of it. But, what they'd learned was distant and abstract, totally impersonal. The real lessons were still as missing from their lives as were some six million Jews missing from Eastern Europe.

ACTOR #3: Tonight, many of Bremenhaven's best and bravest teachers decided that these missing lessons should finally be taught, properly.

(THE THREE ACTORS now stand, side by side, center stage, as if STUDENTS at a lecture. Their faces reflect the shock they feel.)

ACTOR #1: What the students heard that night, sent icy shivers through their hearts.

ACTOR #3: The students were young, and not from wealthy families. Most of them had never travelled outside of Germany.

ACTOR #2: They didn't know that most of the world hated them for what their grandparents had done.

ACTOR #1: They didn't know that they were being blamed for their nation's history.

ACTOR #2: Many of the students assembled had seen the American film *Schindler's List,* a few years earlier, but, somehow, thought that the Nazis, as depicted in the film, represented only an isolated few Germans. Many had dismissed the film, altogether, as "Hollywood-Jewish propaganda." Again, the Holocaust was distant, abstract, impersonal.

ACTOR #3: Their teachers, brave men and women, all, told them everything they knew to be true. Not from books, but from their own lives. Stories of their parents and grandparents, stories of neighbors and family friends, stories of normal German people.

(ALL THREE ACTORS step forward as TEACHERS. THEY will speak in overlapping phrases, imaging their "memories"...)

ACTOR #1: My father, Heinz Hinde, was assigned to a train depot that handled Jews being shipped to Buchenwald...

ACTOR #2: My grandmother, Uta Krebs, called the police and told them that a family of Jews was hiding in her building...

ACTOR #3: My mother and father assured me the Holocaust never happened. They assured me it was a Jewish invention...

ACTOR #1: His job was closing the boxcars doors. He had a wooden bat to hit Jews who wouldn't move forward to make room.

ACTOR #2: The Jewish family had lived in my grandmother's building all their lives. She was jealous of them, because their children wore fancy clothes. She called the police.

ACTOR #3: The day I started kindergarten, my parents sat me down and told me that Jews were demons who printed money, and bought the Holocaust-Denial Law in Germany, so that no German could ever legally question "the Jewish lie."

ACTOR #1: He and his friends used to make jokes about the people they hit with their bats. They knew these people were being taken to the ovens. They knew.

ACTOR #2: She knew that this entire family would be murdered by the Nazis, but, she called the police, anyway.

ACTOR #3: They made me promise to tell my friends, but, never let on they were the ones who told me. Because of the Jewish Law, I could get them in trouble.

ACTOR #1: When I was ten years old, I found a box of snapshots my father had taken during the War, and had saved as momentoes. There was picture after picture of Jewish people crammed into boxcars, some with bleeding heads from being hit by my father and his friends.

ACTOR #2: My grandmother told me she had no regrets, whatsoever, and that she would gladly call the police and turn them in, again, now, if a similar occasion presented itself.

ACTOR #3: To this day, they still believe it is a Jewish lie. They believe it with all their hearts.

ACTOR #1: One by one, the teachers told their stories...of their parents' and grandparents' unthinkable cruelty...

ACTOR #2:...Of how the German people were Hitler's partners in the slaughter of the Jews. Normal, upstanding German citizens were Hitler's most willing butchers.

ACTOR #3: Normal people...

ACTOR #1: Normal people...

ACTOR #2: Normal people...

ACTOR #3: My parents had a perfect marriage. They were loving, considerate, and sensitive. My childhood was ideal.

ACTOR #1: My father is a veterinarian. He loves animals. He's such a gentle, kindly man...such a loving father.

ACTOR #2: My grandmother taught piano to children, all her life. Children loved her. Her school, Charlottenburg Kinder-Flügel, was quite well-known: There was always beautiful music playing in her house...Bach, Beethoven, Brahms.

ACTOR #3: Every single one of us in this room has had someone in each of our families who we loved, deeply, who directly participated in the slaughter of six million Jews.

ACTOR #1: Normal people...

ACTOR #2: Normal people...

ACTOR #3: After the lecture, many students stayed in their seats and wept.

ACTOR #1: On the stage, their teachers embraced one another, each weeping with great relief that his or her darkest secret was so incredibly similar to the darkest secrets of all.

ACTOR #2: When Anna Geisling got home, later that night, she was a changed woman...

ACTOR #3: (As ANNA; sobbing.) How could you not tell me? How could you not tell me?

ACTOR #2: I told you *not* to go to the meeting! I *told* you!

ACTOR #3: Mother? (Sobs.) Mother?

ACTOR #1: Berta Geisling took her daughter in her arms, and held her, wordlessly. Together, they wept...

(ACTOR #3 turns upstage, her back to the AUDIENCE. SHE wraps her arms around her own body; "embraces" herself. ACTOR #2 watches, wordlessly.)

ACTOR #1: Gustav Geisling watched his wife and daughter weeping, together. He said nothing, but, he knew that his life was changing.

ACTOR #2: *(To AUDIENCE, as NARRATOR.)* South of Jerusalem, in the center of Israel, in Beersheba, quite near the border of Jordon, Zev Golem's wife, Reba, cautiously gave her husband upsetting news from his family in America…

ACTOR #3: *(As REBA GOLEM. SHE holds a letter in her hand.)* Your sister's son, the one who's living in Massachusetts…married to the "schikt-sa"…He's taking the offer.

ACTOR #1: *(As ZEV GOLEM.)* What offer? What are you telling me, Reba? What offer?

REBA: The, uh, German offer. That's what your sister says in her letter…Her son, Michael…he and his family.

ZEV: My sister's son is moving to Germany?

REBA: Soon. She says she knows six others…children of her friends. Here, read…

(REBA offers the letter to ZEV.)

ZEV: No!…I won't read it!…No.

(ZEV bows his head. LIGHTS CROSSFADE TO…ACTOR #2, down-stage. HE will now play two different characters, in rapid alternation, by literally changing hats. When HE wears a tattered cloth cap, HE will be playing an old Jew named MAXIMILLIAN ZYLBERSTEIN. When HE wears a fancy-dress hat, HE will be playing an old Jew named AXEL ROSENSWEIG. Both MEN will speak English with essentially Eastern European accents, but with a trace of Australian accent, as well. As the scene begins, SNOW falls on to the two old men.)

ZYLBERSTEIN: It's snowing, Rosensweig.

(ACTOR #2 changes from cap to hat. HE is now playing ROSENSWEIG.)

ROSENSWEIG: Yes, by goodness, it is, Zylberstein. I'm amazed.

(ACTOR #2 changes back from hat to cap; playing ZYLBERSTEIN, again.)

ZYLBERSTEIN: Why are you amazed, Rosensweig?

(Hat trick, again. And so it goes.)

ROSENSWEIG: Because I didn't think it was snow that was falling on me. I thought it was something else.

ZYLBERSTEIN: I know I'm going to be sorry for asking this, but, what did you think was falling on you, Rosensweig?

ROSENSWEIG: Your bloody *dandruff*, Zylberstein!…

ZYLBERSTEIN: Here we go!

ROSENSWEIG: I've told you fifteen times, this week, alone…Head and Shoulders Shampoo! But, do you listen? Do you *ever* listen?

ZYLBERSTEIN: *(Covers his ears.)* I'm not listening!

ROSENSWEIG: The "goyem" look at us, and what do they see? What do they *think?*…

ZYLBERSTEIN: I'm not listening!

ROSENSWEIG: They're thinking "Fifty per cent of all Jews have dandruff!"

ZYLBERSTEIN: I'm hearing nothing!

(ROSENSWEIG sees that ZYLBERSTEIN has covered his ears. HE is disgusted. HE harumphs, gruffly.)

ROSENSWEIG: *Harumph!*

(The OLD JEWS freeze, as ACTOR #3 steps forward, addresses AUDIENCE as NARRATOR…)

ACTOR #3: In Australia, in a tiny Northern village in the Tableland, there lived two old Jews…Zylberstein…

(ACTOR #2 dons Zylberstein's cap.)

ACTOR #3: And Rosensweig…

(Cap changes to dress hat.)

ACTOR #3: Rosensweig and Zylberstein were both concentration-camp survivors. When the war ended, the concentration camps were opened and survivors were released. Both Rosensweig and Zylberstein had to be relocated. Both men had lost everything…Family, homes, all worldly possessions.

ACTOR #1: With funds from the American Joint Distribution Committee, both men were sent to Australia to live.

ACTOR #3: By chance, they were settled in the same tiny village of fifty families, one hundred miles north of Cairns.

ZYLBERSTEIN: Rosensweig opened the village's only general store and fleeced everybody, charging way too much for everything he sold. But, people had no choice, and the "mumzer" made a fortune!

(Cap changes to dress hat.)

ROSENSWEIG: Zylberstein, the "putz," could never learn to speak a good English. He opened a business as a Mr. Fix-It. He should have called his business "Mr. Break-It-Worse!" He could never keep a dime in his pocket for more than five minutes, so, he ended up bumming money from Rosensweig.

ACTOR #1: They were the only Jews in the entire area, so, they were forced into a workable "enemyship," which has lasted, so far, for nearly sixty years.

ACTOR #3: They hated each other!…

ACTOR #1: In their way.

ACTOR #3: Their personalities were as different as different can be.

ACTOR #1: Rosensweig was compulsively neat, never seen without a fresh white shirt and a tightly tied necktie.

ACTOR #3: Zylberstein was, in a one-word euphemism…

ZYLBERSTEIN:…*Relaxed.*

ACTOR #3: His clothing was constantly spotted with meals from a fortnight earlier.

(ZYLBERSTEIN finds speck of dried food on his trousers; eats it.)

ACTOR #1: He often forgot to wear his socks.

ROSENSWEIG: Where are your socks?

ZYLBERSTEIN: On my feet.

ROSENSWEIG: They certainly are not!

ZYLBERSTEIN: They certainly are!

ROSENSWEIG: They certainly are not!

ZYLBERSTEIN: *(Looks down. No socks.)* They were there, this morning.

ACTOR #1: Each of them bore his history, quite differently. Rosensweig suffered, quietly. If the subject of the War (or, God forbid, the Camps) ever arose, Rosensweig had a ready response.

ROSENSWEIG: We don't talk of those times. Those times are passed.

ACTOR #3: But, Zylberstein constantly tried to joke the horror out of his aching memory.

ACTOR #1: Zylberstein was a neverending symphony of Holocaust jokes.

ACTOR #3: Witness Zylberstein's favorite joke.

(ACTOR #2 steps forward, as ZYLBERSTEIN…tells a joke.)

ZYLBERSTEIN: Two Jews, Goldberg and Finkle, survived Buchenwald, together. Goldberg settled in New York City, and made millions. Finkle settled in Russia, and had a miserable life. A few years ago, Goldberg had to go on a business trip to Moscow. Because of the time-change, he woke at 5 A.M., and couldn't get back to sleep. Having nothing better to do, he took a walk through the empty streets of Moscow. He spotted an old man walking in the opposite direction, and he was positive it was Finkle. Suddenly, a KGB van pulled up to the curb and six KGB men got out, grabbed Finkle, and beat Finkle to a bloody pulp. Then, the KGB men drove away in their van as quickly as they had come, leaving Finkle for dead, face down on the pavement. Goldberg ran across the street and knelt beside Finkle. He cradled the old Jew in his arms, and whispered to him, gently…"Finkle, Finkle, open your your eyes! It's me, Goldberg, from Buchenwald!" Finkle opened his eyes, and looked up. And he murmured to Goldberg, smiling, happily...*(Joyously; compared to life in Moscow, a cherished memory.)*..."*Ahhhhhhhhhh, Buchenwald! Those were the days!*"...

(ACTOR #2 changes cap for hat; speaks, now, as ROSENSWEIG.)

ROSENSWEIG: That is not a joke, Zylberstein. That is an *abomination!*

ZYLBERSTEIN: *(Flatly Beckettian.)* If you don't laugh, you cry.

ROSENSWEIG: I laugh when things are funny.

ZYLBERSTEIN: What's funny?

ROSENSWEIG: *Things* are funny.

ZYLBERSTEIN: What things?

ROSENSWEIG: When you see me laughing, you'll see what things.

ZYLBERSTEIN: I've known you for fifty-six years, Rosensweig. I've never once seen you laugh.

ROSENSWEIG: Very few things have been funny.

ACTOR #3: And then, without warning, Zylberstein said the first thing he had ever said to make Rosensweig laugh...

ZYLBERSTEIN: I'm taking the Germans up on their offer, Rosensweig. I'm moving to Germany.

ROSENSWEIG: Excuse me?

ZYLBERSTEIN: You can't hear? You've got waxy ears? I'm taking the Germans up on their offer. I'm moving to Germany.

ACTOR #1: And for the first time since 1937, since the Nazis entered his house and killed his father *(Drumbeat.)*, mother *(Drumbeat.)*, sisters *(Drumbeat.)*, brothers *(Drumbeat.)*, Grandmother and Grandfather *(Drumbeat.)*, Axel Rosensweig rolled back his head, and laughed.

(ROSENSWEIG has a pained reaction to each item in NARRATOR'S list, above. but, then, HE laughs, lightly, at first. His laughter grows, until HE is crippled by his own laughter. Beat. And then...)

ACTOR #3: The first Jews to arrive in Germany under the new "Jewish Homecoming Law" were two Frenchmen from Nancy, in the north of France. They arrived in Bonn a day before the government's offical welcoming ceremony, and reported to Project homecoming's sign-in station, set up in a lovely house that had been Beethoven's birthplace.

(ACTOR #1 steps forward, as PIERRE CHAMBRAY, a flamboyantly gay young Frenchman; wears bright red cap.)

PIERRE CHAMBRAY: Je m'appelle Pierre Chambray. Ahhh, mais, oui!...Je m'excuse. Il faut que je parle votre langue. *(Hesitantly...)* I am...named ...Pierre Chambray.

(ACTOR #2 steps forward as JACQUES BURSTIN, Pierre's gay lover. HE wears a matching bright red cap.)

JACQUES BURSTIN: And I am Jacques Burstin. Pierre and I are married.

(PIERRE and JACQUES kiss, coquetteishly.)

PIERRE CHAMBRAY: Jacques and I have been married depuis longtemps.

JACQUES BURSTIN: *(Kisses PIERRE's cheek, sweetly.)* Almost ten years.

PIERRE CHAMBRAY: We are here to live.

ACTOR #3: There was an astonished silence, broken by Katrina Keitel, first Assistant to Dr. Ludwig Hess, Rudolph Stroiber's most-trusted friend and Executive Chairman of "Project Homecoming." Katrina stepped forward and saved the moment, graciously…*(Changes voice; now speaks as KATRINA KEITEL, puts on band embossed with word "WILLKOM-MEN.")* We are thrilled that you have chosen Germany as your new home.

PIERRE CHAMBRAY: *(Completely unable to understand what KATRINA has said.)* De quoi vous parlez? *(To JACQUES.)* Qu'est-ce qu'elle raconte?

JACQUES BURSTIN: *(Smiling broadly.)* I am…Jacques Burstin…and he is Pierre Chambray.

PIERRE CHAMBRAY: We are married.

JACQUES BURSTIN: We come to live here.

PIERRE CHAMBRAY: Nous sommes Juives…

JACQUES BURSTIN: Ahh, ouais! C'est ça! We are…Jewish!

(JACQUES and PIERRE kiss each other, again, happily.)

ACTOR #3: While Katrina Keitel continued to speak, Project Homecoming's Executive Chairman, Dr. Ludwig Hess, an enormously fat man, who had, thus far, remained silent, with his eyes and mouth opened to their widest, extricated himself from the ceremony, hastily improvising a universally acceptable reason to leave…

(ACTOR #1 enters as DR. LUDWIG HESS. HE carries/wears his "official" portrait, padded with enormously fat stomach. HESS's head and hands poke through cut out holes. HE speaks…)

ACTOR #1: I have to pee.

(HESS runs two full circles around the stage, in a mad sprint. He holds his belly with both hands.)

ACTOR #3: Despite his remarkable corpulence, Dr. Hess sprinted, nonstop, from Project Homecoming's headquarters, across the market-square, to Project Homecoming's main office in the baroque 15th-century building once occupied by radical German students protesting the War in

Vietnam. Chancellor Stroiber was there, confronted by a stack of two hundred and sixty thousand Citizenship Applications.

DR HESS: Rudolph! Rudolph! The first two Jews are gay!

(ACTOR #1 looks up. HE, too, wears his "official" portrait. HE speaks as STROIBER…tired, annoyed.)

RUDOLPH STROIBER: I'm sure they are. Why wouldn't they be?

DR HESS: No, no, no! They're French queers, Rudolph! They're holding hands and kissing!

(STROIBER realizes what is being said. HE slaps his forehead.)

ACTOR #3: Within the hour, Jacques's and Pierre's immigration papers were less in order than they had seemed to be at the outset. They were sent home to Nancy…driven, in fact, in Chancellor's Stroiber's own white limousine.

(ACTOR #3 takes a TOY LIMOUSINE, looks into windows. PIERRE and JACQUES sitting in chairs, acting as if they are on the rear seat of the limo. THEY giggle; hold hands, thrilled to be in a limo.)

PIERRE CHAMBRAY: C'est vachement chic.

JACQUES BURSTIN: Oui. Trés agréable.

KATRINA KEITEL: *(Into windows of toy limo.)* Uhhh…C'est juste une toute petite formalité de plus avec vos documents d'immigration.

ACTOR #2'S VOICE ON TAPE: *(Over sound system in auditorium.)* Translation: There's just one more little formality with your immigration documents.

KATRINA KEITEL: Ce n'est pas du tout grave! On vous revoit, ici, dans deux semaines. *(In her own voice, to AUDIENCE.)* Translation: It's not at all serious. We'll see you back here, again, in two weeks.

PIERRE CHAMBRAY: Oui, d'accord! A dans deux semaines! Merci!

JACQUES BURSTIN: Merci. A dans deux semaines!

KATRINA KEITEL: Au revoir, Jacques! Au revoir, Pierre!

JACQUES AND PIERRE: *(IN UNISON.)* Au revoir, Katrina!

JACQUES BURSTIN: Elle est mignonne!

PIERRE CHAMBRAY: Elle est adorable! Elle est chou!

ACTOR #3: *(To AUDIENCE, as NARRATOR.)* Dr. Hess personally hand-chose the "official" first arrivals. He settled on an American-Jewish family and inttroduced them to the country on national television.

(LINSKY FAMILY holds TV "frame" in front of their faces. THEY are being telecast, nationally. ACTOR #2 leans forward into TV frame, speaks With working-class Boston accent, as MIKE LINSKY…)

MIKE LINSKY: Hi. Michael Linsky. I'm really, really, uh, honored.

(ACTOR #1 leans forward, speaks with similar accent, as SAMMY...)

SAM LINSKY: Sam Linsky...I just wanna' go on record as saying I'm here because my parents made me come here! I...

(ACTOR #3, as LIZZIE LINSKY, saves the moment, shoves SAMMY out of frame...)

LIZZIE LINSKY: I'll talk, Sammy!...Hi, I'm Liz Linsky! Michael's wife and Sammy's mom. I just want to say that we are truly thrilled to be the first Jewish family to be welcomed to Germany in your Project Homecoming. We are all pretty scared. It's new and we don't speak German. Obviously.

MIKE LINSKY: But, we're gonna' learn!...

LIZZIE LINSKY: We're gonna' try to learn.

(SAMMY is bored, picks his nose, off-camera. WE HEAR...STAGE MANAGER as TV INTERVIEWER, offstage.)

TV INTERVIEWER'S VOICE: What kind of music do you like, Sammy?

SAM LINSKY: (Shocked, pulls finger from nose.) Beastie Boys...Luscious Jackson...Smashing Pumpkins are totally whack!...

TV INTERVIEWER'S VOICE: And you, Frau Linsky. What are your favorite pastimes?

LIZZIE LINSKY: Me? Oh, well, I'm into aerobics and horseback riding. I love to ride. My family comes first, of course. We do a lot of things, together...as a family. Course, this is the biggest thing we've ever done, together...as a family...Movin' here. I hope we make some friends.

TV INTERVIEWER'S VOICE: Herr Linsky, could you tell us about yourself?

MIKE LINSKY: Oh, yuh, sure...First off, I guess, I'm a lumper. That's what you call a "docker." I grew up in a fishing town in Masachusetts. My father was a fisherman. I started working on the docks when I was maybe eight or nine...with my father. I started lumpin' when I was about fourteen. I was always a strong kid. I liked the physical, outdoor life kinda' thing. I also liked earning "the big bucks"...The money. (Smiles at LIZZIE.) Lizzie and I went all through school, together, first grade right through high school. Our fathers fished together for years and years. Lizzie — Elizabeth — she's not Jewish. We're bringing Sammy up Jewish, though. He was Bar Mitzvahed, back home, at the local synagogue, same as me. And Lizzie comes to synagogue with us on the High Holidays. She fits in, easy. (Beat.) We're very proud to be the first family welcomed to Germany under this Project Homecoming. I'm praying that there's work for me in my field...on the docks. I love my work. It all dried up back home. Truthfully, I was out of work for the last couple of years. I'm prayin' things are better here. That's why we came. *(Smiles.)* I'm a hard worker, I'm honest…and now, I'm here.

ACTOR #3: *(Speaks to AUDIENCE, as NARRATOR.)* The Linsky family's first national TV appearance was an estimable success. Mike seemed no different from any German dockworker; Elizabeth came across as bright and kind and sexually nonthreatening. Sammy was an instant heartthrob for high school girls all over Germany.

ACTOR #1: Germans liked Americans, and they liked the Linsky family, enormously.

ACTOR #3: Chancellor Rudolph Stroiber's popularity rating went up six points in one day.

ACTOR #2: *(As STROIBER, wearing portrait, giving interview.)* It is too soon for self-congratulations. All we know is that the first family is here, and they are nice people.

ACTOR #1: *(As NEWSMAN at press conference.)* Herr Chancellor Stroiber, how long do you think it will take before six million new Jewish citizens are fully integrated into German life?

RUDOLPH STROIBER: Truthfully? Years and years. We can bring the people here, we can help them get started with their lives, but, full integration — the *reunion* that is my dream — that is a matter of spirit. That is a matter of time.

ACTOR #3: The Linskys were located in Bremenhaven. Mike was given one of the few full-time jobs on the Bremenhaven docks.

(ACTOR #3 CHANGES voice to TV INTERVIEWER.)

TV INTERVIEWER: Herr Linsky, how is it going?

MIKE LINSKY: It's going really well! I was scared stiff about the language part of it, but, ya' know, it turns out that lumpin' is lumpin'. I mean, the containers come in and they've got to be unloaded. It's pretty much exactly the same here as it was back home. So, I do my work. If something complicated comes up, I watch the other guys, and I just copy what they're doin'…

(ACTOR #1 enters with pen and paper, gets LINSKY's autograph.)

ACTOR #1: Danke.

MIKE LINSKY: Bitte. *(To CAMERA.)* Hey, I'm workin'! I'm happy.

ACTOR #3: *(As NARRATOR.)* Most of Germany applauded Mike Linsky. They liked him. They liked his New England work ethic, his American openness. And they especially liked what they came to call his "Judish Bärme"…his "Jewish warmth."

ACTOR #1: The image of the Linsky family's successful relocation was telecast around the globe. Within two weeks of their arrival in Germany, a million five hundred thousand other Jewish families, inspired by the Linskys, made application for German citizenship.

ACTOR #2: One million eight hundred and seven thousand people had arrived in Germany, already, to live their new lives.

ACTOR #1: *(As PIERRE...)* Including Pierre...

ACTOR #2:...And Jacques!

(ACTORS #1 and #2, enter. THEY wear red caps, hold hands...)

PIERRE CHAMBRAY: *(Smiling brightly.)* Coucou! C'est nous!

JACQUES BURSTIN: *(Smiling brightly.)* Coucou! Nous sommes là!

ACTOR #3: But, everyone in Germany was not smiling.

ACTOR #1: *(As FRENZIED GOVERNMENT WORKER, wearing official portrait...)* Chancellor Stroiber, I'm so sorry to interrupt your conference, but, we're having a problem with the *Jews*.

RUDOLPH STROIBER: What is it?

FRENZIED GOVERNMENT WORKER: There are approximately five hundred thousand new Jewish citizens with no place to sleep, tonight.

RUDOLPH STROIBER: Get them hotel rooms.

FRENZIED GOVERNMENT WORKER: Who will pay for that?

RUDOLPH STROIBER: Ask the hotels to donate their empty rooms. If they refuse, get the best price you can and the government will pay.

FRENZIED GOVERNMENT WORKER: Yes, sir. I'll do my best, sir.

ACTOR #3: In Bremenhaven, an outraged Gustav Geisling attended a meeting of unemployed dockworkers.

(ACTOR #2 steps forward as GUSTAV GEISLING; raises his hand...)

GUSTAV GIESLING: I'd like to speak. For those of you here I don't know, my name is Gustav Giesling. I was born in Bremenhaven, morthree streets away from here, and I've worked on the docks all my life...well, since high school...I was Vice-Chairman of the Dockers' Union for ten years. I've been a paid-up Union member for nearly thirty-five years. What I'm going to say, now, will not be popular.

ACTOR #3: The membership leaned forward in their seats. Over the years, they'd known Giesling to be a hard worker, and a brutally honest man, afraid of absolutely nothing.

GUSTAV GIESLING: What my father did in the War was his affair, not mine. I was born in 1949, into the worst possible chaos. When I was 16, to find a job was next to impossible. I found a job. Here. On the docks. I worked to make this country as great as it is, today. I intend to work to *keep* this country great. If our government wants to give our country away to six million Jews without jobs, I say "No!"...I say "Stop!." I say "There are six million *Germans* without jobs. Take care of Germans, first!" *(On tape, we hear...CHEERS and APPLAUSE from two hundred people.)*

ACTOR #3: Gustav Giesling's meeting was but one of a thousand similar meetings taking place in Germany, that night. Unemployed German workers were outraged that their government would create jobs for Jews, instead of creating them for Germans. Worse, in some instances, German workers were being *replaced* by Jews.

(ACTOR #1 steps forward, as GÜNTER FRIEDLANDER, wearing a cashmere overcoat draped over shoulders. HE smokes an Havana cigar; approaches MIKE LINSKY, smiling...)

GÜNTER FRIEDLANDER: Guten Morgen. You're Mike Linsky?

MIKE LINSKY: Yuh. I am.

GÜNTER FRIEDLANDER: Sehr erfreut. I'm Günter Friedlander. I own the docks.

MIKE LINSKY: Oh, *hiiii!* I've heard your name.

(THEY shake hands.)

GÜNTER FRIEDLANDER: I want you to know that I'm really happy you're working here.

MIKE LINSKY: I'm really happy, too. Thanks.

GÜNTER FRIEDLANDER: You're kind of a star.

MIKE LINSKY: Oh, God, well, not really. I mean, I didn't do anything to, you know...

GÜNTER FRIEDLANDER: Business is actually *up*. We're getting two more container-ships, this week, than we got, last week.

MIKE LINSKY: That's *great!*

GÜNTER FRIEDLANDER: I think it's mostly your doing.

MIKE LINSKY: How could that be?

GÜNTER FRIEDLANDER: I think it would be good for everybody if I pushed you up front a little.

MIKE LINSKY: How so?

GÜNTER FRIEDLANDER: I just had a TV reporter in my office asking how you were doing. I told him we're thinking of promoting you.

MIKE LINSKY: Are you kidding?

GÜNTER FRIEDLANDER: I'd like to bring you into the office, maybe team you with salespeople. I know you can't really speak a lot of German, yet, so, we'll have to...

MIKE LINSKY: Please, don't!…I don't want to be inside. I want to stay outside.

GÜNTER FRIEDLANDER: You do?

MIKE LINSKY: I do. I appreciate what you're saying and all, but, I want to
stay working outside.

DOCKOWNER: How about crew chief?

MIKE LINSKY: How so?

GÜNTER FRIEDLANDER: When I tell the TV interviewer you've turned
me down for the office-job, I want to be able to tell him something else
is happening…some other kind of promotion.

MIKE LINSKY: God! Crew chief would be *great!* What about the boys?

GÜNTER FRIEDLANDER: Are you kidding? The boys love you!

ACTOR #3: Herr Friedlander was right. Most of Mike Linsky's co-workers
adored Mike. He worked hard, and he was, after all, a celebrity. But,
Götz Burger, who was being replaced by Mike as Crew Chief, was less
than adoring.

ACTOR #2: *(As GÖTZ BURGER, furious…) This is a gewalttätigeit! An out-
rage!*

GÜNTER FRIEDLANDER: Götz, for God's sake, calm yourself! You'll
burst a blood vessel! I'm not taking any money away from you! I'm just
putting you back in the crew for a while.

(ACTOR #3 enters, as SECRETARY, with coffeepot.)

SECRETARY: More coffee, Herr Friedlander?

GÜNTER FRIEDLANDER: Bitte.

SECRETARY: Guten tag, Herr Berger.

GÖTZ BURGER: Guten tag, Frau Jauslin.

(SECETARY refills mugs; exits.)

GÜNTER FRIEDLANDER: This will all blow over. For the moment, the
Jews are very, very popular. We happen to have a very famous one, and
business happens to be picking up. For the good of the dock — for your
fellow workers — let this happen! It's my right as dock-owner to make
it happen, with your blessing or without your blessing. Give this thing
your blessing, Götz. Use your brain. Be smart.

GÖTZ BURGER: *No!…I will not!*

ACTOR #3: But, the dock-owner did indeed have the right to replace a crew
chief. And replace he did. While Michael Linsky was telling his wife
Elizabeth his good news, and while Götz Burger was telling his wife
Miriam his bad news, Sammy and Anna were meeting for the very first

time…*(Smiles at AUDIENCE.)*…As you must have known, all along, would happen.

SAM LINSKY: Hi. Do you, uh, speak any English?

ANNA GIESLING: I do, yes.

SAM LINSKY: Great! That's a major relief!

ANNA GIESLING: Why?

SAM: 'Cause, I've been staring at you in Biology class, nonstop, for about three days, and I was really hoping you'd, you know, speak English.

ANNA: Well, I do.

(An embarrassed pause.)

SAM: That's great. I'm Sam Linsky.

ANNA; I know. Everybody knows that. I mean, all you have to do is turn on your TV, or read the local newspaper.

SAM: I guess.

ANNA: I'm Anna Giesling.

SAM: I know. I copied your name down from your Biology paper.

ANNA: I saw you doing that, yuh. *(Beat.)* Do you speak any German, yet?

SAM; Not too much. Just the basics. Like, Where's the bus to Frederickstraße…*Wo fährt (excuse me) ein Bus ab Frederickstraße?* I had to learn that, first day, or I never would have gotten home from school. I also know *"Wann fährt (excuse me) der nächste Bus?"*…When's the next bus? And basic food—German. *"Ich hätte gern Schinkenspeck, Hackfleisch"*…

ANNA; You eat Schinkenspeck?

SAM: Yah, yah…Schinkenspeck. Every morning, with my eggs. Schinkenspeck's a totally funny word. German's full of funny words. Sometimes, I think Germans must stand around laughing about how funny they sound.

ANNA: Is that why you say "excuse me" after you say "fährt?"

SAM: "Fährt?" Is that how you say it? "Fährt?" Oh, *God!*

ANNA: I thought Jews were against eating Schinkenspeck?

SAM: I dunno. I guess. We eat it. Maybe, 'cause my mother's not Jewish. She does the cooking. 'Course, my father's Jewish, and he always eats it, too. But, he's not religious at all. I am. Religious. Not too much, but, more than my father. 'Course, I throw back the old Schinkenspeck, same as him. We call it "bacon."

ANNA: I know. Bacon.

SAM: I've been eating bacon and eggs with my father, at four o'clock, every morning, ever since I can remember.

ANNA: You get up at four in the morning?

SAM: For breakfast with my dad. Then, he goes to work and I go back to bed, til I have to get up for school. My mother does the same deal...up at four, goes back to sleep, til she has to get up at seven-thirty with me. It's totally ridiculous.

ANNA: We all get up at four, same as your family. My father has to be to work at five, too.

SAM: What's he do?

ANNA: He's a docker. He works on the docks, unloading ships. Same dock as *your* father.

SAM: You're kidding!

ACTOR #2: *(To AUDIENCE, as NARRATOR.)* Sam and Anna stayed together, for the next four hours, discovering all their amazing similarities — and differences. They skipped taking der nächste Bus ab Frederickstraße, opting to walk, together, talking...falling in love.

ANNA: Do you really like the Beastie Boys?

SAM: They're genius! They totally rule!

ANNA: Maybe I'll give them another try.

SAM: I'll take you through a couple of cuts on "Paul's Boutique." You've got to have the lyrics out, when you listen the first five or six times, otherwise, you can't understand anything they're saying.

ANNA: That's exactly what happened to me! I couldn't hear the words so well.

SAM: I'll take you through it.

ANNA: That'd be great. I could help you with extra German lessons, if you'd like.

SAM: You could? You would? *Really?*

ANNA: Sure.

ACTOR #2: *(To AUDIENCE, as NARRATOR.)* Sam stared at Anna. He wanted to kiss her more than he wanted to breathe. He didn't dare. He breathed, instead.

SAM: *(Exhaling.)* You're really beautiful.

ANNA: I'm *not!*

SAM: Oh, God, you so totally *are!* Back home, you'd be elected head cheerleader, hands down. *Shit!* I mean, *Sheisse!* That's so dumb, what I just said!

ANNA: I don't know what what you said means.

SAM: Trust me.

ANNA: I do trust you.

ACTOR #2: What Anna said next took Sam by surpise.

ANNA: You're very handsome, Sam.

SAM: Go on!

ANNA: I can't go on. That's it. That's all I have to say. I guess you hear you're handsome a lot...from a lot of girls.

SAM: Just you and Elizabeth.

ANNA: Who's Elizabeth?

SAM: My mother. Oh, yuh, Selma, too...My Grandmother. She always pinches my cheek...

(SAMMY pinches his own cheek, imitates his Grandmother's voice...)

SAM: *Oy, Sammy, you're so handsome! (Smiles.)* Those three girls...Liz, Selma, and, now, you.

ACTOR #2: It is often said that great loves are made in their differences, not in their similarities. Sam never knew what Anna was going to say next. She often shocked him.

ANNA: Do you think we should stop talking and do the kissing? I don't know your morality-position on boys and girls kissing during their first meeting.

SAM: I have no morality-position, because it's not a subject that comes up a lot. Oh, yuh...There was this one girl, Maxine, who moved into town in eighth grade. I kissed Maxine the first time *we* met. We were walking home across the beach and I, uh, kissed her.

ANNA: What happened?

SAM: She stopped talking to me. She started walking home with Brian O'Donnell.

ACTOR #2: Sam asked Anna if she'd had a lot of boyfriends.

ANNA: Not at all. I'm not allowed to have boyfriends.

SAM: Really? Are you, like, some kind of German *nun*?

ANNA: *(Laughs.)* No, my father's really strict with us.

ACTOR #2: Anna told Sam about her parents, about her brothers and sisters. And then, Sam talked about *his* family...

SAM: I'm an only child. I had a brother, but he died.

ANNA: Oh, no!

SAM: It was before I was born. He drowned when he was little. He fell off my uncle's boat. He was two, I think.

ANNA: How terrible!

SAM: Deep down, I always thought it was a good thing for me. My parents really wanted me. They kept telling me that.

ACTOR #2: Anna asked Sam if being an only child put a lot of pressure on him...

SAM: Not really. Maybe. I guess it made me learn how to be a good swimmer.

(ANNA laughs.)

ANNA: That's *terrible*, to say that!...You're so funny.

SAM: You think so?

ANNA: I *know* so.

SAM: Then, it's definitely okay for us to kiss.

ANNA: Because I laugh at your jokes?

SAM: Because you laugh at my jokes.

(THEY kiss.)

ACTOR #2: And that's how Sam Linsky, American, Jewish, and Anna Giesling, German, Lutheran, came to kiss a perfect first kiss...full of exploration, full of gentleness and caring...and totally without guilt.

(THEY break from their kiss.)

SAM: Oh, God! That was really good! I'm really glad we did that!

ANNA: Me, too! Before the first kiss, you're always worrying about whether to do the kissing or not.

SAM: It was definitely the main thing on *my* mind, I can tell you that!

ANNA: I always think, "After you kiss the boy, you can begin to talk and get to know each other!"...You must promise you'll never tell my father I said any of this!

SAM: I promise. As long as you promise to never tell my grandmother you're German.

ANNA: What should I tell her I am?

SAM: We'll think of something. Maybe Korean. How do you feel about *second* kisses?

ANNA: Very favorably.

(THEY kiss, again. As soon as their lips meet...LIGHTS SHIFT TO...ACTOR #2, downstage...)

ACTOR #2: At the very moment Anna and Sammy's lips made contact for the 2nd time, Max Zylberstein arrived at Project Homecoming's sign-in center in Bonn. He was exhausted. *(Puts on tweed cap; speaks, now, as MAXIMILLIAN ZYLBERSTEIN.)* You know how many hours it takes to fly from Cairns, Australia, to Bonn, Germany? I'll tell you. A *hundred!* You know how many peanuts you eat in a hundred hours?!

ACTOR #3: Maximillian Zylberstein had the distinction of being the oldest of the new citizens to arrive under the Project Homecoming Law.

ACTOR #1: He was also the first concentration camp survivor to claim German citizenship under the new law.

ACTOR #3: He was also the first new citizen to have actually been a German citizen, earlier in his life, in pre-Hitler Germany.

ACTOR #1: *(Playing SIGN-IN CENTER CLERK.)* Where were you born, Herr Zylberstein?

ZYLBERSTEIN: Here and there.

SIGN-IN CENTER CLERK: Here and there?

ZYLBERSTEIN: Here and there.

SIGN-IN CENTER CLERK: Here and there, in which country?

ZYLBERSTEIN: I can't remember.

SIGN-IN CENTER CLERK: Do you have any clue at all?

ZYLBERSTEIN: None. I've been in Australia for nearly sixty years.

SIGN-IN CENTER CLERK: Shall we put down "Australia?"

ZYLBERSTEIN: I wasn't born there. I was relocated there.

SIGN-IN CENTER CLERK: Could you have been born in Poland?

ZYLBERSTEIN: I could have been.

ACTOR #3: Zylberstein was, in fact, born in Berlin...in a working-class neighborhood called Charlottenburg.

ACTOR #1: Zylberstein remembered his childhood, vividly. His father had been an actor in the same company in which Bertolt Brecht's earliest plays were first performed.

ACTOR #3: His father, Zelly Zylberstein, was gaining popularity, in 1930, just as Hitler was gaining political power.

ACTOR #1: The Zylbersteins weren't a rich family, but, they were well-off. They had a small house, overlooking the River Spree. They were loving, educated, and sophisticated.

ACTOR #3: Zelly Zylberstein was arrested, on stage, in the midst of a comic peformance as the forgetful butler in a German adaptation of a George Bernard Shaw play.

ACTOR #1: He had told his family a thousand times that what was happening to other Jews in Germany could never happen to them. They were Germans. Intellectuals. They were safe.

ZYLBERSTEIN: He was incorrect.

ACTOR #1: Hitler made a shabbily dramatic example of Zelly Zylberstein's crime against the state. The popular Jewish actor was arrested and humiliated in front of an astonished audience.

ACTOR #3: His understudy was rehearsed and ready to take over Zylberstein's role, midperformance. And he did.

ZYLBERSTEIN: My father was taken away in handcuffs. Hitler's people in the audience were yelling "Judle! Judle!"…"Kike! Kike!." My father was crying.

ACTOR #3: The understudy entered, stage left, as Zelly Zylberstein exited, stage right. And the show went on.

ACTOR #1: At 8:15 PM, precisely the same moment of Zelly Zylberstein's arrest, Police entered the Zylberstein family's home in Charlottenburg, and arrested Zelly Zylberstein's wife *(Drumbeat.)*, daughter *(Drumbeat.)*, mother *(Drumbeat.)*, his dying father *(Drumbeat.)*, his sister *(Drumbeat.)*. Zylberstein's small son, Maxie, was not in the house.

ACTOR #2/ZYLBERSTEIN: *(To AUDIENCE, as NARRATOR.)* The little boy…seven years old…was sitting on the carpeted steps in the back of the theatre, scared, weeping, watching his father being led away by the Police…hearing people planted in the audience by Hitler screaming "Judle! Judle!"…*(To CLERK, as ZYLBERSTEIN.)* I can see you've had a difficult day. Let's put down "Poland." Poland is a fine place to be born.

SIGN-IN CENTER CLERK: That's ever so nice of you, Herr Zylberstein. *(Types information into computer.)* "Poland" it is. *(Looks on computer screen.)* Let's find you a place to stay. Any preferences? Would you rather live in the country, or in the city?

ZYLBERSTEIN: Berlin, please.

SIGN-IN CENTER CLERK: Berlin? Let's have a look.

(CLERK looks at computer screen.)

SIGN-IN CENTER CLERK: There is a small guest-house in the Charlottenburg district. The listing indicates they can take you for a few weeks, maybe longer, if you're willing to help out on the desk.

ZYLBERSTEIN: Yes.

SIGN-IN CENTER CLERK: I can put you up here in Bonn, for tonight, in a very nice hotel, just here on the market-square. You can travel to Berlin, in the morning.

ZYLBERSTEIN: I'd prefer to go to Berlin, now, if you please.

SIGN-IN CENTER CLERK: Are you sure?

ZYLBERSTEIN: Quite sure.

ACTOR #3: Within the hour, Zylberstein was driven from Bonn to Cologne, where he boarded a Lufthanza flight to Berlin.

ACTOR #1: By all that was holy, a man of Zylberstein's age should have been exhausted by his journey, but, he was not at all. In fact, Zylberstein felt more energetic than he had at any time during several prior decades.

ACTOR #2: *(As NARRATOR.)* He had a purpose. He had a plan.

ACTOR #3: In Beersheba, Israel, Zev Golem, had a plan, as well.

ZEV GOLEM: I firmly believe that we must monitor Germany's "Project Homecoming." I and many, many others believe this project is neo-Nazi based...designed to complete Hitler's mission: the elimination of world Jewry. Our organization must maintain the strongest possible military presence in Germany, at this time.

ACTOR #3: Zev Golem had organized a meeting of one hundred trusted Jewish militants, members of a worldwide secret Jewish army called "Jews, Forever." Among them, we meet a Czech, Rifka Borenstein, head of the Women's Committee.

(ACTOR #3 now speaks to AUDIENCE as RIFKA, angry, dangerous...)

RIFKA: If you think they do not plan to slaughter six million *more* Jews, you are insane! They are Germans! They are *born* to kill Jews! They are *defined* by killing Jews!

ACTOR #2: May we ask Rifka Borenstein and Zev Golem what they are proposing to the Executive Committee, specifically?

ZEV GOLEM: We must organize our people in Germany, immediately!

RIFKA: I will personally go to live in Germany, as soon as possible, for this purpose.

ZEV GOLEM: As will I.

RIFKA: We're both speaking a good German, so we can stay undercover, easily.

ZEV GOLEM: We propose that we go to live in Germany as new German citizens under the Project Homecoming program.

RIFKA: Our people on the inside can deal with the necessary paperwork. I've checked everything. Zev Golem and I have already been preapproved.

ZEV GOLEM: Once we're living there, we can organize our people, properly.

RIFKA: We must be able to disseminate news, worldwide, immediately, if and when the Germans begin to kill Jews, again.

ZEV GOLEM: We must be ready to strike back, militarily, as well.

RIFKA: This is our job.

ZEV GOLEM: We are the policemen of the world's Jews.

ACTOR #2: You'll have no opposition from anyone on this committee. We back you, entirely. May God be with you, as well.

ACTOR #3: *(As NARRATOR.)* And that is how Rifka Borenstein and Zev Golem came to emigrate to Germany as new Jewish citizens.

ZEV GOLEM: *(To RIFKA; urgently.)* Rifka! Pay attention! I think this fat one is our clerk! *(To SIGN-IN CLERK #2.)* My name is Allen Schwartz.

RIFKA: And I'm his wife...Mrs. Schwartz.

(ACTOR #2 plays SIGN-IN CENTER CLERK #2)

SIGN-IN CENTER CLERK #2: You're both American-born?

RIFKA: Yes. Both of us. But, we've been living in Israel for several years, so, our English is a little rusty.

SIGN-IN CENTER CLERK #2: Your German is not bad.

ZEV GOLEM: Thank you.

RIFKA: Thank you.

SIGN-IN CENTER CLERK #2 *(Puts rubber-stamp mark on several official citizenship-papers…)* Fine. Fine. Fine. Fine. Fine. Your papers are in order. Welcome to Germany…fellow citizens.

RIFKA: *Vielen Dank.*

ZEV GOLEM: *Danke.*

SIGN-IN CENTER CLERK #2: Bitte.

(SIGN-IN CENTER CLERK looks up at imagined line of people, waiting.)

SIGN-IN CENTER CLERK #2: Nächste?

ACTOR #3: Mike Linsky spent his first day as crew chief with a smile from ear to ear. At dinner, that night, he had nothing but praise for their new country.

MIKE LINSKY: Can you imagine? Can you imagine? Here I am, runnin' a crew of fifty men, TV cameras, everywhere…Three container-ships in a nest, waitin'! Can you imagine this? Business is gettin' better and better, and everybody's givin' me the credit! *Everybody!* Herr Friedlander… Günter…I'm s'pose'ta call him by his first name, Günter… He owns the docks…He gave out this interview sayin' that he's gonnna' be bringing back fifty jobs…He's gonna' be hiring twenty-five new men… all new citizens…Jews! Can you imagine?…

ACTOR #3: But, everybody in Bremerhaven wasn't as euphoric as Michael Linsky. Gustav Giesling, for example, was totally offended by Günter Friedlander's decision to hire twenty-five Jewish citizens to work the docks.

GUSTAV GIESLING: There are ten million Germans out of work! Ten million! And out of fifty new jobs, twenty-five are going to Jews? I say "No!" I say "Strike!"…*Strike! Strike!*

ACTORS #1, #2 AND #3: *Strike! Strike! Strike!*

ACTOR #3: There were five hundred union workers gathered together in the hall. Those with jobs were hesitant. *(Calls out as FISH-PACKER.)* I waited a year for my job! I don't want to strike!

GUSTAV GIESLING: You can't be so greedy! This is a union, not a rat race! We must protect our brothers and sisters who are out of work, as well as those who are working. Strike! Strike!

ACTORS #1, #2 AND #3: *Strike! Strike! Strike!*

ACTOR #3: Götz Burger spoke, briefly, but convincingly.

GÖTZ BURGER: My name is Götz Burger. Many of you know me from the docks. I have been demoted as crew chief, so that a Jew can take my place! So that a Jew could be put in the spotlight! A Jew has taken my job from me. Soon, Jews will have everybody's jobs! That is our government's plan! That is why we must strike!

ACTOR #3: And, one by one, the workers were frightened or shamed into joining together...

ACTOR #1: *(To AUDIENCE, as NARRATOR...)* Heroes and villians alike are too often born of hopelessness and humiliation.

ACTOR #2: In Berlin, a cable-television installer named Allen Schwartz got an urgent message to return a call from his his wife at her office.

(LIGHTS SHIFT TO...ZEV GOLEM, as if talking on telephone.)

ZEV GOLEM: I need to speak with Mrs. Schwartz. This is her husband.

RIFKA: *(As if on telephone.)* Hello?

ZEV GOLEM: It's Zev, Rifka. Issak said it was urgent.

RIFKA: We must meet, immediately, Zev. There's trouble.

ACTOR #1: Zev Golem went to Bremenhaven, immediately, along with Rifka and sixteen other "new citizens," all members of the rapidly growing underground army, "Jews, Forever."

ZEV GOLEM: Are you Herr Linsky?

MIKE LINSKY: I am, yuh.

ZEV GOLEM: I'm Allen Schwartz. I'm assigned to your crew.

MIKE LINSKY: Hey, that's great. *(THEY shake hands.)* Call me "Mike," Al, okay?

ZEV GOLEM: Fine...Mike.

MIKE LINSKY: You speak English, huh?

ZEV GOLEM: I do, yes, Mike.

MIKE LINSKY: How come?

ZEV GOLEM: I speak many languages, Mike.

MIKE LINSKY: Have you worked on the water at all?

ZEV GOLEM: Excuse me?

MIKE LINSKY: Hey, no problem. You speak any German?

ZEV GOLEM: I speak German.

MIKE LINSKY: Great! I'm gonna' put you with Hans on that first containership. We're a little short-handed, today. We've got some union problems. Nothin' serious. The boss is workin' on it.

ACTOR #3: Mike Linsky's assessment of the situation as "nothing serious" was grossly and absurdly hopeful, given the fact that Gustav Giesling, Götz Burger, and several other union men were now carrying guns.

GUSTAV GIESLING: *(Brandishing pistol.)* Under no circumstances do our guns come out unless *their* guns come out!…Is that clear?

ACTOR #1: Clear, Herr Giesling.

ACTOR #3: Clear, Herr Giesling.

ACTOR #1: Absolutely clear, Herr Giesling.

ACTOR #3: Each morning, at five A.M., Maximillian Zylberstein woke, and left his warm bedroom at number 25 Hardenbergstra(e, and walked six blocks to stop and stare at number 16 Tribestra(e, a small one-family house overlooking a tiny tributary of the river Spree, and a large park, Charlottenburg Schlosspark, beyond. Zylberstein had spent his boyhood in this house, until his father was arrested. This morning, Zylberstein walked for nearly forty minutes along Otto-Suhr-Allee, to an undistin-guished four-story apartment house at 12 Frederickstra(e. This is where little Maxie Zylberstein lived when *he* was arrested and, subsequently, sent to Buchenwald. He opened the front door and he went inside. He climbed the steps to the third floor and he knocked on the door. A sixty-five-year-old woman answered. Her name was Esla Krebs.

(ACTOR #3 now talks to ZYLBERSTEIN as ESLA KREBS.)

ZYLBERSTEIN: Max Zylberstein.

ESLA KREBS: You're much older than I thought you'd be. You must be near-ly my mother's age.

ZYLBERSTEIN: Fifteen years younger. I'm very healthy.

ESLA KREBS: I'm glad to hear it. Truthfully, there's very little to do, other than to look in on her, from time to time. And, of course, to call me, if there's a reason.

ZYLBERSTEIN: I see you have a piano.

ESLA KREBS: We have many pianos. Two in the apartment, here, and sev-eral in storage. My mother taught piano to children for years and years. She had her own school…just two streets away…the Charlottenburg Kinder-Flügel. It was quite well-known. When I was growing up, in this very apartment, there was always beautiful music in the air. Bach, Beethoven, Brahms. Do you play the piano?

ZYLBERSTEIN: I did…a bit…when I was a child.

ESLA KREBS: Where did you grow up?

ZYLBERSTEIN: Here and there.

ESLA KREBS: Here and there?

ZYLBERSTEIN: Here and there.

ESLA KREBS: I'll have to get to work, soon. It's terrible, our job situation in Germany, just now. I've had to take a job nearly two hours from here.

ZYLBERSTEIN: So you told me on the telephone.

ESLA KREBS: It's terrible. still and all, it's better to work than to not work.

ZYLBERSTEIN: Much.

ESLA KREBS: It's a matter of dignity, don't you think?

ZYLBERSTEIN: I do think dignity matters, greatly, Frau Krebs.

ESLA KREBS: Let me take you into mother's room.

(ESLA KREBS moves upstage, as if leading ZYLBERSTEIN into her mother's bedroom. ACTOR #1 is now totally swarthed in lacey sheets and blankets, as UTA KREBS.)

ESLA KREBS: She's just there. She won't talk to you, at all. She can't do much more than just lie there. She can hum, a bit. She does that from time to time. If she weeps, don't worry yourself. There's nothing can be done. You want to listen that she's still breathing…or for anything, you know, quite unusual. Call me, immediately, if something quite unusual, you know…

ZYLBERSTEIN: *(Completes her thought…)*…Happens?…

ESLA KREBS: *(Smiles.)* Happens.

ZYLBERSTEIN: I assure you I will.

ESLA KREBS: I rest assured. Let me show you the kitchen and the bathroom. Oh, yes…This is the nasty part of your job.

ZYLBERSTEIN: Cleaning her.

ESLA KREBS: Changing her bag. She has a bag attached.

ZYLBERSTEIN: It won't be a problem.

ESLA KREBS: You've seen them before?

ZYLBERSTEIN: I've seen everything you could possibly imagine in life that anyone might call "nasty."

ESLA KREBS: Oh, dear!…That's life, I suppose.

ZYLBERSTEIN: Yes, Frau Krebs. I suppose that is life.

ESLA KREBS: Well, then, good luck. There's plenty of food in the fridge…Take whatever you want. The TV is ordinary. The books are for reading. Whatever is here is yours to use. Feel free.

ZYLBERSTEIN: Oh, I do, thank you.

ESLA KREBS: Well. I'll be off, then. I'll call you in a while to see if everything's all right.

ZYLBERSTEIN: You can rely on me, Frau Krebs.

ESLA KREBS: I'm sure I can, Herr Zylberstein. You seem a most reliable man.

(Changes voice, again, to NARRATOR: speaks to AUDIENCE.)

ACTOR #3: And Esla Krebs went off to work, two hours away, relieved to have found anyone at all willing to sit and watch her mother, Uta Krebs…94, feeble, and failing.

ACTOR #1: Maximillian Zylberstein stood staring at Uta Krebs for a full two hours, without moving or talking, until he realized that he had to urinate. Saying nothing, he peed on Uta's bedroom floor.

(ZYLBERSTEIN urinates on the floor. NOTE: ACTOR #3 enters carrying squeeze-bottle of water, holds it aloft, drips water, slowly, on to the floor in front of UTA KREBS…)

ACTOR #3: And then, once he'd relieved himself of his urine, he began talk to Uta Krebs, quietly, thoughtfully, relieving himself of thoughts he'd kept hidden within for years and years. At first, Zylberstein's voice was like a child's…

ZYLBERSTEIN: Hello, it's me, Frau Krebs…Maxie Zylberstein…from upstairs. I've come down for my lesson.

(ZYLBERSTEIN plays a child's two-handed exercise on toy piano.)

ZYLBERSTEIN: It was my left hand that bothered you, wasn't it, Frau Krebs? You always called my left hand "lazy," yes?…

(ZYLBERSTEIN continues to play the piece, lightly, talking to UTA, underscoring his words…)

ZYLBERSTEIN: It is an amazing thing what the brain chooses to shlep through this life, isn't it? I mean, it just *amazes* me what I've been stuck having to remember. *(Beat.)* I remember your breasts…your nipples, especially. You were feeding your daughter during my piano lesson. You couldn't have been more than twenty-five. I was eleven. You know, I expected to show up here, this morning, and have your daughter look like you. I was ready to be shocked by the similarity. But, she's nearly three times the age you were when I last saw you, isn't she? I mean, she looks more like your *grandmother* looked than like you looked, doesn't she? *(Beat.)* Your breasts were full and white, crisscrossed with blue veins. Your nipples were enormous. *(Beat.)*

You caught me looking and you liked it. "Want a drink, little man?" you asked me. You were smiling with a kind of sexy smile. *(Beat.)*

In fact, I was weeping. I didn't know, at the time, why seeing your milky breasts and nipples made me so sad, Frau Krebs, but, I know now. *(Beat.)*

I don't think you knew my mother, did you? Tante Elke wasn't really my tante. She was my father's cousin, I think. I don't think you ever met my mother. My mother's breasts were enormous. I can still smell them. Imagine! Almost eighty years later, and I can still smell them. *(Beat.)*

Sometimes, I go for a long time without bathing, so I can have the same smell on my own body. *(Beat.)*

It was so nice of Tante Elke to take me in, wasn't it? She was so kind to me. She never tried to be my mother, not once. She used to say it to me, just like that: "I'm not your mother, Maxie. I'll never be your mother. Your mother was an angel." *(Beat.)*

So was Tante Elke, Frau Krebs. She took me into her family like I was one of her own. She held me in her arms at night until I fell asleep. And sometimes, when I'd have the dream and wake up crying, she'd already be at my bed…As if she knew I was having the dream, and she'd come to my bed, to be ready for me when I woke up, crying. *(Beat.)*

I found a cure for my bad dreams, Frau Krebs. I never sleep. If you don't sleep, you can't dream…you can't wake up, so frightened. *(Beat.)*

Tante Elke said you called the police and turned us in, because you were jealous of our clothes. Tante Elke made the most beautiful clothes for us. *(Beat.)*

Tante Elke said we should forgive you for calling the police. Tante Elke said there was no good in hating people. It was like a poison, to hate people. That's what my Tante Elke tried to teach me, the same way you tried to teach me to play this piano. Both of you failed!…*(Beat.)*

They killed Tante Elke and all of her children. I was saved because Major Daniel Reitz saw my father play in an Ernst Toller play, three times. My father made him laugh, three times, so, he let his son live. *(Beat.)*

In Buchenwald, for a long time, I was frightened that I would die. And then, I was frightened that I would live. *(Beat.)*

For the last seventy years or so, I thought I would find you, one day, and kill you, Frau Krebs. It was a kind of pleasant daydream for me to imagine you, just there, and me, just here, able to kill you, so easily. *(Beat.)*

I won't kill you, Frau Krebs. I'll come here, every day, and I'll tell you everything that I remember. And you'll listen. *(Beat.)*

I know you can hear me, Uta. I'm sure of it.

(ESLA KREBS re-enters.)

ESLA KREBS: You're playing the piano?

ZYLBERSTEIN: Yes, I've played for her, most of the day.

ESLA KREBS: Oh, lucky mother!

ZYLBERSTEIN: She ate very little.

ESLA KREBS: She would starve to death if I let her.

ZYLBERSTEIN: You mustn't let her!

ESLA KREBS: Oh, I won't! *(Sees wetness on floor.)* It's wet.

ZYLBERSTEIN: I'm afraid she had an accident.

ESLA KREBS: I'll clean it up.

ZYLBERSTEIN: You don't mind?

ESLA KREBS: I don't mind at all.

> *(SHE gets rag, wipes up puddle of urine from floor.)*

ESLA KREBS: You didn't mind being here?

ZYLBERSTEIN: I didn't mind at all. I enjoyed talking with your mother.

ESLA KREBS: You did?

ZYLBERSTEIN: I did indeed.

ESLA KREBS: Did she respond at all?

ZYLBERSTEIN: I think she did.

ESLA KREBS: Lucky mother! *(To IMAGINED MOTHER on imagined bed.)* We're so lucky to have Herr Zylberstein with us, aren't we, Mother? *(WE HEAR…A WOMAN'S MOAN from ACTOR #1.)*

ESLA KREBS: Are you speaking, Mother? *(To ZYLBERSTEIN.)* I think she's trying to thank you.

ZYLBERSTEIN: She probably is.

ESLA KREBS: So, you'll come back, tomorrow?

ZYLBERSTEIN: Tomorrow and every day. It's my pleasure.

ESLA KREBS: I'm so pleased, Herr Zylberstein.

ZYLBERSTEIN: I'm so pleased to have pleased you, Frau Krebs.

ESLA KREBS: This is so special for my mother.

ACTOR #1: And with a great gentlemanly flourish, Zylberstein took Esla Krebs's hand in his hand, bowed…

ESLA KREBS:…And *kissed* it! *(To AUDIENCE, as ACTOR #3.)* Esla Krebs was shocked, but she allowed her hand to linger in the old man's hand for a full minute. It was more affection than Esla Krebs had felt in years. *(ACTOR #2 steps into spotlight…)*

ACTOR #2: Sam Linsky and Anna Giesling were negotiating a kiss of their own. They were on bikes, on their way to a school picnic. The route to the picnic was somewhat circuitous. They stopped on a small, brown sandy beach, on the edge of the harbor, directly opposite Mike Linsky's dock. *(LIGHTS SHIFT TO…ANNA and SAM.)*

ANNA: Shall we park our bikes for a while?

SAM: Are you tired?

ANNA: No...yes. A bit.

SAM: Fine. If you're tired, we should stop.

ACTOR #2: Anna and Sam held hands, timidly. They both knew that they were about to make love for the first time in their lives, in the paper-white light of the glistening spring sunshine, on the banks of Anna's beloved River Weser.

ANNA: I love the River Weser. I look at it every day of my life. I can't imagine spending a day, alive, and not.

SAM: That's like me, back home in Gloucester. I walk on Good Harbor Beach, every day, no matter what.

ANNA: You miss Gloucester, a lot, don't you?

SAM: I guess. Mostly at night.

ANNA: I'd love to see Gloucester.

SAM: I'd love you to. Someday, maybe I could take you there.

ANNA: I'd love to, so much!

ACTOR #2: Without a word, they lay down on the sand, side by side, knowing that they would both remember this day, vividly, for the rest of their lives. Neither hurried the event.

SAM: *(To ANNA.)* Good Harbor Beach is awesome. There's this brook at one end that goes under this wooden footbridge. When the tide's goin' out, you can ride the current. It's fantastic!

ANNA: *Wie ist der Strand...* What's the beach like? *Sandig, steinig, felsig?...*

SAM: Oh, right! *Strand* is beach.

ANNA: *Sandig?...*

SAM: Sandy.

ANNA: Right.

SAM: Good Harbor beach is totally *sandig*. It's all really soft, white *sandig*. It's beautiful. So are you.

ANNA: *Kann man hier ohne Gefar schwimmen?*

SAM: "Schwimmin" has got to mean "swimming," right?

ANNA: Right. Kann man hier ohne Gefar...Is it safe for....

SAM: *Schwimmin*! Good Harbor Beach is definitely safe for *schwimmin*.

ANNA: *Ist dort ungefährlich für Kinder?*

SAM: What's "*ungefährlich?*"

ANNA: "Safe."

SAM: Oh, yuh. Totally *ungefährlich für Kinder*. *I* started *schwimmin* there, alone, when I was a little Kinder.

ANNA: *Gibt es gefährliche Strömungen?*

SAM: Wait! Wait! If ungefährlich mean "safe," then does "gefährlich" means "dangerous?"

ANNA: You're so clever!

SAM: Selma said that, too.

ANNA: I hope I meet Selma.

ACTOR #2: And then, Sam told Anna a small, sad bit of truth.

SAM: Grandma Selma's not real crazy about Germans. She had German and Polish cousins that got killed by the Nazis.

ANNA: That's terrible. Why?

SAM: They were Jewish. I'm Jewish. Remember?

ANNA: I forgot. I forgot that. It's nothing to me that you're Jewish.

SAM: It's nothing to my father, too, but, it's not nothing to me. *(Beat.)* My Grandfather Nathan was really religious. He died, two years ago. Grandpa Nathan was my best friend...before you.

ANNA: You always say such nice things to me!...I wish I knew your grandfather.

SAM: Me, too. I guess you do, kinda'. There's a lot of him in me. At least, that what Grandma Selma's always sayin'. Grandpa Nathan was the reason I got Bar Mitzvahed...That's when a Jewish boy becomes a man...a Jewish man, like, officially. My father didn't really want to get me Bar Mitzvahed, and my mother isn't Jewish, so, she didn't care, either way. But, my Grandpa Nathan, he insisted. Grandpa Nathan told me there have got to be Jews on earth, no matter what, and I totally agree. When I have children, I really hope they study Hebrew and get Bar Mitzvahed.

ANNA: I would never object.

SAM: Really?

ANNA: Really. I think it's important to have religion in a family. We're not at all religious in my house, not like some of my friends are, and I'm always jealous of them. Having my children be Jewish would be fine.

SAM: It would?

ANNA: Sure. Why not? I never met a Jewish person before I met you. From things my father said, I thought you might be very different from what you are.

SAM: What am I?

ANNA: Everything I admire. Except for your Deutsch. You didn't finish your sentence in Deutsch.

SAM: I know. There was a word at the end...

ANNA: *Strömungen*...It means strong waters...current.

SAM: Oh, right. There's a little island that's just off the beach, where the water gets wick'id rough. There's this cross-*Strömungen* that gets ya', if you're not careful. *(Without warning.)* If you weren't here for me, I would've been *schwimmin* home, already…*ungefährlich*, or not.

ANNA: I'm glad you feel that way.

SAM: What did your father say about me?

ANNA: My father doesn't know you. If he knew you, he would admire you the way I do.

ACTOR #2: Anna changed the subject, abruptly, moving from The Preliminaries to The Main Event.

ANNA: Can we do some kissing, now?

SAM: Is that like a German thing?…Girls asking for the kissing?

ANNA: Oh, is it wrong for me to do the asking?

SAM: No, no, no! I'm just really nervous about the kissing going further. I mean, I *want* it to go further, but, I don't wanna' mess things up between us. I mean, I'm frightened that if I lose you, I won't have *anything*.

ANNA: You won't lose me.

SAM: I'm really glad to know this. You won't lose me, either, Anna. No chance.

ANNA: Can we do the kissing?

SAM: You're really into the kissing, huh?

ANNA: I've never met anybody I've wanted to do the kissing with so much, before you.

SAM: Oh, my God. That is like such a fantastically beautiful thing you just said. *(Beat.)* Anna, this is the first time in my whole life that I ever kissed anybody I was in love with.

ANNA: *Mein Gott!*

SAM: What?

ANNA: That is such a fantastically beautiful thing you just said.
      (THEY kiss.)

ACTOR #2: Sam and Anna snuck away, together, almost every afternoon for the next three weeks, to the same small, secluded beach, for secret kissing-sessions, with occasional breaks for language lessons exchanged in German and in English. Anna taught Sammy her favorite poem, a verse from a sonnet by Rilke.
      (SAM and ANNA lie on their stomachs on the inclined ramp — their "beach" — side by side…)

SAM: *Und fast ein Mädchen wars und ging hervor…*

ANNA: She was nearly a woman…

SAM: *Aus diesem einigen Glück von Sang und Leir…*

ANNA: She sprang forth from a beautiful song and the sound of a lyre…

SAM: *Und glänzte klar durch ihre Frühlingsschleir…*

ANNA: Shining through clear veils of Springtime…

SAM: *Und machte sich ein Bette in meinem Ohr.*

ANNA: She made a bed for herself in my ear.

SAM: *Und schlief in mir.*

ANNA: And she slept inside me.

ACTOR #1: *(To AUDIENCE, as NARRATOR.)* Sammy never told Anna how sad he was, how much he missed his beloved Gloucester, Massachusetts… his school friends…his English language.

ACTOR #3: *(To AUDIENCE, as NARRATOR.)* And Anna never told Sammy how her father raged at the dining table, every night, railing against Germany's new Jewish citizens.

ACTOR #1: Gustav Giesling promised to help cleanse Germany of what he called its "disgusting blight."

ACTOR #3: Anna knew enough to say nothing. Not a word.

ACTOR #2: The situation on the docks at Bremerhaven worsened, each day.

ACTOR #1: Inspired by Mike Linsky's well-publicized success, Jewish laborers began to arrive in Germany looking for work, many looking for Linsky, himself, who had become a kind of symbol of Project Homecoming's promise.

ACTOR #3: Linsky was now overall boss of three active docks, second only to Günter Friedlander, himself.

ACTOR #2: Thus, a fair number of Jewish laborers…more than a thousand new citizens, in all…came directly to Bremerhaven, to live and to work.

ACTOR #1: Any new citizen who was ready to do an honest day's labor found a job waiting on Mike Linsky's dock, even though it almost always meant displacing an existing German worker.

(ACTOR #2, as MIKE LINSKY, talks to AUDIENCE, as if talking to CREW CHIEFS.)

MIKE LINSKY: I've called this meeting of crew chiefs because I want each of you to make sure the guys we're layin' off in each of your crews know that their layoff is only temporary. We've gotta' get the new citizens on the books, right away. This we know. Chancellor Stroiber is watching us, personally. But, as soon as things settle down, I'm positive there's gonna' be work enough for everybody, and the guys we've laid off will have first crack! Herr Friedlander definitely backs me up on this.

ACTOR #3: *(To AUDIENCE, as NARRATOR.)* Was Mike Linsky really as trusting and as innocent as he seemed? A week before the event that the good people of Bremerhaven would come to call "The Dock Six Catastrophe," over an evening meal of roast chicken and parsleyed potatoes, with Sammy off with a school friend named Anna, getting what he called "a one-on-one German lesson," Michael Linsky spoke his thoughts to his wife.

(ACTOR #3 speaks to MIKE; as LIZZIE...)

LIZZIE LINSKY: More potatoes?

MIKE LINSKY: Yuh, thanks.

(LIZ serves potatoes to MIKE, who eats, and speaks his mind to his wife, thoughtfully...)

MIKE LINSKY: I dunno, Liz...I think I'm changing. I used'ta think: if the world says it doesn't like Jews, okay, then, fine, I'm not gonna' be a Jew!...When I was in fourth grade, walking home, these kids from St. Ann's Sister School jump out from behind this big bush and they grab me, yelling "You Jews killed Jesus! You Jews killed Jesus!" It was like a joke. I yell back "That was two thousand years ago!" and they go "Yuh, but, we just heard about it!"...They muckled me. Eight of 'em. I didn't wanna' advertise I was Jewish, too much, after that. You see what I'm sayin'? *(Beat. Following speech builds in its passion...)*

But, I'll tell ya' the honest-ta'-God truth, Lizzie: I think it's the kids from Saint Ann's, Hitler, and the Germans that are finally gonna make me more stand-up. I spent too much time, when I was a kid, listenin' to my mother and my grandmother talkin' horror stories about Germans and Jew-haters. You see what I'm sayin' on this? I don't know about "retribution." That's a fancy word. What I feel in my heart is simple: Germans owe us, big time, and I got no problem takin' a job from any one of them, or givin' a job to any New Citizen that comes on to my dock lookin' for an honest day's work. What's goin' on here is just about bringin' us back to scratch! *(Embarrassed by his emotion...)* Hey, what do I know, huh?!...Pass me some more roast Hühnchen, huh? It's *delicious!*

ACTOR #1: The ship-building industry in Bremerhaven, once powerful and prosperous, had been all but invisible for nearly ten years.

ACTOR #3: To the shock and amazement of out-of-work shipbuilders, Chancellor Rudolph Stroiber announced the re-opening of Bremerhaven's largest shipyard. *(New voice...official, ominous.)* Ladies and gentlemen, the Chancellor of the German Republic, Rudolph Stroiber!...

(ON TAPE...APPLAUSE and CHEERS.)

RUDOLPH STROIBER: *(Wears his "official" portrait...)* It is our intention that the Bremerhaven shipyard will be manned entirely by our new citizens. Work on a fleet of lifeboats will begin, immediately.

ACTOR #3: And now, the good citizens of Bremerhaven were stunned.

ACTOR #1: Gustav Giesling and Götz Burger found support in every corner of Bremerhaven. Five hundred of Bremerhaven's unemployed workers marched to the docks to protest the first day of shipbuilding.

ACTOR #2: Many of these angry people carried guns and knives.

ACTOR #3: The re-opened shipyard was located just opposite Mike Linsky's dock.

GUSTAV GIESLING: *(Making a speech to the assembled WORKERS.)* We mustn't back down! We will teach these Jews the lesson they should have learned sixty years ago!

(ON TAPE...sounds of an angry mob.)

ACTOR #3: Zev Golem and seventy worldwide members of "Jews Forever" were among Gustav Giesling's angry mob.

ACTOR #1: They allowed Giesling to fire the first shot...

(GIESLING fires his pistol...)

ACTOR #3: And then, they shot him dead with a volley of more than three hundred bullets.

(DRUM BEATS, or hammer strokes on wood, like gunshots...A loud barrage. GIESLING flies upstage, heaving and bobbing with every bullet that passes into and through his body.)

ACTOR #1: The angry mob stopped, dead in their tracks, stunned by Giesling's bloody death...and by the seventy guns now pointed at their faces.

ACTOR #3: Rifka Borenstein made the announcement...*(As RIFKA, SHE screams, madly...)* We've have killed your leader and we will kill any man, woman, or child who shows us a gun, a knife, or even an angry word! Go back to your houses and we will let you live. The victim-Jews of the past are dead! We are the new Jews of the world, and if you threaten us, we will kill you, without a moment's hesitation!

ACTOR #1: Every man and woman in the angry mob heard Rifka's words.

ACTOR #3: They turned from the shipyard and they went to their homes.

ACTOR #2: Gustav Giesling lay dead. And just across the river from the dock, on a tiny, brown sandy beach, on the edge of River Weser, Anna Giesling lay dead, as well...

(LIGHTS FADE UP ON...ANNA and SAMMY, locked in a kiss.)

ACTOR #2: While she and Sammy lay together, making love, Anna's life was stopped by a single bullet, gone astray, as bullets do, into the hearts and heads of the innocent…Perhaps it was a bullet intended for Gustav Giesling? Perhaps, it was a bullet from Giesling's own gun?…We'll never know.

(Suddenly, a final gunshot. ANNA flinches, screams…)

ANNA: *Uggghhhhhh.*

SAM: Anna? What's happening?…Anna?…

(ACTOR #2 walks to ANNA, places a red silk square on her breast.)

ACTOR #2: When Sammy turned Anna's limp body over, there was a flooding river of blood on her dress, just above her breast.

SAM: *ANNNNNNNNNNAAAAAAA!*

ACTOR #2: Anna Giesling's funeral captured the imaginations of the people of the world. Her death was compared to the death of another young Anna…

ACTOR #1: Anne Franck.

ACTOR #3: And, once again, the same agonized words were heard, whispered by mourners through their tears…

ACTOR #2: *Tragisch.*

ACTOR #1:…*Une tragedie…*

ACTOR #3: Tragic.

ACTOR #2: *Unbrauchbar.*

ACTOR #1:…*Inutile…*

ACTOR #3: A useless waste.

ACTOR #2: *Undenkbar.*

ACTOR #1:…*Impensable…*

ACTOR #3: Unthinkable.

ACTOR #1: Sammy spoke at Anna's funeral, invoking the words of the German poet, Rainer Maria Rilke, from his delicate "Sonnet to Orpheus"…

(HE now speaks as SAMMY, directly to AUDIENCE. HE is weeping.)

SAM: *Aus diesem einigen Glück von Sang und Leir…*

(WE hear ANNA's VOICE, on tape, translating the Rilke sonnet…)

ANNA'S VOICE: *(ON TAPE)* She sprang forth from a beautiful song and the sound of a lyre…

SAM: *Und glänzte klar durch ihre Frühlingsschleir…*

ANNA'S VOICE: *(ON TAPE)* Shining through clear veils of Springtime…

SAM: *Und machte sich ein Bette in meinem Ohr.*

ANNA'S VOICE: *(ON TAPE)* She made a bed for herself in my ear.

SAM: *Und schlief in mir.*

ANNA'S VOICE: *(ON TAPE)* And she will sleep inside me…

SAM:…Forever and ever.

ACTOR #2: Anna Giesling's ashes were scattered on the River Weser. Sammy moved back to Gloucester, within the month, to live with his grandmother, who had never doubted for an instant that something terrible would happen, if her son Michael moved his family to Germany.

ACTOR #1: Mike Linsky became Gunter Friendlander's business partner, and, eventually, gained majority control of Bremerhaven's docklands, employing New Citizens, almost exclusively, for the enterprise Germany came to call its "Jewish waterfront."

ACTOR #3: Liz and Mike Linsky stayed married for ten more years, before their marriage dissolved, and Liz moved back to Massachusetts to live near her family and friends.

ACTOR #2: Mike remarried, five years later. His new wife was German-Jewish, a New Citizen.

ACTOR #3: In Hamburg, Pierre Chambray and Jacques Burstin lived together in their tiny, chic apartment above their flower-shop...
(ACTOR #1 and ACTOR #2 hold hands, kiss...)

ACTOR #1: Married...

ACTOR #2: They stayed faithful to each other, loyal and loving til the end of their lives.

ACTOR #3: And in Berlin, a full year after Maximillian Zylberstein first began his daily visits to Uta Krebs, Uta breathed her last.

ACTOR #2: After Uta's death, Zylerberstein saw little reason to continue, and he died, as well.

ACTOR #3: Esla Krebs buried Maximillian Zylerberstein next to her mother.

ACTOR #2: They stayed together, side by side, into eternity.

ACTOR #3: And in Berlin, a few months after Rudolph Stroiber's death, after more than fifty failed attempts, the German government unveiled its first-ever official monument honoring World War II's German-Jewish dead, built on Prinz-Albrecht-Terrain, former site of the Gestapo's headquarters, where the killing began.

ACTOR #2: And facing the 21st Century, Germany now tries to lead Europe into unification—for economic power, for living space...*Lebensraum.*
(MUSIC IN...)

ACTOR #1: This play has no ending, happy or sad.

ACTOR #3: Art has no answers, no solutions, or resolutions...

ACTOR #1: Art has only vision and revision...

ACTOR #2: Art has only hope and more hope...again and again, against circumstance and history...

ACTOR #1: What we hope life might be, again and again, against what we see it has been.

ACTOR #3: In hope, there is a reason to continue.

ACTOR #1: This play was written with a special love for Jews and for Germans. History is written and cannot be changed. But the future is being written by us...now. It is a time to understand what has passed, to join hands, and to move forward, to forgive, and to never forget.

ACTOR #2: The lights begin to fade...We actors step forward for out bows, and think about food and rest, and tomorrow night's performance of our play.

ACTOR #1: But, all over Germany, new citizens are living their lives, and Jews, once again, have begun to call Germany "home."

ACTOR #3: And in a tiny river-port called Bremenhaven, Jews and Germans join hands in a tiny chapel overlooking the harbor. Together, they speak the words "Nimmer wieder," over and over...

(The THREE ACTORS will now move forward and drop pieces of their various costumes on to a pile, downstage center. THEY will speak in the various voices of the characters they are releasing...)

ACTOR #2: *(As GIESLING.)* Nimmer wieder.

ACTOR #3: *(As LIZZIE LINSKY.)* Never again.

ACTOR #2: *(As MIKE LINSKY.)* Never again.

ACTOR #1: *(As SAMMY.)* Nimmer wieder.

ACTOR #3: *(As ANNA.)* Never again.

ACTOR #2: *(As ZYLBERSTEIN.)* Never again.

(THE THREE ACTORS now stand in a line, facing front.)

ACTOR #1: Our story is told.

ACTOR #3: *(Simply...)* The play is over.

(The lights fade out.)

End of Play.

One Under

For Oliver, Ken, and Rocco —
May your short games improve.

INTRODUCTION

Prologue: England, last year. A frustrated golfer, after hitting his ball from sand trap to sand trap, threw his entire bag of clubs into the pond next to the clubhouse and stormed off to the parking lot, in full view of a dozen lunching golfers. Within minutes, he returned to the pond, waded to his sunken golf bag. The onlookers thought, "Yuh, sure, good show, but, he'll never quit playing golf. No one ever does…" All watched, smugly, as the man found his bag, unzipped a side pouch, removed his car keys, threw the bag back into the pond, and walked to his waiting car…smiling, peacefully.

It is remarkable how our lives take small, unexpected turns to places we'd never really imagined we'd visit. And how we go with it…how we accept our new surroundings with a simple shrug and a "Life's like that." Because it's simply true: Life's like that.

When I was young, I used to start a play with a specific ending in mind, saying to myself "I'll take this play from here to there"…Now that I'm snowy on top, I start a play and wonder "Where will this play will take me?…"

As *One Under* is a brand new play, about to go into rehearsal for its World Premiere, the most I can do by way of introduction is to share my new-play anxiety with you…i.e., Why would the world *want* such a play?…and some of the impulses I felt when I first set out to write the thing.

A few years ago, my eleven-year-old son Oliver took up golf. There was a summer golf program for kids being offered by the City of Gloucester, Massachusetts, and Oliver had been watching overmuch golf on TV during the year and had asked permission to enter the program. After a few weeks, there were several dozen divots in the front yard, and golf balls underfoot, everywhere. Gillian (Oliver's mother, my wife) quietly collected the golf balls, each evening, and set them out in a neat grouping for Oliver's morning practice. Gillian is a professional athlete and takes no sport casually. She added in private golf lessons for Oliver at a small public course in nearby Essex. After one lesson, the pro told me that Oliver "has the goods."

I got my late father's old clubs from my mother's basement, cleaned off the cobwebs, and went out for my first round of golf in twenty-five years. As a kid, I had caddied at a profoundly restricted club in Hamilton, Mass., called (get this) Myopia Hunt Club. I had some interest in golf, but had only played a few rounds, and with almost no discernible skills.

As Oliver's interest in golf deepened, his talent became obvious. By the end of his first summer of play, he'd won a couple of trophies, and talked of almost nothing but golf.

During the following winter (last winter), a friend of mine, Gary Foster, produced a film called *Tin Cup*. Many of the top golf pros were working in the film in cameo roles, and Gary, knowing of Oliver's interest, invited us down to the set in Texas, for a couple of days "to play some golf and meet the pros." I knew that Oliver would be thrilled, so I accepted Gary's offer, and off we went to Dallas; he with his new set of shiny kid-clubs, and I with my ancient plaid bag of antiques—*mashie niblick*, included, for a two-day jaunt that would take my life—and Oliver's—on still another small surprising turn...

We played two 18-hole rounds of golf a day, and visited with the pros for some thirty minutes of chat and autographs, in between. Somewhere during the second day, out on the course with what seemed like endless green on green on all sides...and in the middle, Oliver and I, walking together, talking about life, my son's hand in mine, walking from his shot to my shot...I thought to myself "It gets no better than this."

And after we said our good-byes and walked toward our rent-a-car, Oliver, autographed golf ball in hand, looked up at me and said, "No matter what, I'll never have a happier two days in my whole life, Dad. I know this." And so did I.

And back in NYC, when we discovered the super-secret, brilliant NYC Public Courses—Van Cortland, Pelham, Split Rock, South Shore, Silver Lake—unthinkably beautiful oases of green on green, minutes from the center of the Western World's most hectic city, I had such a strong reaction. No, it wasn't at all a surprise when I set out to write a new play set in the world of golf. That endless green on green seemed to me so *theatrical*, so rife with dramatic possibility...a gaming field, a meadow, a graveyard...a place of pain and pleasure, winning, losing, endless fantasy of heroism, battleground, comedy, tragedy...

So, okay, another year has passed, I belong to two private golf clubs and, yuh, I've got this hook, and the need to break 90 has faded like my 3-iron shots into this need to break 80. Oliver is starting to collect as much hardware for his sport as Gill has for hers. And I've got this play...about a New Yorker who goes one under par and kills himself...

That was the first surprise turn in the road...Why was the play, born in green and sunlight, becoming so dark? And then, I remembered...

When I was Oliver's eleven years of age, I caddied for a young man named (I still remember) Guy Haskell. He was a commercial airline pilot, twenty-nine years old, big, tall, the right kind of Protestant for Myopia...It was nearly six P.M., all the other caddies had gone home, and it was possible for a shrimp like me to get a round. (In those days, a caddie earned $2.50 for an 18-hole round...$4.50 if you carried two bags.)

Mr. Haskell played badly, distractedly so. He lost ball after ball, which I found for him in poison ivy-laden woods. On the fifth hole, he skulled one into the tall grass. "Can't find it!" I yelled, scooping the ball into my pocket.

I would sell it, tomorrow, for a dime. Sixth hole, he sent a major slice into a nearby hobbit. I grabbed it, pocketed it, same scream, "Can't find it!"

On the seventh green, Guy Haskell, tall, handsome, privileged, lay down and began to die. Through profound pain and bucketing perspiration, in a barely audible voice, he whispered "Get help, caddie...I'm very sick." I ran to Bromberg, the caddie-master..."Mr. Haskell's sick, he's really sick, get help!"...We rode out to the course in an ancient gas-powered golf cart, alongside two equally ancient Hamilton policemen in an 1950 Chevrolet station wagon. As best they could, they loaded Mr. Haskell's huge, immobile body into the back of their van, but refused to even start the engine until the back gate was firmly closed. In time's penultimate nick, as the rear-gate's window was being cranked upward, I tossed the two sellable golf balls into the van with the man, himself, and flew my bike homeward.

I said nothing to my parents, afraid they might not let me caddie if they knew the inherent dangers of the job. At midnight, I snuck from my bed and called Beverly Hospital..."I'm calling to ask about Guy Haskell. He was brought in around 7:30 with a heart attack."

"Are you family?" they asked.

"I'm his caddie."

"Mr. Haskell passed away."

I put down the phone and turned to see my mother and father standing in the doorway behind me...loving, concerned...

Read the play.

Gloucester, Mass.
July, 1997.

ORIGINAL PRODUCTION

The original production of *One Under* was produced at Gloucester Stage, August 20, 1997. Israel Horovitz, Artistic Director; Ian McColl, Managing Director; Lisa Pegnato, Scenery and Costume Design; Ian McColl, Lighting; Kristin Pierimarchi, video design; Donald Christy, Stage Manager; with the following cast

Bennie Foss	Peter Berkrot
Randolf	Joseph Garland
Xavier	Ricardo P. Engerman
Allie, Miranda, and Smitty	Katrina Stevens

THE PEOPLE OF THE PLAY

RAN, Late 20s to late 30s, average height, white, kindly, appealing.
X, Late 20s to late 30s, large, black, handsome, athletic.
BENNIE, Late 20s to late 30s, small, balding, handsome, nervous, dapper.
ALLIE*, Mid 20s to mid 30s, dark-haired, stunningly beautiful.
MIRANDA*, Mid 20s to mid 30s, ginger-haired, sweet.
SMITTY*, Mid 20s to mid 30s, blonde, sporty.

*NOTE: Same actress, using wigs, plays all three women.

THE PLACE OF THE PLAY

Various locations around New York City, including golf course, graveyard, coffee shop, various apartments.

THE TIME OF THE PLAY

The time of the play alternates between the late 1980s and the present. The action of the play is continuous, without an intermission.

A NOTE FROM THE AUTHOR

This play is designed to be produced imaginatively, rather than expensively. Only one actress should be used to perform the three female roles. The stage should be, essentially, an expanse of green (blue, if you're French and superstitious about using green on stage), doubling as a golf course and a graveyard. There should be a putting green with flag and cup, downstage left; an elevated driving tee, upstage right. The elevated driving-tee should double as the NYC balcony, although it should be constructed on railroad ties, rocks, sod, grass, and a railing of ages 2'x4' lumber: clearly golf-course materials. There is another driving tee, downstage right, that can double as various apartments. A few rustic benches (gold course variety) suffice to create a coffee bar and/or living room furniture. A telephone in an actor's hand should be enough to create the sense of an office. From time to time, numbered flags can pass by, upstage, carried by an offstage actor, to indicate the passing of time/advance of place in the golf game that frames/contains much of the action of this play. The use of real golf balls should be forbidden, so that the audience is safe from injury, and the golf game onstage might achieve perfection in the imagination of the beholder (i.e., the audience). A large cloud painting is hung, upstage, and used for projected videos. Also upstage, a small sculpture depicting New York City, off in the distance, should be spotlighted.

Scenes should flow, one into the next, without interruption. Use of imaginative music, sound effects, lighting, props, costumes, wigs, *is* imperative. The entire play should occupy approximately 90–95 minutes, played straight through, without intermission. Lighting should never be general. Spotlights are to be used, almost entirely, to light the play. Costumes should be minimal, costume changes are unnecessary.

About the play's odd time structure. *One Under* exists, in a sense, in X's and Ran's final golf game, after Bennie's death. As such, the entire play could be seen as Ran's and X's memories of Bennie and their lives with Bennie. Thus, the final golf game between X and Ran could be defined as both Epilogue and as "real time." There are, of course, some scenes dramatized which neither Ran nor Bennie could have witnessed, directly. These moments beg suspension of disbelief...i.e., Dramatic License.

I.H.,
Nov. 1996 – August 1997.

One Under

MUSIC IN…Bach, played by a single cello, loud, elegant, terrifying…SIN-
GLE SPOTLIGHT FADES UP ON…BENNIE FOSS, 30s, small, hand-
some. HE wears an expensive silk bathrobe. HE trims and lights a Havana
cigar, inhales deeply; uncorks a bottle of 1966 Châteauneuf du Pape, fills a
glass to its brim, drinks; refills the glass, drinks, again.

> *HE moves to a video camera, flicks a switch on. BENNIE's image comes*
up on an overhead TV-monitor. Thus, HE is seen on stage, and, simultane-
ously, on monitor, as HE records his thoughts…)

BENNIE: I leave these thoughts to my children, to my wife, and to my
friends…As I see it, life and golf are endless flat things, from which occasional shafts of glory rupture through, rise like rockets, before falling
back to boredom. I seize, this day, this rising rocket. I fly with it, up, up,
and never, again, down to Earth. Try to understand, it's nothing any of
you did that was wrong. It's just me ending it, doing something right,
finally.

> *(HE takes a pistol from his pocket, loads it, puts the end of the pistol in his*
mouth, prepares to kill himself, as…MUSIC CHANGES TO…FM-
RADIO…LIGHTS CROSSFADE DOWNSTAGE TO…TABLE, COF-
FEE BAR, early morning. Two men at a table for three await a third.
THEY are XAVIER and RANDOLPH, both are the same age as BENNIE.
XAVIER is large, black, handsome. RANDOLPH is thin, white, handsome.
THEY were both wealthy at age twenty-eight, broke at age thirty-two. Their
clothing reflects both their wealthier past and their moneyless present. THEY
wear NYC-style golf gear…caps are backwards, baggy trousers, etc. Their
golf clubs are in evidence, nearby. THEY drink coffee as they chat.)

RANDOLPH: As far as I'm concerned, it's the first real women's movie
Hollywood's ever made. Hard to believe Hollywood was brave enough
to make a movie like that. It's great when you can be like *proud* of
Hollywood, for being *responsible*…looking at women, you know, *prop-*
erly, for a change. *(Looks out front.)* Two more of the same, please!

XAVIER: I agree. Men have got to start thinking with their *big* heads, 'stead
of their *little* heads. Maybe a popular movie will have a little moral
impact.

RANDOLPH: A *little* "Moral impact?" This movie's gonna' gross over two hundred-million, worldwide!...*(Looking at watch.)* Where the hell *is* he? Every goddam time!

XAVIER: The man was born without a Be-On-Time Gland.

RANDOLPH: It's nothing but rude. You remember the time we played Split Rock with this little Japanese guy they put with us to round out the foursome...Were you there?

XAVIER: Was I there? I shot a 42 on the front nine! You, me, Eddie Bonzo, and this little Japanese guy...Isuzu.

RANDOLPH: Isamu.

XAVIER: Right, Isamu. Bennie must've been an hour late.

RANDOLPH: Shows up on the fifth tee, wants us to boot Isamu.

XAVIER: Bitches us for a month, after, for not doing it.

RANDOLPH: Thinks his money and his power rule!

XAVIER: What money? What power?

RANDOLPH: Even when he did! Nobody ever gave a goddam who was rich or not. Not in golf.

XAVIER: Not the way the game works.

RANDOLPH: That's what I'm saying. Poor homeless guy drops an 80-foot putt, the ball stays in, yes?

XAVIER: Totally. I love Bennie, don't get me wrong, but, the game speaks for itself. Bennie's got to learn this.

RANDOLPH: Eddie was telling me he played with Bennie, last month, over Staten Island. The starter matches 'em up with two strangers for a pick-up foursome. Bennie's like giving advice to everybody on the first tee. Loud. To total *strangers*...The first guy hits one in the water, Bennie goes "You're fallin' off the ball like a *beginner*, that's why you're slicing." Second guy tees up, starts his swing, Bennie goes "You're lined up toward Jersey!" Guy steps away, tells Bennie ta' shut the hell up.

XAVIER: I heard.

RANDOLPH: Bennie himself tees up...You know the first tee at South Shore?

XAVIER: 'Course I know it! Right at the clubhouse. Always twenty guys watchin', minimum.

RANDOLPH: This day, maybe *forty* guys.

XAVIER: Bennie tees up in front of 'em, smokin' a $50 Cuban cigar, right?

RANDOLPH: Exact. After he's been givin' advice, pissin' everybody off.

XAVIER: Everybody's thinkin' "Let's see what the asshole with the cigar can do"...

RANDOLPH: Totally. He's wearin' all his brand-name Bennie-shit...

XAVIER: Polo slacks, Ping shirt, Callaway cap, Foot-Joy saddle shoes…

RANDOLPH: Looks like Nevada Bob!…

XAVIER: *(Laughs, affectionately.)* Bennie.

RANDOLPH: Sees everybody watchin', thinks he's the Jewish Tiger Woods, takes a monster swing, tries to crush it…

XAVIER: Misses!

RANDOLPH:…Whiffs! *(Beat. And then…)* You *knew* this story?

XAVIER: *(Laughing.)* He's lookin' out towards the first green, goin' "I never saw it come down! Anybody see my ball come down?"

RANDOLPH: You *knew* this goddam story?

XAVIER: His ball's still sittin' on the tee!

RANDOLPH: You let me tell this whole goddam story, you knew the end?

XAVIER: Eddie Bonzo told us, together!

RANDOLPH: *When?*

XAVIER: Couple'a weeks ago. *(Looks at watch.)* Now, *I'm* gettin' nervous! Van Cortland's 100% booked! We miss our tee time, we're screwed!

RANDOLPH: We give him til ten past. He's not here, we head on up without him.

XAVIER: I'll back you. We miss our tee time, we're standin' in Van Cortland watching a thousand other people play golf.

RANDOLPH: Bennie comes here, we're on the train without him, he'll never shut up!

XAVIER: Bennie'll never shut up, anyway, train or no train!

RANDOLPH: This is true. Remember Alvy What's'is when they wouldn't let us on the first tee three minutes late? Where was that?

XAVIER: Pelham. He went ballistic.

RANDOLPH: He could've gotten himself disbarred.

XAVIER: He could've gotten himself dis*membered*.

RANDOLPH: What, dismembered? Pelham's a public golf course.

XAVIER: Dismembered! Dismembered! Dick, arms, and legs cut off!

RANDOLPH: Oh, right.

   (Beat.)

RANDOLPH: Alvy *was* disbarred, wasn't he?

XAVIER: I think you're right. He yelled at a judge.

RANDOLPH: He *struck* a judge!

XAVIER: Crazy bastard, Alvy. Plays good golf, though.

RANDOLPH: Not so great.

XAVIER: Pretty great. Plays to an eight.

RANDOLPH: In your wettest! He shot a one-oh-six, last time we played Silver Lake, and that was with about fourteen mulligans.

XAVIER: I think you're right.

RANDOLPH: 'Course, I'm right! *(Looks at his watch.)* Two more minutes, we make our move.

XAVIER: Alvy had major money.

RANDOLPH: Nothing like Bennie.

XAVIER: After Bennie.

RANDOLPH: Somebody told me twenty.

XAVIER: Alvy? Twenty, easy.

RANDOLPH: Poor son of a bitch had nothin' at the end.

XAVIER: Unlike us?

RANDOLPH: Yuh, but, imagine losing twenty?

XAVIER: How about Bennie? Imagine bein' Bennie?
    (BENNIE enters, carrying golf clubs, wearing Polo slacks, Ping shirt, Foot-Joy saddle shoes, Callaway cap. His lip is bloodied.)

BENNIE: What the fuck are you, *deaf?!* You didn't hear me screaming?!

XAVIER: Hey, Bennie? What happened?

BENNIE: I just got mugged, about two inches from here! I was screaming your fucking names, top of my lungs! You didn't hear anything?

XAVIER: The door's closed and the air-conditioning's goin'.

RANDOLPH: You okay?

BENNIE: *(Cleaning lip with napkin…)* Do I *look* okay? Fucking Polo slacks cost $185!…*(Takes out a cigar. It's broken.)* Pure Havana. Box of these cost more than X's clubs!

XAVIER: What's the matter with my clubs?

BENNIE: *(Lights bottom half of broken cigar.)* Lookit me! My hands are shaking! *(Calls out to Counterman, offstage.)* Double-double tall de-caf' latté with 1% milk, one and a half Sweet'n'Lows, to go, with a sip-lid.

RANDOLPH: Jesus, Ben! How many were they?

BENNIE: One, but, he was monster huge.

RANDOLPH: Gun?

XAVIER: Knife?

BENNIE: He was speaking some goddam language I never heard! I didn't even know what the hell he wanted for the first ten minutes!

XAVIER: How'd you figure it out?

BENNIE: He was hitting me!

RANDOLPH: He get your wallet?

BENNIE: He wanted my clubs.

XAVIER: Jesus! Your clubs?

RANDOLPH: He get anything?

BENNIE: Matched set of titanium-head-graphite-shaft Great Big Berthas? You think I'm gonna' let some greaseball foreigner get away with a matched set of titanium-head-graphite-shaft Great Big Berthas? They're the only truly beautiful things I've still got!

RANDOLPH: You've got your kids.

XAVIER: *(Amazed.)* Jesus, Ran!

BENNIE: Jesus, Ran!

XAVIER: *(Saving the moment.)* How'd you get away from him, Ben?

BENNIE: I didn't! I told ya's! I was right outside the door here, screaming for you guys, for maybe twenty minutes!...

XAVIER: We didn't hear a thing!

RANDOLPH: Nothing!

BENNIE: It was like a Mexican standoff! He just kept hitting me and I just kinda kept myself wrapped around my bag, taking it.

XAVIER: Protecting your clubs.

BENNIE: Exact. I guess he got tired, and he got up off me and left.

RANDOLPH: He was Mexican?

BENNIE: *(To XAVIER, about RANDOLPH...)* Shut him up!

XAVIER: Jesus, Bennie, didn't anybody, like, *walk by?*

BENNIE: Only a million people!

RANDOLPH: Nobody did anything?

BENNIE: Oh, yuh, sure.

XAVIER: Goddam city's getting worse!

RANDOLPH: Unbelievable.

XAVIER: You gonna' be okay to play, still?

BENNIE: 'Course, I'm okay ta' play! When I'm not okay ta' play golf, I'm a dead man!

XAVIER: That's the truth.

RANDOLPH: Definitely.

XAVIER: Definitely.

BENNIE: *(Suddenly...)* Jesus! Do you see what time it is?!
    (A telephone rings. LIGHTS SHIFT TO...BENNIE's OFFICE, night, some years earlier. Telephone is ringing...and ringing. BENNIE crosses to desk; calls out...)

BENNIE: Mrs. Chandler! Anybody still working here? *(Picks up phone.)* Yuh?
    (SPOTLIGHT UP ON...ALLIE, downstage, at restaurant table. SHE is

30 years old, stunningly beautiful. SHE holds a flip-phone in her hand. There is an uneaten fruit tart on plate in front of her.)

ALLIE: You're still working?

BENNIE: Nobody else is!…Can you believe this? I made two point six million dollars, last month, and I'm answering my own phone!

ALLIE: It's ten o'clock, Bennie. You're two hours late.

BENNIE: It's nothing *like* ten o'clock. You're kidding! *(Looks at watch.)* Jesus, it is! Where are you?

ALLIE: I'm at Zucchini's.

BENNIE: Oh, my God! I'm really sorry, Allie. Maybe you should eat something and…

ALLIE: I already did. An hour ago. I've been here since quarter to eight. I finished reading my novel.

BENNIE: Must have been a thin book.

ALLIE: *Bonfire of the Vanities*—647 pages!

BENNIE: Don't move. I'm coming.

(LIGHTS CROSS WITH…BENNIE, as HE jogs across the stage to ALLIE.)

BENNIE: You hate me.

ALLIE: I don't hate you. I'm just majorly pissed off.

BENNIE: You love me, but you're majorly pissed off.

ALLIE: I'm lyin' on the street. I'm dying. You're with me. You start running for an ambulance. I'm waiting for you to get back, lyin' on the street, life or death. A guy calls out to you, says he's got a takeover deal, you can see a quick four or five million. What do you do? Go for the ambulance or stop and do the deal?

BENNIE: *(Tries to kiss ALLIE.)* Allie, I love you. I wanna spend my life with you.

ALLIE: What do you do?

BENNIE: I stop, I do the takeover deal, then, I pick you off the street, spend one-point-four million bringing you back to life with the best medicine money can buy. You recover, you're fine, we live happily ever after, with an after-tax profit of, say, two-six. Tax credits…Your medical bills are totally deductible, right off the top. You have a piece of a sprout between your teeth.

ALLIE: I don't. You're just saying that.

BENNIE: Look at me, Allie: I'm twenty-eight years old, I'm the seventy-first richest man in the United States. I could have any woman in the world

after the other seventy pick theirs. And I'm looking at you, Alison
Resnick, saying "I want to spend the rest of my life with you."

ALLIE: Fuck you, Benjamin.

BENNIE: Exactly why I'm here.

ALLIE: Did you ever read *A Christmas Carol?* When he's young, Scrooge has
a girlfriend...a fiancé...She breaks off their engagement. She tells him
"You have someone you love more than me."

BENNIE: Money.

ALLIE: Money.

BENNIE: So, he loses the girl but he gets Tiny Tim.

ALLIE: *(Angrily...)* What are you *talking* about?

BENNIE: He's English. He likes little boys.

ALLIE: You're ridiculous.

BENNIE: I am, I'm ridiculous. I'm also really, really sorry I'm late. Allie, listen to me...It's like I'm playing birdie-golf, nonstop. I don't know why
it's happening, why I'm hitting 'em so good, but I know I've gotta' keep
playing the game while it's working. You know what I mean by this? It's
gonna stop, sooner or later. But, til it does, I'm gonna' keep workin',
'round the clock, and I guess you're stuck with it, if you wanna be stuck
with me.

ALLIE: What if I don't?

BENNIE: Wanna be stuck with me?

ALLIE: Wanna be stuck with *it*. How much money do you need, Bennie?

BENNIE: A lot, Alison. As much as I can get. *(Beat.)* Are you planning to
eat that fruit tart?

(BENNIE eats fruit tart, as...THE LIGHTS SHIFT TO...XAVIER,
yamulkah on his head, at BENNIE'S GRAVE, day.)

XAVIER: I've never been to a Jewish funeral, before. It seems like a big rush
to me, getting Bennie buried so quick. I guess it's the rules, but, it just
seems so...rushed. *(Beat. XAVIER holds back his tears.)* Bennie and I first
met at PS75, first day of kindergarten. Bennie tried to sell me a ballpoint
for more than he paid for it, so, I hit him. We were best friends, ever
since then. Best friends, every *day*, since then. Bennie and I and
Ran...Randolph. *(Beat.)* Randolph bought the ballpoint. *(Smiles.)*
Bennie's the first friend I've ever had die. There were neighborhood kids,
but, never anybody so close to me...never somebody I always rush to the
phone to tell news to. Like now, I keep wanting to call Bennie up and
tell him who died. *(Beat.)* I don't know what I would have been without
Bennie. I'm a lawyer and I certainly wouldn't have been that. I've got two

brothers. They've both been in jail, already. *(Beat.)* Bennie showed me how to study. He also showed me why. *(Beat.)* Bennie was the first kid I knew to make a million. More accurately, Bennie was the first kid I knew to make a hundred million. Also the first kid I knew to *lose* a hundred million. *(Sobs.)* I love you, Bennie. I'll never stop thinking about you. I'm always gonna' make my moves thinking "What would Bennie do in this situation?"…I wish you didn't kill yourself, Bennie. It's gonna be so weird playing golf without your noise. My short game is just getting good. *(Beat.)* Peace, bro.

(THE LIGHTS SHIFT TO…BENNIE on the tee. HE calls across to X…)

BENNIE: Don't spend an hour lining up your shot, X. Just put "I can do this" in your head and hit the ball.

(LIGHTS WIDEN TO…XAVIER, who moves to tee, exasperated, driver in his hand. The full stage is now lit, and we see that it is more or less an expanse of green grass. There is a tee area, replete with blue-and-white men's markers, upstage center. There is a large bench, that is the centerpiece of this particular set. Downstage center, we see a circular "green," replete with flag and cup. BENNIE's GRAVE is visible, well upstage of the action.)

XAVIER: *(To RANDOLPH, about BENNIE…)* Shut him up, okay?

BENNIE: I'm just tellin' him what he already knows. How's my lip? Still bleeding?

XAVIER: *(Without looking up from his ball…)* Mutilated. You're gonna' have a hideous purple scar.

BENNIE: Are you gonna hit, or should I hit?

XAVIER: I'm hitting.

RANDOLPH: Why don't you let me hit, first, X? Calm yourself down.

XAVIER: I'm calm. I'm hitting.

(XAVIER addresses the ball; hits. SFX: WE HEAR: a whack, and then, a "Raspberry," i.e., a fart sound, indicating that a bad shot has been hit. NOTE: When a good shot has been hit, we will hear a pleasing, congratulatory sound effect: a whack, and then, a bell being rung. After the "raspberry" sound, RANDOLPH and BENNIE exchange a knowing glance. XAVIER stomps his feet in disgust. These sounds should be produced, live, by the stage manager, with clap-stick, whistle, bell, etc.)

XAVIER: Shit!

RANDOLPH: Hit again, after us.

XAVIER: *(Hopefully.)* We playing a mulligan on the front nine?

BENNIE: Not since third grade.

XAVIER: *(Loses it.)* Drop dead, Bennie! You deliberately yapped, just to get my timing off!

BENNIE: Yuh, right, for the buck a point. I need the seven dollars.

XAVIER: It isn't the money! You think Greg Norman or Corey Pavin or Nick Faldo are playing for *money?* Bullshit! It's the *win!* And in your case, it's also the seven bucks.

BENNIE: As I've said many, many times before, "Fuck you, X!"...

RANDOLPH: You guys are something. One ball off the tee, so far, and listen to yourselves!

BENNIE: What ball is off the tee? You call his drive "off the tee?"

XAVIER: It's playable.

BENNIE: Crossing two other fairways, sideways, is not "playable," it is totally out of bounds!...*Look, look, look!* The kid on the hot dog cart just picked your ball up, X.

XAVIER: *(Suddenly, screams, to OFFSTAGE PERSON.) That's my ball! Hey! HEY! That's my ball!*

BENNIE: Too late, X. *He's selling it!* See him?

XAVIER: Fuck you, Bennie, huh? *(Yells.) HEYYY! HOT DOG CART MAN! THAT'S MY BALL!*

RANDOLPH: He heard you.

XAVIER: *THAT'S MY BALL! (And then...) THANKS!*

RANDOLPH: You made great contact, X, you just lacked direction.

XAVIER: Fuck you, too, Ran, okay?

RANDOLPH: You'll hit again, after us.

XAVIER: Fine.

BENNIE: Two strokes, out'ta bounds.

RANDOLPH: One stroke.

BENNIE: Come on, Ran, will ya'? Out of bounds is out of bounds! We're not beginners, here. I mean, let's face it: If it were me who hit the hot dog cart, we'd be writing down two strokes, yes?

RANDOLPH: One stroke, Bennie.

BENNIE: Fine. You hit.

RANDOLPH: You can go.

BENNIE: I'm not hitting when I'm pissed off.

RANDOLPH: Fine. I'll go.

> *(RANDOLPH lines up to hit his drive. HE addresses the ball, checks his line. And then...)*

XAVIER: I've known you all your life, Bennie. When *aren't* you pissed off?

BENNIE: People are different with different people, X.

XAVIER: Touché.

BENNIE: Is that a multilingual non-retort I heard?…

XAVIER: No, it was connilingual.

BENNIE: There are torts and there are *re* torts. That was a…

    (Suddenly, RANDOLPH steps away from the ball; loses it; screams.)

RANDOLPH: *Shut up, both of ya's! Shut up! Shut up! Goddamit!*

    (Beat.)

BENNIE: I'll hit. I'm cool.

RANDOLPH: I'm hitting! Just shut up!

XAVIER: Don't hit when you're razzled, Ran. You saw what happened to me.

RANDOLPH: I'm not razzled! I'm just telling ya's both to shut up. I'm hitting my drive, okay?

XAVIER: Okay, Ran.

BENNIE: Okay, Ran.

    (RANDOLPH goes through a lengthy address of the ball, checking his line, etc. XAVIER and BENNIE avoid eye contact with one another, for fear of getting the giggles. XAVIER is the first to giggle…just as RANDOLPH is ready to hit. RANDOLPH starts his swing, steps away from the ball, disgusted.)

RANDOLPH: *Godammit!*

XAVIER: Sorry.

BENNIE: Sorry.

RANDOLPH: Fine.

    (RANDOLPH steps back into position, swings at ball, makes contact. WE HEAR…Sound of a farting "raspberry.")

RANDOLPH: Great. Thank you. It's a joy to play golf with you guys, really.

XAVIER: It rolled right next to mine. We can walk, together, Ran.

BENNIE: At least the kid won't be able to sell it.

RANDOLPH: What is that supposed ta' mean?

BENNIE: Nothin'.

RANDOLPH: What?

BENNIE: Nothin'.

RANDOLPH: *WHAT?*

BENNIE: You're not playing sellable balls, that's all.

RANDOLPH: Hit, Bennie.

BENNIE: I'm ready.

RANDOLPH: I wish you the best, Bennie.

BENNIE: I know you do, Ran.

    (BENNIE addresses the ball, hits. SFX: sweet sound of bell ringing.)

XAVIER: Good hit, Bennie.

RANDOLPH: Good hit, Bennie.

BENNIE: *(Smiles.)* Thanks, guys.

> *(THE LIGHTS CROSSFADE TO…BALCONY overlooking East River, night. A party is in progress, off. WE HEAR…Late '80s house music. WE DISCOVER…MIRANDA. SHE is 30, ginger-haired, beautiful. NOTE: SHE is played by same actress (be-wigged) who plays ALLIE. MIRANDA carries a drink to a potted tree, discreetly pours the contents of her glass into pot. RANDOLPH calls across to her.)*

RANDOLPH: Saw that. I'm going to have to turn you in for giving alcohol to an underage Ficus tree.

> *(MIRANDA looks up, laughs.)*

MIRANDA: Oh, hi. Yuh, I panicked. I got talked into trying a whiskey drink called "Sex On The Beach." It's horrible!…

> *(RANDOLPH pulls on a floppy sport jacket; crosses to MIRANDA.)*

RANDOLPH: Never judge a book by its cover.

MIRANDA: Sorry?

RANDOLPH: "Sex On The Beach."

MIRANDA: Oh, no, it's not a book, it's a drink. *(Laughs. And then…)* Oh, shit! That's what you meant. I'm not drunk, I'm just naturally slow reacting to jokes. It's an emotional thing. My father told a lot of jokes. I never really satisfied him with my reaction. I never really…got them…his jokes.

RANDOLPH: My father did, too. Told jokes all the time. Same deal. I never really got them. We both worry about not getting the joke. That's our connection, probably.

MIRANDA: Connection in what sense?

RANDOLPH: There's always a psychic connection, especially when there's a strong sexual attraction…*(Without pause…)* I cannot believe that I just said that, out loud.

MIRANDA: That was pretty amazing.

RANDOLPH: I apologize.

MIRANDA: It's okay. Your id and ego are in place. You just need a superego.

RANDOLPH: In what sense?

MIRANDA: You're without moral restraint.

RANDOLPH: That's the other connection.

MIRANDA: Meaning we're both in treatment.

RANDOLPH: *(Holds up his hand, like a student answering a question.)* Five years.

MIRANDA: *(Holds up her hand...)* Six, here. On the couch.

RANDOLPH: On the couch. Five days a week.

MIRANDA: I was five, I'm down to three. How old's your doctor?

RANDOLPH: How *old* is my doctor?...He's eighty-one.

MIRANDA: Amazing!

RANDOLPH: Yours is old, too?

MIRANDA: Eighty-one.

RANDOLPH: She's exactly eighty-one?

MIRANDA: He. Exactly eighty-one.

RANDOLPH: *(Nervously.)* Where's your guy?

MIRANDA: Where's his office?...In the Village.

RANDOLPH: What street, he asked, beginning to perspire profusely.

MIRANDA: Eleventh.

RANDOLPH: What number Eleventh?

MIRANDA: *(Holds up four fingers on each hand.)*

RANDOLPH: Jesus! West or East?...*West?*

MIRANDA: West.

RANDOLPH: Beyond amazing. Excuse me, I mean, this is really kind of embarrassing, but, like the song says, "Hello, I love you, won't you tell me your name?"...

MIRANDA: Miranda. Mandy. I prefer "Man" or "Mand."

RANDOLPH: You're kidding!

MIRANDA: Why?

RANDOLPH: Randolph. Randy. I prefer "Ran" or "Rand."

MIRANDA: How would you feel about us getting out of here?

RANDOLPH: Us? Together? Like, leaving together, now, kind of thing? *(SHE nods, affirmatively. HE smiles.)* Comfortable. I would feel comfortable...Mand.

MIRANDA: Me, too, Rand.

(MUSIC IN...LIGHTS CROSSFADE TO...THE GAME. THREE TINY SPOTLIGHTS ON...THREE GOLF BALLS, teed up, ready to be hit.

LIGHTS WIDEN TO INCLUDE...BENNIE, XAVIER, and RANDOLPH, golf clubs in hand, swinging at their golf balls, several times, each, in a ballet of golf shots.

Each shot gets an overdramatic reaction from each player...and an appropriate sound effect...a whacking sound, and then, farting raspberries, or, the most welcome sound of affirmative bells.

This sequence should last about one minute and should communicate to the audience that four holes have been played, that BENNIE is leading, RANDOLPH is not far behind, and that XAVIER is in deep trouble. Therefore, we will have heard Bennie yelling "Yessss!" and "Bingo!"; Ran yelling "Not bad" and "I can work with that"; and X yelling "Oh, my God!" and "Oh, shit!"

At completion of ballet, RANDOLPH exits, BENNIE and XAVIER move to the green. BENNIE's ball is next to the pin.)

XAVIER: Fantastic shot, Ben. Where's Ran?

BENNIE: In the woods, still, looking for his ball.

XAVIER: He thinks he gonna *find* that shot? He must've gone a hundred and fifty yards, straight in!

BENNIE: Please, X, in the last ten years, have you ever known Ran to lose a ball?

XAVIER: Yuh, but, c'mon, will ya'? He's not gonna' drop a ball a hundred and fifty yards into the woods, yell "I've found it," and think we're gonna' believe...

(Suddenly...RANDOLPH's VOICE...)

RANDOLPH *(Offstage.) Found it!*

(BENNIE and XAVIER exchange a glance.)

RANDOLPH *(Offstage.)* Look sharp! I'm hitting!

BENNIE: I'll bet he tees it up.

XAVIER: Unbelievable!

(WE HEAR...WHACK!...then the sweet sound of a bell...RANDOLPH's "Yessss!"...His ball drops on to the green. BENNIE and XAVIER exchange another knowing glance.)

XAVIER: I'm laying five, he's teeing up in the woods!

(RANDOLPH enters, smiling happily.)

RANDOLPH: That was lucky. It was sitting up nice on a clump, right out in the open. I caught it nice.

BENNIE: Nice shot, Ran.

XAVIER: Nice shot, Ran.

RANDOLPH: Thanks, guys.

(BENNIE moves to his ball, putter in hand. XAVIER moves to the flag...)

BENNIE: Pull it. Let me put this away.

(XAVIER pulls the flag.)

RANDOLPH: *(As Bennie lines up his putt...)* Birdie putt, Ben. Take your time.

BENNIE: Eagle putt, Ran. Add again.

RANDOLPH: *(Remembering Bennie's strokes...)* Great drive, monster three-wood put you on in regulation...

BENNIE: What hole are we on, Ran?

RANDOLPH: Five.

XAVIER: Eagle putt, Ran.

BENNIE: What's the par on five, Ran?

XAVIER: Bennie's got an eagle putt, here, Ran.

RANDOLPH: *(Realizes.)* Jesus, Bennie! You're having the round of your life!

BENNIE: *(Calmly.)* Now, then, I'm going to putt...and I'm going to ask you both to shut your mouths...otherwise, I will have to kill you.

(XAVIER and RANDOLPH exchange a glance. After a few moments of setting up his shot, BENNIE putts. In our imaginations...the ball travels a long distance...disappears in hole. Bell rings.)

BENNIE: *(Simply.)* Bingo.

(XAVIER and RANDOLPH exchange another glance, as...LIGHTS CROSS TO...ALLIE, in a black dress, black veil. SHE is speaking at BENNIE's funeral.)

ALLIE: Bennie Foss was one of a kind. When our marriage was good, there was none better. When our marriage was not good, there was none worse. Bennie's only constant was contradiction. His energy was boundless, but his exhaustion was profound. His lust for life was unfathomably great, but, sometimes, absolutely nonexistent. His life could be incandescent or, terrifyingly dark. His words were either crystal clear, or, totally enigmatic. But, his death was pure. Pure Bennie. Theatrical, startling...unforgettable. *(ALLIE sobs. Beat. ALLIE regains her composure, opens her prayer book...)* I would like to lead you, now, in the prayer for the dead... *Yiskadal, v'yiskadal, shmrai rabbah...*

(Men's voices join in short, prayer, as...LIGHTS CROSSFADE TO...SPOTLIGHT ON...BENNIE, in silk smoking jacket. HE lights a long Cuban cigar.)

BENNIE: Cigar?

(LIGHTS WIDEN TO INCLUDE...XAVIER and RANDOLPH, wearing tweed sport jackets. BENNIE gives them each a cigar.)

RANDOLPH: These are good ones.

BENNIE: Sixteen bucks, apiece.

XAVIER: What's up, Ben? We celebrating something?

BENNIE: I sold the company.

RANDOLPH: What's this?

BENNIE: You got waxy ears? I sold the company to a Japanese cartel. I'm totally free.

(XAVIER and RANDOLPH exchange a glance.)

XAVIER: That's great, Ben.

RANDOLPH: You get your price?

BENNIE: I got my price.

XAVIER: Jesus, Bennie, that's fantastic!

RANDOLPH: How much.

BENNIE: I'll clear a hundred.

XAVIER: A hundred? *(A bell sounds.)*

BENNIE: A hundred.

(There is an astonished silence. And then...)

RANDOLPH: Jesus, Ben, I feel like I'm gonna' cry! It's unbelievable that you— that one of us — Jesus, Bennie!

(RANDOLPH hugs BENNIE. XAVIER moves in hugs BENNIE, as well.)

XAVIER: Does this mean that, from now on, you cover our green fees?

RANDOLPH: This is astonishing news, Ben. I'm proud of you, man.

XAVIER: Me, too, Ben.

RANDOLPH: How fast does the deal close?

BENNIE: It's closed. It took about twenty minutes.

RANDOLPH: You're kidding me!

XAVIER: How'd it move so quick?

BENNIE: They took my first price.

RANDOLPH: Think your first price was too low?

BENNIE: Nope. I think they wanted it, and they know how to get what they want. They're Japanese.

XAVIER: You get any kind of kiss-off?

BENNIE: A car and a mill a year for five years. Also...

XAVIER: Fantastic!

RANDOLPH: What are you gonna' hav'ta give them?

BENNIE: I'm not done.

RANDOLPH: Oh.

BENNIE: Also, a buyout for you two.

(XAVIER and RANDOLPH exchange a glance.)

RANDOLPH: What are you saying?

XAVIER: What's up, Ben?...

BENNIE: A mill, apiece, for you both.

(Two bells. There is a substantial pause. And then...)

RANDOLPH: What are you talking about?

BENNIE: I put you both into the sale as my top outside advisors, my out-side council. It's a straight, clean buyout. I have to be available to them for five years, for no more than one meeting a month. You'll have to be available to me, once a week. We can play Split Rock, Van Cortland, South Shore, Dykker Beach, or Pelham. I won't play Mosholu. Nine-Holers aren't worth the effort. *(Beat.)* You guys accept?
(XAVIER and RANDOLPH are stunned by this news.)
XAVIER: Jesus, Bennie...
RANDOLPH: Bennie, I...
BENNIE: I've got two friends in my life...that's it...you two assholes. It's definitely pathetic, but, it's all I've got. I'm a rich man. I've got to have rich friends. So, now I do.
(Beat.)
XAVIER: Bennie, the only thing I can say is if it were reversed...if it were me getting the hundred and giving you and Ran each one, I would defi-nitely be giving you both more than just the one.
BENNIE: *(To RANDOLPH.)* I knew he was gonna' say that.
RANDOLPH: Bennie, there's no better guy than you. You are so great!
BENNIE: Fuck you, Ran.
RANDOLPH: *(To XAVIER.)* I knew he was gonna' say that.
(XAVIER walks to BENNIE, shakes his hand, "street" style, hearts touch-ing.)
XAVIER: I love you, Bennie.
RANDOLPH AND BENNIE: *(In unison.)* Fuck you, X!
XAVIER: *(Half laughing, half crying...)* I wanna' go home and tell Smitty, face to face. *(Looks at BENNIE.)* Nobody's ever had a better friend, Ben. I mean this.
(LIGHTS CROSS TO...BALCONY, Bennie's penthouse, night. MUSIC IN...1980s HOUSE MUSIC, new tune, or, perhaps, Beastie Boys' "FIGHT FOR YOUR RIGHT TO PARTY." WE DISCOVER...SMITTY, née COURTNEY HOGG-SMITH, 30, blonde, beautiful...played by same (be-wigged) actress who plays ALLIE and MIRANDA.)
XAVIER: People call me "X"...
SMITTY: Is that like a racial thing?
XAVIER: Short for Xavier.
SMITTY: Xavier...Nice name.
XAVIER: Thanks. My whole name's Xavier Bouvier.
SMITTY: *Tu parle Français?*
XAVIER: Uh uh. You?...

SMITTY: *Oui.* I lived in Paris for two years.

XAVIER: I've just got a really French name…Bouvier…but, I speak *trés mauvais français.* I'm not related to Jackie Kennedy, either.

SMITTY: I'm Smitty. My whole name's Courtney Hogg-Smith. I'm not related to Michael Lindsay-Hogg.

XAVIER: Who's that?

SMITTY: You ever see the Beatles' movie, *Let It Be?* He directed it. How did you ever get a name like Xavier Bouvier and not speak French?

XAVIER: My parents are French…from Martinique, originally.

SMITTY: Oh, cool. And now?

XAVIER: Where do they live, now? Here. Midtown.

SMITTY: Whose apartment is this?

XAVIER: My friend Bennie Foss.

SMITTY: Which one's Bennie Foss.

XAVIER: He's not here.

SMITTY: Who's the host?

XAVIER: He's the host. Bennie Foss. He's just not here. He works a lot.

SMITTY: So, his parties just happen, anyway, without him?

XAVIER: A lot of the time, yuh.

SMITTY: He's a close friend?

XAVIER: Since kindergarten.

SMITTY: You're a lawyer?

XAVIER: You hate lawyers?

SMITTY: I do, actually.

XAVIER: What do you do for a living?

SMITTY: Lawyer.

XAVIER: Oh. Right. Yuh, me, too. What kind of law?

SMITTY: Legal Aid. How about you? What kind of law?

XAVIER: Basic corporate doo-doo. Ran, my roommate, does entertainment law. Ran and I and Bennie, the host, we all went through school, together, first grade right through law school.

SMITTY: Same firm?

XAVIER: Ran and I, yuh. Bennie's on his own. He's a hyphenate…a lawyer-hyphen-raider.

SMITTY: Oh. Right. *(Beat.)* I was thinking lawyer-hyphen-football-player, first…

XAVIER: Oh, right. Uh uh. Bennie's definitely not that kind of Raider. He's a pretty good golfer, though.

SMITTY: You, too? You play golf?

XAVIER: The three of us...Ran, Bennie, and I...We've been playing golf, together, since we were kids. Ran's father played, and he used to take the three of us out with him, Saturdays.

SMITTY: Really? You don't hear about golf a lot in New York. Where do you play?

XAVIER: There are a bunch of New York City-owned courses. We've been playing the city courses for years and years.

SMITTY: We'll never get married.

XAVIER: Excuse me?

SMITTY: You and I. We'll never get married. My father's a big golfer. My mother made me promise...

XAVIER: ...Never to marry a golfer?

SMITTY: Exactly. *(SMITTY smiles, looks out at city.)* Nice view. Your friend must be rich.

XAVIER: Big time.

SMITTY: How old is he?

XAVIER: Same as me: 28.

SMITTY: How'd he make his money? Raiding?

XAVIER: Raiding and ridiculous good luck. He once bought into a gold mine for a 2-for-1 tax write-off on the loss. They struck gold. Bennie made, like, mega-money!...

SMITTY: Are you rich?

XAVIER: Don't feel you're being indiscreet.

SMITTY: I don't.

XAVIER: Pretty rich, yuh. How about you? What do you do?

SMITTY: I told you...

XAVIER: Law. Right. Are you rich, or just beautiful?

SMITTY: *(Smiles.)* Men.

XAVIER: Sickest people on Earth.

SMITTY: Not rich, not yet. Not poor, not rich. But, I went to a good school.

XAVIER: How good?

SMITTY: You don't want to know.

XAVIER: I went to City College. We all did. Me, Bennie, Ran.

SMITTY: You guys planning to marry the same girl?

XAVIER: Why'd you say *that*?

(Beat. And then...)

SMITTY: I think the first time you get married, you pick the kind of person your parents want you to marry. The second time, you pick somebody for yourself.

XAVIER: I guess. I lived with somebody for four years…a woman from the Islands. Bajan…from Barbados. Really smart. Teaches high school English at Trinity School. Really, really nice person.

SMITTY: But, boring.

XAVIER: *(Smiles; nods.)* A little boring, yuh. *(Beat.)* You? Any serious coupling?

SMITTY: I married a guy I knew from Princeton.

XAVIER: You went to Princeton.

SMITTY: Princeton High School. I grew up there.

XAVIER: In Princeton.

SMITTY: Near Princeton.

XAVIER: Didn't work out?

SMITTY: The marriage? Uh uh.

XAVIER: That's too bad. When did you get divorced?…

SMITTY: I didn't.

XAVIER: Separated?

SMITTY: No. How about you?…When did you and your girlfriend break up?

XAVIER: We didn't.

SMITTY: You want to get out of here?

XAVIER: Sure. Where to?

SMITTY: I've got an invitation to a gallery opening down in Soho. It's this young guy I'm interested in. Jean-Michel Basquiat.

XAVIER: He's the best.

SMITTY: You know his work?

XAVIER: I know *him*.

SMITTY: How come you're looking at me funny?

XAVIER: It's hard when you don't really know somebody and you're like *drawn* to them. With us, for example, it's hard to tell if you're the love of my life, or if you're an ax-murderer.

SMITTY: Isn't it kind of the same thing?

(XAVIER smiles.)

(THE LIGHTS WIDEN TO…BENNIE and RANDOLPH sitting on bench. BENNIE lights the other half of his broken cigar, RANDOLPH tallies the score for the first four holes. XAVIER sulks, nearby.)

XAVIER: *(Looking out, forward.)* Do you think I'll hit as far as those two guys down there?

BENNIE: Not the way you've been hitting 'em, today.

(XAVIER gives BENNIE his worst silent stare.)

RANDOLPH: Bennie's 36, I'm 41…

XAVIER: I don't wanna' know!

BENNIE: You've gotta' know. How you gonna' play best-front-nine if you don't hear your score?

XAVIER: 53.

RANDOLPH: 54.

XAVIER: How do you make it 54?

RANDOLPH: Nine sixes.

XAVIER: I just got a five!

BENNIE: Six.

RANDOLPH: You got a six, X. You skulled your drive, your hooked your 3-wood, five iron next to the pin…

XAVIER: Fine.

BENNIE: Three putts.

XAVIER: I said "fine!" *(XAVIER looks out at golfers up ahead.)* They're still looking for the old guy's ball in the stream.

BENNIE: Relax. It's not your honor, anyway.

XAVIER: I wanna' be able to play the full eighteen.

BENNIE: Why wouldn't you play the full eighteen? I've got the best round of my life, goin' here!

XAVIER: I've got a thing I gotta do.

RANDOLPH: What kind of thing?

XAVIER: I'm meeting up with Smitty.

RANDOLPH: You are?

BENNIE: How come?

XAVIER: I dunno. *(Beat.)* We bumped into each other.

BENNIE: When?

XAVIER: Couple'a days ago.

RANDOLPH: You didn't say anything.

XAVIER: Yuh, well, so, I didn't.

　　　(BENNIE and RANDOLPH exchange a look. XAVIER sees this.)

XAVIER: Something wrong with me and Smitty meeting up for a drink?
　　　(BENNIE and RANDOLPH shrug.)

XAVIER: You don't live with somebody for seven years, and just, like, turn your back on them.

BENNIE: She in some kind of trouble?

XAVIER: Why'd you ask that?

BENNIE: You just said "You don't live years and years with somebody and turn your back on them."

XAVIER: Yuh, so?

BENNIE: Nothing, X.

XAVIER: *(To RANDOLPH.)* She was askin' about Mandy.

RANDOLPH: What did you tell her?

XAVIER: You know…that you guys were havin' your problems.

RANDOLPH: You can tell her anything. I don't give a shit.

BENNIE: *(Looking out front.)* They're hitting.

RANDOLPH: *(Looks.)* Finally.

XAVIER: *(Looks.)* Finally. *(To BENNIE.)* Your honor.

BENNIE: *Still* mine?

    (Smiles; moves to the tee.)

RANDOLPH: Up yours, Bennie.

XAVIER: Up yours, Bennie.

BENNIE: I'm gonna' take that as a compliment.

    (RANDOLPH and X exchange an amazed glance, as…LIGHTS CROSS-
    FADE TO…ALLIE, on balcony to Bennie's penthouse, years earlier, night.)

ALLIE: This place is beautiful!

BENNIE: Yuh, it's not bad.

ALLIE: What does your father do?

BENNIE: My father?

ALLIE: I'm just interested.

BENNIE: When I last saw him, he was selling shoes.

ALLIE: You don't see him much?

BENNIE: *(Smiles.)* No.

ALLIE: Does he like *manufacture* shoes?

BENNIE: I don't think so.

ALLIE: I feel like I'm touching some really tender places, here. I'm sorry if
    I'm prying, or getting into stuff I shouldn't be getting into. If it helps, I
    can tell you that my parents had a bloodbath of a divorce. I was in court
    more than twenty times before I was ten, with them fighting through
    lawyers. My father's been married four times since my mother. He's got
    six more kids.

BENNIE: What kind of court?

ALLIE: Excuse me?

BENNIE: You were in court. Were they fighting over money or over you?

ALLIE: Over me.

BENNIE: Who won?

ALLIE: Who *won?* *(Smiles.)* Not *me.* I can tell you that!…*(Beat.)* My mother got
    me four days a week, my father the rest.

BENNIE: My mother and father were in court fighting over me…but, not quite the same way your parents were fighting over you. Mine were fighting to force the other one to get stuck with me.

ALLIE: What?

BENNIE: I was what they called a "hyperactive" child. I talked a lot. I was nervous.

ALLIE: I'll bet.

BENNIE: They each petitioned the court to have the other one get me.

ALLIE: My God!…Who won?

BENNIE: Me. I got put with my mother's cousin Iris.

ALLIE: She was nice?

BENNIE: She was paid well.

ALLIE: Oh. God. How old were you?

BENNIE: Ten, when I moved in with her; fifteen, when I left.

ALLIE: You left?

BENNIE: My sister was living with my mother. She's five years older. She got a place of her own, when she turned twenty, not far from my mother's, and I moved in with her…with my sister.

ALLIE: And that worked out?

BENNIE: Sure. Why not?

ALLIE: Are you, like, close with her?

BENNIE: My sister? No.

ALLIE: Oh. How about your mother or father? Did you make peace with either of them?…

BENNIE: Never had to.

ALLIE: Me, neither. I went off to boarding school when I was fourteen and I never looked back. I'm really good at that: never looking back.
(There is an embarrassed pause.)

ALLIE: So!…Now, that we're both completely naked in front of each other, to our bones, I think I'd like to say something finite about you and your parents, from *my* point of view.

BENNIE: Be my guest.

ALLIE: Whatever you lived through, you lived through. However you got where you are, you got there. I don't know you at all, really, I mean, we've just met, but I feel as if I know you, totally. You're self-assured, you're creative, you're totally open and vulnerable, and you're really, really, really good-looking…so, like, fuck them if they can't take a joke, right?
(BENNIE sings Joe Cocker's "You are so beautiful (to me)" to ALLIE, a cappella.)

BENNIE: "You are so beautiful to me. You are so beautiful to me…Can't you see? You're everything I dream of, you're everything I need."

ALLIE: *(Laughing.) Stoppp!*

BENNIE: "You are so beautiful…to meeeee!"

ALLIE: You have a terrible voice!

BENNIE: I do. I know I do.

ALLIE: Oh, Goddddd!…Excuse me, if I seem really dumb asking this, but, who's place is this? I can't figure it out. Are you, like, *house-sitting*? Did you, like, *borrow it* for our date, tonight?

BENNIE: It's mine.

ALLIE: Yours.

BENNIE: Mine.

ALLIE: You *own* this place?

BENNIE: I own this place, I own a house on the Island, I have a limo and a driver.

ALLIE: You're…rich?

BENNIE: Rich.

ALLIE: I'm amazed. I mean, sure, why not? It's just that I didn't have a clue.

BENNIE: That's the way I wanted it.

ALLIE: I guess…sure…I'm just surprised.

BENNIE: You can understand, can't you?

ALLIE: Sure. It's just that I feel a little, I dunno, tricked.

BENNIE: Can we kiss and make up?

ALLIE: *(Considers this. And then…)* Sure.
        (BENNIE moves to her.)

ALLIE: Is there anything else I should know?

BENNIE: About me?

ALLIE: About you, about me, whatever.

BENNIE: You're going to marry me, and we'll probably have two kids, maybe three.

ALLIE: Excuse me? I'm going to *what?*
        (LIGHTS SHIFT BACK TO…XAVIER and RANDOLPH on the tee. ALLIE stays on balcony, back turned to audience.)

XAVIER: *(Looking out front at GOLFERS, ahead.)* It looks like he's given up looking for his ball in the stream. He put a new ball down and he's hitting. Get set up, Bennie.
        (BENNIE moves to tee; addresses ball; lines up shot…RANDOLPH interrupts…)

RANDOLPH: *(Looking out front.)* You can reach. Better wait up til he hits. Maybe we ought to ask to play through, next hole. This is stupid!

BENNIE: *(Matter-of-factly.)* My divorce becomes final today.

XAVIER: No kidding?

(ALLIE exits balcony. RANDOLPH and XAVIER exchange a glance.)

RANDOLPH: You buyin' drinks?

BENNIE: I've been doin' that already for twenty years, haven't I? *(SFX: WE HEAR…a distant whack and fart-sound. BENNIE looks out front.)* Shit! You see that?

RANDOLPH: I saw him hit. Where'd he go?

BENNIE: Back in the water.

XAVIER: Back in the water.

BENNIE: *(Steps away from his ball.)* Allie called me, this morning, to remind me. I'd forgotten.

XAVIER: She happy about it?

BENNIE: Seems to be.

RANDOLPH: Just a piece of paper, Ben. Nothing really changes.

BENNIE: Hey, I got no problem with any of it. I was just telling ya's.

XAVIER: How are the kids?

BENNIE: Great. Why'd you ask?

XAVIER: No reason.

BENNIE: Roddy's doing a lot better.

XAVIER: Great.

RANDOLPH: He'll be fine.

BENNIE: *He won't! He'll get worse and worse! (There is a small silence. And then…)* You gotta' face up to things, Ran. I mean, you can't keep fooling yourself, pretending that what is, isn't. What is, is. *(Beat.)* Roddy's doing better. He's sleeping through most of the night.

XAVIER: That's great.

RANDOLPH: How's Cody?

BENNIE: Cody's a winner.

XAVIER: Totally.

RANDOLPH: Great kid.

BENNIE: We playin' golf, here, or we doin' a talk show?

XAVIER: We're waiting for you to hit, Ben.

BENNIE: No, you're not. You're deliberately bringin' up shit ta' psych me out of a good golf-head.

(XAVIER looks at RANDOLPH.)

RANDOLPH: Want me to hit first, Ben?

BENNIE: *(Addresses his ball.)* Fuck you, Ran, huh?…You, too, X. Both'a ya's keep tryin' ta bring me down. *(Hits. SFX: Whack. Then, sweet sound of a bell being rung. BENNIE smiles.)* I'm happy to say it isn't holding me back from Greatness.

XAVIER: Good ball, Ben.

RANDOLPH: Nice shot, Bennie.

BENNIE: Thanks, guys. *(Turns to them; smiles.)* Who's up?

> *(LIGHTS SHIFT TO…ALLIE, downstage, in kitchen of BEN and ALLIE's townhouse.)*

ALLIE: Are you sure it's definite? You tend to exaggerate. You…

BENNIE: It's definite, Allie.

> *(There is a substantial pause.)*

ALLIE: If we're poor, we're poor. It could be interesting.

BENNIE: Don't be ridiculous! We've never been poor, either of us. What the hell makes you think it could be interesting?

ALLIE: When will it happen?

BENNIE: It happened. It's over. Everything I used to try to shore up the company stock is gone. I could give you the technical details, but the bottom line is it's over. The market's bottomed out. It's all gone.

ALLIE: The company?

BENNIE: Us, personally, Allie. The company doesn't exist, any more, as of noon, today.

ALLIE: Ben, is it definite that you used the house as collateral against the loan? What I'm asking is…

BENNIE: Both our houses, my mother's apartment, X's house, Ran's apartment…all of it.

ALLIE: Will we have to move?

BENNIE: Yes.

ALLIE: When?

BENNIE: We can probably stall six months, maybe a year, but, no more.

ALLIE: What about the kids' schools?

BENNIE: Aren't they paid up?

ALLIE: Just til the end of the term.

BENNIE: So, that'll be it. I mean, we can just keep rolling bills for a while. Nobody'll believe it, really. I've seen other big money guys on the slide. They still get credit. They can still…*(Beat.)* It's gonna' be in tomorrow's papers.

ALLIE: Oh. *(Beat.)* How do you know this?

BENNIE: This guy from the *Times* called me, first thing, this morning.

ALLIE: Could you ask him to hold off printing anything, til we tell our family, ourselves...some friends?

BENNIE: *(Sardonically.)* No newspaperman ever held off from printing anything, if he thought he could cause some serious pain...

ALLIE: I mean, it'll be really difficult for the kids...

BENNIE: I know. I pointed that out, but, it just turned him on, all the more.

ALLIE: Bennie, I don't care. I really don't.

BENNIE: We'll see.

ALLIE: What does that mean?

BENNIE: We'll see. That's what "We'll see" means. It means "We'll see."

ALLIE: Are you okay?

BENNIE: Yuh. Never better.

ALLIE: How about Ran and X? Was it just their houses, or did you borrow money from them, too?

BENNIE: Everything, like us. They've lost everything.

ALLIE: Oh, God...*(Beat.)* Are they okay?

BENNIE: I haven't told them yet.

> *(LIGHTS CROSS TO...RANDOLPH on the tee, preparing to drive. BENNIE calls to HIM.)*

BENNIE: You're gonna' hav'ta keep your head down.

> *(THE LIGHTS WIDEN TO INCLUDE...XAVIER, on bench, watching RANDOLPH on tee...)*

XAVIER: Keep your head down, Ran, we'll watch your ball.

RANDOLPH: *(Stepping away from his drive.)* Thanks for talking, guys. Really. Thanks a lot. It helps my game, enormously, to have you break my concentration and remind me that I skulled my last two drives.

XAVIER: Sorry, Ran, sorry.

BENNIE: *(Crossing to THEM...)* Just trying to help, Ran. When you're on a bad roll, something's gotta' change, if you're ever gonna' break your luck.

RANDOLPH: *(To XAVIER.)* Can you shut him up?

> *(XAVIER signals BENNIE, who shows RANDOLPH his palms, then, sits on bench next to XAVIER. THEY both stare at their shoes, trying to be perfectly silent and motionless, as RANDOLPH once again prepares to drive. Suddenly, WE HEAR...)*

OTHER GOLFER: *(Offstage.)* FORE! FORE! *(Yelled by stage manager or actress playing ALLIE.)*

> *(RANDOLPH, XAVIER, and BENNIE all duck and cover their heads, as a golf ball flies at them, hitting RANDOLPH.)*

RANDOLPH: Jesus! I got hit!

BENNIE: Jesus! Ran got hit!

XAVIER: You okay, Ran?

RANDOLPH: I guess. It whacked into my side.

BENNIE: You okay?

RANDOLPH: I'm fine! I know it hit me, but, it didn't hurt. It just like hit me hard.

XAVIER: Where'd it go?

RANDOLPH: I don't know! *(And then...)* Jesus! It went in my pocket!

XAVIER: You kidding?

BENNIE: In your pocket?

RANDOLPH: It's in my pocket! Look!

(RANDOLPH reaches into his pocket and takes out a golf ball.)

XAVIER: That's not *yours*?

RANDOLPH: Uh uh.

BENNIE: That's not your ball?

RANDOLPH: Definitely not. I'm hitting a Pinnacle.

XAVIER: Amazing!

BENNIE: It went in your goddam *pocket?!*

RANDOLPH: I didn't feel anything but my pants get heavy. *(Looking at ball.)* That is amazing!

BENNIE: Hit *that* ball.

RANDOLPH: How so?

BENNIE: Pick up your own ball and hit that one. It'll change your luck. Go with it, Ran! Do it!

RANDOLPH: You tryin' ta' sucker me into something?

BENNIE: I'll give you a mulligan if it doesn't work! Try it! Jesus, Ran, I'm leading you by twenty-two strokes and I just drove the green. *Do it!*

XAVIER: Go on, Ran. Why not?

(RANDOLPH replaces ball on tee with new ball.)

RANDOLPH: Nice and easy...*(Addresses ball.)* Tempo...

(Hits. WE HEAR...SFX: WHACK! and then...SWEET SOUND OF BELL.)

BENNIE: Bingo.

RANDOLPH: Wow!

XAVIER: Looks great.

RANDOLPH: Is it fading?

BENNIE: Just off to the left, on the apron, pin-high. See it?

RANDOLPH: My God!

XAVIER: Your best drive of the day, Ran!

BENNIE: Beautiful shot, Bro!

RANDOLPH: *(Smiles.)* Wow! *(Nods, happily.)* Wow! *(Small fist of victory.)* Easy game, golf. Nothing to it.

(LIGHTS CROSS TO…MIRANDA, downstage, in RAN's apartment. SHE calls upstage…)

MIRANDA: Are you *always* going to be with Bennie and X so bloody much of the time?

RANDOLPH: *(Crossing to HER…)* Does that really really bother you, Mandy?

MIRANDA: Not really really, no. I mean, it's not without its attraction.

RANDOLPH: Meaning?

MIRANDA: They're both attractive guys…they're clever, funny…

RANDOLPH: And?

MIRANDA: It's just that I feel like I'm sometimes, I dunno, back living in the main dorm.

RANDOLPH: I guess we do log in a lot of time, together.

MIRANDA: Can I just say it?

RANDOLPH: Sure.

MIRANDA: I don't want to play Yoko Ono to the Beatles, Ran.

RANDOLPH: God, you won't, Miranda! Nothing like that! X and Bennie are both crazy about you! So's Allie and Smitty! It's no different than if we were family, except X, Bennie, and I *chose* to be brothers. We don't have all the sibling bullshit! We really love each other. We really love each other's wives and girlfriends, too.

MIRANDA: Did you, like, ask Ben and X about marrying me?

RANDOLPH: Did I *ask* them? *Of course not!* Jesus, Mandy! How could you even *think* I'd do something like that? I'm asking you. I love you. I want you to be my wife. Nobody's more important to me than you, and nobody's ever going to *be* more important to me than you! I'm asking you to be my *wife!*

MIRANDA: Okay, I'll do it.

RANDOLPH: What? You will? You're saying you will?

MIRANDA: Yes.

RANDOLPH: Oh, my God!…I feel like I'm going to cry.

MIRANDA: Me, too.

RANDOLPH: You won't ever be sorry, Mand. I promise you.

MIRANDA: You won't be, either, Rand.

RANDOLPH: I love you so much, Miranda. I can't imagine living my life without you.

MIRANDA: I love you, so much, too, Ran.

(RANDOLPH exits...SPOTLIGHT UP ON...BENNIE, alone, down-stage...)

BENNIE: I wish I had died when I was on top.

MIRANDA: *(Moving downstage to BENNIE.)* On top of what?

BENNIE: You're a funny lady, Mandy. On top of my game. When I was first mega-mega-loaded, when Allie and I were still loving each other...when we still had a lot of big plans...

MIRANDA: What are you saying, Bennie?

BENNIE: Sooner or later, it catches you, Miranda. Life sets up against you. You run out of reasons for being alive...Love dies.

MIRANDA: Not everybody, Bennie.

BENNIE: Everybody, Mandy. Everybody.

MIRANDA: You're a terrible cynic.

BENNIE: It's true. I am. I'm a terrible cynic.

(THEY kiss, lightly.)

MIRANDA: What's the matter with us all, Bennie? Why are we all so unhappy?

BENNIE: Because we're people, and people are unhappy, Miranda. If we could have been born, say, artichokes or pussy willows.

(RANDOLPH re-enters.)

RANDOLPH: Hey, Bennie! What are you doing in such humble surround-ings? *(Kisses MIRANDA.)* Hi, sweetie. *(To BENNIE.)* I call her "sweet-ie." My grandfather called my grandmother "sweetie." My father called my mother "sweetie." She married into a long line of sweeties. *(Sees BENNIE's upset.)* What's the matter, Bennie?

BENNIE: *(To MIRANDA.)* I'm gonna' need to talk to Ran, alone, Mandy, just us.

MIRANDA: Oh.

RANDOLPH: What's up?

BENNIE: Please, Mandy. It's guy-stuff, dick-talk.

(MIRANDA looks at RANDOLPH.)

RANDOLPH: Do you mind?

MIRANDA: No. It's fine.

(MIRANDA backs out of the lights, exits.)

RANDOLPH: What's up, Bennie? You look awful.

BENNIE: We wiped out, Ran.

RANDOLPH: How so?

(THE LIGHTS SHIFT TO...XAVIER, upstage.)

XAVIER: They're calling it *Black Monday*? Like they haven't blamed us for everything else?

(BENNIE moves to XAVIER.)

BENNIE: I'm sorry, X.

XAVIER: *(Punches into his own fist.) This is so fucked up! (And then...)* Is it *mostly* gone, or *all* gone?...

BENNIE: All gone.

XAVIER: How deep did you put me in?

BENNIE: All the way.

XAVIER: Ran?

BENNIE: Same.

(XAVIER exhales. There is a substantial pause. And then...)

XAVIER: Mother*fucker!* I was lookin' at this badassed Mercedes, yesterday. Would've been nice...

BENNIE: It wouldn't have mattered.

XAVIER: *(Angrily...)* Wrong! Incorrect! It would've fuckin' mattered! I would've liked to have...*shit! (And then...)* So what's the deal, man? You give me the fucking million, then, you take it back? Like it wasn't really fuckin' mine, it stayed fuckin' yours?

BENNIE: That's not exactly it, X...

XAVIER: *(Enraged.)* What's exactly it, then? I mean, I gotta' know where this is goin', man! Yo, it's a funky million, today, but, what's down the road, tomorrow: my fuckin' *soul?*

BENNIE: *(Blows...as angry as X.)* What soul? What fuckin' soul? You and Ran have had your hands in my pockets since fuckin' kindergarten! You've had a better ride off me than you would'a had off'a any fuckin' Mercedes I can...

XAVIER: I never asked for nothin' from you, Bennie! Nada! Not a fuckin' thing!

BENNIE: What are you, mentally fucking challenged? I begged you ta' take the fuckin' money for law school?! I begged you ta' take the fucking eight-hundred-thousand for a fucking townhouse off Central Park West?! Get real, X! I am the tit you've been sucking on all your life!

XAVIER: I want *off*, motherfucker!

BENNIE: *You are off! I'm broke, man! I got nothin' but my fuckin' friends!*
(Long pause.)

XAVIER: How's Ran? He okay?

BENNIE: He's okay.

XAVIER: How's Bennie? He okay?

BENNIE: He's okay, too.

XAVIER: How am I? Am I okay?

BENNIE: You're okay, X.

(Suddenly, X screams, punches air violently. And then…)

XAVIER: You're probably right, bro. I don't need the fucking Mercedes. I've had the ride.

BENNIE: You gonna' start to hate me, now, X?

XAVIER: What do ya' mean "start to hate you," asshole? I've been hating you since the first time I saw you, when you tried to screw me with the Bic ballpoint.

BENNIE: I thought you didn't buy that. I thought Ran bought that.

XAVIER: He did. He's been hating you since the very same day.

BENNIE: I don't know what to say, X. It went so fast, man. I couldn't control it…

XAVIER: My house, too?

BENNIE: Everything.

XAVIER: Jesus! *(Beat.)* Bennie? Can I?

BENNIE: Do it.

(XAVIER winds up; punches BENNIE in the stomach. It is an enormous swing. WE think BENNIE will be a dead man…but, it is a game these two friends have played, many times before. XAVIER has pulled the punch. BENNIE is untouched.)

BENNIE: Feel better?

XAVIER: Made you flinch.

BENNIE: Bullshit I flinched! That'll be the day Bouvier could make Bennie Foss flinch!

XAVIER: *(Brightly…)* I never really liked that house.

(BENNIE smiles, moves to bench next to X; sits.)

BENNIE: Can you sit with me for a while, X?

XAVIER: Sure.

(The TWO OLD FRIENDS sit on the bench, side by side, not touching, not speaking, staring downward, each holds a golf club. Five count, and then… LIGHTS SHIFT TO… ACTRESS playing MIRANDA, ALLIE and SMITTY in rapid alternation. We will see MIRANDA, first, angry… NOTE: MEN enter from corners.)

MIRANDA: But, how in bloody hell could you have allowed him to invest *everything*?

(RANDOLPH steps into the light, facing MIRANDA…and the AUDIENCE.)

RANDOLPH: It's not a matter of allowing anything with Bennie. Bennie just goes ahead and does what Bennie wants. If Bennie wants permission, Bennie takes permission.

MIRANDA: Randolph, get real! Bennie couldn't have put up our house as collateral on his loans without your permission!...

(Beat.)

RANDOLPH: *(Quietly.)* I guess I gave it.

MIRANDA: Excuse me?

RANDOLPH: I said I guess I gave it.

MIRANDA: You *guess* you gave it?

RANDOLPH: I gave it. He put this paper in front of me to sign and...

MIRANDA: You signed it.

RANDOLPH: I signed it.

MIRANDA: He forced you, Ran? He had a gun? A knife? A gang of Iraqis...

RANDOLPH: Jesus, Mandy! Bennie gave me the money to begin with! He paid all the taxes on it! It's not like it was ever really *mine!* X is in exactly the same boat. Both of us were practically broke, before Bennie gave us money. I mean, who knows if either of us would have had a pot to piss in, on our own, without Bennie! Who knows?

MIRANDA: That is the *sickest!* Ran, do you realize what you're saying?

RANDOLPH: It's hard, Mandy. Bennie and X and I have had this same relationship since first grade. Bennie's the mover, the king; X plays the "Yessir-boss-you're-the-greatest" sycophant, and I play the dumb "whatever-you-want's-fine-with-me" boring shlepp. I hate it, I've *always* hated it, but I can't break out of it. Neither can X.

MIRANDA: Well, you'll either break out if it, now, Ran, or you'll break out of our marriage.

RANDOLPH: I can't get the money back, Mandy.

MIRANDA: *(Screams.)* I don't give a fuck about the money!

RANDOLPH: Don't delude yourself, Miranda. You care a lot about the money.

MIRANDA: Yuh, well, maybe I do. *(Beat.)* Thank God we don't have children.

(LIGHTS SHIFT TO...XAVIER, downstage, facing actress, who changes wig — and character — and now plays SMITTY.)

XAVIER: Excuse me?

SMITTY: I said "Thank God we don't have children," X.

XAVIER: It's funny, Smitty. It's really ironic, 'cause I'm feeling kind of the opposite thing. I'm feeling like maybe if we had children, we'd have this in some kind of perspective.

SMITTY: Meaning?

XAVIER: Meaning money is only money. It's not life, it's not happiness.

SMITTY: Money is only money, life is only life, happiness is only happiness, and you don't let any-fucking-body give away any of the above if it's yours.

(Beat.)

XAVIER: I love you, Smitty. That's what's Number One in my mind. We're pretty young, still, we're still healthy, we're still looking ahead. I'll be making more money. I'm sure of it.

SMITTY: I'm leaving you, X.

XAVIER: You're what?

SMITTY: I'm leaving you.

XAVIER: When?

SMITTY: Now.

XAVIER: Why?

SMITTY: I *knew* you were going to ask me why! I fucking knew it! It's not the money. It's a pity the timing is what it is, because you'll always think it's the money, but, that's only the tip of the iceberg. I would have left you, anyway, X.

XAVIER: This hurts.

SMITTY: I'm leaving you, I'm leaving Ran, and I'm leaving Bennie. I'm leaving the whole problem.

XAVIER: What are you talking about, Smitty?

SMITTY: If you ever want to be married to anybody else, you're going to have to choose, X. The wife or the boys.

XAVIER: That's total bullshit!

SMITTY: If you think it is, it is.

(LIGHTS SHIFT TO…BENNIE facing ALLIE, the same actress, her back remains turned toward audience).

BENNIE: I'm moving out, Allie.

ALLIE: Why?

BENNIE: I have to.

ALLIE: Why?

BENNIE: I can't take it, any more…

ALLIE: Take *what* any more?

BENNIE: I dunno…The shame.

ALLIE: The *shame?*…That's ridiculous, Bennie.

BENNIE: I'm a ridiculous guy.

ALLIE: And that's the reason?

BENNIE: I don't think I love you, any more.

ALLIE: You don't *think* you love me, any more?

BENNIE: I don't want to be married to you.

ALLIE: Oh. *(ALLIE chokes back a tear.)* What about the kids?

BENNIE: I won't be far away.

ALLIE: Is there somebody else?

BENNIE: No.

ALLIE: I can't blame you. I've wanted to move out, myself, about a thousand times.

BENNIE: Why didn't you?

ALLIE: The kids. I dunno. I didn't. That's why: 'cause I didn't.

BENNIE: Because of the money falling apart?

ALLIE: What?

BENNIE: Is that when you started wanting to move out? When the money thing fell apart?

ALLIE: Uh uh, no. In fact, I thought it might be fun to be broke with you.

BENNIE: You're dead wrong.

ALLIE: Yuh. Maybe I am.

BENNIE: You would have hated me for it.

ALLIE: *(Interrupts, screaming…)* Don't talk any more! Don't fucking tell me what I would hate! Just don't talk any more!…
(ALLIE runs from BENNIE, in a balletic, graceful dance. SHE circles the stage. Suddenly, WE ARE HEARING…WEDDING MUSIC played on organ. COLOR OF LIGHTING CHANGES to pinks and blues…WE HEAR…CLERGYMAN'S VOICE, over loudspeaker…)

CLERGYMAN: *(V.O.)* Do you, Xavier Bouvier, take this woman as your lawful wedded wife? To love, honor, and cherish, til death do you part?
(ALLIE stops, downstage center, her back to the AUDIENCE. XAVIER steps forward, facing ALLIE.)

XAVIER: I do.

CLERGYMAN: *(V.O.)* Do you, Randolph Shimma, take this woman as your lawful wedded wife? To love, honor, and cherish, til death do you part?
(RANDOLPH steps forward, beside XAVIER, faces ALLIE; speaks…)

RANDOLPH: I do.

CLERGYMAN: *(V.O.)* Do you, Benjamin Foss, take this woman as your lawful wedded wife? To love, honor, and cherish, til death do you part?
(BENNIE steps between RANDOLPH and XAVIER; speaks, confidentially.)

BENNIE: I certainly do.

CLERGYMAN: *(V.O.)* I now pronounce you men and wife. Til death do you part. Did you hear me? Til death do you part. Til death do you part. Til death do you part. Til death do you part. You're hearing this? Til death do you part. Til death do you part. Til death do you part. *(Beat.)* Okay, guys. Kiss the bride.

(BENNIE, RANDOLPH, and XAVIER step forward and kiss ALLIE, one at a time. Each pulls her away from the prior kisser, kisses her. SHE dances from one man/kiss to the next in a nightmarish ballet. The CLERGYMAN's VOICE is heard, again…)

CLERGYMAN: *(V.O.)* Kiss her again, guys.

(The three men move in a line toward ALLIE, arms outstretched. SHE screams and whirls downstage into new light. SHE is terribly upset. BENNIE now sits in chair, opposite, facing upstage. HE wears a grey beard. He is now playing SIGMUND FREUD. ALLIE lies on back, on bench, opposite, weeping, using Kleenex.)

ALLIE: Oh, my God, Herr Dr. Freud, it was *horrible!*…I dreamed I was getting married to all three of them at once.

FREUD: *(Thick accent.)* All three? At once? At the same time?

ALLIE: In quick alternation.

FREUD: In bed? Doing the hoopie?

ALLIE: *(Angrily.)* No! Who said "bed?" I didn't say "bed!" *You* said "bed!" It wasn't *sexual!* It was *horrible!* There's a difference!

FREUD: Where was this taking place, Frau Foss?

ALLIE: I think it was in a synagogue on West End Avenue. Bennie, Ran, and X were in a line, facing me, and this sort of rabbinical voice was coming from Heaven, conducting the wedding service.

FREUD: Were your mother and father there?

ALLIE: Oh, goodness, no. I don't think so.

FREUD: Were you dressed?

ALLIE: Of course, I was dressed!

FREUD: In white?

ALLIE: No, I was wearing all black.

FREUD: Like you're wearing now?

ALLIE: *(Realizes.)* God!…Yes.

FREUD: Did they all kiss you at the end of the service?

ALLIE: They did, yes.

FREUD: At the same time?

ALLIE: In quick alternation. It was terrifying. But, not unexciting.

FREUD: This is quite a significant dream, Frau Foss. Was there anything else unusual about the wedding service, other than the fact that there were three grooms…your husband and his boyhood friends?

ALLIE: No, not really. The rabbi's voice kept repeating the "til death do you part" part.

FREUD: How many times?

ALLIE: Seven or eight.

FREUD: I see. Was there any talk of death during the day, Frau Foss?

ALLIE: Bennie did say he wished he'd killed himself when he was on top.

FREUD: "On top," in what sense, Frau Foss?

ALLIE: Jesus, Dr. Freud! You've got a dirty mind!

(BENNIE removes the Freud-beard; speaks with his own voice, directly to ALLIE.)

BENNIE: Hold me, Allie. I'm really scared.

ALLIE: What?

BENNIE: I had this dream, Allie…It was frightening.

ALLIE: Jesus! I was *asleep*! I was *dreaming*!

BENNIE: Look at me, Allie, look at me: I'm shaking.

ALLIE: I was having this amazing dream, Bennie!

BENNIE: I lost everything. I was totally broke. Ran and X, too. I used all their money to try to shore up the stock in my company. Nothing worked. The market kept going down and down. Finally, everything was gone.

ALLIE: Bennie? Are you here?

BENNIE: I've got to kill myself, while I'm still on top, Allie! I don't want to be one of these pathetic-loser-used-to-be's. I can't face it, Allie. It's not me. It's not who I am.

(BENNIE backs out of the light. ALLIE is alone on stage. SHE rubs her eyes, terrified, as if, only now, finally, waking from her nightmare, realizing it was all a dream, remembering what has really happened in her life. SHE screams out…)

ALLIE: *Bennie! Don't be dead, Bennie! Bennnieeeeee!*

(THE LIGHTS CROSSFADE TO…RANDOLPH, at BENNIE's grave, delivering eulogy…)

RANDOLPH: I guess X told you, already…The day Bennie and I met for the first time, I bought this red Bic ballpoint from him for a dollar. He'd just bought it in the store across from the school for fifty-nine cents. I gave him my money, and then pointed out to him that he was screwing me. He gave me a sheet of paper from his backpack, and told me to draw a picture of this old guy who was sitting on the curb, right next to us…with the pen. I did and he sold my picture for a dollar to the old guy. He told him I was a great artist. He gave me fifty cents and kept fifty cents. So, I ended up getting my fifty-nine cent pen for fifty cents and Bennie made ninety-one cents for himself. I know there's sales tax to factor in, but, in the simplest possible terms, I made nine cents and Bennie made ninety cents. Somehow, at the end of the incident, I was happy, Bennie was happy, the guy with the picture was happy, and the guy in the candy store who sold Bennie the pen was happy, too. This incident sort of defined our lives together for the next thirty-something years. *(Beat.)*

I don't know if knowing you was a good thing or a bad thing, Bennie. Sometimes, I think, without you, I would still be saving my pennies for the pen. Or maybe still trying to decide between the red one and the blue one. Or maybe I would have figured out how to do things on my own? I don't know. I really don't. All I know now is that you're gone, and there are so many things you did for me that I'm going to have to figure out how to do for myself. It scares me, Bennie. I'm really scared. *(Beat.)*

I really miss you, Bennie. You know how some people have these reoccurring nightmares that they're dying? Well, I had this reoccurring nightmare that *you* were dying. Now, it's come true.
(THE LIGHTS CROSSFADE TO…XAVIER and SMITTY, in Smitty's apartment…)

SMITTY: I'm so sorry, X.

XAVIER: I didn't know if you heard.

SMITTY: Mandy called me, right away. Then, Allie, a couple of minutes later.

XAVIER: She okay?

SMITTY: Not great.

XAVIER: It hasn't sunk in. I mean, it's perfect Bennie, right? He's not gonna', like, *grow old and die*…like normal people kind of thing.

SMITTY: Not Bennie.

XAVIER: *(Suddenly…)* I miss you, so much, Smitty. I want us to be together, again. I want to have kids with you.

SMITTY: You do?

XAVIER: So much.

SMITTY: Oh, God, X…

XAVIER: Can we try to be together, again? Can we, please?

SMITTY: X, I'm pregnant. *(Beat.)*

XAVIER: You are?

SMITTY: I am.

XAVIER: *(Quietly.)* I'm scared stiff to open my mouth, 'cause I don't wanna' say the wrong thing, here...the really dumb thing I'm thinkin'. I'm fighting all this macho street-shit, inside, right now. I...I...

SMITTY: *(Rescues XAVIER...)* It's definitely our baby. No chance it's anybody but you.

(Beat.)

XAVIER: What I was choking on was to say it wouldn't matter if it wasn't me. I dunno', maybe it would...It might drive me apeshit if we had this little Korean kid or whatever...

SMITTY: Or Bennie's kid?

XAVIER: Or Bennie's kid. Jesus. It wouldn't matter, Smitty. It wouldn't, deep down, matter, it wouldn't, 'cause I love you that much, Smitty. I really love you that much...I really do.

(THEY kiss.)

(LIGHTS CROSS TO...BENNIE, on the tee, driver in hand. As HE talks, HE lines up his drive, addresses the ball...)

BENNIE: The thing about this game is that you never know when it's coming...the perfect round. You go along, hitting 'em okay, week after week, chippin' away at your score, but, you're pretty much playing the same game. And then, for no reason you can figure, this day comes...when you can do no wrong.

(MUSIC IN...BENNIE drives. His swing is huge, powerful. WE HEAR...a solid WHACK, and then, THE SOUND OF A BEAUTIFUL BELL. THE LIGHTS WIDEN TO INCLUDE...RANDOLPH and XAVIER. BOTH are amazed.)

RANDOLPH: Jesus, Bennie, what a belt!

XAVIER: Monster drive, Bennie! Monster! John Daley time!

BENNIE: *(Smiles.)* Thanks, guys.

(BENNIE sobs, suddenly. RANDOLPH and XAVIER exchange a glance.)

XAVIER: You okay, Ben?

RANDOLPH: Bennie?

BENNIE: *(Profoundly sad. HE smiles, bravely.)* I'm fine.

(BENNIE goes to his bag, takes his three-wood, lines up his shot, hits...WE HEAR...a solid WHACK, and then, THE SOUND OF A BEAUTIFUL BELL.)

XAVIER: Jesus, Bennie! *You're going on!*

RANDOLPH: *You're on!*

XAVIER: *Go in!*
RANDOLPH: *Go in!*
BENNIE: In!
RANDOLPH: You're in!
XAVIER: You're in!
RANDOLPH: *(Adding the scores...)* One under, Ben.
XAVIER: One under? Jesus, Bennie, I can't believe it! One under!
RANDOLPH: Congrats, Ben!
XAVIER: Fantastic, bro!
    (They all hug.)
BENNIE: Thanks, guys, I...*(Stops himself. HE is quite emotional.)* Sooner or
    later, it comes back.
    *(MUSIC IN...Bach, played by a single cello, loud, elegant, terrifying...It is
    the music that opened the play. LIGHTING CHANGES COLOR...BEN-
    NIE looks at RANDOLPH and XAVIER, sadly.)*
BENNIE: I'm going.
RANDOLPH: What's up?
XAVIER: You okay, Ben?
BENNIE: I'm fine. I just wanna' go. I've got to go do a thing.
RANDOLPH: We're not celebrating this?
BENNIE: Later. Is that okay? We'll celebrate later, okay?
XAVIER: Sure.
RANDOLPH: Later's fine.
    *(LIGHTS SHIFT TO...MIRANDA, downstage, in Miranda and
    Randolph's apartment. RANDOLPH moves to her, as SHE speaks...)*
MIRANDA: There's someone else, Ran.
RANDOLPH: There is?
MIRANDA: I didn't plan it...I mean, I didn't *expect* it...I wasn't *looking* for
    somebody else.
RANDOLPH: No. I'm sure you weren't.
MIRANDA: I mean, it's not like we didn't give it our best effort.
RANDOLPH: You and he?
MIRANDA: You and I.
RANDOLPH: This is a definite thing?
MIRANDA: I'm in love, Ran. I've been in love for some time.
RANDOLPH: Oh. I see. What does "some time" mean? Two or three days?
    Two or three years?
MIRANDA: Longer.
RANDOLPH: Longer?

MIRANDA: I want us to be friends, Ran. In some crazy way, I need your *approval*. I…

RANDOLPH: Please, don't.

MIRANDA: I never wanted to hurt you, Ran, that's why I never…

RANDOLPH: Miranda, could you please stop talking?

MIRANDA: I'm sorry, Ran.

RANDOLPH: *No! Not even that! Just shut your fucking mouth!*

   (*MIRANDA looks at RANDOLPH and nods, as if to say "I'm being quiet."*)

RANDOLPH: Good-bye, Miranda.

   (*LIGHTS SHIFT TO…BENNIE, upstage…HE wears an expensive silk bathrobe. HE trims and lights an Havana cigar, inhales deeply; uncorks a bottle of 1966 Châteauneuf du Pape, fills a glass to its brim, drinks; refills the glass, drinks, again. HE moves to a video camera, flicks a switch on. BENNIE's image comes up on an overhead TV-monitor. Thus, HE is seen, on stage, and, simultaneously, on the monitor, as he records his thoughts…*)

BENNIE: You cannot imagine what it's felt like to be me, these past six years…to go on living all this time after my ship, you know, went down. *(Beat.)*

   Not the kind of thing you ever think about when you're up there, when people are constantly telling you you're the greatest thing since night baseball. But, five minutes after it's gone…when you're first on your ass, when you first start looking backwards, you figure it out, real fast…You get the joke. It's you. You're the joke. You make people nervous, just by being there. You hear the story of your life, every time you turn a corner, in whispers, everywhere you go…*(Whispers, imitating gossips…)* "That's Bennie Foss…used'ta have two hundred million…stupid shit's got nothin'…*nada…rien.*" *(Beat.)*

   Well, guess what happened, today, folks? Guess what I did that a couple'a guys I know would pay a good couple'a million to do? I went one under. I could do *no fucking wrong!* Every time I hit the ball, I was, like, *Mozartian*…I was, like, *Nureyevian!* I was Sylvester fucking *Stallonian!* I was greatness. Wait wait wait…I shouldn't be modest, 'cause I was so much better than greatness! I was profound. I was *sublime.* *(Beat.)*

   So, now, I've got the second chance to end all second chances. *(Beat.)*

   Much as we avoid admitting this, folks, there is a tremendous connection between what we know and what we do. So, here goes.

You hear about Bennie Foss? Son of a bitch went one under and then, *bah boom*. One fucking under and *bah boom!* Go figure." *(Smiles.)*

What I had with me at the end was a glass of 1966 Châteauneuf du Pape, a hand-rolled Havana cigar, memories of a lot of laughs...ending a very pleasant day in which I went one under. It should only happen to you. This is the American Dream come true, friends...rich, successful, and forever young.

(BENNIE takes a pistol from his pocket, loads it, puts the end of the pistol in his mouth, prepares to kill himself, backs out of the light, off stage. On the TV SCREEN, the image of Bennie, gun in mouth, freezes.

A moment passes. And then, WE HEAR...clap-stick, whistle, bell. On screen, BENNIE lies dead, in pool of blood.

TV SCREEN IMAGE freezes. LIGHTING CROSSFADES TO...ALLIE, in spotlight, watching video. SHE holds groceries, and TV set on; screams out...)

ALLIE: *(Screaming, sobbing...)* This is total macho bullshit, Bennie! You've got kids! What the fuck am I supposed to tell our kids?! Am I supposed to tell them that you had an excellent round of golf, so, now, they'll never see you, again? That's brilliant, Bennie, fucking brilliant!

(LIGHT FADES UP ON...BENNIE, on floor, upstage, facedown, dead, gun in hand...blood puddles from head. ALLIE continues her railing, directly at HIM, instead of his on-screen image...)

ALLIE: Look at the mess you've made, Bennie! You've made a miserable mess!...I'm always cleaning up after you...Ever since I met you, I've had to clean up after you! *(Sobs.)* Now, I'm gonna' have this in my head... every night, every time my head hits the pillow, I'm gonna' see you, I'm gonna' remember you this way...and it's gonna' scare me, Bennie...It's gonna' make me feel so angry! *(Beat.)*

How am I supposed to get to sleep after this, Bennie? How? You get to sleep into *eternity*, but, how am I? *Answer me!* Did you ever fucking think about anybody besides yourself? *DID YOU?*

(TV SCREEN UNFREEZES...A NEW VIDEO begins to play...BEN-NIE, facing camera, directly, speaking quietly, calmly...)

BENNIE: This tape is just for you, Allie...for you and the children...Please, never show it to anybody else...Please. I just want people to see the other one. Promise me, please...(Beat.)

My company insurance runs out, tomorrow. I haven't got a hope in hell of making the premium. It's huge. I've had a 30-day grace period.

It's gone tomorrow. I've hustled around to try to scrape together the money. Not a chance. I tried everybody. *(Beat.)*

Allie, Sooner or later, I would've done this...ended it...it might as well be now. At least, this way, you and the kids are gonna' be covered...It's a lot of money, Allie. X'll be doing the details...He'll bring you this tape with the forms to sign. *(Beat.)*

Roddy and Cody...I want you to know how much I love both of you. I never ever wanted to be away from you, it's just that I stopped remembering how to make enough money to take care of you...I used to know how, but, I think I must have forgotten...and now, today, I've got this chance, and I've got to take it. In no way were you guys responsible and in no way will I ever stop loving you, and I hope you'll never stop loving me. I'll always be with you, just not in the same way, just not in a day-to-day kind of thing. *(Beat.)*

Allie, it finally comes down to this last time to speak to you, these last words...No matter what you think, no matter what I ever said or did, believe me, Allie...you were the love of my life.

(VIDEO FADES OUT...LIGHT FADES OUT ON...BENNIE. HE exits in the dark...LIGHT UP ON...X, downstage left. HE wears a black armband; moves to ALLIE; speaks, softly, quietly...)

XAVIER: The package was waiting for me when I got home. The doorman gave it to me. A second one, an exact dupe of the tape and a Xerox of the letter, came in the mail this morning. He planned it out pretty good.

ALLIE: I guess he did.

XAVIER: The policy's ten years old, way over the two-year exclusion for suicide. Bennie checked it all out...*(Beat. X holds back his tears...)* All in, it'll be about seventeen million, after the taxes are paid. I should have the paperwork by Thursday.

(ALLIE sobs.)

XAVIER: He left Ran and me something, too...about six hundred thousand, apiece...plus, his old clubs...also, golf lessons.

ALLIE: I didn't want money, X, I wanted Bennie. I never cared about money.

XAVIER: I know.

ALLIE: I wanted Bennie.

XAVIER: I know.

ALLIE: Goddam country...it fucks people up...gives people all the wrong values.

XAVIER: Some people, yuh.

ALLIE: Almost everybody I know, X. Almost nobody escapes it.

XAVIER: Call me, Allie, no matter what you need, call me.

ALLIE: Thanks.

XAVIER: Promise?

ALLIE: I promise.

> *(LIGHTS SHIFT WITH…XAVIER as HE crosses to RANDOLPH on the tee. HE takes his driver from his bag, sits on bench, opposite RAN.)*

RANDOLPH: It feels weird, just us.

XAVIER: Totally weird.

RANDOLPH: Bennie would like this, though…

XAVIER: Our doin' this? Playing so soon, after? Totally.

RANDOLPH: He's smiling down at us.

XAVIER: *(Correcting…)* Up at us.

RANDOLPH: *Up* at us.

XAVIER: Totally. No doubt about it.

RANDOLPH: If it had been you or me or both of us…

XAVIER: Bennie'd be out here…

RANDOLPH: Playing golf…

XAVIER: Same afternoon…

RANDOLPH: Totally…

XAVIER: Out of respect…

RANDOLPH: To honor us. *(Beat.)* Did you see it?

XAVIER: The video? Uh uh, no. You?

RANDOLPH: Not yet.

XAVIER: Allie said maybe after a couple'a more weeks, she'll let me look.

RANDOLPH: Same here. Mandy saw it.

XAVIER: She did? *(RANDOLPH nods.)* You guys are talking?

RANDOLPH: Mandy and I? Yuh, sure.

XAVIER: Good.

RANDOLPH: We're going to try, again. It'll be like walking on eggs, but, I want to try. I think she does, too.

XAVIER: *(Looks at RANDOLPH, worriedly.)* Oh, yuh? No kidding?…That's great, Ran.

RANDOLPH: I told her about you and Smitty trying, too. She's really happy about it. She wants me to tell you that.

XAVIER: Thanks. Smitty's been hanging out with Mandy and Allie. You must know that, huh?

RANDOLPH: I know. They had lunch, together, Tuesday. Funny, huh? The girls are getting close.

XAVIER: Ran, what I'm hearing is not that you guys are getting back together.

RANDOLPH: *(Caught in his lie; humiliated...)* Yuh, well, nothing's definite.

XAVIER: When you lose a ball in the woods, Ran, it's lost. You put down another ball, it costs you two strokes. That's the game. That's the *rule*. That's what's *real*.

RANDOLPH: I know, X...I know.

> *(RANDOLPH breaks down, sobs. XAVIER stands by, watching. And then...)*

XAVIER: You okay, bro?

RANDOLPH: Sure.

XAVIER: No matter what, I'm there for you, Ran. You're my brother.

RANDOLPH: Is this the bottom, X? Am I on the bottom?

XAVIER: Probably not. We've both still got old age and death ahead of us.

RANDOLPH: *(Smiles.)* This is true.

XAVIER: We might move, Ran. *(RANDOLPH looks up.)* Smitty and I. Nothing definite. We just sort of talked about it. She thinks it might be better for us in a new...situation.

RANDOLPH: What do *you* think?

XAVIER: I could use living in a new place. We're talking about Seattle.

RANDOLPH: Seattle? Wow!...

XAVIER: Won't happen tomorrow.

RANDOLPH: That's major.

XAVIER: I dunno, Ran...it feels like it's time to try stuff. *(And then, without warning.)* Do I ever sound black to you, Ran?

RANDOLPH: What?

XAVIER: It's something Smitty said, when she was really mad at me.

RANDOLPH: How's black supposed to sound?

XAVIER: I don't know.

RANDOLPH: You *are* black. What the hell did she mean?

XAVIER: I think she meant that I sound like you...and Bennie.

RANDOLPH: Maybe *we're* black?

XAVIER: I dunno, Ran...When I was little, I knew who I was. Since then, I've been spendin' so much time chasing after Bennie...imitating Bennie...tryin' to *be* Bennie...I dunno...I don't exactly know who I am, anymore, Ran. I really don't.

> *(Beat. And then, RANDOLPH moves his life to a new place...)*

RANDOLPH: Mandy was seeing somebody all the time we were married.

XAVIER: I heard this.

RANDOLPH: X, I knew Bennie was gonna' kill himself, sooner or later, once the money was gone. I just keep wondering if somebody...

XAVIER: Don't say it out loud. *(Chokes back a tear, and then...)* Jesus, Ran, do you really think we could have stopped him? Do you think we should have seen it coming and maybe got him help?

RANDOLPH: You can't climb into somebody's else head, X — you can't! You think you can. You think love gets you there, but, it doesn't...It maybe gets you close, but not *there*, never *there!* In the end, you never really know what's going on in anybody else's head — not your wife's, not your best friend's, nobody!

XAVIER: *(Looking out front at golfers, up ahead.)* They put the pin back in. You can hit.

RANDOLPH: *(Addresses his ball.)* My club feels heavy.

XAVIER: Stay down on the ball.

> *(RANDOLPH swings, hits. WE HEAR...a solid WHACK, and then, THE SOUND OF A BEAUTIFUL BELL. RANDOLPH and XAVIER exchange an astonished look...)*

XAVIER: Beautiful.

RANDOLPH: Jesus! That's the best drive of my life!

XAVIER: Fantastic shot, Ran!

RANDOLPH: It's that same ball, X...the one that went in my pocket...from last week's game with Bennie. I kid you not.

> *(RANDOLPH turns away; in pain. XAVIER goes to the tee, driver in hand.)*

XAVIER: It hurts, huh?

RANDOLPH: It hurts a lot.

XAVIER: *(Readying his drive.)* Okay...I'm hitting. Listen to me, ball...chase Ran, okay? Just lay up close to Ran's ball. Tempo, X, follow through... you can do this...belt buckle to the green...tempo... tempo...

> *(XAVIER swings. We hear...a solid WHACK, and then THE SOUND OF A BEAUTIFUL BELL.)*

RANDOLPH: Jesus, X! Fantastic!...Right at the pin!...You're on!...You're rolling perfect!...

> *(RANDOLPH and XAVIER react, as Xavier's drive goes in the cup...hole in one.)*

XAVIER: Jesus!

RANDOLPH: Jesus, X, I think you went in! *Jesus, X!*

XAVIER: *Jesus, Ran, both of us! Look at this! Look at what we just did on our own, Ran! Just us, on our own, Ran! We did this! We...*

> *(Suddenly, WE HEAR...)*

VOICES: *(Offstage.)* FORE! FORE!

RANDOLPH: *Watch it!*

XAVIER: *Heads!*
> (*Thud! RANDOLPH flinches. HE has been hit by a golf ball. And then, another thud! XAVIER flinches. HE, too, has been hit by a golf ball. THEY realize that they are both unhurt. RANDOLPH reaches into his pocket, extracts a golf ball. And then, XAVIER reaches into his pocket, extracts a golf ball, as well.*
>
> *RANDOLPH and XAVIER exchange a worried glance. THEY look above, to heaven, freeze...lights shift to...BENNIE, center. He speaks to Audience...*)

BENNIE: In childhood, life is constantly heroic...Almost every new day brings new battle, new challenge. Adult life is repetition on repetition...a long, slow walk to the graveyard. By playing golf, we keep our childhoods alive. Me, personally, I need to stay a child...I need some hope that I can meet my mother and father again, and set things straight. I also need the battle. On the golf course, I am a warrior. I approach the ball like it is the first, ever, rife with possibility. I look out at the endless green on green and I see a gaming field, a meadow, a graveyard...a place of pain and pleasure, of winning, of losing, of endless fantasy, of endless heroism...I am not a spectator in this sport. I am a player. There are no excuses, no mitigating circumstance. It's just me, trying to create one moment of wordless grace. If I was stranded on a desert island with one club and one ball, I would set out a course, and I would play golf...and the game would be no different than anywhere else...difficult, maddening, joyous...(Smiles.) Of course, like Ben Hogan said, I always try to play golf with friends, but we never play a friendly game.
> (*Behind BENNIE, on video screen, we see...THREE CHILDREN on a golf course. ONE of them sets up his shot, swings. His ball flies to the green, rolls up to the pin, goes in. The CHILD leaps in the air, joyously. The other TWO CHILDREN fall to the ground, comically, as if they have fainted.*)

End of Play.

ISRAEL HOROVITZ is author of more than 50 produced plays, of which several have been translated and performed in as many as 30 languages, worldwide. Among Horovitz's best-known plays are *The Indian Wants The Bronx, Line* (now in its 22nd year, off-Broadway, at the 13th St Repertory Theatre), *Rats, It's Called The Sugar Plum, Morning, The Primary English Class, The Wakefield Plays* (a 7-play cycle, including *Hopscotch, The 75th, Stage Directions, Spared, Alfred the Great, Our Father's Failing,* and *Alfred Dies*), *The Good Parts, Mackerel,* and the "Growing Up Jewish" trilogy, *Today, I Am A Fountain Pen, A Rosen By Any Other Name,* and *The Chopin Playoffs*. Other recent Horovitz work includes a cycle of Massachusetts-based plays, including *North Shore Fish, Henry Lumper, Sunday Runners In The Rain, Strong-Man's Weak Child, The Widow's Blind Date, Park Your Car In Harvard Yard, Year Of The Duck, Fighting Over Beverley, Unexpected Tenderness, Barking Sharks,* and, most recently, *Captains and Courage*, a stage adaptation of Kipling's *Captains Courageous*; and two new plays that had their world premieres at Gloucester Stage, summer, 1996, *My Old Lady,* and *Lebensraum,* which re-opens in NYC in October, 1997. His newest play, *One Under,* has just had its world premiere at Gloucester Stage in August, 1997. Off-Broadway, this past season, saw *Israel Horovitz Times Two: Free Gift and The Former One-On-One Basketball Champion.* Mr Horovitz's screenplays include *The Strawberry Statement, Author! Author!, A Man In Love* (written with Diane Kurys), *Believe In Me,* and, recently, screenplays for two upcoming Warner Bros films: *James Dean,* based on the life of the actor; and for a new version of *A Star Is Born,* as well as a new film-version of *Captains Courageous.* He has also completed screenplays for film-adaptations of his stage-plays *Strong-Man's Weak Child, North Shore Fish* (just aired on Showtime), *The Widow's Blind Date* (which Horovitz will direct), and *The Taste of Sunshine* with famed Hungarian film-maker Istvan Szabo. He is now adapting *Fighting Over Beverley* for the screen. As an actor, Horovitz recently starred in several new films, *Dead Letters Don't Die; Trifecta,* HBO's *Subway Stories,* in which Horovitz played opposite Lili Taylor; a French film, *Corps Plongés;* as well as a cameo performance in *North Shore Fish.* He also starred in the BBC (England) production of his own new play *The Chips Are Down,* and, on stage, off-Broadway, in Nicole Burdette's *Mighty Bad Day.* He is currently completing film of the lead role in *The First Seven Years,* based on Bernard Malamud's award-winning short story. Horovitz has won numerous writing awards, including the OBIE (twice), the EMMY, the Prix de Plaisir du Théâtre, The Prix du Jury of the Cannes Film Festival, The Prix Italia, The Christopher Award, The Drama Desk Award, an Award in Literature of the American Academy of Arts and Letters, The Elliot Norton Prize, a Lifetime Achievement Award from B'Nai Brith, The 1996 Literature Prize of Washington College, an honorary Doctorate in Humane Letters from Salem (Massachusetts) State College, and many others. Mr Horovitz is founder and Artistic Director of Gloucester Stage Company, and of the New York Playwrights Lab. Horovitz is the father of five children: film producer Rachael Horovitz, novelist/screenwriter Matthew Horovitz, Beastie Boy Adam Horovitz, and unemployed 11-year-old twins, Hannah and Oliver Horovitz. He is married to Gillian Adams-Horovitz, former British National Marathon Champion. The Horovitz family divides its time among homes in NYC's Greenwich Village, London's Dulwich Village, and the seaport city of Gloucester, Massachusetts. Mr Horovitz visits France, frequently, where he often directs French-language productions of his plays. He is the most-produced American playwright in French theatre history. (Sept., 1997.)